EPIC LAND

Namibia exposed

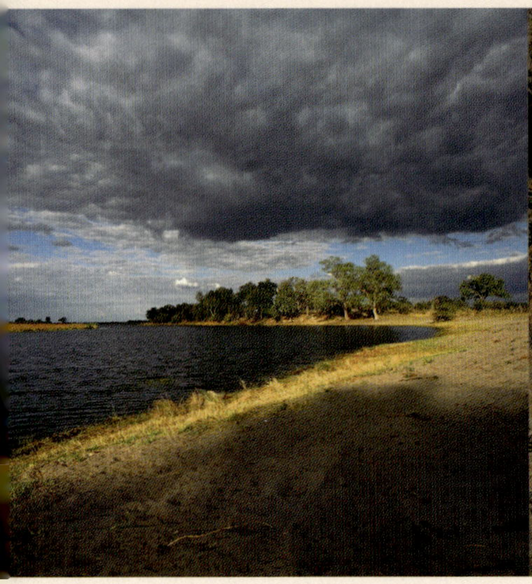
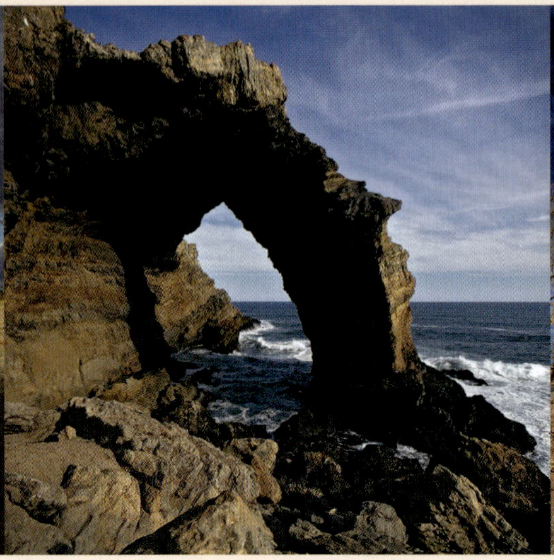
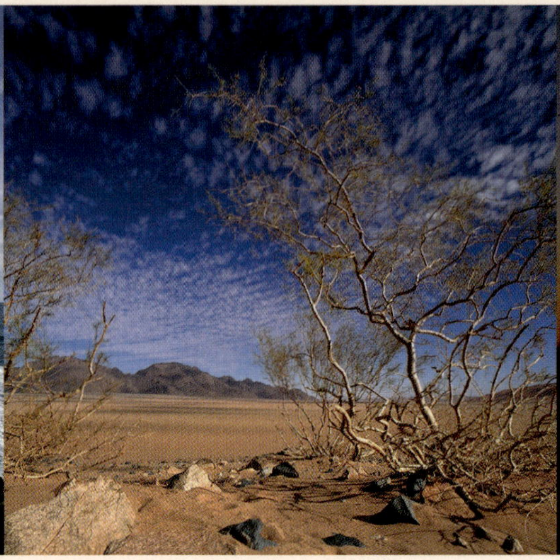
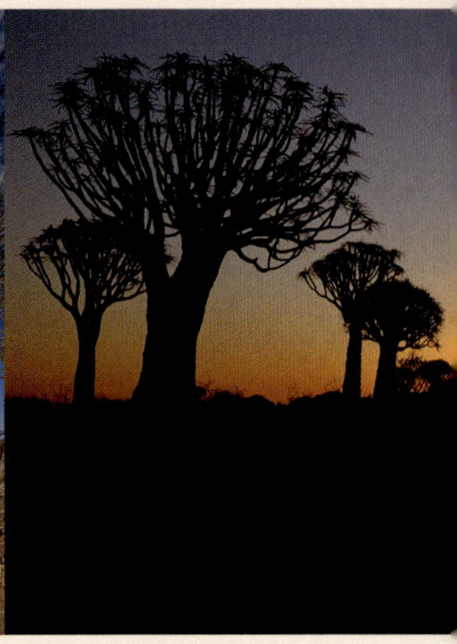

EPIC LAND

Namibia exposed

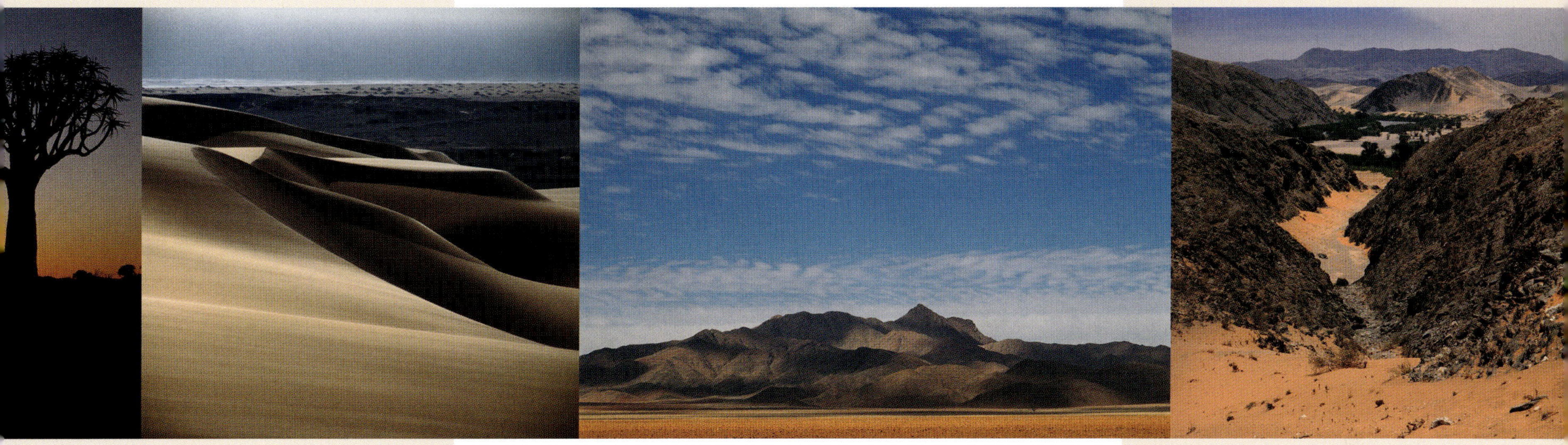

AMY SCHOEMAN

with text contributions by

Massimo Baistrocchi, Danie Botha & André du Pisani

Protea Book House
Pretoria
2015

Epic Land: Namibia exposed – Amy Schoeman

First edition, first impression in 2015 by Protea Book House
PO Box 35110, Menlo Park, 0102
1067 Burnett Street, Hatfield, Pretoria
8 Minni Street, Clydesdale, Pretoria
protea@intekom.co.za
www.proteaboekhuis.com

EDITOR: Danél Hanekom
PROOFREADER: Carmen Hansen-Kruger
COVER AND BOOK DESIGN: Hanli Deysel
SLIDE REPRODUCTION: Silvertone International (Pty) Ltd, Johannesburg
TYPOGRAPHY: Gaba & Futura
PRINTED AND BOUND: Craft Print, Singapore

ISBN: 978-1-86919-844-2

This publication was made possible by the contributions of the National Arts Council of Namibia, Silvertone International, Bank Windhoek and Herman van Wyk.

To the people of Namibia

Land of “bottomless” lakes,
the highest dunes,
the oldest desert

Publications

Non-fiction

Skeleton Coast, Macmillan South Africa, Johannesburg, 1984

Tones & Textures, photopoetry from Namibia, Clifton Publications, Cape Town, 1987

Notes on Nature Nature (omnibus), Gamsberg Macmillan, Windhoek, 2002

Kolmanskop – past & present (text), Klaus Hess Publishers, Göttingen, Germany, 2004

Namibian Elegy (photographs), Macmillan Namibia, Windhoek, 2008

Skeleton Coast, update by Venture Publications Windhoek & Protea Book House, Menlo Park, South Africa, 2010

Fiction

Short story in *ACCLAIM* magazine, UK, 1992

Short story in *Impressions of Independence*, Gamsberg Macmillan, Windhoek, 1991

Anthology *Mirage & other stories*, Gamsberg Macmillan, Windhoek, 2003

Novel *This is not a Flowerpot,* Wordweaver Publishing House, Windhoek, 2013

Photographic accreditations

SAIP (South African Institute of Photographers) Licentiate, 1983

SAIP Associate, 1986

PPSA (Professional Photographers of Southern Africa) Fellowship in Environmental Photography, 1998; Fellowship in Fine Art Photography, 2000

Current accreditation: FPPSA (Dux)

Based in Windhoek, Namibia, Amy Schoeman started her professional career as journalist/photographer for the Department of Nature Conservation in 1977. She has written prolifically about the country and has 65 solo exhibitions to her name, culminating in the Amy Schoeman Retrospective presented in the Sasol Art Museum in Stellenbosch in South Africa.

Key photographic portfolios

Skeleton Coast Images	Desert Classics
Namib from the Air	Last Light
Presence of the Past	Now & Zen
Womandala	Desert Textures
Sea Namibia	Hiroshima Namibia
Yin-Yang	Mystic Desert

The Five Seasons (with fashion designer Melanie Harteveld-Becker)

Eleven (with fashion designer Melanie Harteveld-Becker)

Key photographic awards

Acceptance of *Dune* for the Cape Town Triennial Art Competition, 1988

Gecko Award for *The Five Seasons – Autumn & Winter,* Windhoek, 2002

Standard Bank Biennale Photography Award, Windhoek, 2003

/Ae//Gams Arts & Culture Festival–Bank Windhoek, Overall Winner of the Namibia Today Art Exhibition with *Isis*, Windhoek, 2007

Fujifilm Southern Africa Photographic Awards, Johannesburg: two Gold, 2004; three Gold, 2006; two Gold, 2007; Gold and Image of the Year for *Presence of the Past* (title image), 2008

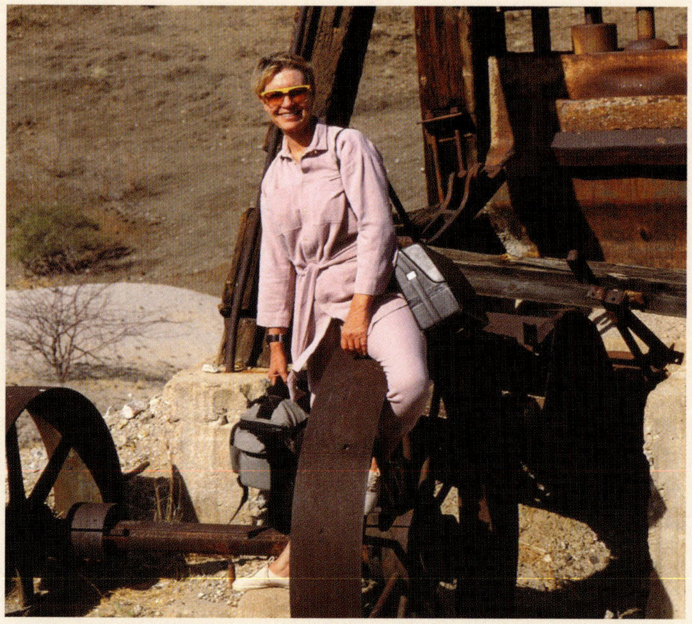

CONTENTS

PREFACE

Rock of Ages

Some young countries
hide their age
in a mass of foliage,
jungle green,
dripping with mist.
this Namibia lies
bones exposed,
a translucent desert gecko,
reptile on a rock,
crocodile on Kavango,
with latitude and longitude
mapped on its back,
dust colour chameleon
with a long tongue flick along, Caprivi
elsewhere here is mammal land
giving birth to grey shapes
that toughen under sun,
strung between equator
and quarter line.
and mountains rise
ringed in age
lined long before
and tortoise built its shell
and crawled ashore
or the first dinosaur print
was signed in stone.

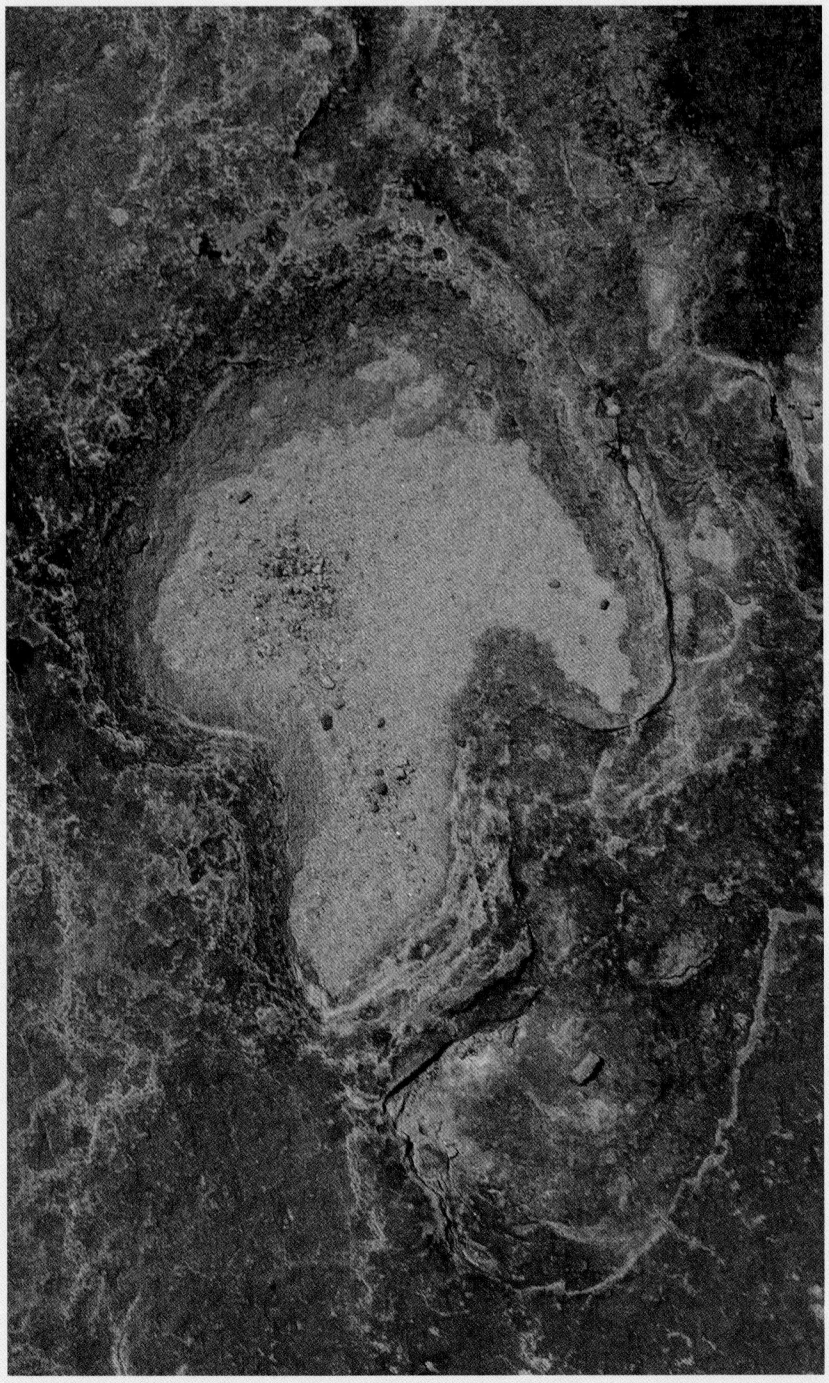

Dorian Haarhoff
Aquifers and Dust
Justified Press, Johannesburg, 1994

FOREWORD

In *Epic Land* photographer Amy Schoeman reflects not only on the extraordinary scenic beauty and diversity of the Namibian landscape, but also on the perspective-giving qualities it bestows on its visitors. This innovative and seminal interpretation of the Namibian environment through the photographic medium ranges from abstract aerials and close-ups of plants and minerals to computer-manipulated imagery with an inspirational content.

Throughout 35 years of travelling around the country to gather material, she has pointed her camera at her subject matter with passion and an informed knowledge of the Namibian natural world. Her articles have been published in international magazines such as *Travel Africa*, *Reader's Digest* and *De Kat*. They have also appeared in local magazines such as the *SWA Annual* and *Rössing Magazine*, tourism publications including *Namibia Holiday & Travel* and *Travel News Namibia*, and newspaper columns. A recurring theme in her articles has been the long-term conservation of Namibia's sensitive and vulnerable areas, especially the Namib Desert. A photographic artist who has never stood still, she understands above all the concept of illusion. Inspired by her muse, Namibia, her themes have had a natural progression from one focus area to the next.

Amy Schoeman is regarded by her peers as a pioneer in her field due to projects such as *The Five Seasons* and *Eleven*, and the thought-provoking *Mystic Desert* series, the concluding portfolio in this book. She has presented her work to the public in no less than 65 solo and a large number of group exhibitions, and is currently working on a book showcasing the work of multi-faceted Namibian artist extraordinaire J.J. van Ellinckhuijzen.

Adding value to the book are excerpts from historical and contemporary texts selected by André du Pisani and Danie Botha, and the chapter on rock art written by the late Massimo Baistrocchi, the last Italian ambassador to Namibia.

Hon. Professor Peter H. Katjavivi, MP *January 2015*

Professor Katjavivi currently serves as a Member of the Namibian Parliament and Government Chief Whip in the National Assembly. He is the Founding Vice Chancellor of the University of Namibia (UNAM) (1992–2003).

ACKNOWLEDGEMENTS

A large number of people inspired, encouraged and opened doors for me on my quest of some 35 years to accumulate photographic material on Namibia. In the years I worked for the Nature Conservation authorities I was mentored initially by Director Bernabé de la Bat and subsequently by his successor Polla Swart on environmental conservation in the wider sense, during which I became especially aware of the vulnerability of Namibia's wilderness areas, above all the ecologically fragile Namib Desert.

My husband Louw introduced me to the strange beauty and mystique of the Skeleton Coast Park. As pilot and driver, he hosted me on countless photographic missions across the length and breadth of his concession area in the park, in the adjoining Kaokoland and Damaraland, and in the central and southern Namib Desert. In subsequent years on flying trips with his sons Bertus and André Schoeman I further supplemented my visual material on the Skeleton Coast and its hinterland, especially the aerial photographs.

When I went under my own steam, I was on occasion accompanied by friends, among others Eleanor-Mary Cadell, editor of the first edition of *Skeleton Coast*; Elisabeth Braun, author of *Echoes from the Wild*; Esther van Zijl, one of my colleagues at Venture Publications; Sharri Whiting De Masi, author of *Culture Smart! Namibia*; Rianne Selle, Deputy Director of the Namibian Ministry of Information and Broadcasting; and South African sculptor, June te Water. For the patience and encouragement afforded me by these travelling companions I am most grateful.

In later years, several people took me along on 4x4 trips to remote and lesser-visited parts of the country. They were considerate in terms of the space I needed for my bulky equipment, and adapted their travelling schedules to accommodate the "golden" hours of the day. For this my sincere appreciation goes to the late Hennie Diederiks and his wife Coba, Walter and Renate Theile, Herman van Wyk and Hentie Champion, Albi and Stephan Brückner, Heidemarie Rapmund, and the late Paul van Schalkwyk and his wife Riéth.

Epic Land was conceptualised one Sunday afternoon by myself and Danie Botha of the Peace Trust as a vehicle to celebrate the variety and splendour of the Namibian landscape through my photographic images, substantiated by excerpts from contemporary and historical texts relating to the land. A former academic and parliamentarian in Namibia, Danie Botha currently works as a development facilitator and community activist in the private and non-governmental sector in Namibia, South Africa and elsewhere in Africa. He is passionate about promoting reconciliation and understanding among Namibians, and has maintained an enduring interest in Namibian visual arts and literature.

The project proposal and introduction were written by André du Pisani, Professor of Political Studies at the University of Namibia; the chapter on rock art was contributed by Massimo Baistrocchi, Italian ambassador to Namibia from 2001 to 2005; the text excerpts were compiled by Danie Botha and André du Pisani; the poem entitled Rock of Ages for the Preface was contributed by Dorian Haarhoff, a former Professor of English Literature at the University of Namibia and currently a writer, storyteller and personal development speaker based in Cape Town; and my colleague at Venture Publications, Carmen Begley, helped me prepare the visual material to support the project proposal.

I am most grateful for the professionalism, forbearance and good humour of Andreas Kahlau at Silvertone International in Johannesburg while scanning the transparencies and negatives; coding them in sequence for the seven portfolios; and handling the proofing process. Thank you to Nicol Stassen of Protea Book House for undertaking to publish *Epic Land*; to Danél Hanekom for editing the text and giving thoughtful advice and guidance in the planning stages of the book; and to Hanli Deysel for her imaginative design and layout. Last but not least, I would also like to express my gratitude to the National Arts Council of Namibia, Bank Windhoek and Herman van Wyk for providing the funds that enabled this pictorial journey through Namibia to see the light of day.

Amy Schoeman *Windhoek, 2014*

INTRODUCTION

The publication of *Epic Land* confirms that Amy Schoeman is now an immutable part of art history in Namibia and southern Africa. Over the past four decades, she has helped to form a visual language for nature photography that will continue to inspire those who come after her. The images each have their own energy. They are not uniform other than by subject – and there are images that I can only describe as classically poetic.

Epic Land is a celebration in pictures and words of the arresting beauty of the landscapes of Namibia and of the centrality of land in the culture, history, politics and daily lives of its people. The book seeks to uncover the rare essence that sets the landscape of Namibia apart from all others. Few countries in the world are richer than Namibia in its canvas of natural beauty. The landscape is one of rich and often harsh contrasts with many changing moods. A journey through this landscape is infinitely rewarding, a progression that is depicted within the seven portfolios presented in this book. The dramatic scenery of remote deserts, distant mountains, mystical trees, forbidding rock faces and stormy shores are equal to any. In this transience, the voice of beauty enters the heart of the most awakened of souls.

Variety is the key to abiding fascination, and with exuberant variety comes surprise. As is evidenced in the pages of this singular book, Namibia is a country of many surprises. In the west, among mountains and dunes sculptured over aeons and a coastline abutting the surging swell of the Atlantic Ocean, humans first roamed this impenetrable land. In the south, the bleak tablelands, gaping canyons and expansive plains seem to suggest the Hand of Nature crafting a naked beauty intended for the strong. In the central region, lined, sharp mountains rise into the full glorious fury of the Khomas Hochland. In the north, the great Etosha Pan yields a depth of vision that draws the visitor into an almost untouchable world of clear light and floating animals. In the north-east, the sacred, life-giving waters of the Zambezi and Kavango rivers are a comfort to humans, birds, and animals alike; offering a home to the water spirit and providing solace to the weary.

The image is the global language of our time. Within these pages are pictures that speak across distance; speak with respect of the sanctity of Creation, integrating mind, body, spirit and soul. In 2008, in his Introduction to Amy Schoeman's retrospective exhibition in the Sasol Art Museum in Stellenbosch, South Africa, Doug Taylor wrote: "An artist who is not squeamish about post-production, Amy has truly moved beyond the conventional and taken charge of the frame as a painter does of the canvas. Her confidence and total ownership of her images allow her to use them as raw material for composition or to apply digital effects to them, as her unerring eye sees fit." Indeed, many of Amy's pictures have stood the test of time. More than that, her pictures have shaped our image of the landscapes they recorded. Her poetic vision of nature frames contemporary debates about the intersection of art and environmentalism.

Epic Land is testimony that the material prosperity enjoyed by some in independent Namibia has not blunted the souls of all. Man fits into the Land with all its ancient savagery and power. In the words of South African novelist André Brink: "… the hard flat solid light of this land, its hills and outcrops and dunes, its sky drained of colour, a landscape too old for memory. Here is only silence, a silence of distance and space, too deep even for terror …" (*The Other Side of Silence,* 2002). It is here in the world that the stones themselves appear to glow with the mellowing influence of time. The land is possessed of a power and spirit that rivals anything that the rest of Africa can offer. Peace reigns over this landscape. It is a quality loved by Amy Schoeman, who knows its moods and inner beauty well, so vividly expressed in these poetic photographs.

One of the many redeeming features of the dignified body of work featured in these seven portfolios is that Amy probes, ever deeper, into the essence of the landscape, presenting her work in ways that move the spirit and engage the mind. The interplay between space, form and colour has given her work a painterly quality, reminiscent of the work of the American artist Georgia O'Keefe, whom she greatly admires.

Colour is the carrier of mood to the artist. She mines an eclectic range of colours and contrasts, working in the early morning, shortly before sunset and even at midday, having found that certain colours are strongest at this time of day, traditionally regarded as the worst light possible for taking photographs. An entire spectrum of emotions is embedded in her work, with the pendulum swinging from ecstasy and hope to contemplative longing. True to her craft, Amy also works in black and white. Her reflective series *Presence of the Past*, Portfolio 4 in *Epic Land,* provides as good an example as any of her mastery in this most exacting medium.

The seven portfolios of environmental photography presented in *Epic Land* pay homage to the canyons, deserts, wilderness and imposing skies of Namibia. Like the great Ansel Adams (1902–1984), Amy also points her lens at close-ups of rocks, trees, fissures and driftwood; at the small fragments that help define the natural world; and like Adams, she believes in the spiritually redemptive power of the pristine landscape. In Amy's photographs the Namibian landscape is mysterious and sacred, but never threatening. The rugged timeworn land is her nirvana that we too can reach through these moving images.

This milestone publication also testifies to the fact that Schoeman is not only an accomplished artist in a technical sense, but that her body of work springs from within; from the "intangible qualities" that make us truly human. These seven portfolios are not Namibian bound. They cross boundaries to reach out to humanity in a communicative way that reaffirms our connectedness and oneness.

In *Epic Land* many different voices speak in different languages of the power of the land and its famous rock art. The passages have been selected from the texts of Namibians and other writers referring to Namibia, the dialogue between the images and narrative speaking of respect and reverence for the land, given depth and resonance by dreams, memory and personal experience. Many celebrate the power and spirit of the land; others speak of hope, misery, solitude and loss. We need to rediscover our environment and establish an ethical and socially sustainable relationship with the land and its resources; otherwise the destruction of the land will precede the destruction of ourselves.

The extraordinary photographs reproduced in these pages were taken over three decades using a medium-format analogue Hasselblad camera and negative (slide) film. Fierce, stark and ethereal, they reveal a vision for minimalist landscapes that move and mesmerise. No photograph, however powerful, can reflect what is not within the photographer. This special book on Namibia and its powerful landscape gives credence to the words of Paul Ricoeur in his memorable work *Time and Narrative*: "Time becomes human to the extent that it is articulated through a narrative mode." *Epic Land,* through images, prose and verse, will strengthen our deep connections to Namibia and Mother Earth. Amy Schoeman is the recipient of numerous photographic awards – the most prestigious being the Fujifilm Southern Africa Professional Award, Gold in Fine Art and the Image of the Year in 2008. Her oeuvre is a source of beauty and dignity that is much needed in our post-colonial condition.

In the tradition of Ralph Waldo Emerson, she too, says: "I am the lover of uncontaminated and immortal beauty. In the wilderness I find something more dear and connate than in streets and villages. In the tranquil landscape, and especially in the distant line of the horizon, man holds something as beautiful as his own nature."

André du Pisani — *Windhoek, 2014*

André du Pisani is Professor Emeritus at the University of Namibia (UNAM) and Chairperson of the National Commission on Research, Science and Technology (NCRST). He is a widely published poet and author, was awarded the Chevalier of the Palmes Academiques by the French Government in 2006, and is an accomplished photographer.

ROCK ART IN NAMIBIA

The Epic Land is not only a paradise of biodiversity for its unique ecosystem or a destination for modern hunters looking for trophies with which to satisfy their tribal instincts as men of the twenty-first century, but also a world of graffiti and cave paintings made by our primitive forefathers on the walls of the caves and shelters in which they were dwelling or to where they withdrew to invoke the spirits of the prey they were hunting to feed their people.

Acknowledgement that our forebears who lived in the Epic Land contributed with their obscure albeit enormous work towards enlarging the Cultural Heritage of Humanity was officially recognised worldwide in 2007 by the World Heritage Committee of UNESCO when it inscribed Twyfelfontein (*/Ui-//aes*, in the local language) on its World Heritage List of cultural sites as a location to be protected. Twyfelfontein, however, is only the tip of the iceberg.

The first fresco discovered in the Epic Land was by land surveyor Reinhardt Maack in 1917 while doing appraisals on the Brandberg, an imposing almost-circular granite massif about 30 kilometres long and 25 kilometres wide, with an altitude of some 2600 metres at Königstein, its highest point. Estimated to be 120 million years old, the Ovaherero tribespeople refer to the massif as Omukuruwaro, translated as The Burning Mountain.

But it was not Maack who gave the now famous fresco the name it carries today. It was named in 1929 by a French anthropologist, Abbé Henry Breuil, considered in his day as one of the great Paleolithic art specialists. During a visit to South Africa, Abbé Breuil was awestruck by a replica of the fresco made by Maack. During the World War II years, Breuil made an attempt to visit the Brandberg himself, sending a letter to General J.C. Smuts, the South African Prime Minister at the time, with the following request: "I am sending you a picture of a girl full of charm who has been waiting for us under a rock shelter on the mountain massif Brandberg for about 3000 years: do you think it would be appropriate to make her wait any longer?"

Although his attempt was unsuccessful, Breuil continued studying the replica. He came to the conclusion that the magnificent fresco could not have been painted by local people, who were considered to be "too backward and underdeveloped", but must be the work of individuals of a "superior culture". It followed, for Breuil, that the authors of the wall painting could only have come from the "Mediterranean cradle", and thus have been Minoans, Mycenaeans, Phoenicians or at any rate "Peoples of the Sea".

In 1947 Abbé Breuil made a second even bigger incorrect hypothesis when he interpreted the central figure in the fresco as being a "young female bull-leaper in Crete". In fact, he was convinced that his "lady" was dressed in clothes similar to those on a famous fresco in the Palace of Minos at Knossos in Crete depicting the labyrinth designed by the legendary Daedalus to hold the Minotaur, a creature that was half man and half bull, which was subsequently killed by the Athenian hero Theseus. With this Minoan attribution, he confirmed his earlier hypothesis that the fresco was of Mediterranean origin! It should be noted that the "girl" in question is undoubtedly a male, due to the presence of genital organs (already detected by the discoverer of the fresco, Maack) and that he is brandishing objects that appear in African iconography, as well as in other primitive cultures, which are unmistakably features of the hunter, to wit a bow and arrow.

The frieze found in the Tsisab Valley on the Brandberg depicts a procession of people, animals and mythological creatures as well as other figures resembling hunters. In the centre of the panel, which is occupied by two extraordinary characters, are flute and string-instrument players. The first figure – the famous "White Lady" – is painted in white and brown, with body decorations of leather strips and other beaded ornamentation adorning his arms and wrists, knees and ankles. In his right hand he carries a bow and arrows, and in the left an object that could be a cup or a flower with a long stem. This figure is followed by another – a keeper? a coryphaeus?

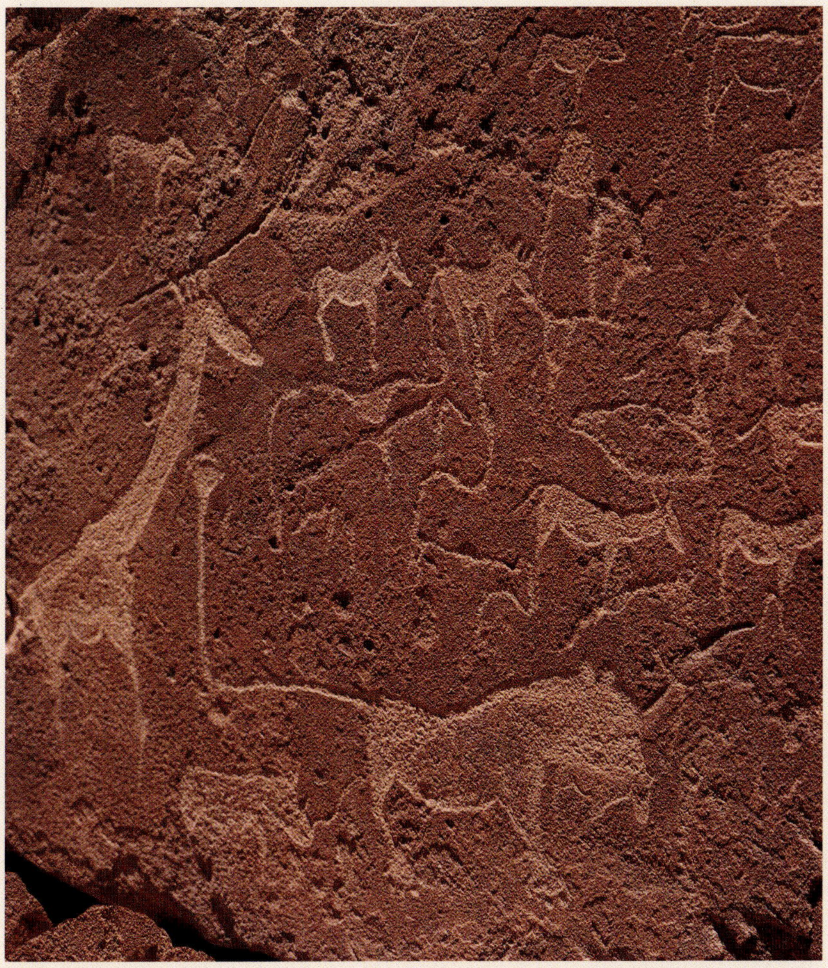

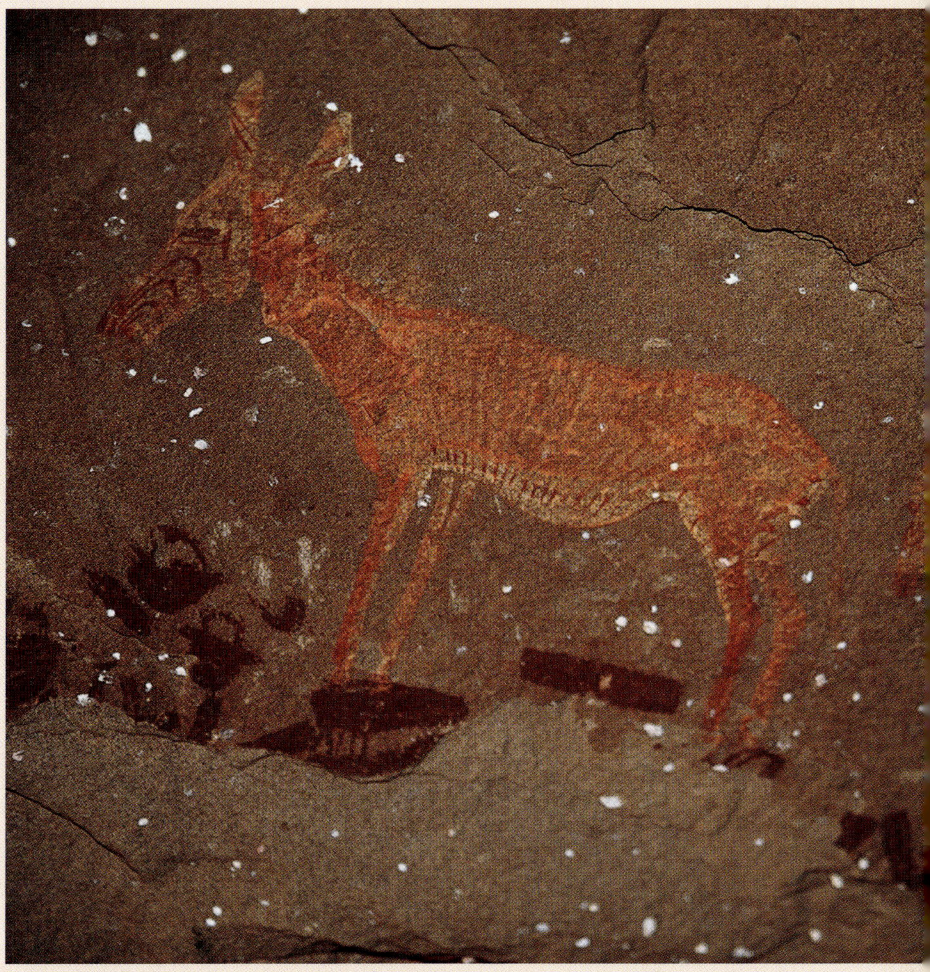

(LEFT) Rock engravings, Twyfelfontein (RIGHT) Rock painting, western Kunene Region

a priest? – painted in dark ochre, whose body is also richly decorated, and seems to be touching the body of the White Lady with a long stick. The scene is completed with a large parade of warriors with bows and arrows, quivers, sandals or shoes, coupled with female figurines, and a large number of animals – kudu, springbok and other antelope, wildebeest, eland and zebra.

An intriguing aspect of the White Lady fresco, and one that is characteristic of the aboriginal rock art of the Koisan people, widely referred to nowadays as the Bushmen, is the presence of anthropomorphic figures with zoomorphic heads, with some having human characteristics, such as human legs. These images are often associated with hunting scenes and different ceremonies, or portraying dream experiences and hypnotic trances held in the rainmaking rituals and ceremonies.

When was the frieze we refer to as the White Lady painted?

Upon scrutiny it becomes obvious that it was created over a long period of time by different hands – this is indicated by the overlapping images that show a diversity of styles and composition. But is it possible to establish when this period was? In rock-art analyses and studies, contrary to work done on archaeological excavations, there are not layers that scholars can pass through a strainer. Rock art locations do not have "garbage sites" where our forefathers dumped their waste, creating trash in which we can find charcoal or other proteins that can be dated using modern techniques, such as C14 tests or radiocarbon dating, or potassium-argon analysis, testing by thermoluminescence, and so on.

In the case of the Brandberg, scholars were unusually lucky. In ancient times a fragment of a painting in a shelter on the Upper

Brandberg fell from the wall, to be discovered at a later date by the researcher Peter Breunig. The coals associated in the deposit layer with that fragment were dated as 2700 years old. And it was possible at a later stage to put that fragment of painting back!

A few hundred kilometres north-east of the Brandberg is Twyfelfontein, one of the other great sanctuaries of Namibian rock art. The name of the site is an Afrikaans word meaning "doubtful spring". It was given by the farmer on whose land it was discovered, due to the source being replenished only sporadically by spring rains.

On 28 June 2007, the World Heritage Committee of UNESCO inscribed Twyfelfontein (*/Ui-//aes* in the local language) on its World Heritage List of cultural sites as part of the protected Cultural Heritage of Humanity. No less than 2500 engravings on about 200 slabs of sandstone were discovered at Twyfelfontein, depicting lion, elephant, rhino, zebra, several kinds of antelope, giraffe and ostrich. Although presented in schematic form, they were engraved with many fine details. On the so-called Ceremonial Rock, a set of large slabs of sandstone detached from the higher slopes, the animals are represented by the footprints they leave on the ground. Easily recognisable are the hoofprints of kudu and gemsbok, ostrich and giraffe, associated with the pawprints of many predators, including African wild cat, lion, leopard and cheetah. Possibly the most famous engraving at the site is the so-called Lion Man, a zoomorphic figure of a lion, but with five toes. This figure is connected to the rituals practised by the indigenous communities of hunter-gatherers that lived in the Twyfelfontein environs.

Although the stone slabs do not have anthropomorphic representation, marks of the hands and feet of human beings can be associated with long lines of paired dots (interpreted by some experts as elements of "games" or "calendars") or abstract designs, with spirals and circular sequences of dots representing the sun or the stars in the sky? Or in heaven? The engravings suggest – as we can read in the communiqué released in 2007 announcing the UNESCO World Heritage List of cultural sites that "... the rock art was linked to the belief system of hunter-gatherers who dominated the area until the arrival of pastoralists around 1000 AD. The site forms a coherent, extensive and high-quality record of ritual practices relating to hunter-gatherer communities in this part of southern Africa over at least 2000 years; and eloquently illustrates the links between the ritual and economic practices of hunter-gatherers."

Some scholars believe that the engravings are older than the paintings in the surrounding areas – a hypothesis that is yet to be verified. However, the objects excavated in two tests of the archaeological site strata of Twyfelfontein (but not related directly to the stone slabs or the engravings), produced ornaments in schist, slices of ostrich eggshells used for necklaces, and other stone artefacts typical of the Stone Age indicated. These artefacts were dated as being between 3000 and 5000 years old.

Until recently the Brandberg massif was considered to be the richest rock-art site in the Epic Land. This has, however, gradually been disproven by the discoveries made in other regions, such as the Erongo Mountains, a vast volcanic caldera located between Omaruru and Karibib. Virtually every farm within or outside the caldera has shelters and caves with a wealth of rock-art paintings and engravings, but the local cattle farmers, until recently, were wary of "opening up" their properties to strangers – tourists and scholars alike.

Anibib Farm, located in the heart of the Erongo Region, is rich in petroglyphs and rock paintings, while a few embers were discovered in the human dumping area of Philipp's Cave on Ameib Farm. These can unfortunately not be associated directly with the paintings, but have been dated back 3370 years.

Close to the Erongo caldera there is another smaller volcanic massif, comprising two groups of mountains known as the Gross (Big) and Klein (Small) Spitzkoppe. An initial systematic survey conducted in 1996 recorded more than 35 rock sites here.

A curious feature of the Spitzkoppe paintings are representations of the so called "sphinxes-griffins", a definition once again given by Abbé Breuil, and attributed by him to a "Semitic, Nilotic and Mediterranean culture". Apart from the imaginative interpretation of the works of art, we must recognise the unusual colour (that of reddish, clayey earth), shape and outline of some smaller figures. The fact that they were painted "under" other icons with which we are more familiar, may provide evidence that these Spitzkoppe "records" are far more ancient than those of the surrounding regions, including the Brandberg and Erongo Mountains. This has yet to be confirmed.

Finally, in the deep south of our Epic Land, close to the Fish River Canyon, comes one of the most interesting rock-art discoveries ever made. Under a shelter in the Huns Mountains, which was christened Apollo 11 (the discovery was made in 1969, the year in which the world's attention was captivated by the moon explorations), German archaeologist Wolfgang Wendt brought to light some of the oldest human artifacts on the entire African continent. These are seven stone slabs on which man painted, with coal, ochre and white kaolin, a rhino and a zebra. The charcoals stored in the layers where the slabs were found made it possible to date the layers as having formed some 27 000 years ago.

Today research on rock art in Namibia, as in many other parts of Africa – considered today as the Cradle of Humankind – is aimed not only at providing a better understanding of our past, but also at preserving and protecting these sites from vandalism, negligence and human stupidity, since a simple graffiti or painting made hundreds or thousands of years ago by an ancestor is without doubt a common heritage for all of humanity. It is our responsibility to conserve, protect and keep it intact for those who come after us.

Massimo Baistrocchi — *Windhoek, 2012*

The late Massimo Baistrocchi, a graduate in Political Science at the University of Milan, was the Italian ambassador to Namibia from 2001 to 2004. While posted in Algeria, he developed an interest in rock art, and started writing on Saharan rock art and African cultures. He was a widely exhibited artist with over 70 exhibitions to his name, and a writer whose essays, short stories and novels have been published in over 30 books.

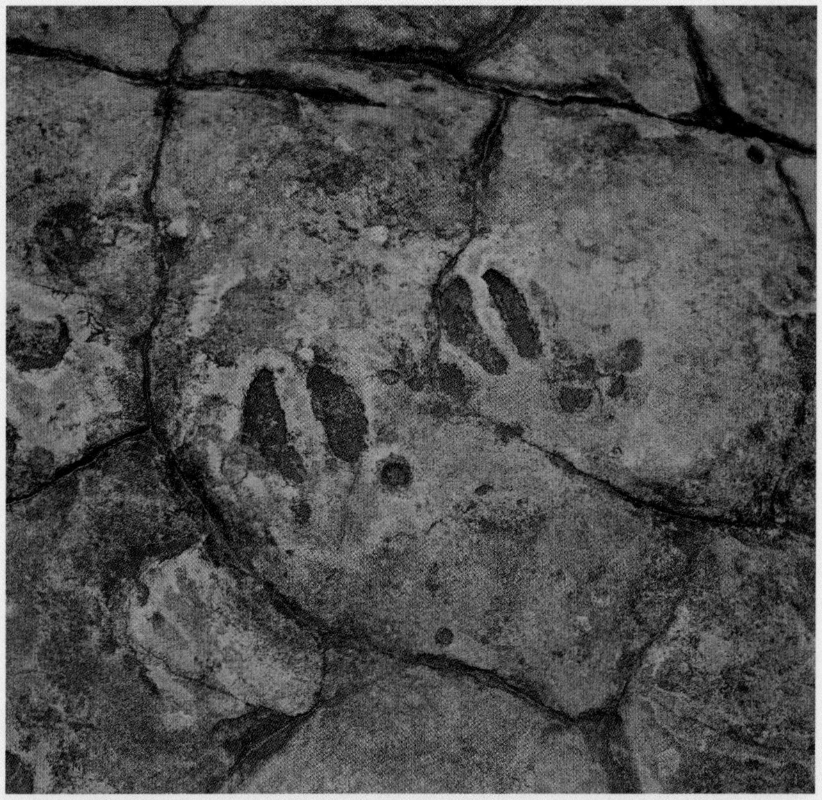

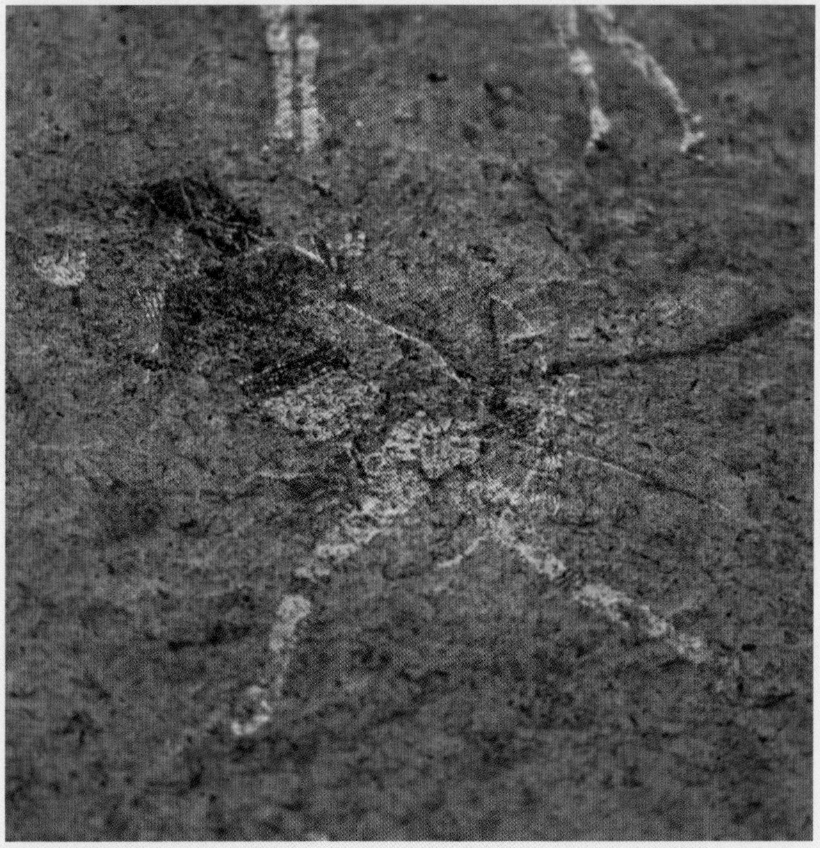

(TOP) Rock engravings by Yellow Bushmen, Waterberg Plateau
(BOTTOM) The White Lady, Brandberg

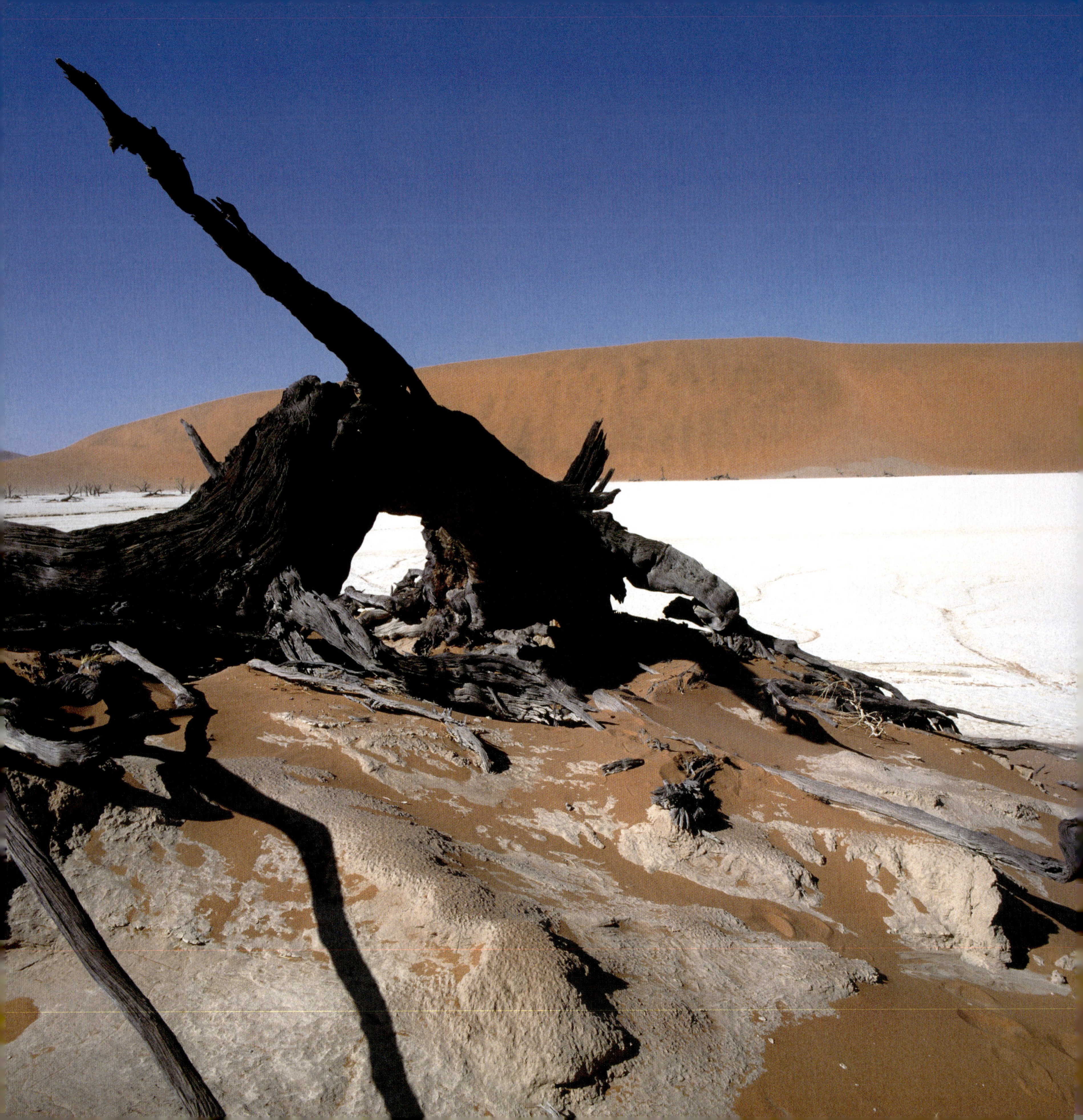

Portfolio 1

EPIC LAND

When selecting the images for the title portfolio, my objective was to represent the great diversity and scenic splendour of Namibia as comprehensively as possible. This meant poring over my light-table with a critical eye for several months, as the many thousands of transparencies in my library represent some 35 years of flying over and driving around in the country. On these photographic missions to gain material on the Namibian environment and its many facets, I drove myself when feasible, enabling me to photograph when I was on my own.

When taking pictures in the northern Namib, I was aided logistically by my late husband Louw Schoeman, who willingly flew me over and drove me through the lesser-travelled areas of the Skeleton Coast, Kaokoland and Damaraland, to "look and see". From time to time we camped in remote locations such as the Hartmann Valley, Marienfluss and Kunene environs, to be "on the spot" in the "golden" early-morning and late-afternoon hours. In later years I was invited to accompany friends to locations such as the Khaudum environs and Kalahari Desert in eastern Namibia, and to Caprivi in the far north-east. On these trips I gained much of the material featured in this portfolio. In my quest to capture the Epic Land through my lens, I found that the landscape photographer embarks on a never-ending journey of discovery.

To quote John Szarkowski in his introduction to the book *The Portfolios of Ansel Adams*: "Serious photographers believe that photography is something larger and more inclusive than the sum of all photographs made thus far, larger even than all those that will be made in future, and that the chief adventure of the medium lies not in using what is known but in learning more."

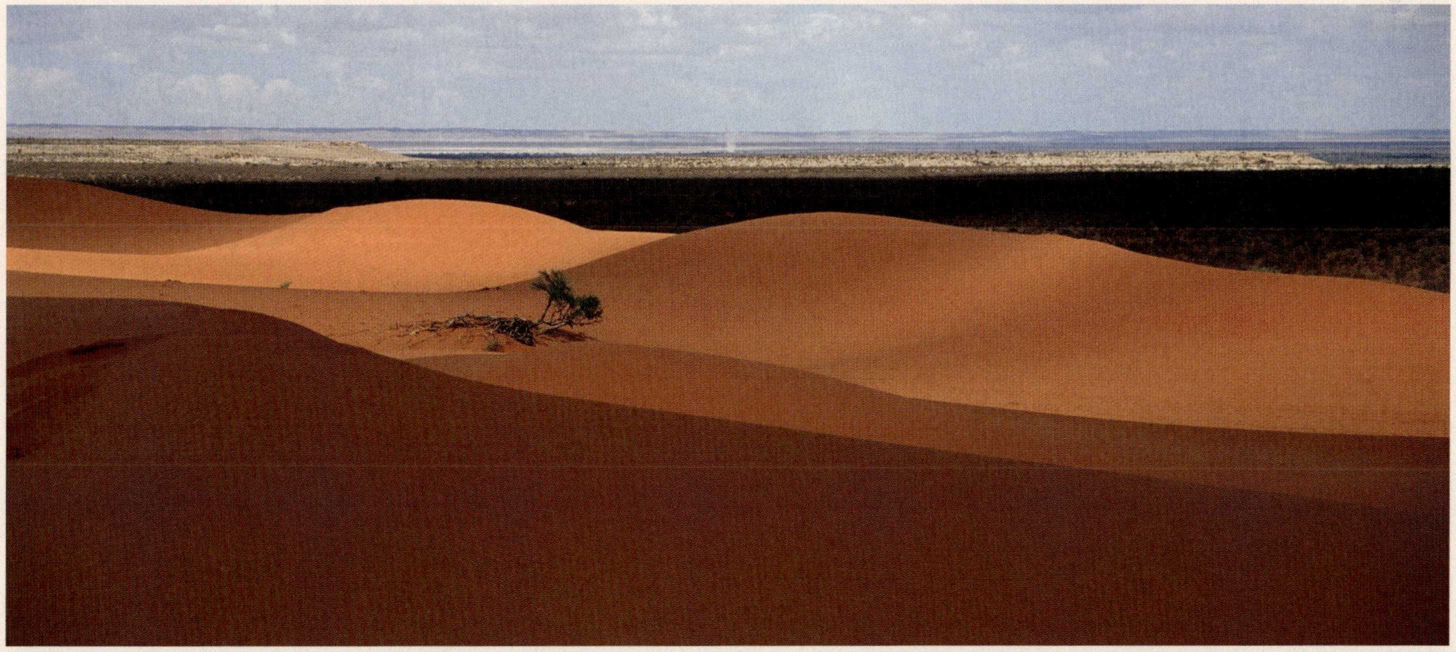

(OPPOSITE) Pointing north, Dead Pan (ABOVE) Kalahari Landscape

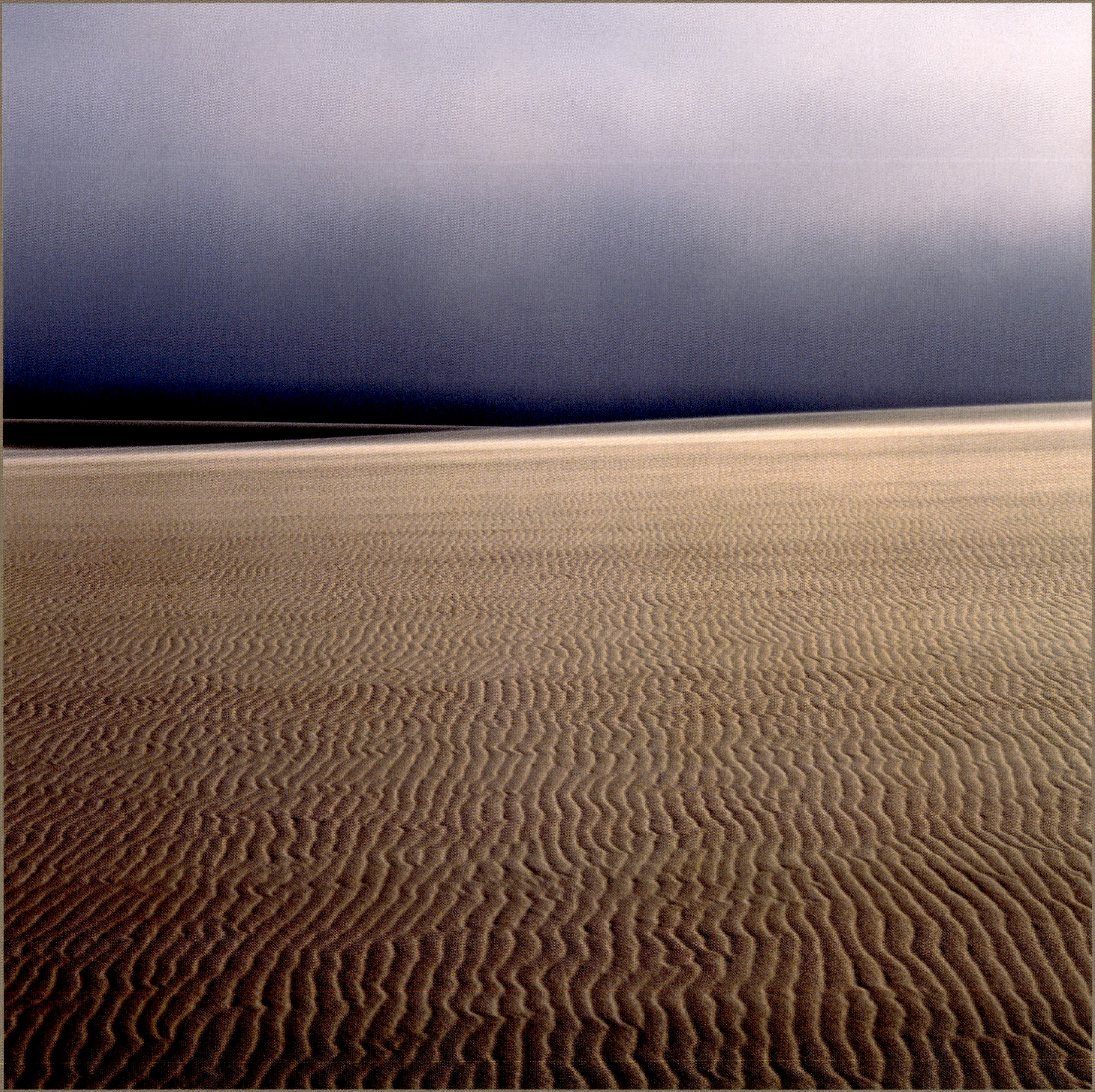

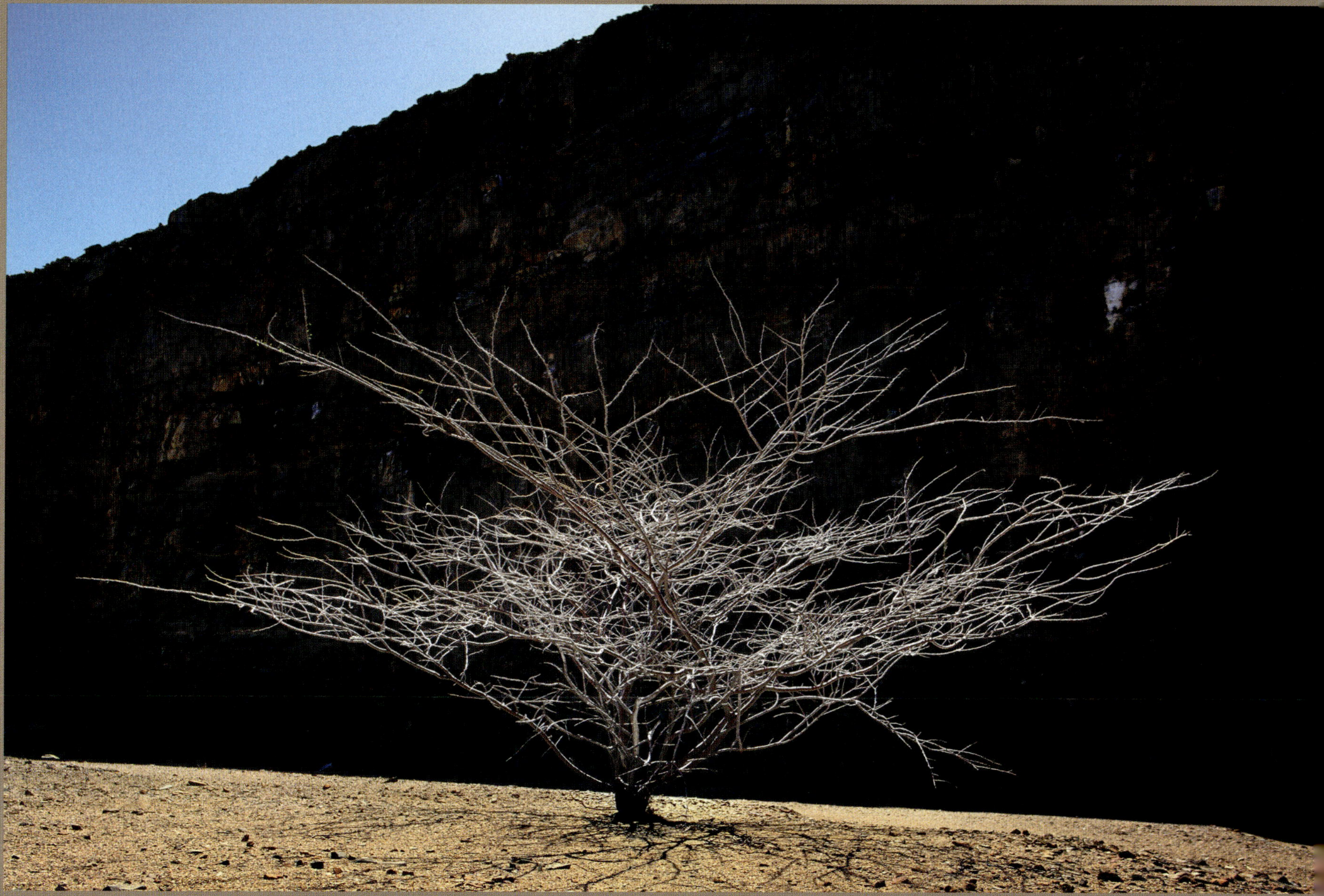

(OPPOSITE) Sea Namibia (ABOVE) Damaraland Tree

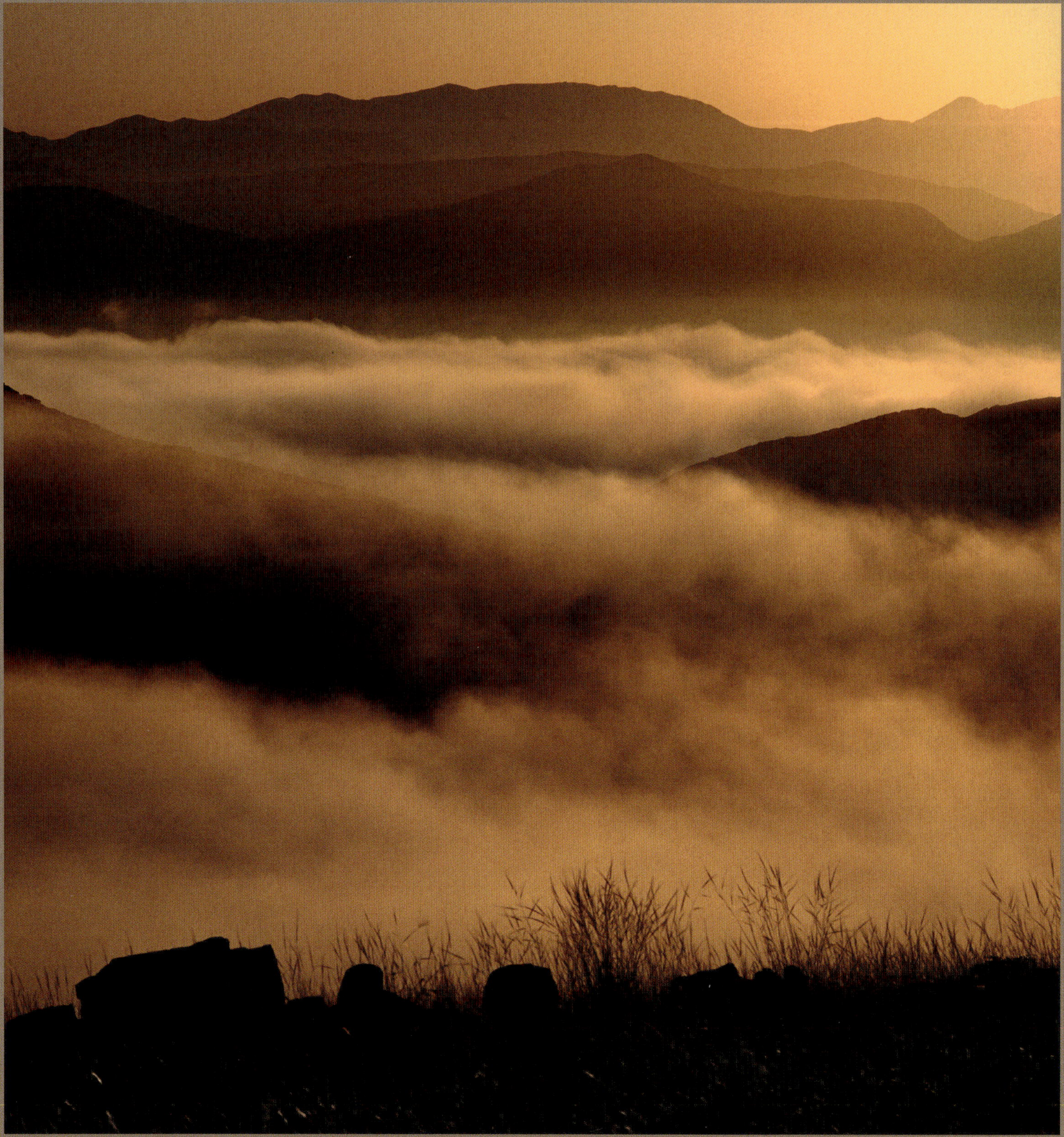

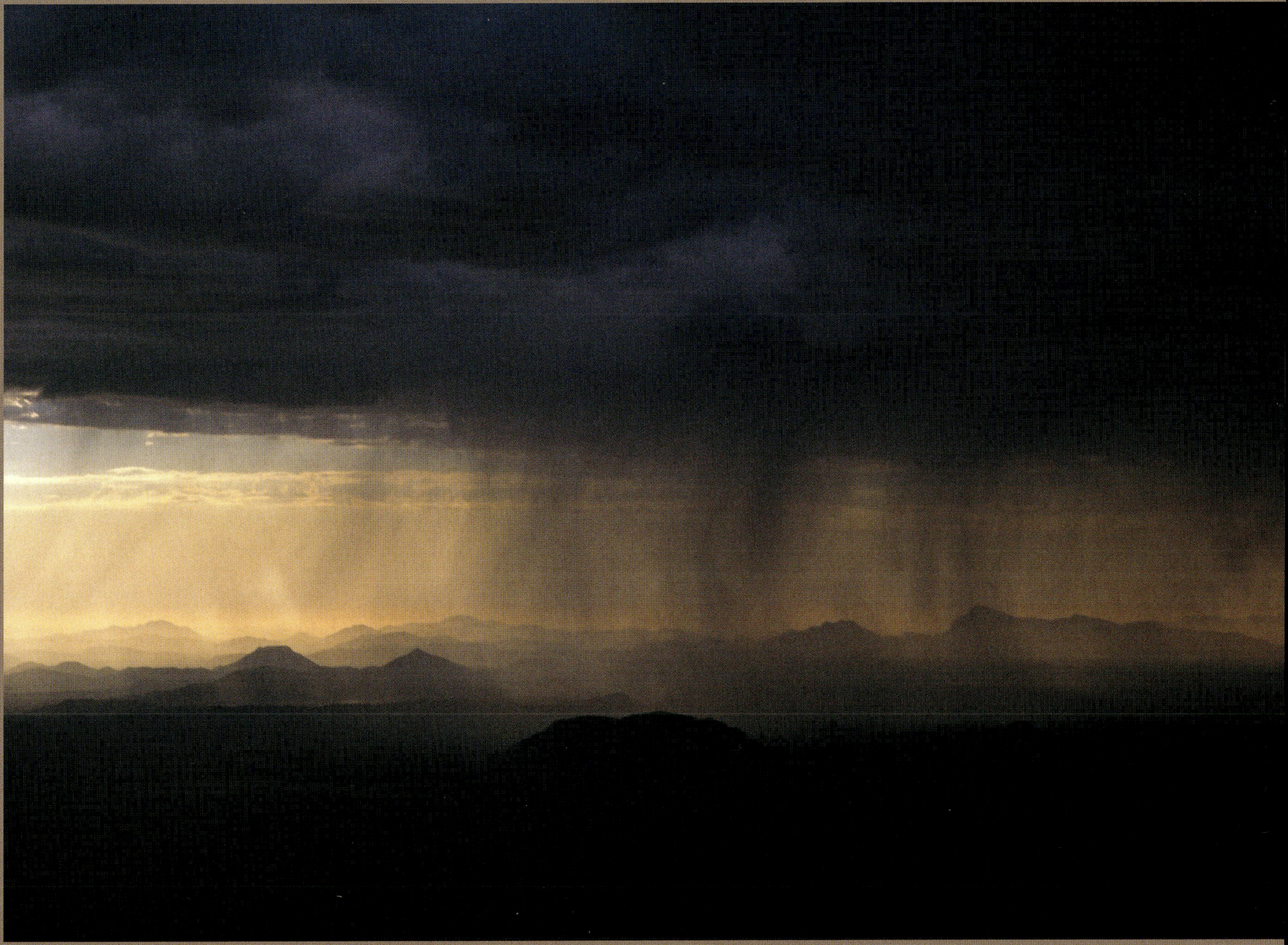

(OPPOSITE) Kunene Dawn (ABOVE) Rain Storm

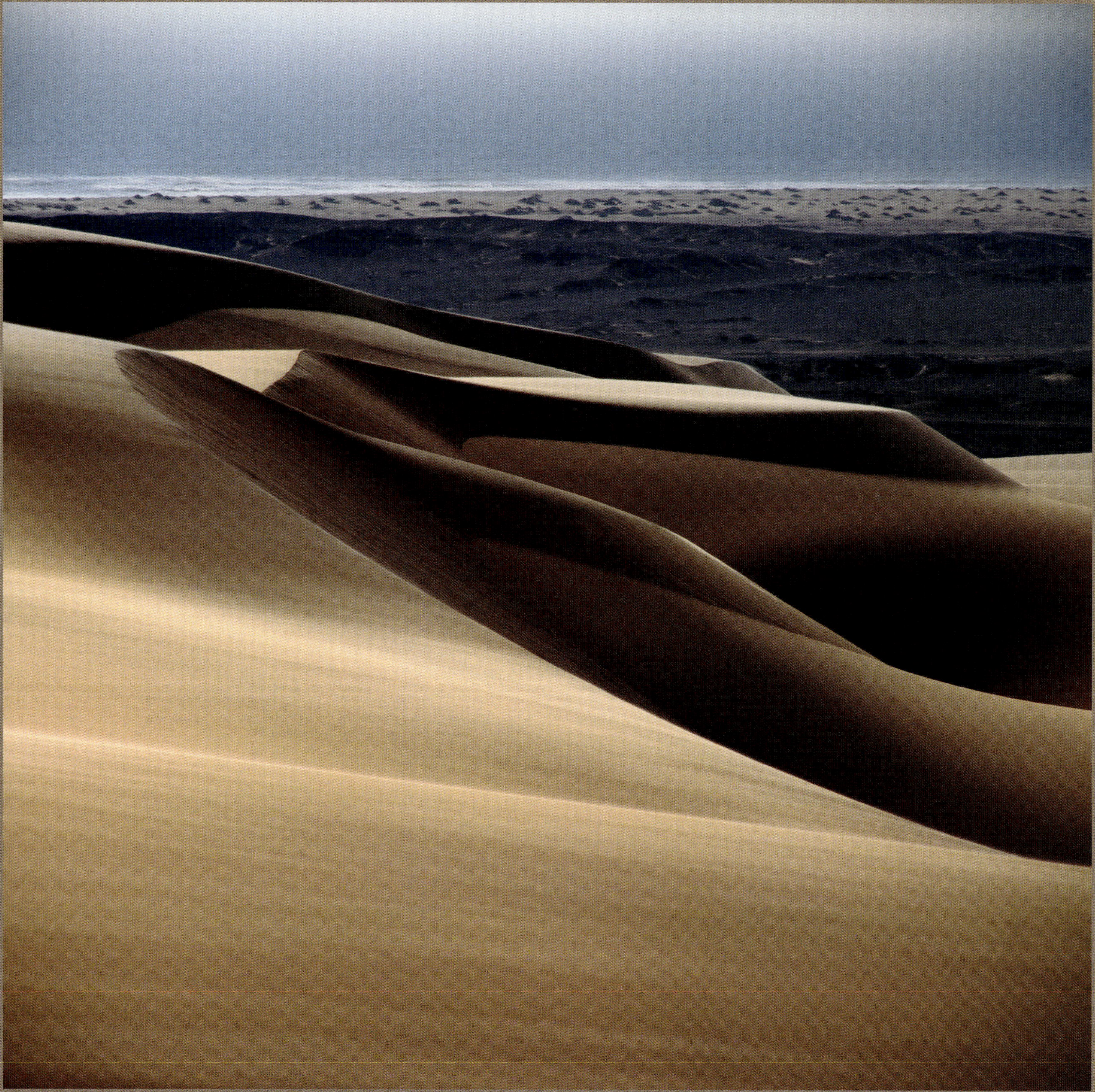

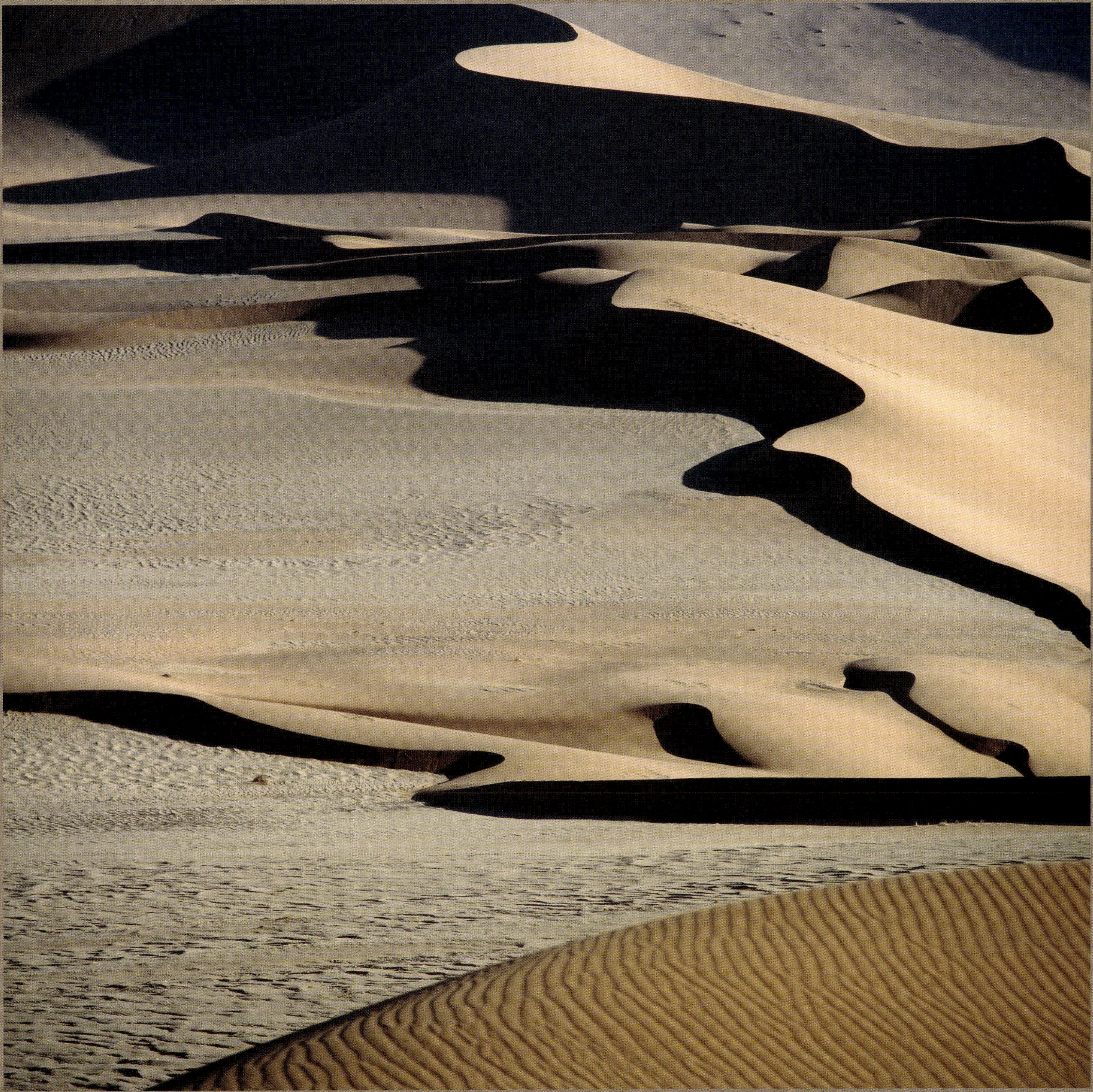

(OPPOSITE) Coastal Dunes (ABOVE) Dunescape, Sossusvlei

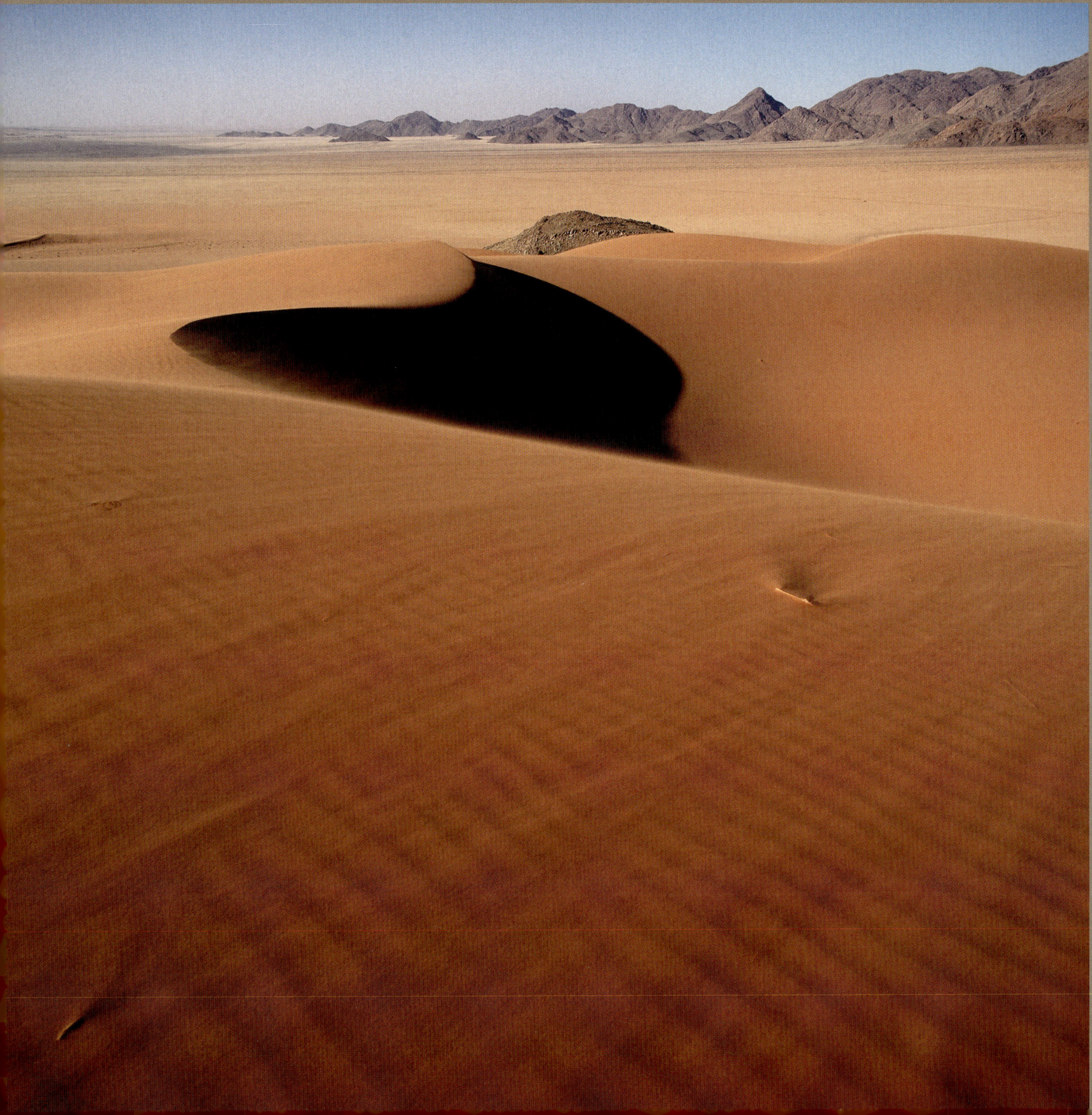

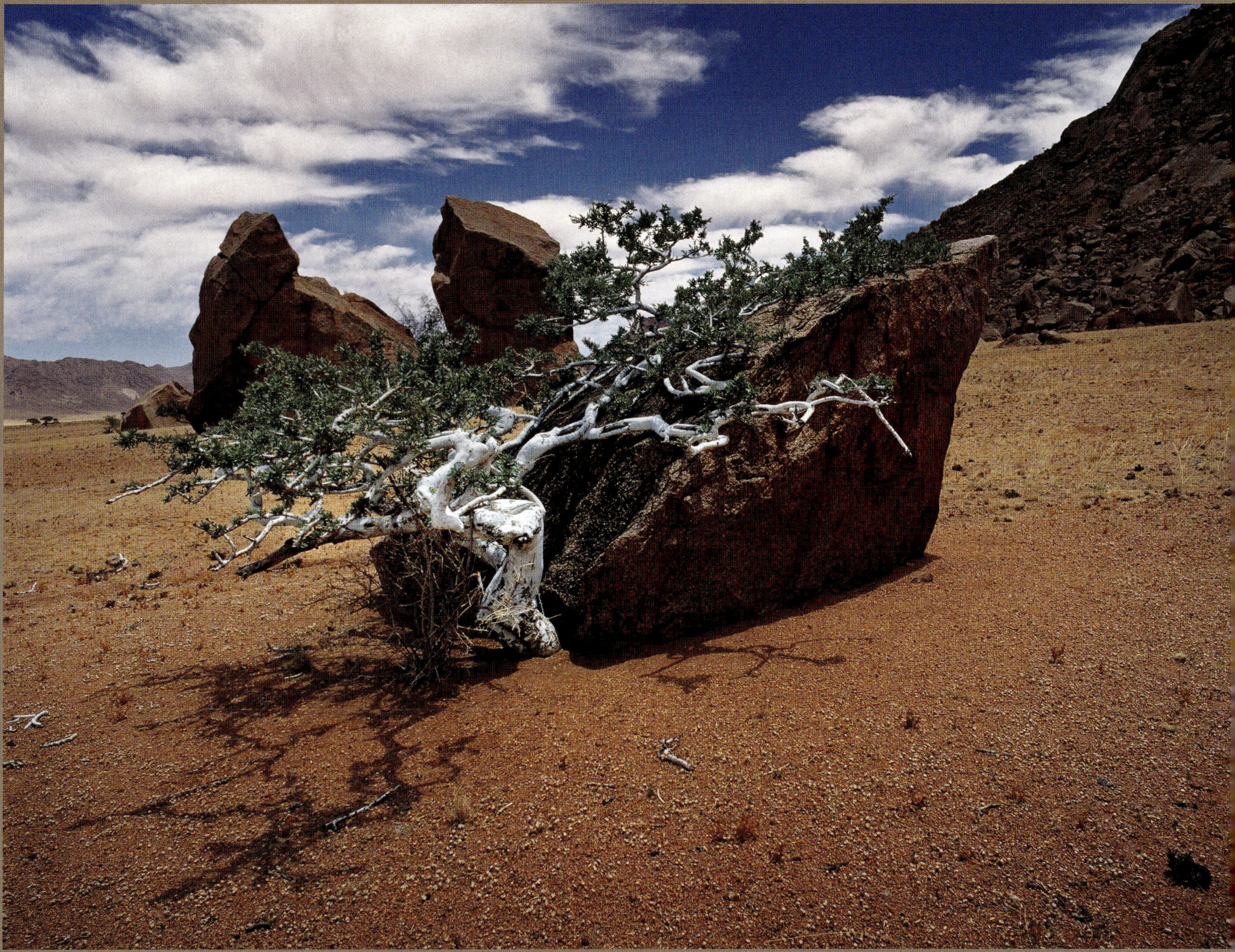

Smoking Dune and Rock-splitting Fig, Namtib Biosphere Reserve

The Namib has many faces,

some of them

forbidding,

some of them

beautiful,

all of them

fascinating.

Henno Martin, geologist and writer

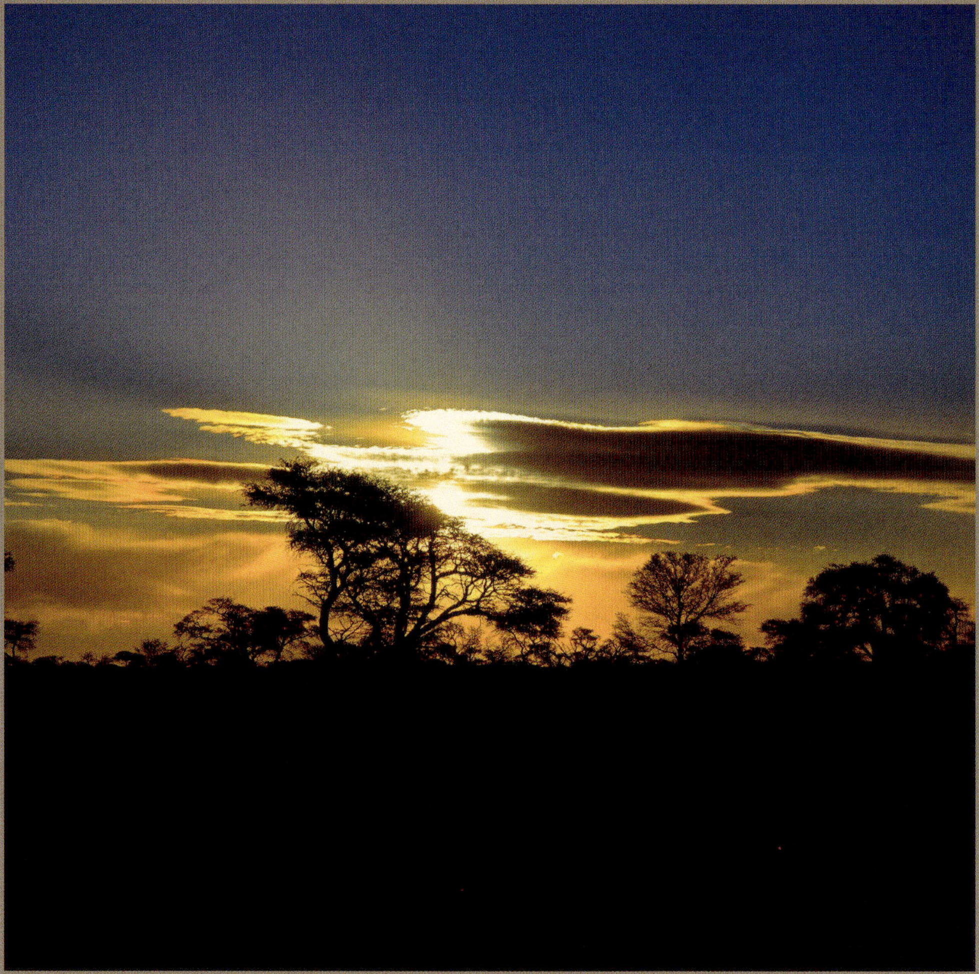

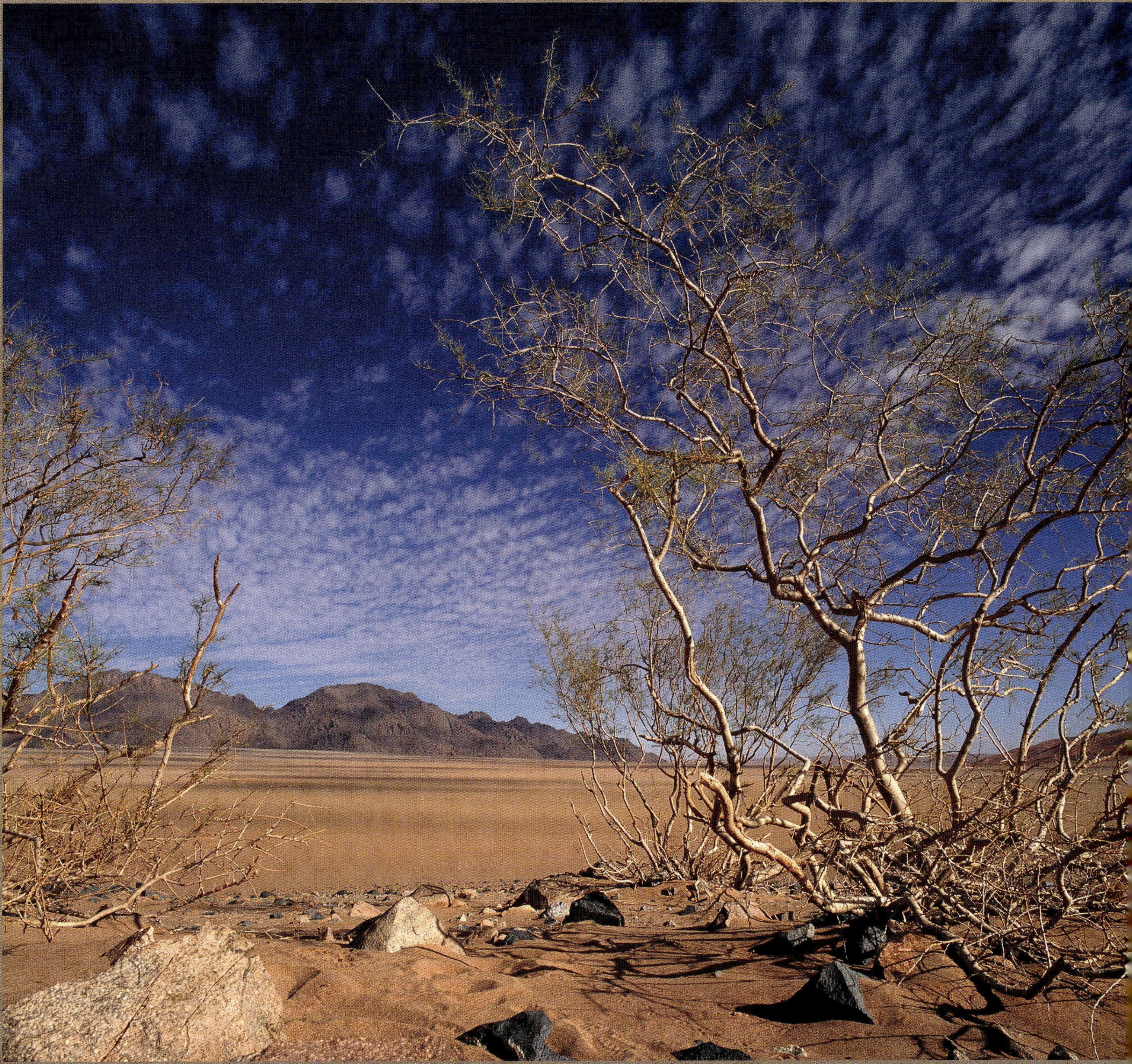

(OPPOSITE) Kalahari Sunset, eastern Namibia (ABOVE) View from Chateau, NamibRand Nature Reserve

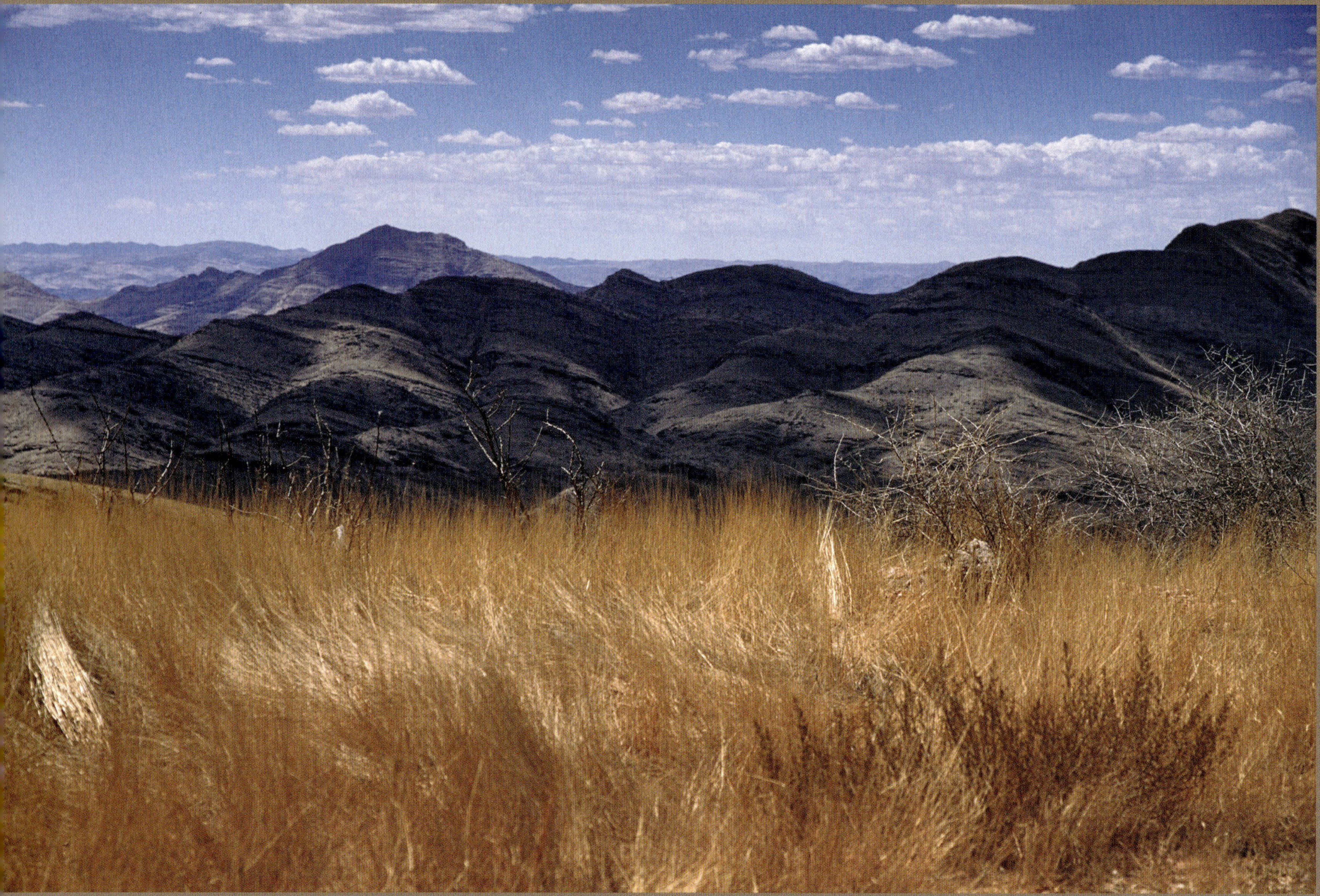

(ABOVE) Khomas Hochland, Central Highlands (OPPOSITE) Fossil Dunes, Dieprivier Farm, southern Namibia

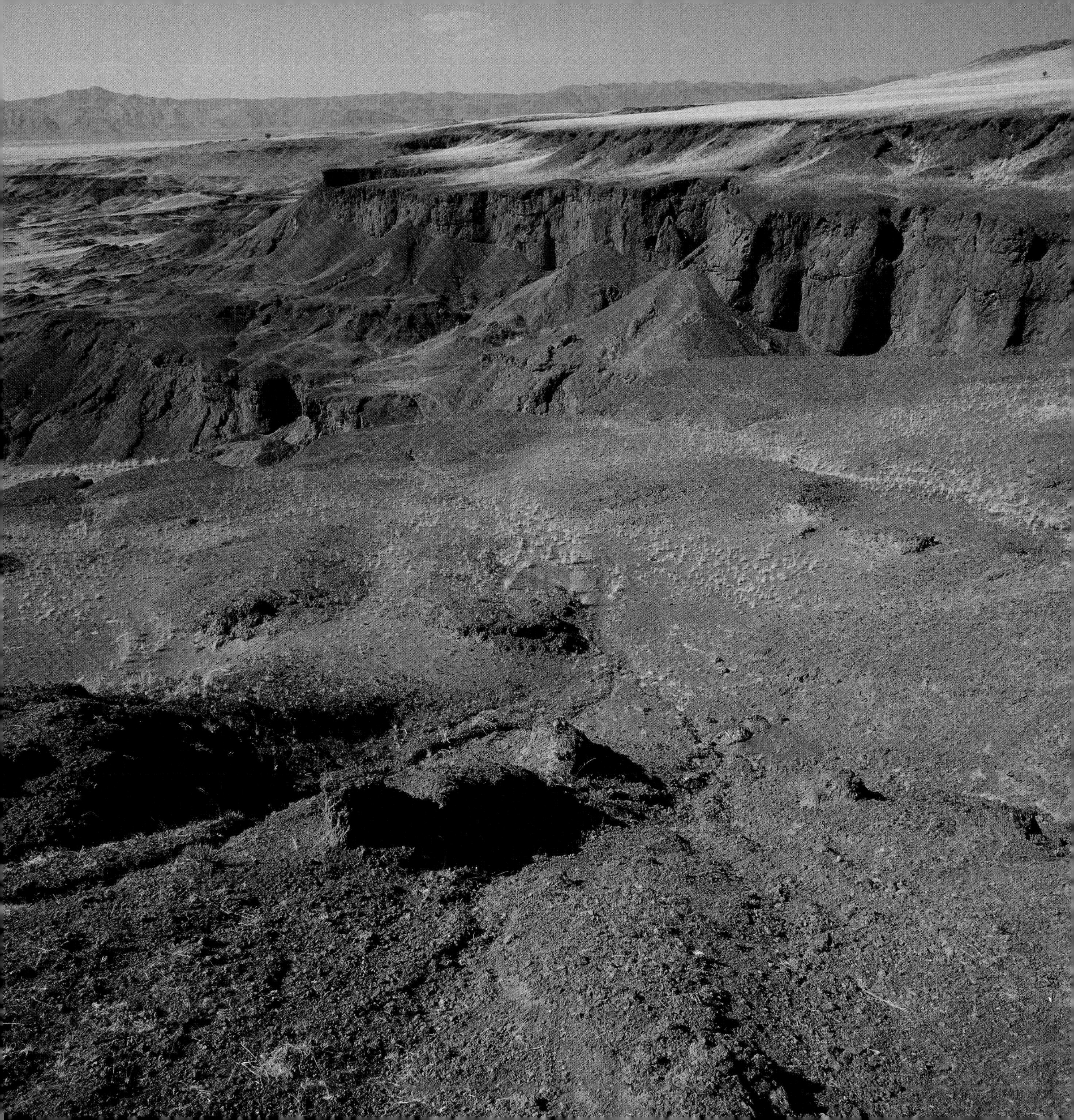

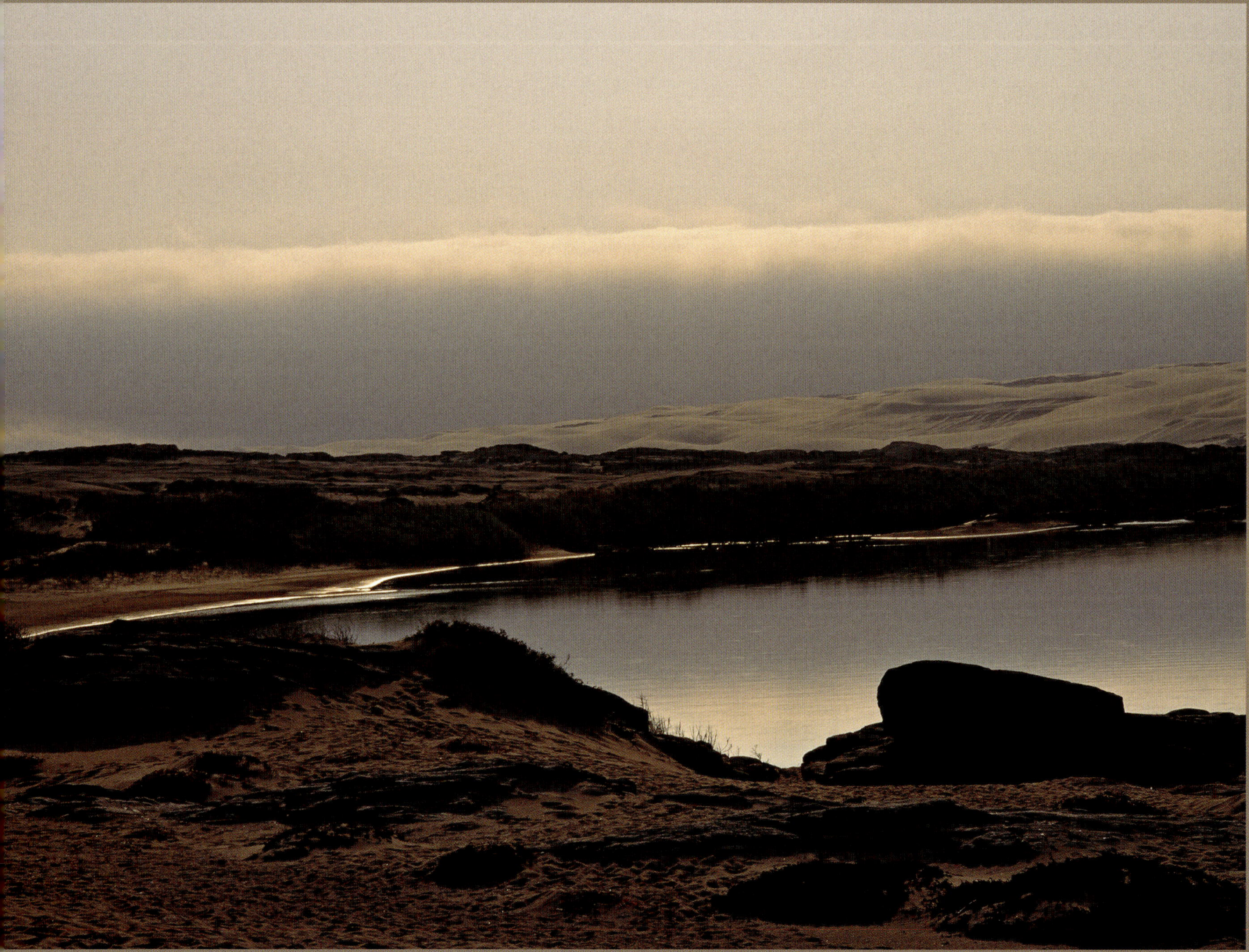

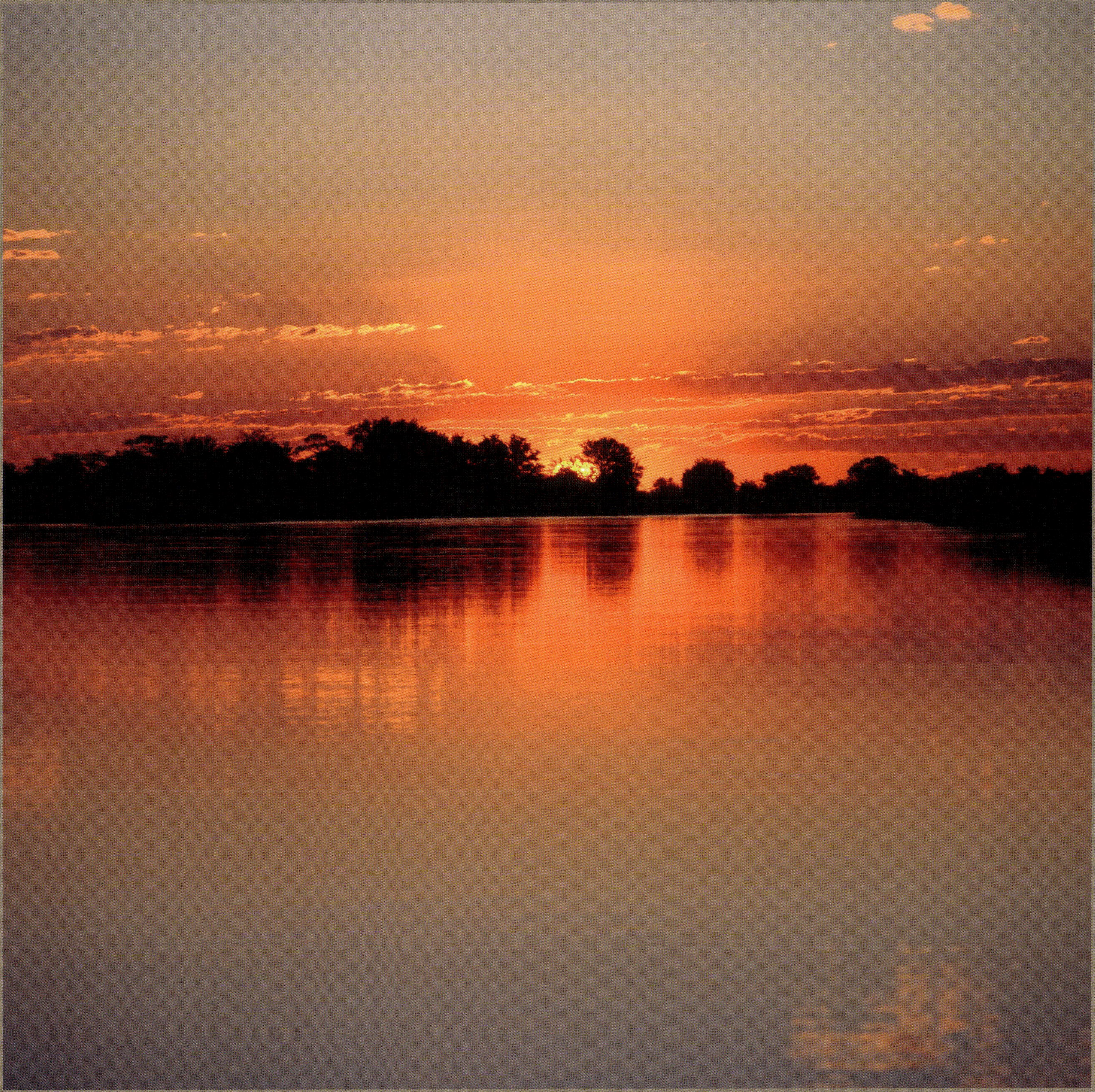

(OPPOSITE) Kunene Mouth, Kaokoland (ABOVE) Cocktail Hour, Kavango Region

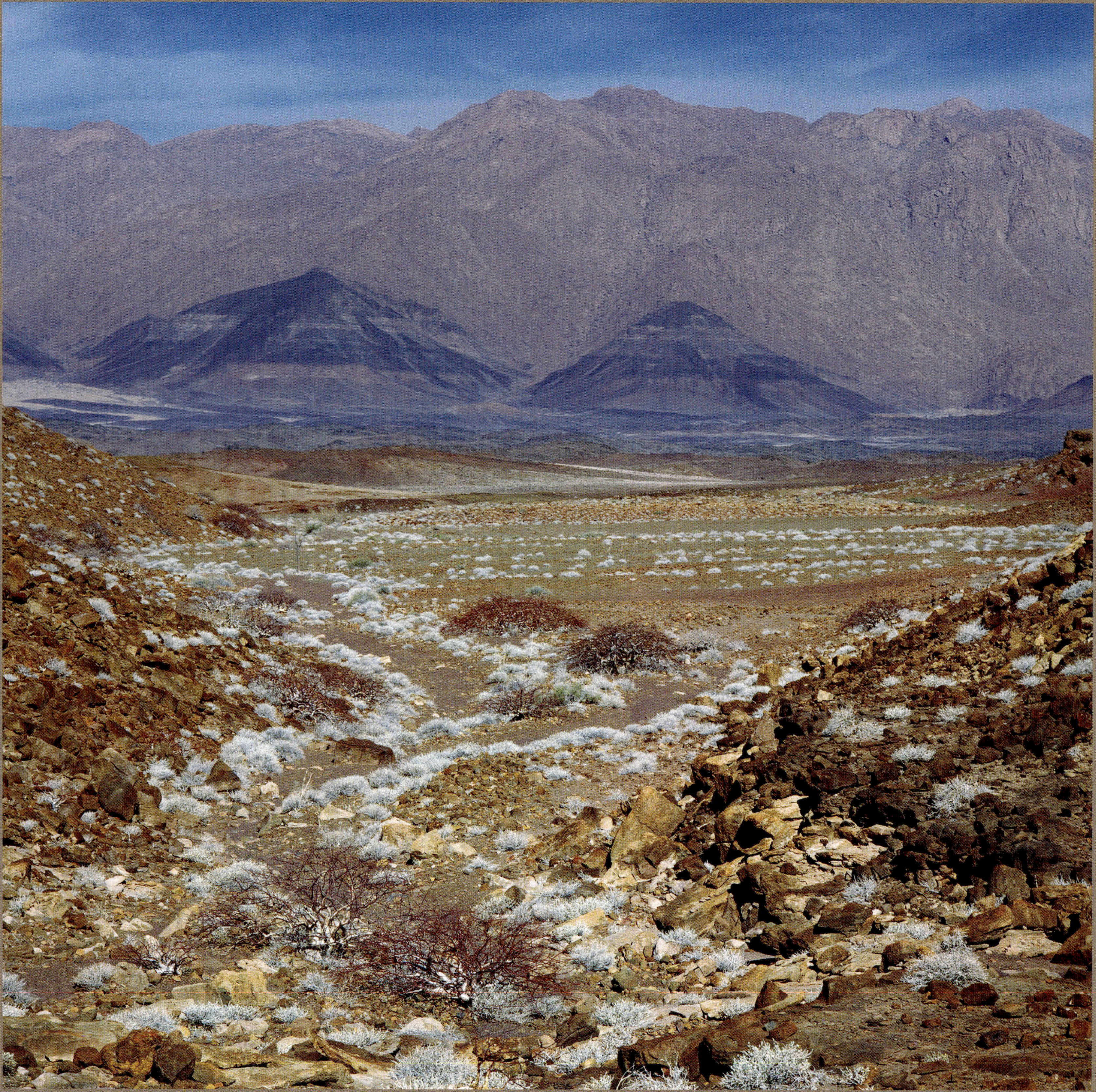

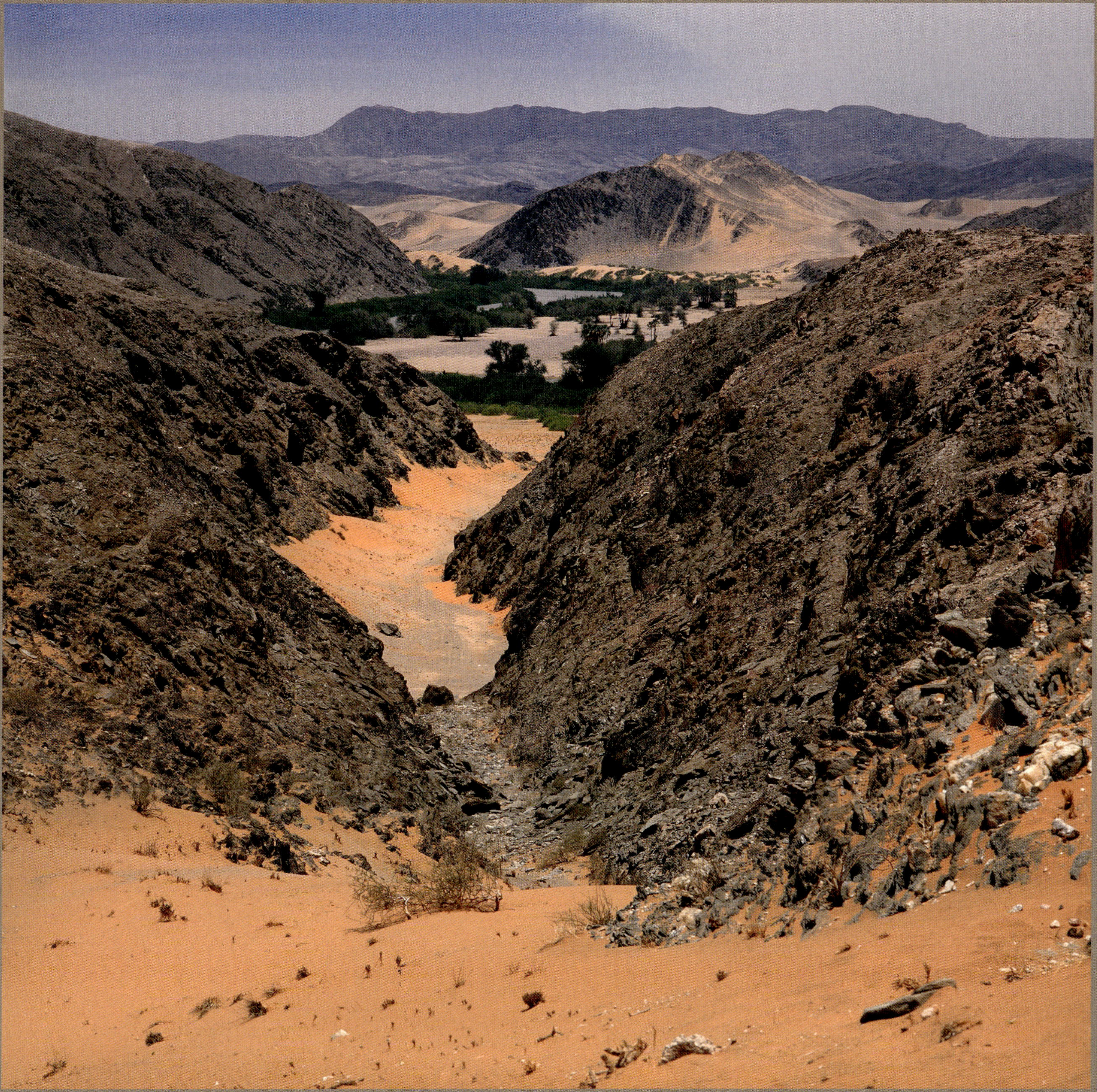

(OPPOSITE) Brandberg Mountain Massif, Damaraland (ABOVE) Kunene View, Hartmann Valley

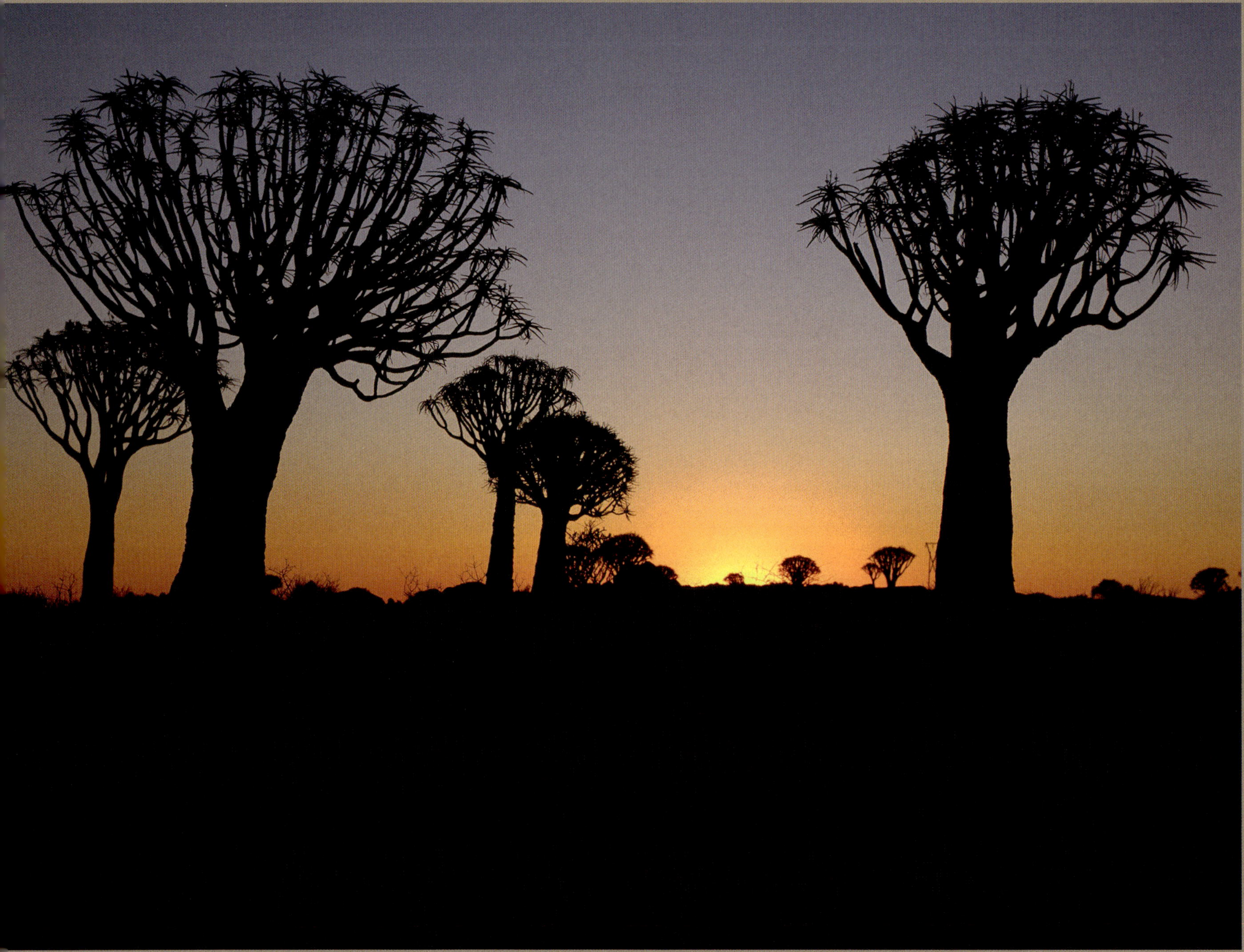

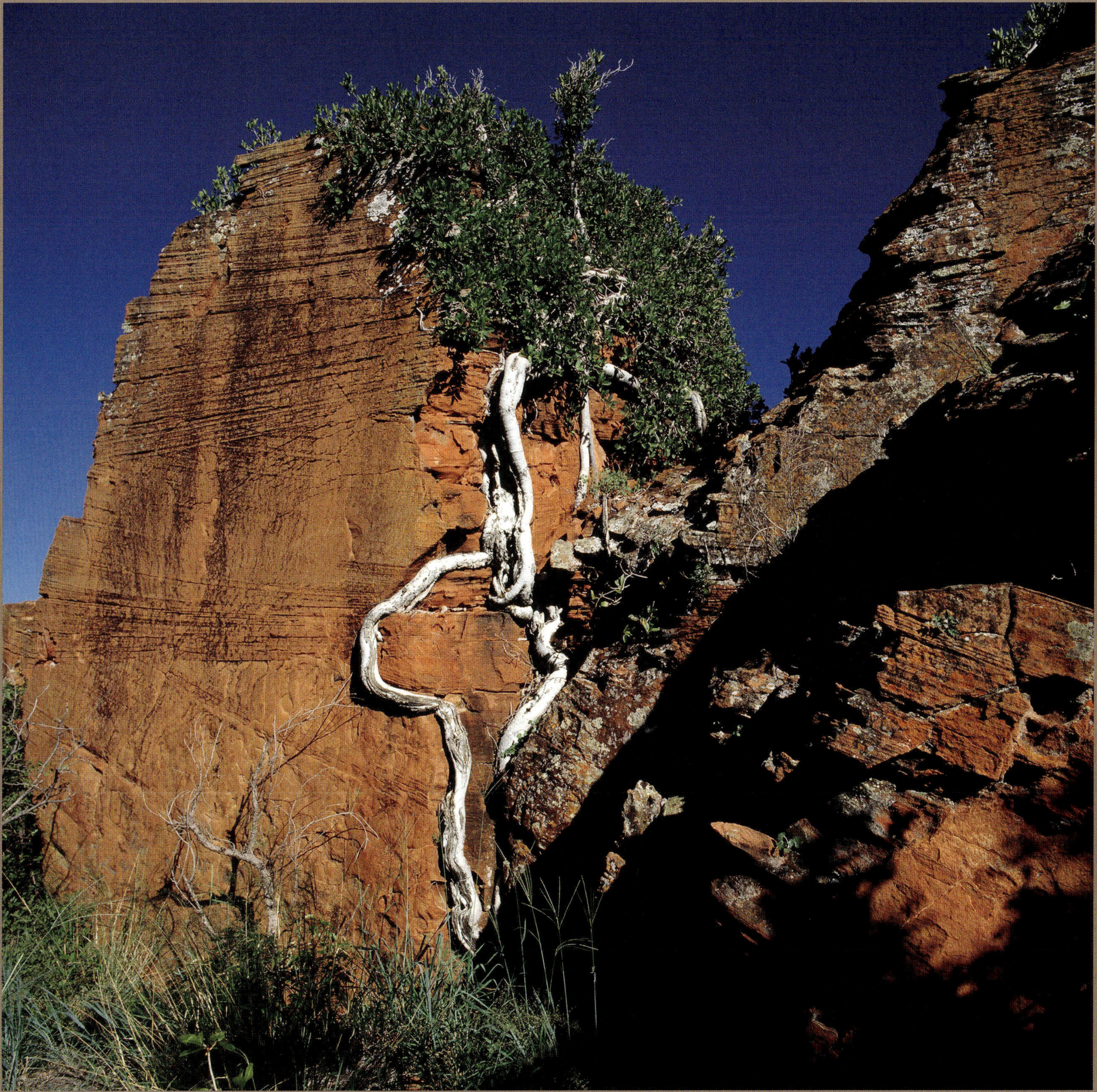

(OPPOSITE) Kokerboom Forest, east of Keetmanshoop (ABOVE) Rock-splitting Fig, Waterberg Plateau

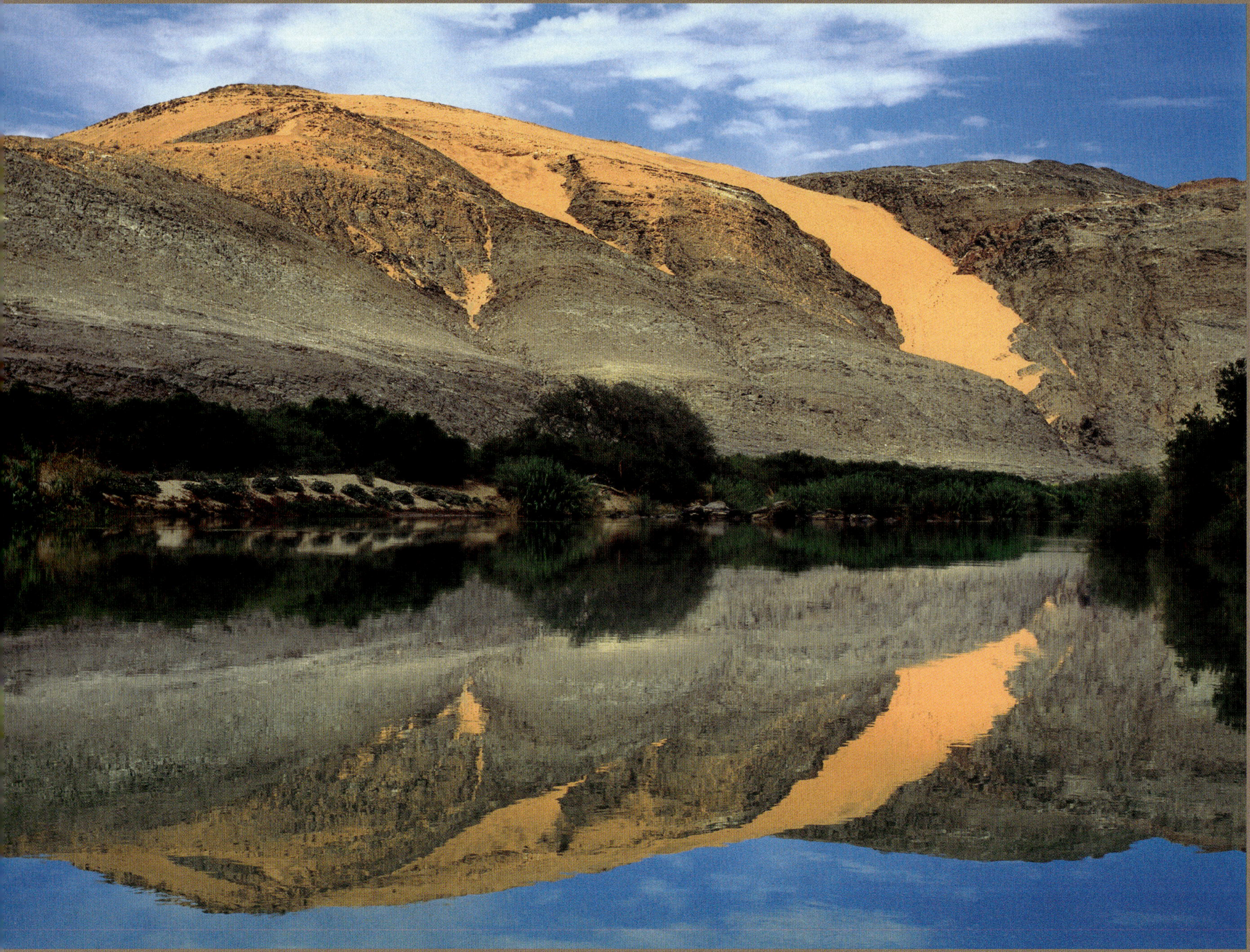

(ABOVE) Kunene Reflections, Kunene Region (OPPOSITE) Bogenfels Rock Arch, Sperrgebiet

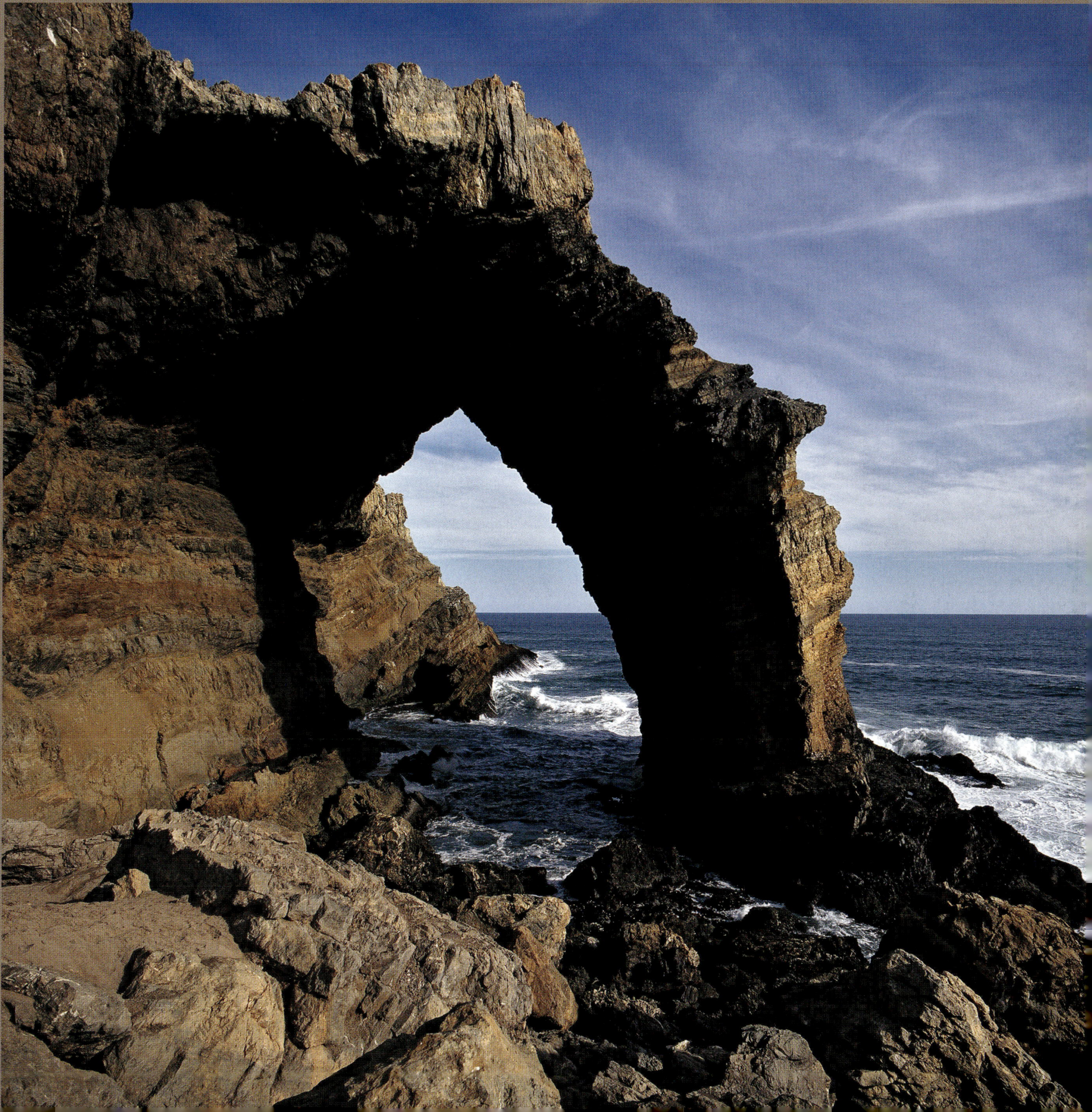

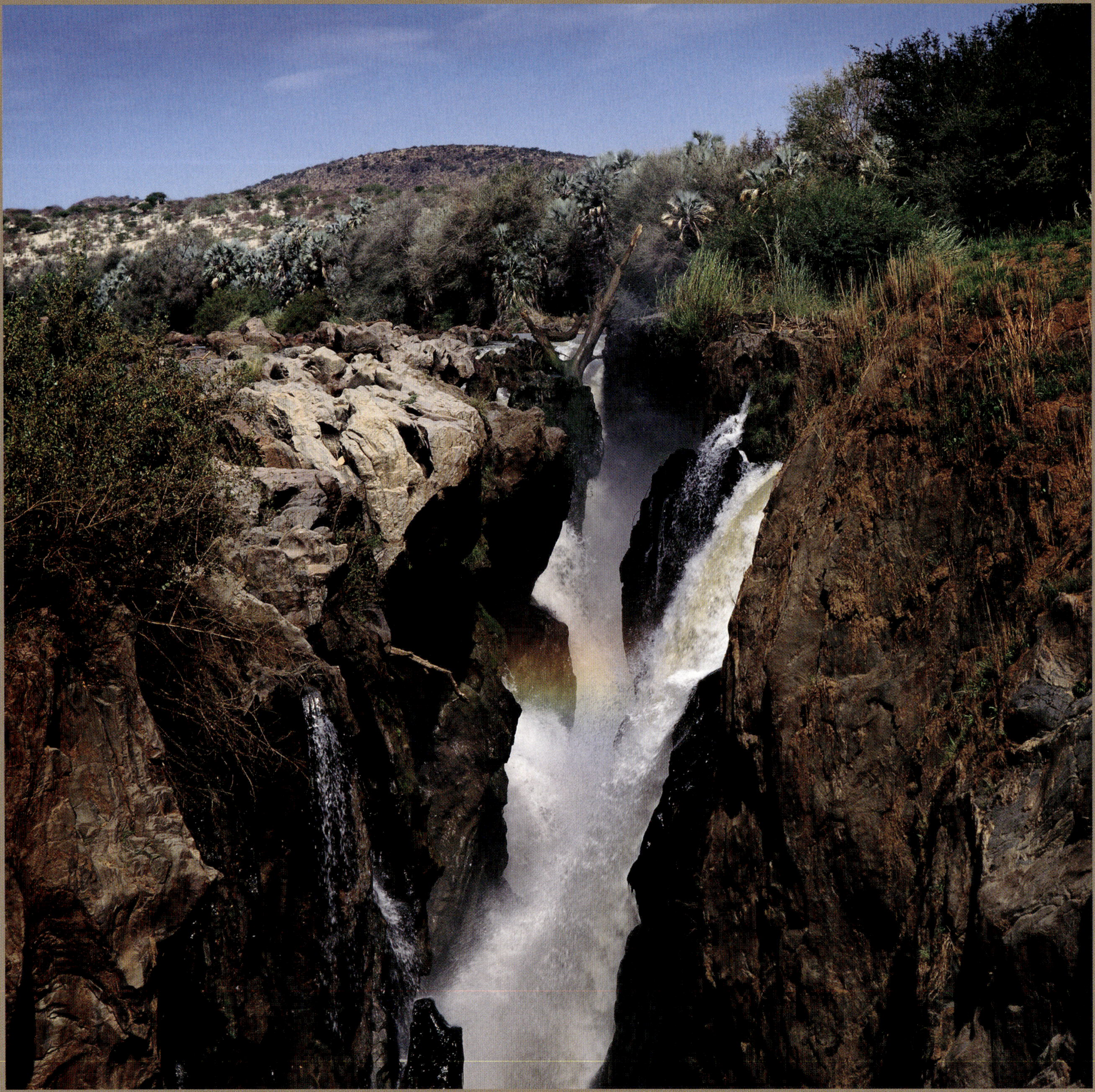

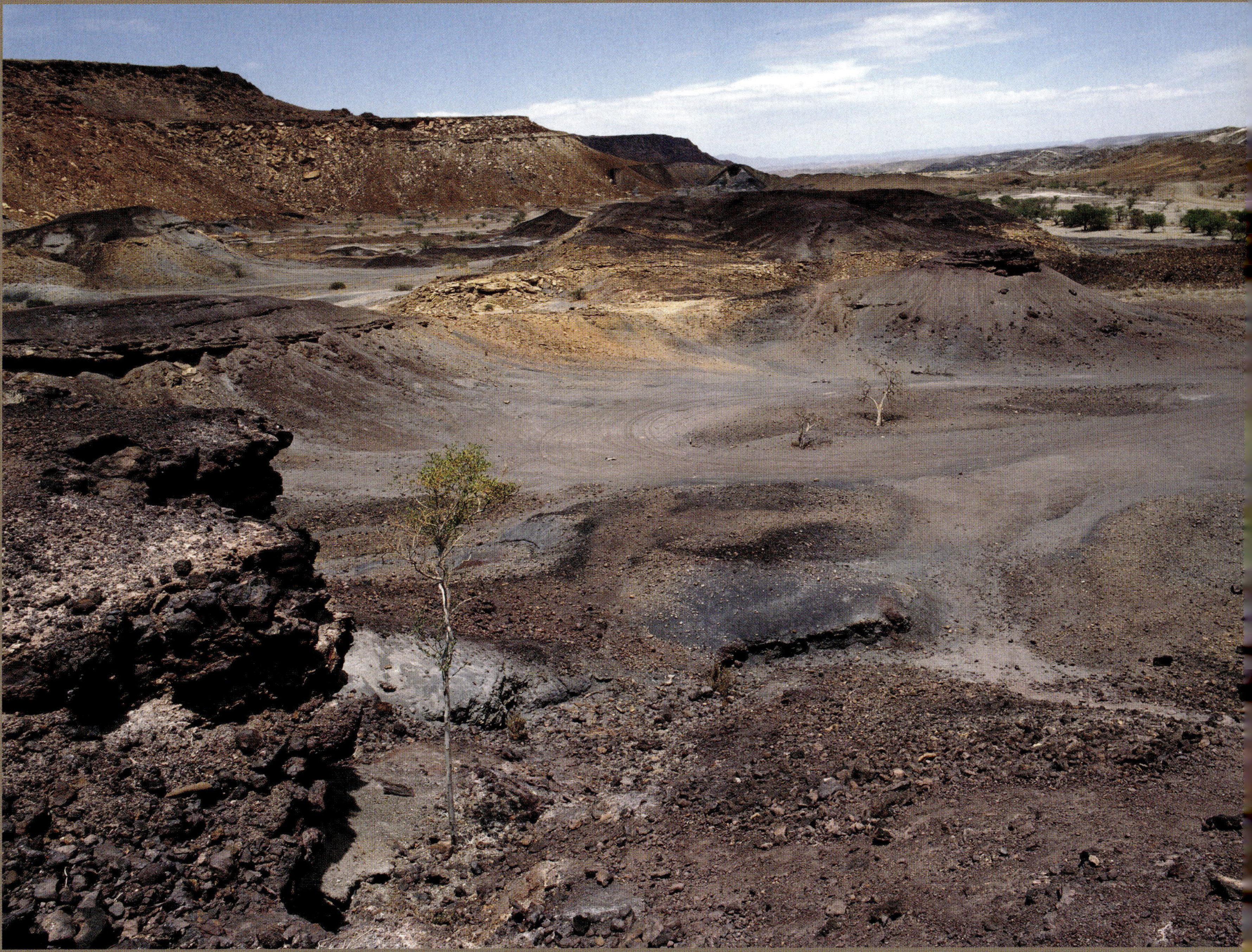

(OPPOSITE) Epupa Falls, Kaokoland (ABOVE) Burnt Mountain, Damaraland

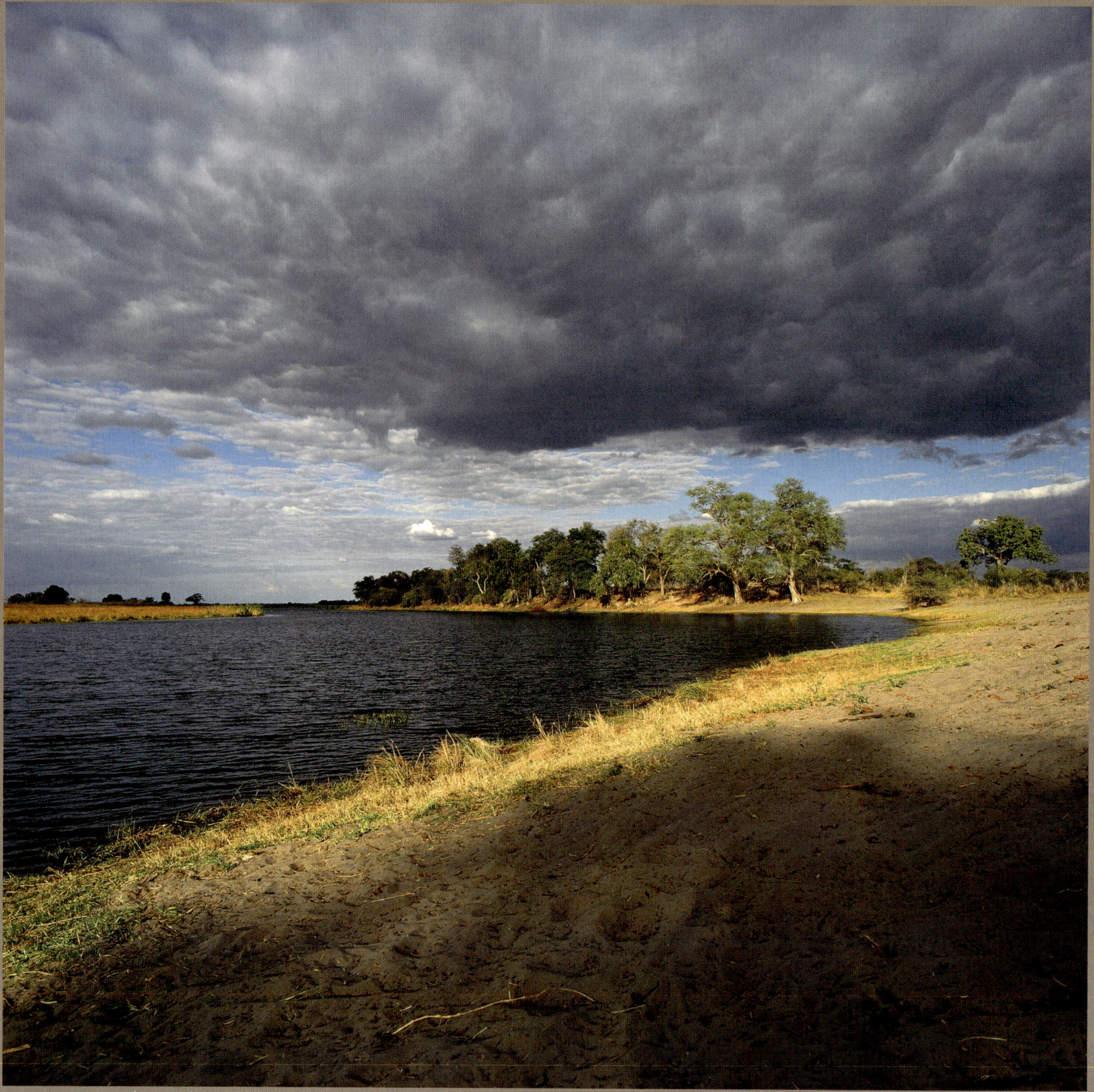

Horseshoe Lake, Golden Triangle, Caprivi

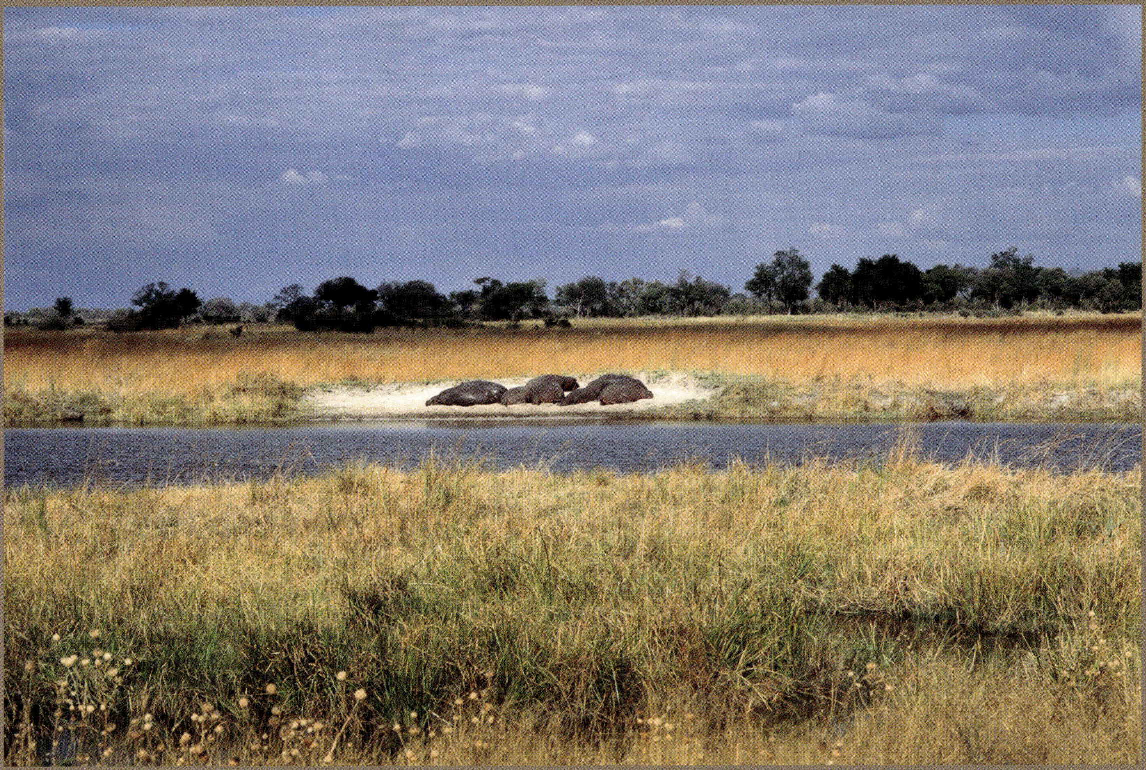

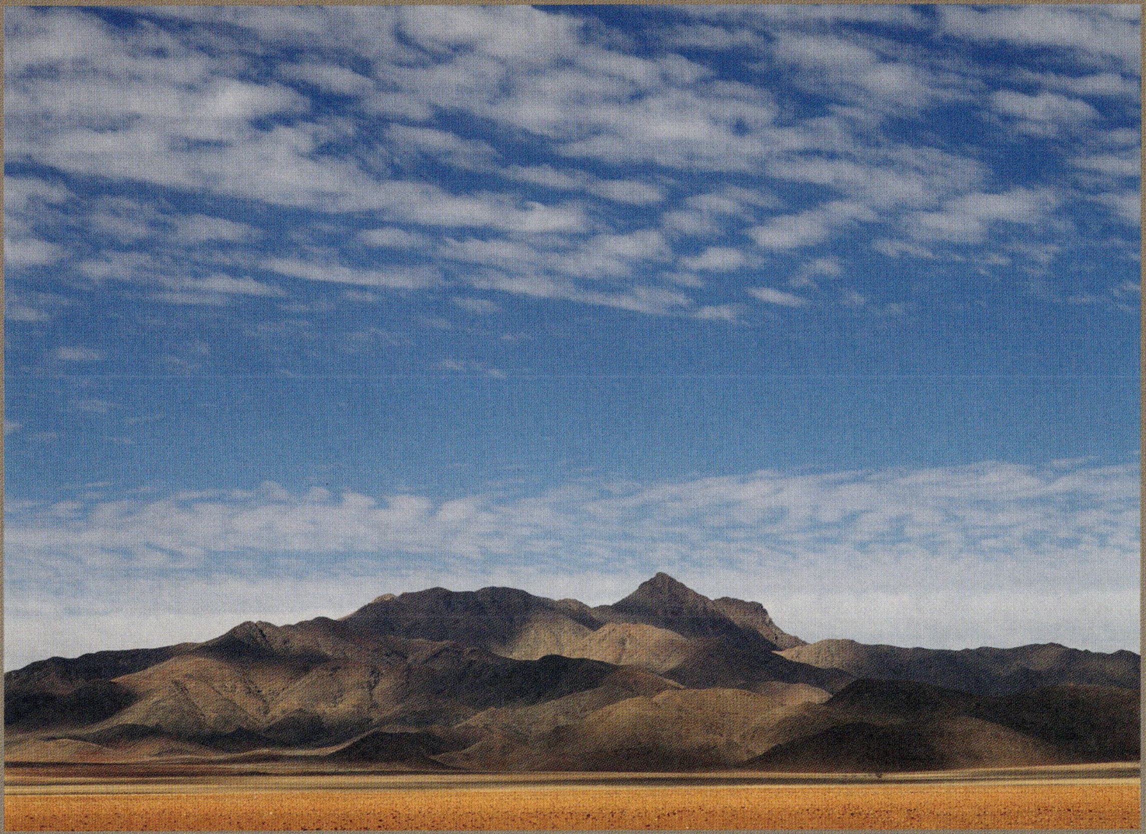

(ABOVE) Hippo Hideout, Caprivi (BELOW) Shadow Mountains, NamibRand Nature Reserve

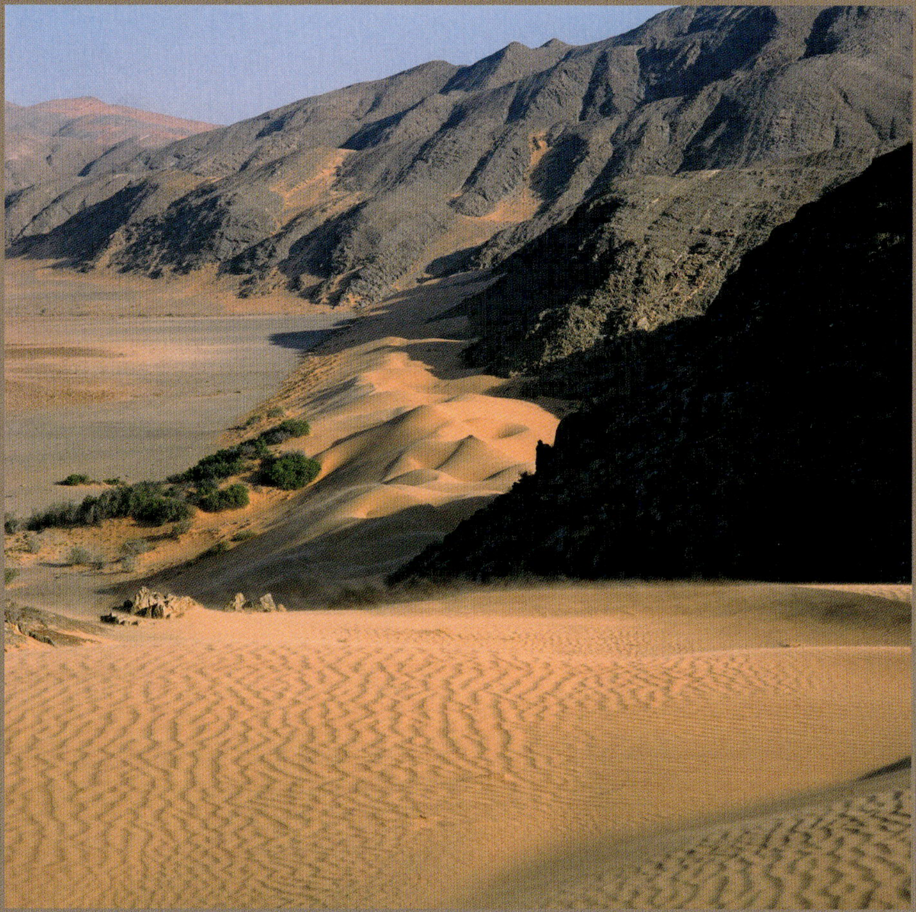

Namibia ist ein Land von beeindruckenden Kontrasten.

Thomas Dressler, Bilder Namibias. Roggebaai, Cape Town: Sunbird Publishers, 2000

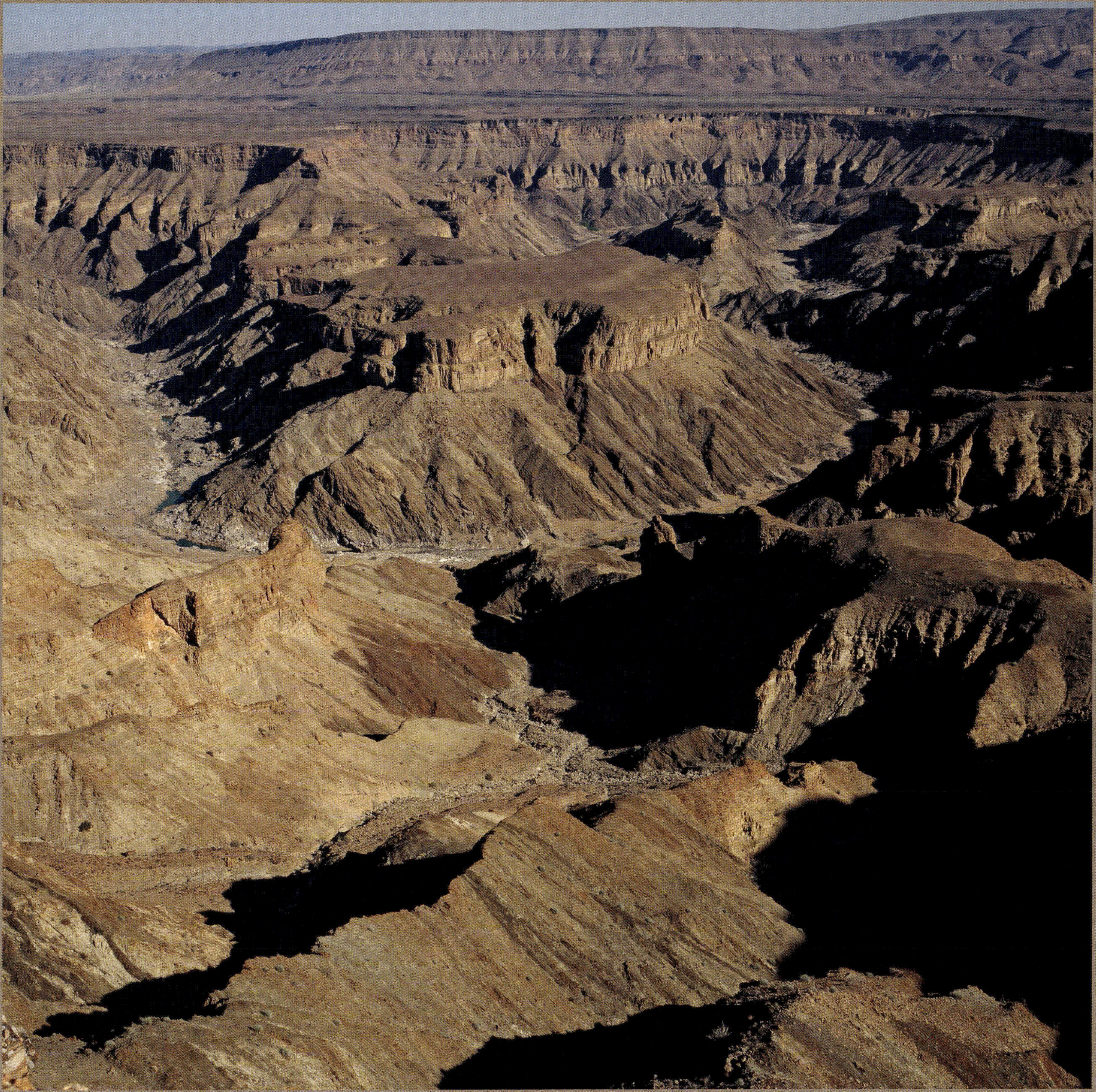

(OPPOSITE) Kunene Descent, Kaokoland (ABOVE) Horseshoe View, Fish River Canyon

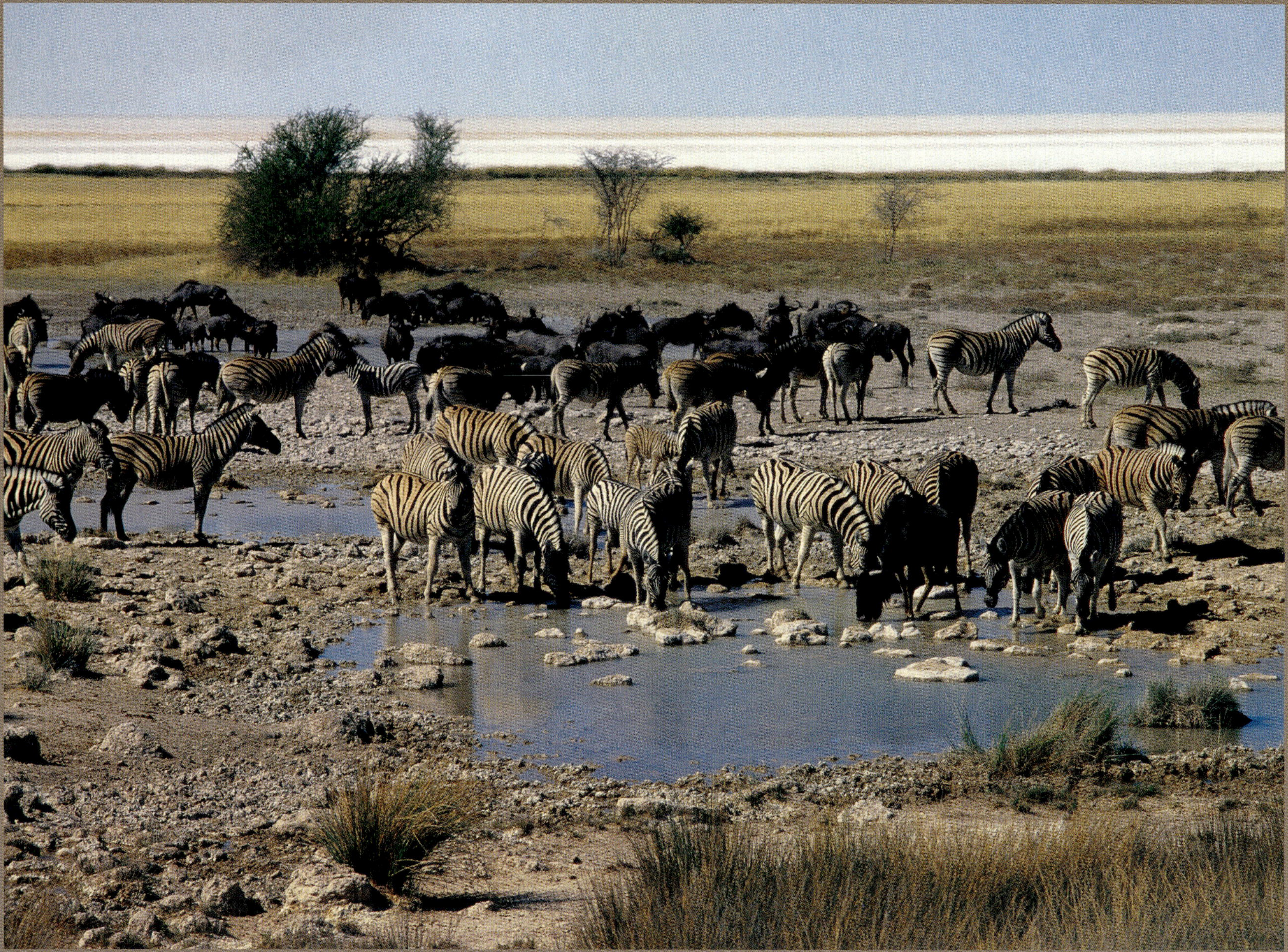

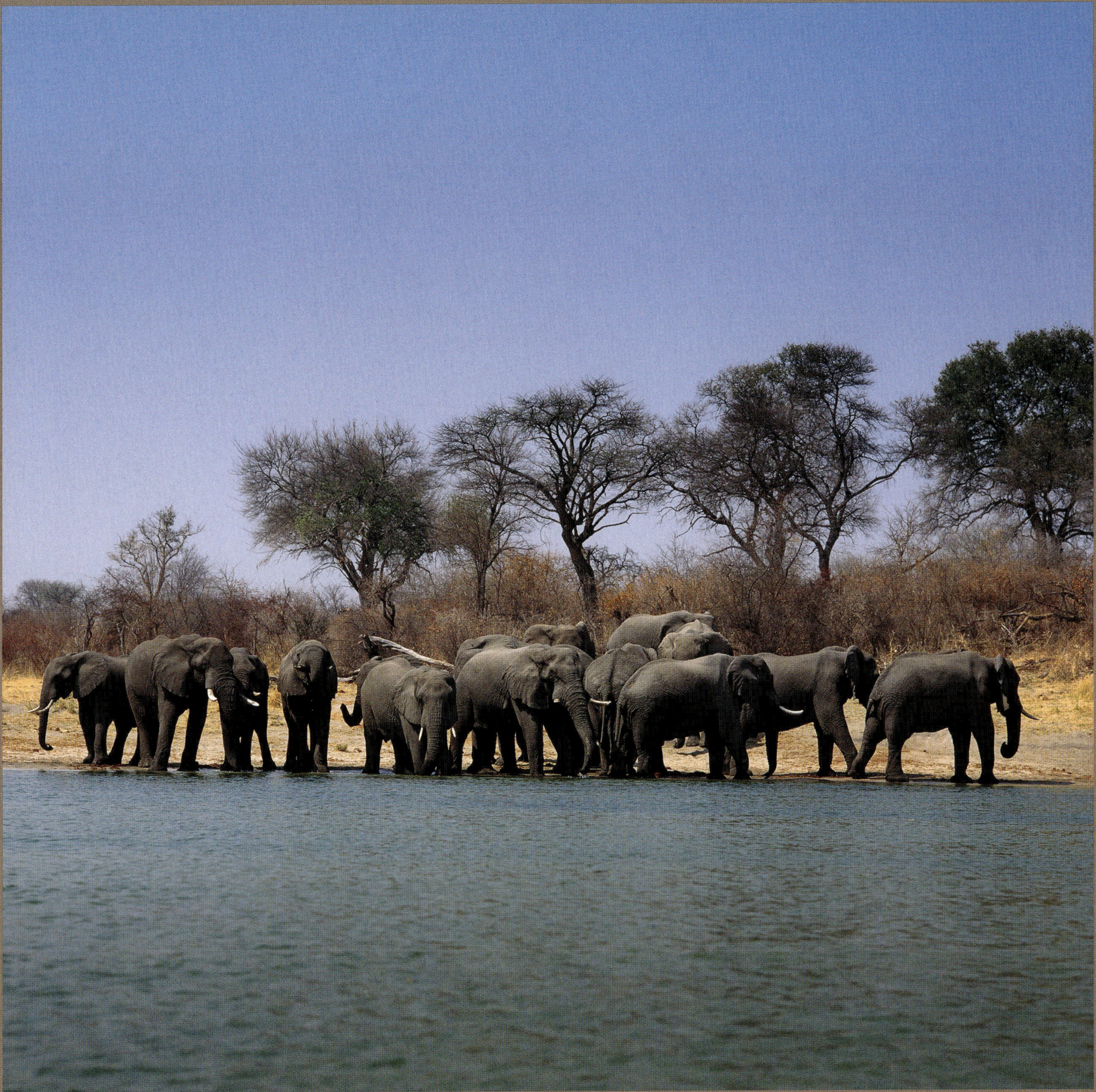

(OPPOSITE) Salvadora Waterhole, Etosha National Park (ABOVE) Kavango Elephants, Okavango River

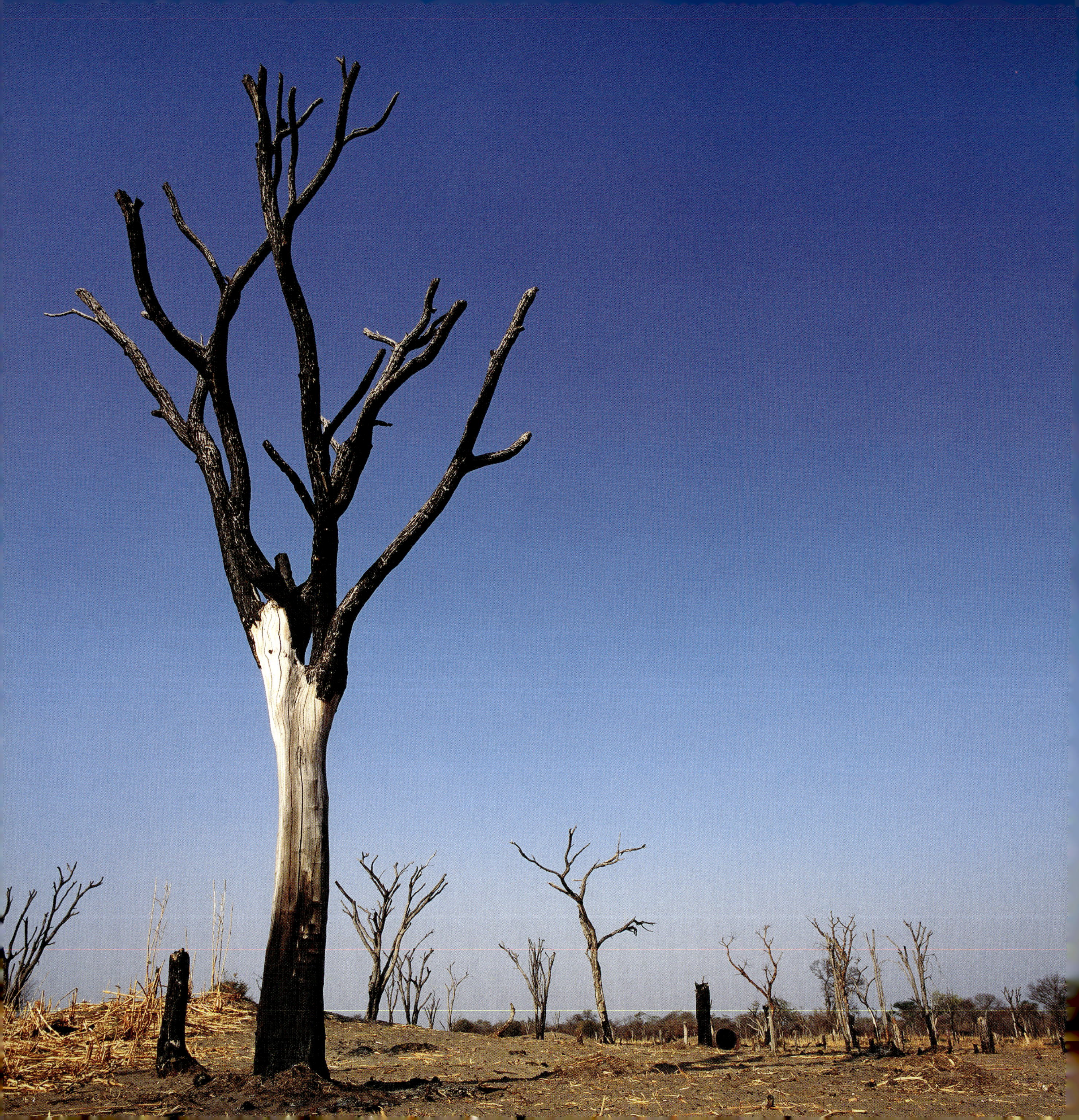

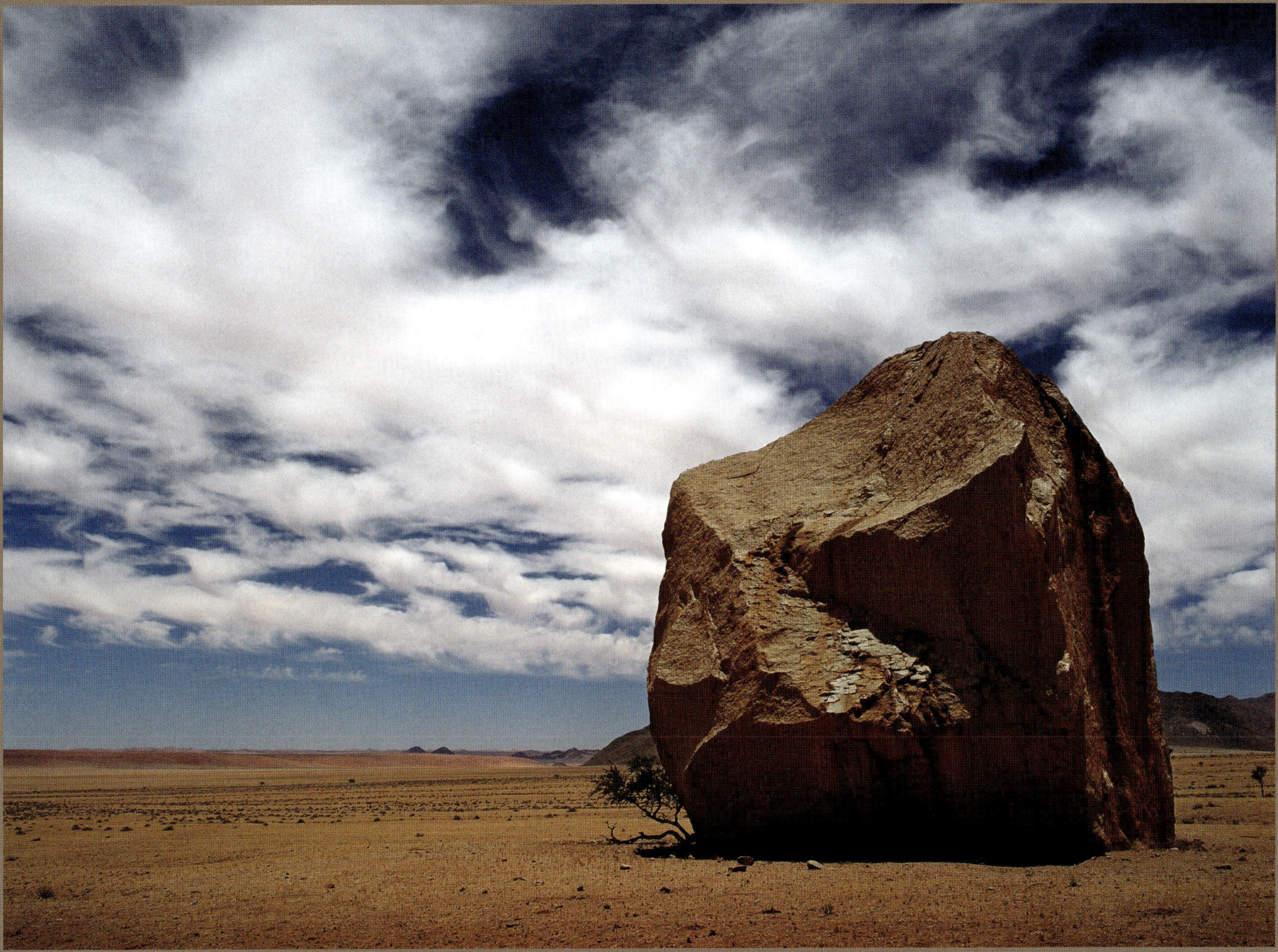

(OPPOSITE) Burnt-out, Caprivi (ABOVE) Hanging Rock, Namtib Biosphere Reserve

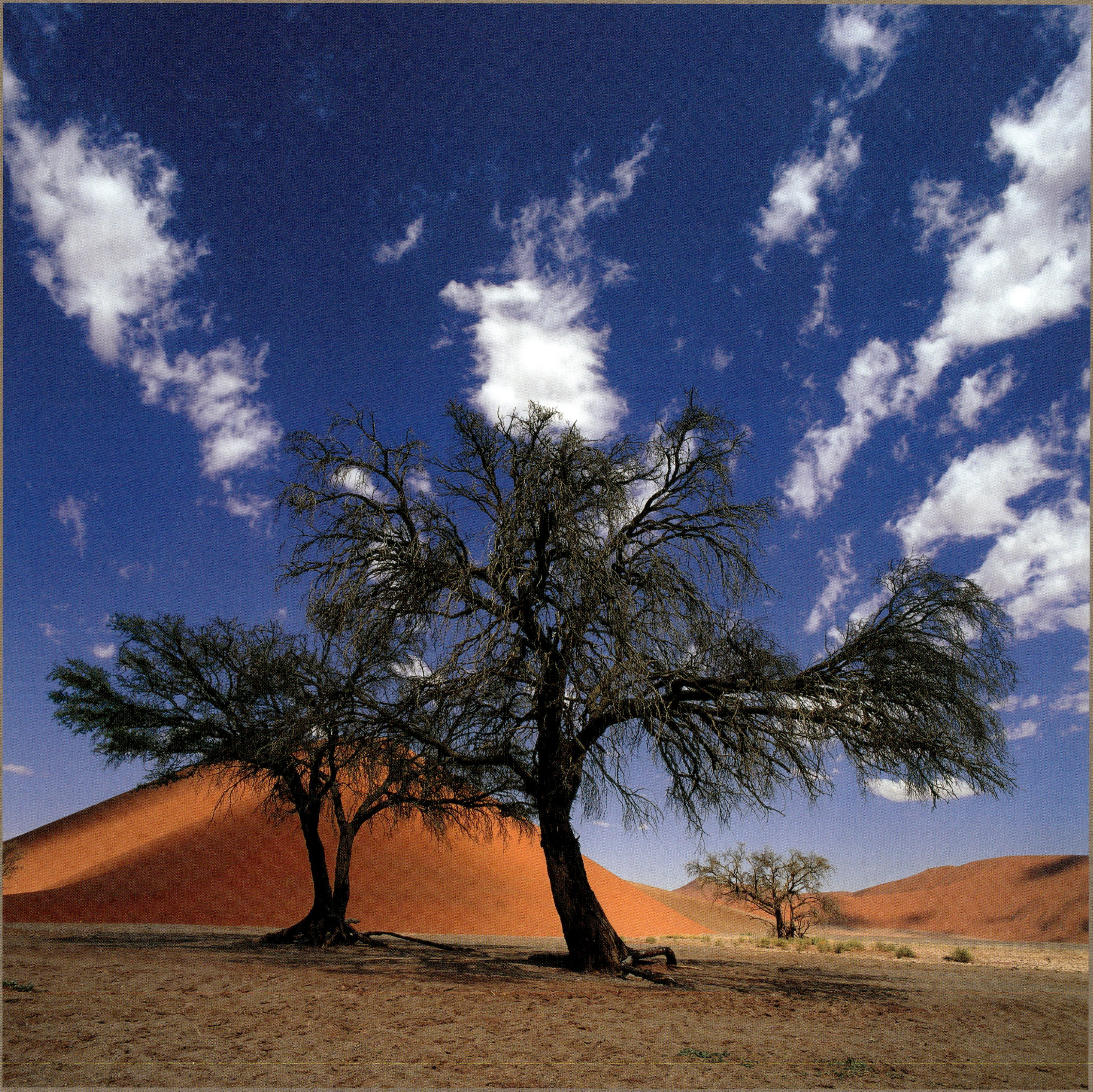

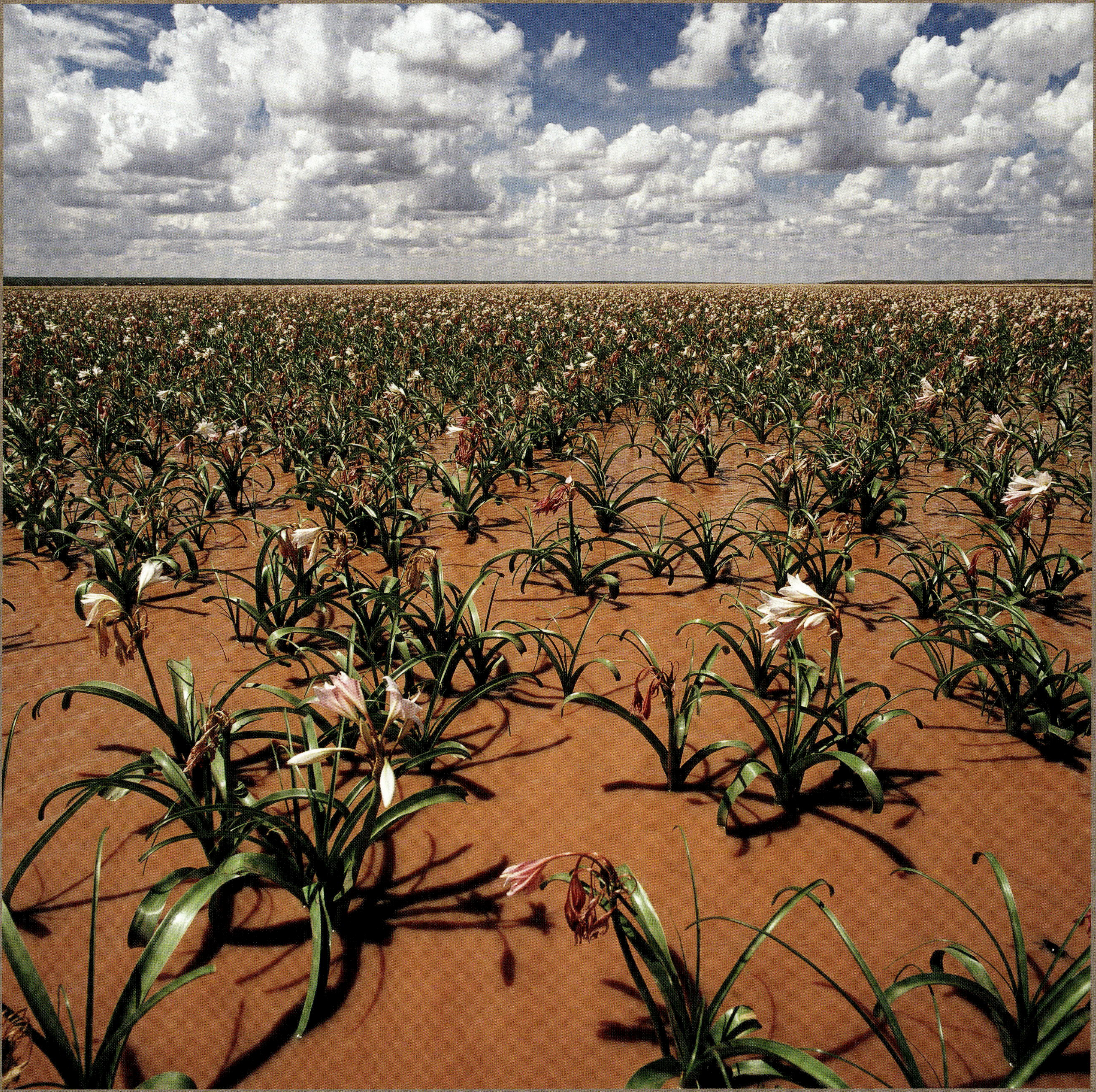

(OPPOSITE) Dune Alley, Sossusvlei (ABOVE) Lily Pan, Sandhof Farm, Maltahöhe District

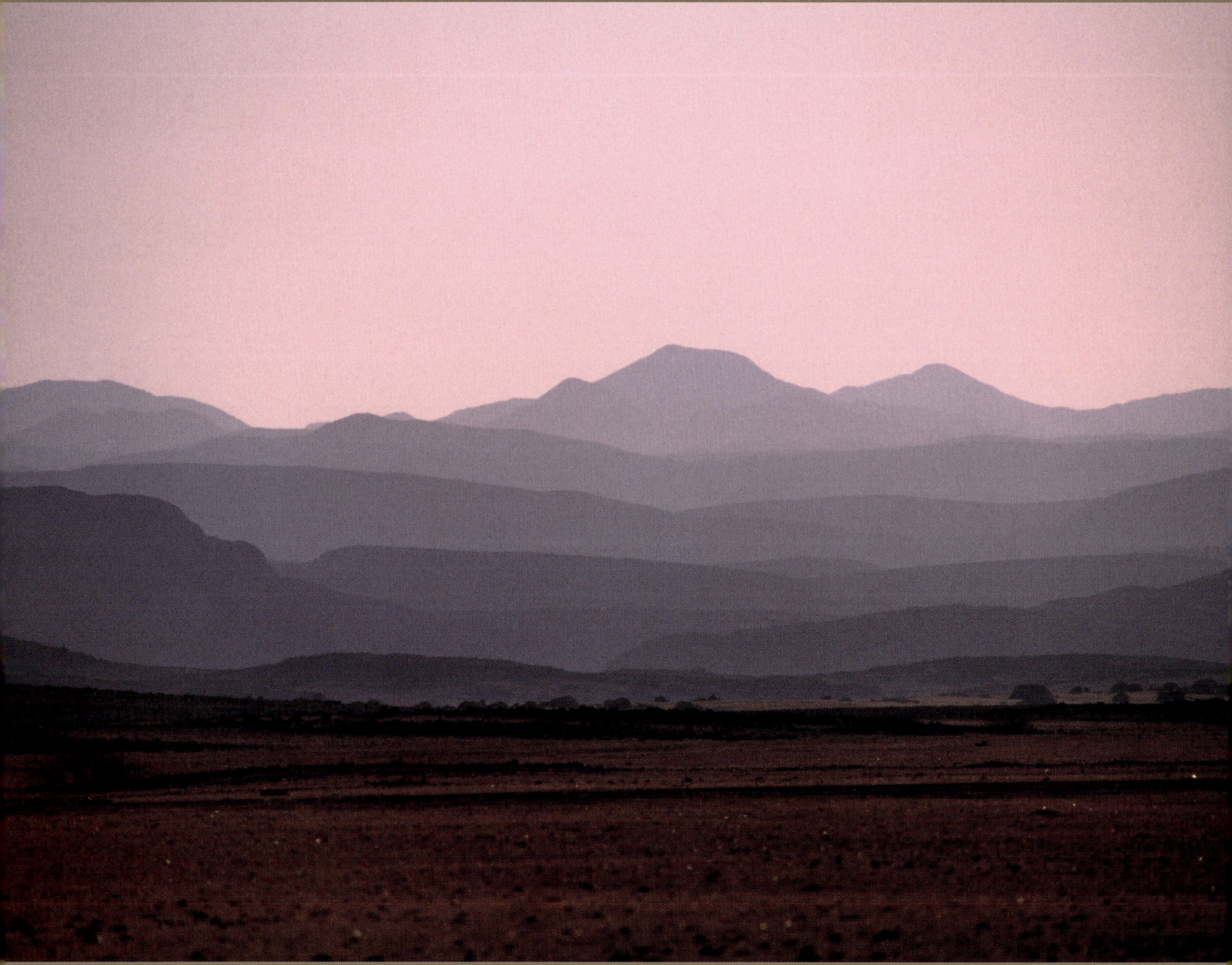

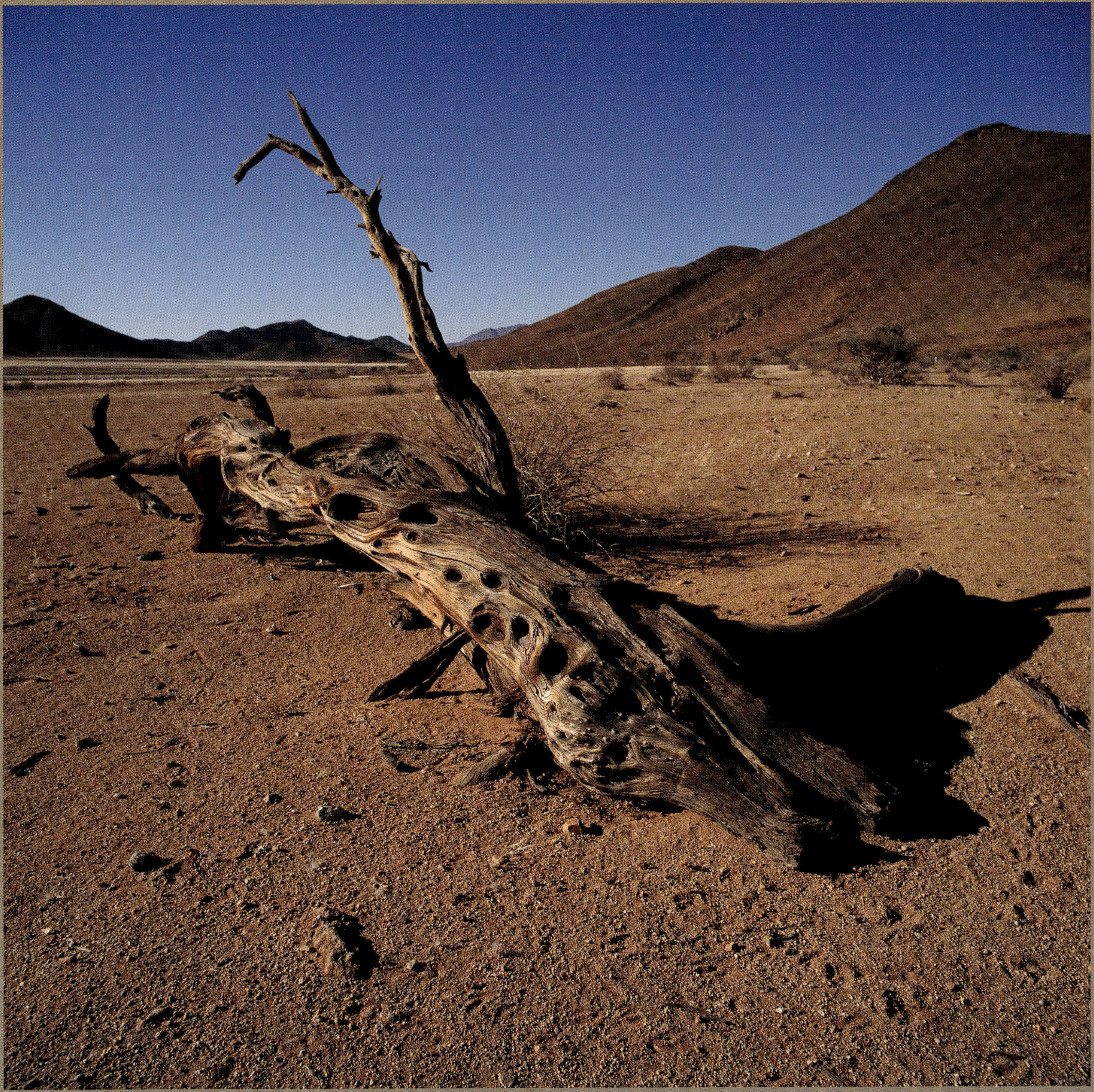

(OPPOSITE) Purple Mountains, Kaokoland (ABOVE) Tree Metropolis, Namtib Biosphere Reserve

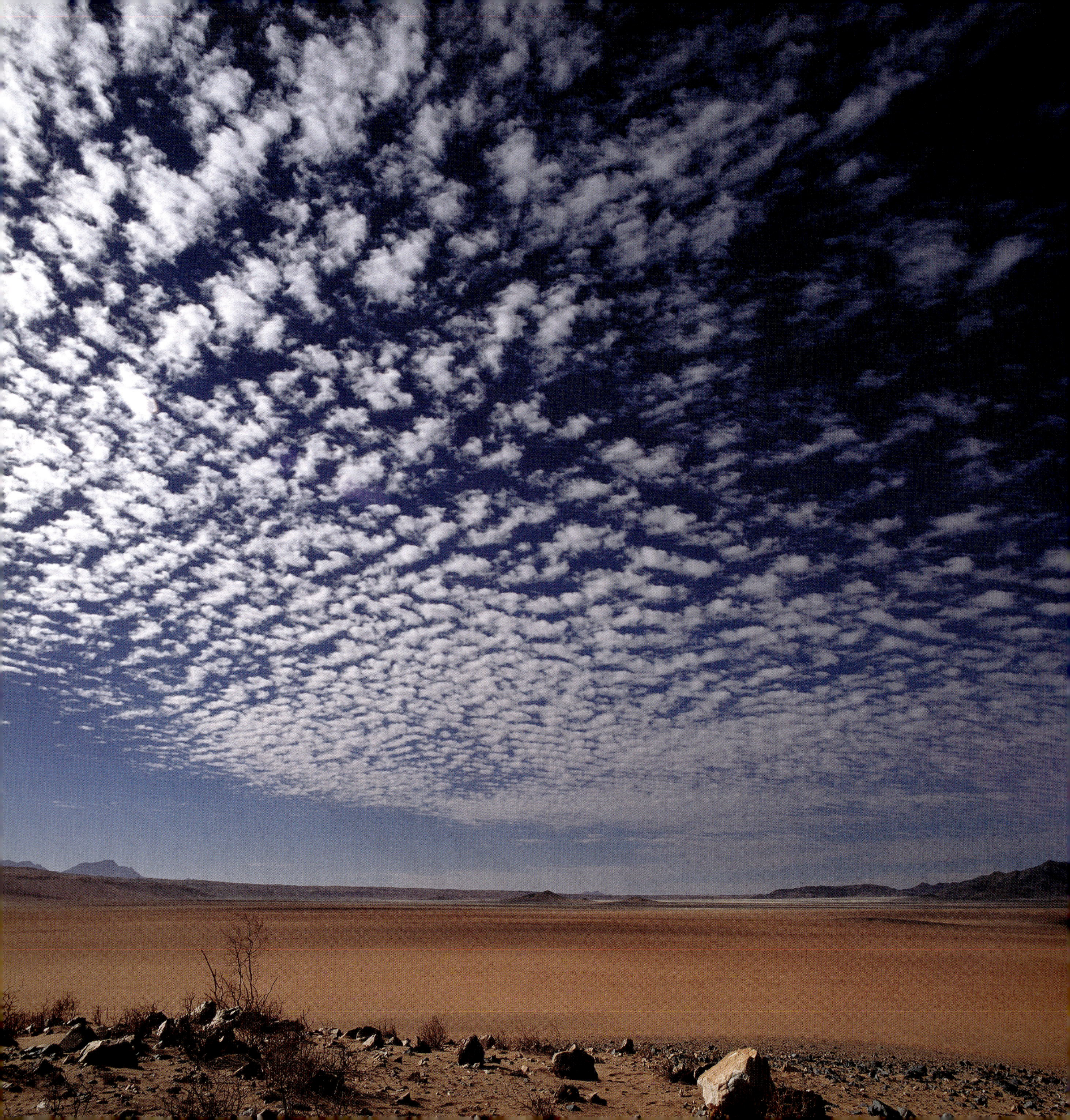

Onguti yaKamushimba
yooNamene Sheepo
(ya tuka) tayi lambele poombunda
dhaambo yaa nevuliko

TRANSLATION:

A dove of Kamushimba
Of Namene's Sheepo
The one that flies up and lands
On the backs of those who break the law

Praise song for King Sheepo (1942–1960) quoted in H. D. Namuhuja, *The Royal Ondonga Kings*, Windhoek: Out of Africa Publishers, 2002: 44

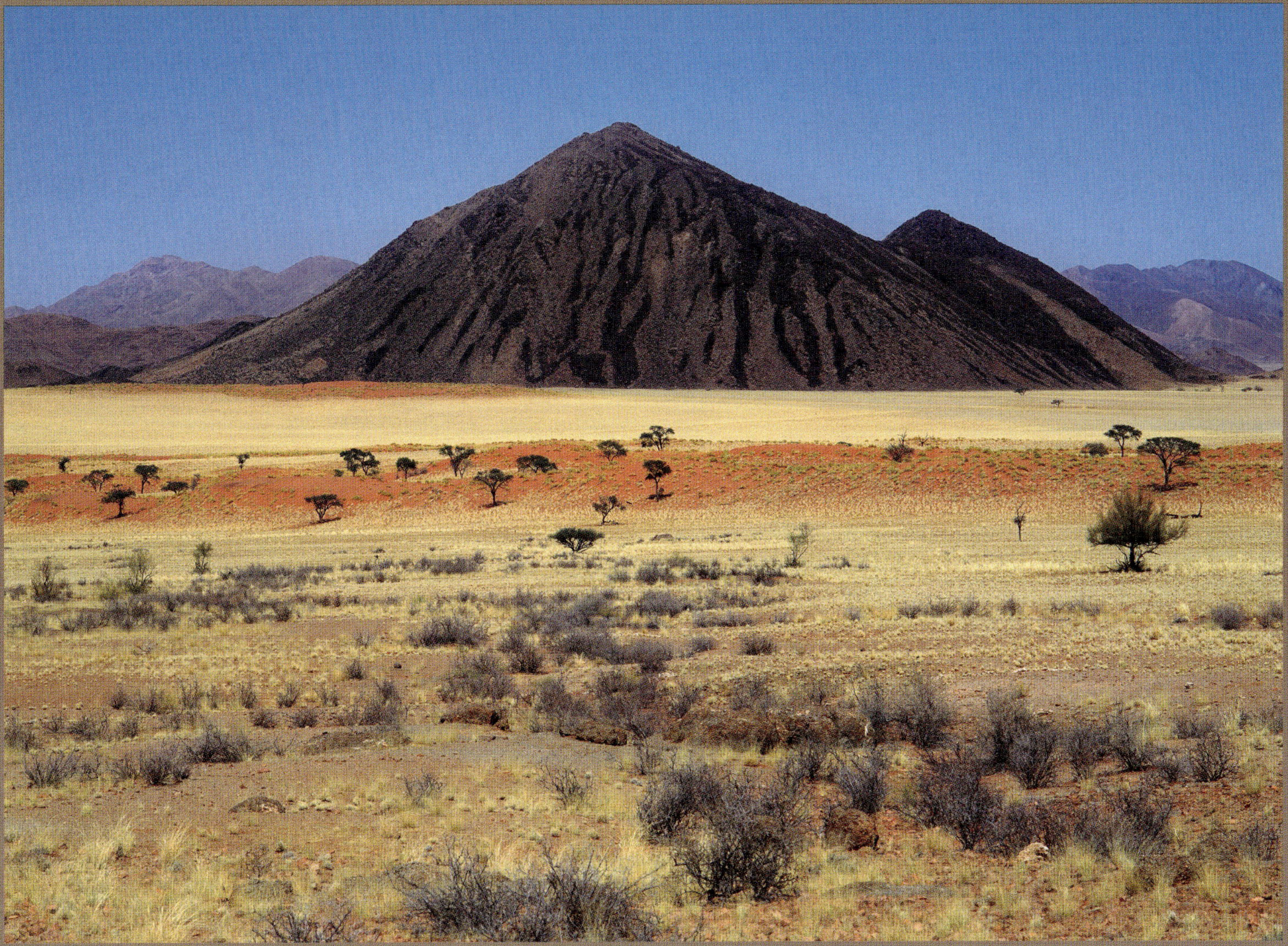

(OPPOSITE) Pregnant Cloud, NamibRand Nature Reserve (ABOVE) Chocolate Mountain, NamibRand Nature Reserve

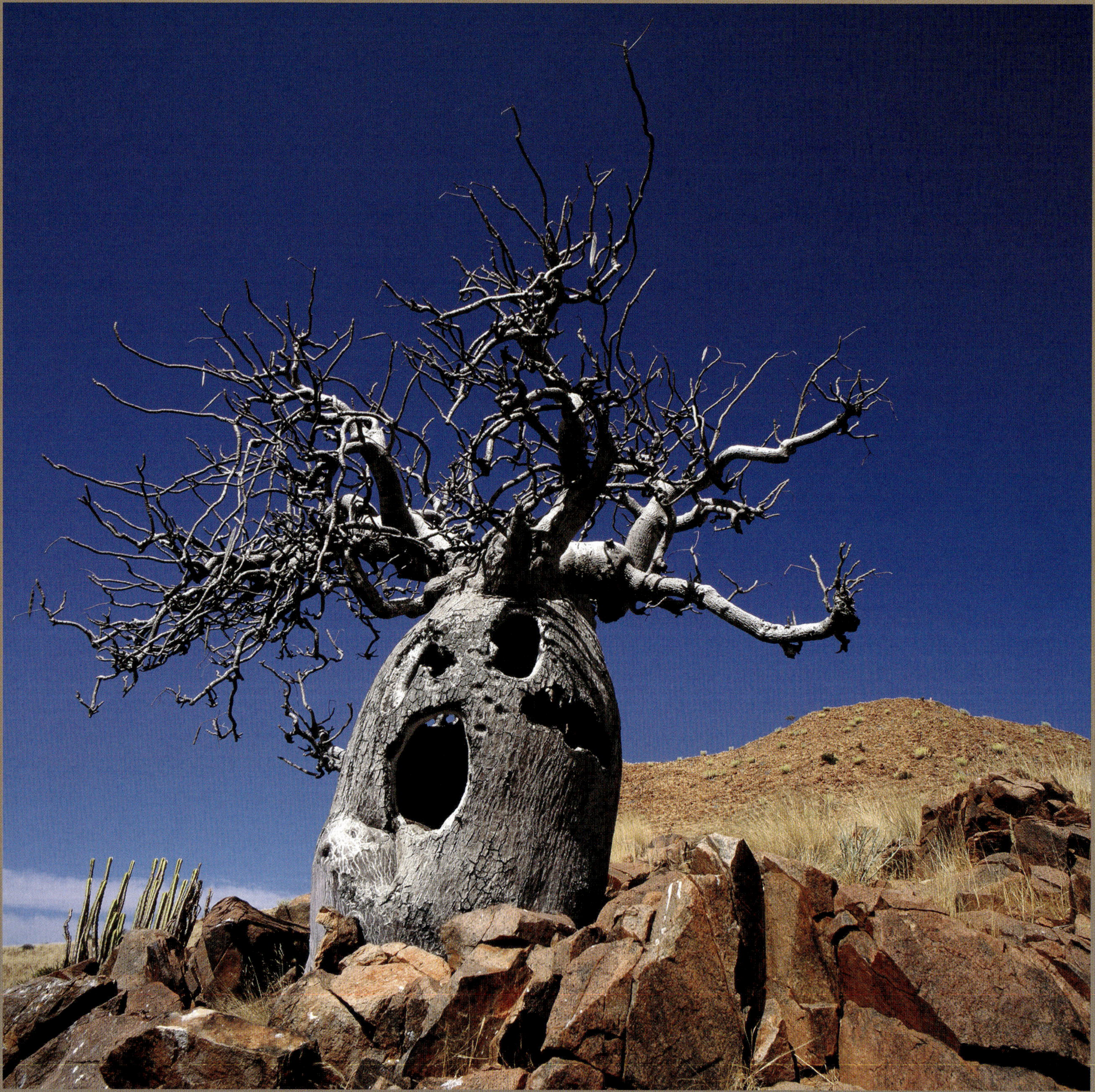

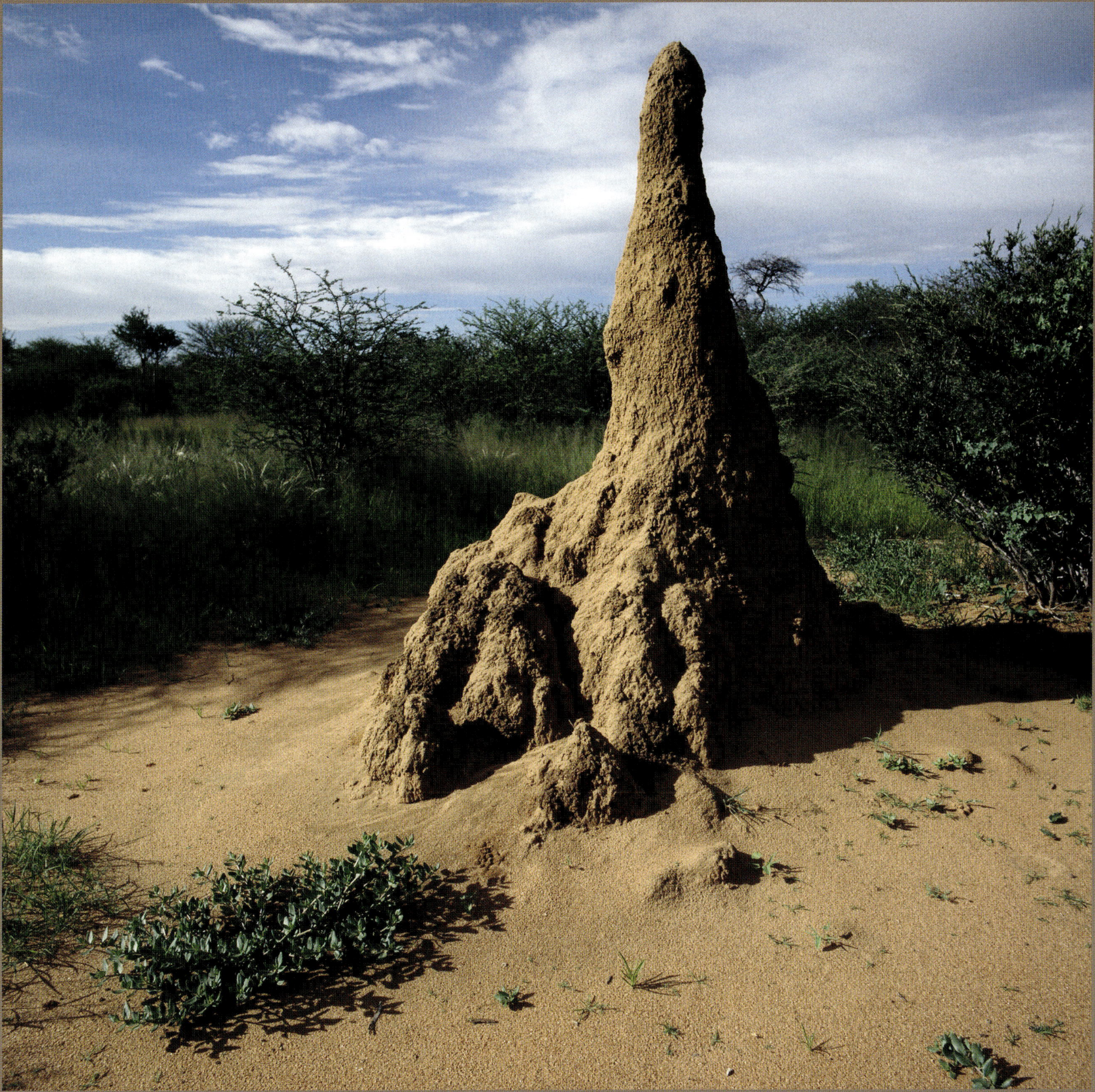

(OPPOSITE) Ghostly Hideout, NamibRand Nature Reserve (ABOVE) Termite Tower, Waterberg surroundings

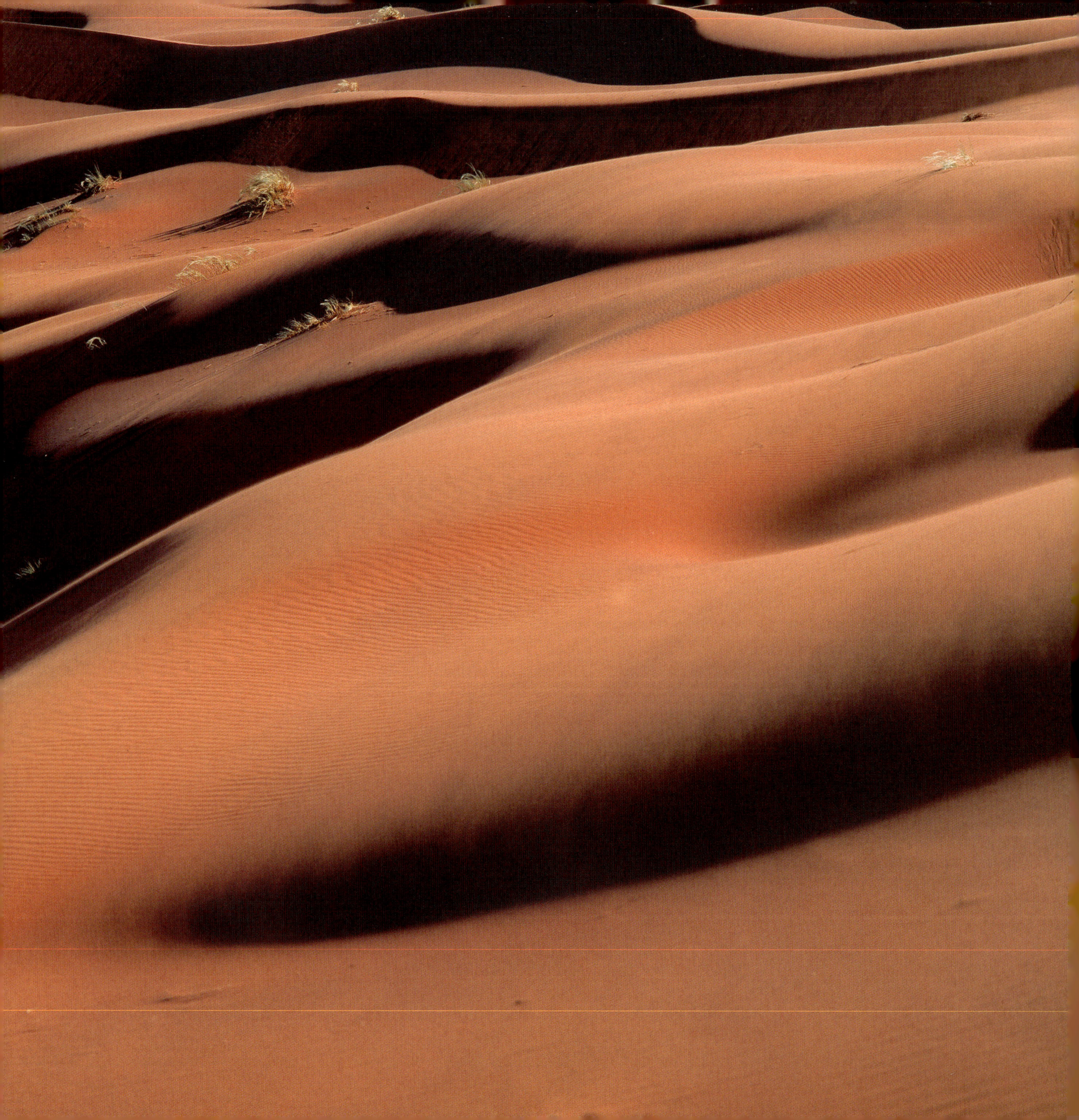

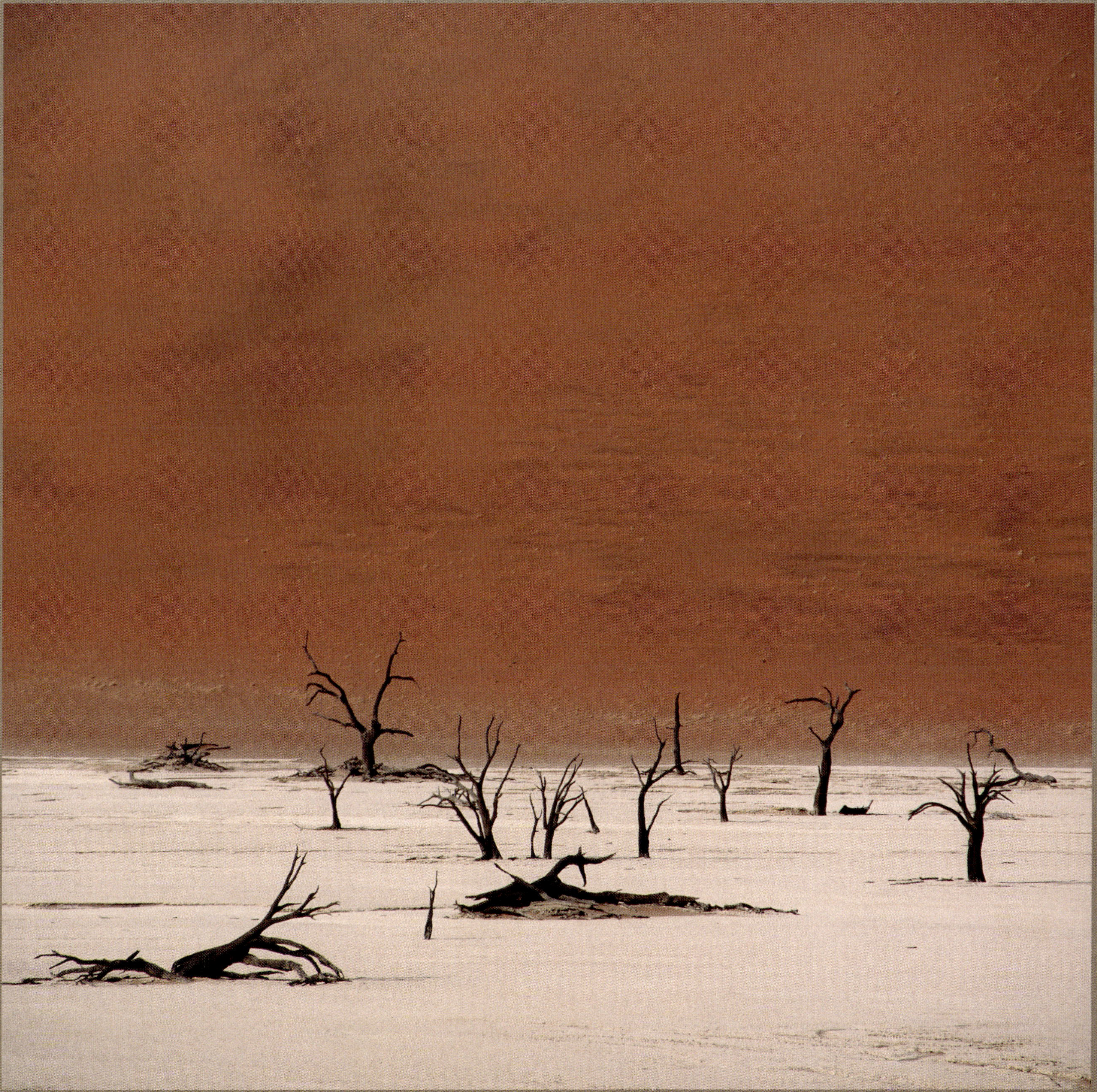

(OPPOSITE) Dune Continuum, Namib-Naukluft Park (ABOVE) Dead Pan, Namib-Naukluft Park

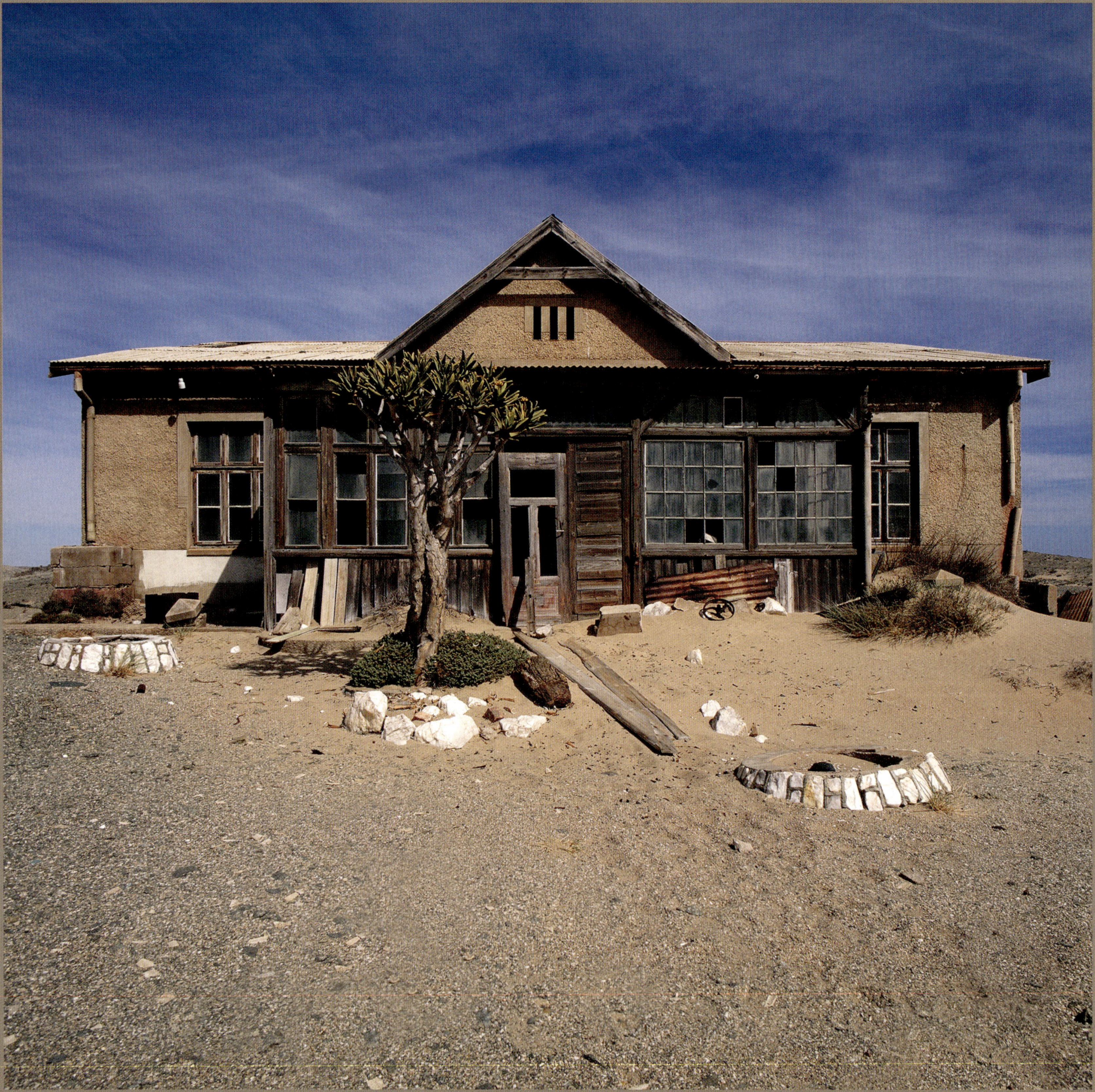

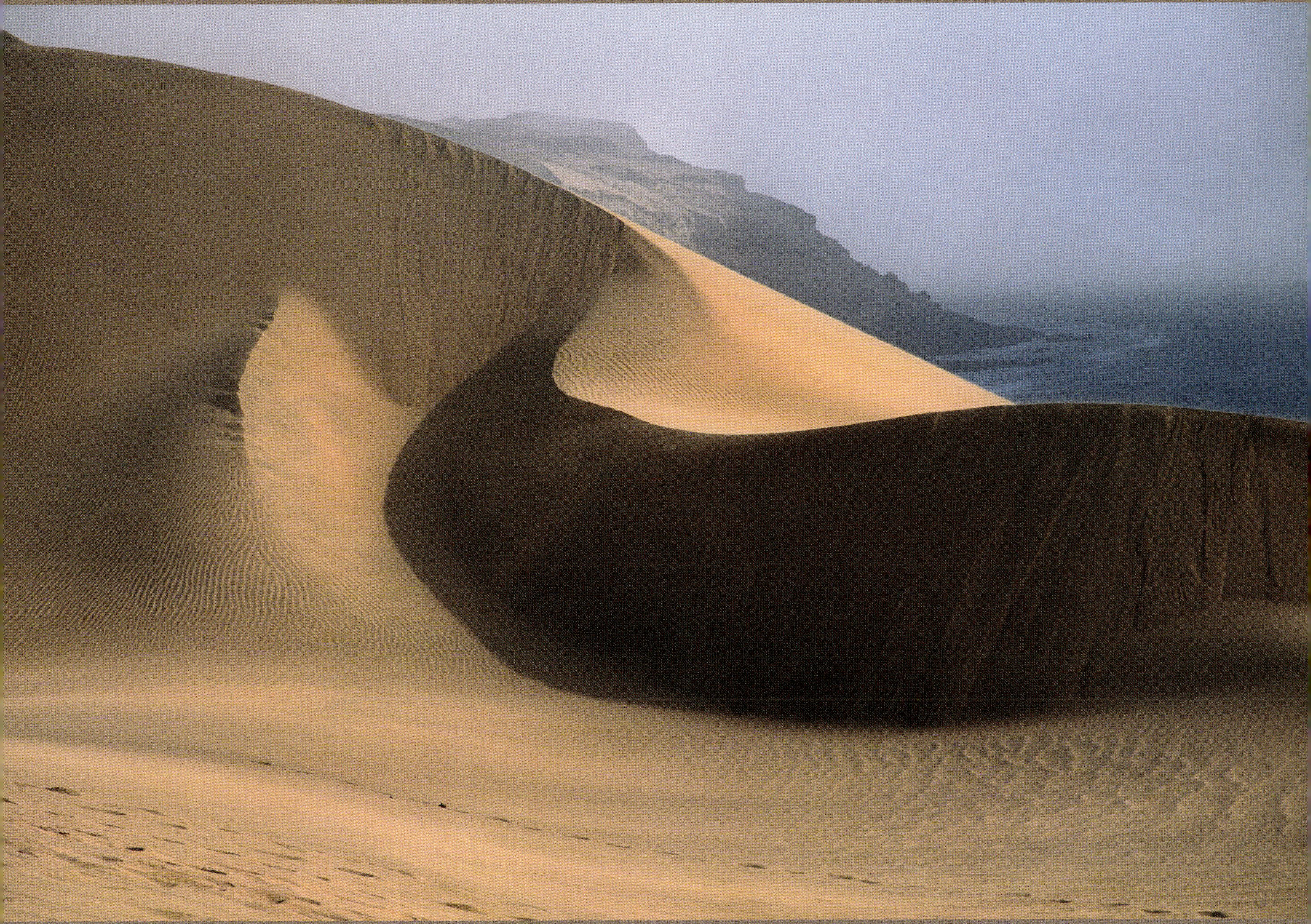

(OPPOSITE) Pomona Ghost House, Sperrgebiet (ABOVE) Sylvia Hill, Sperrgebiet

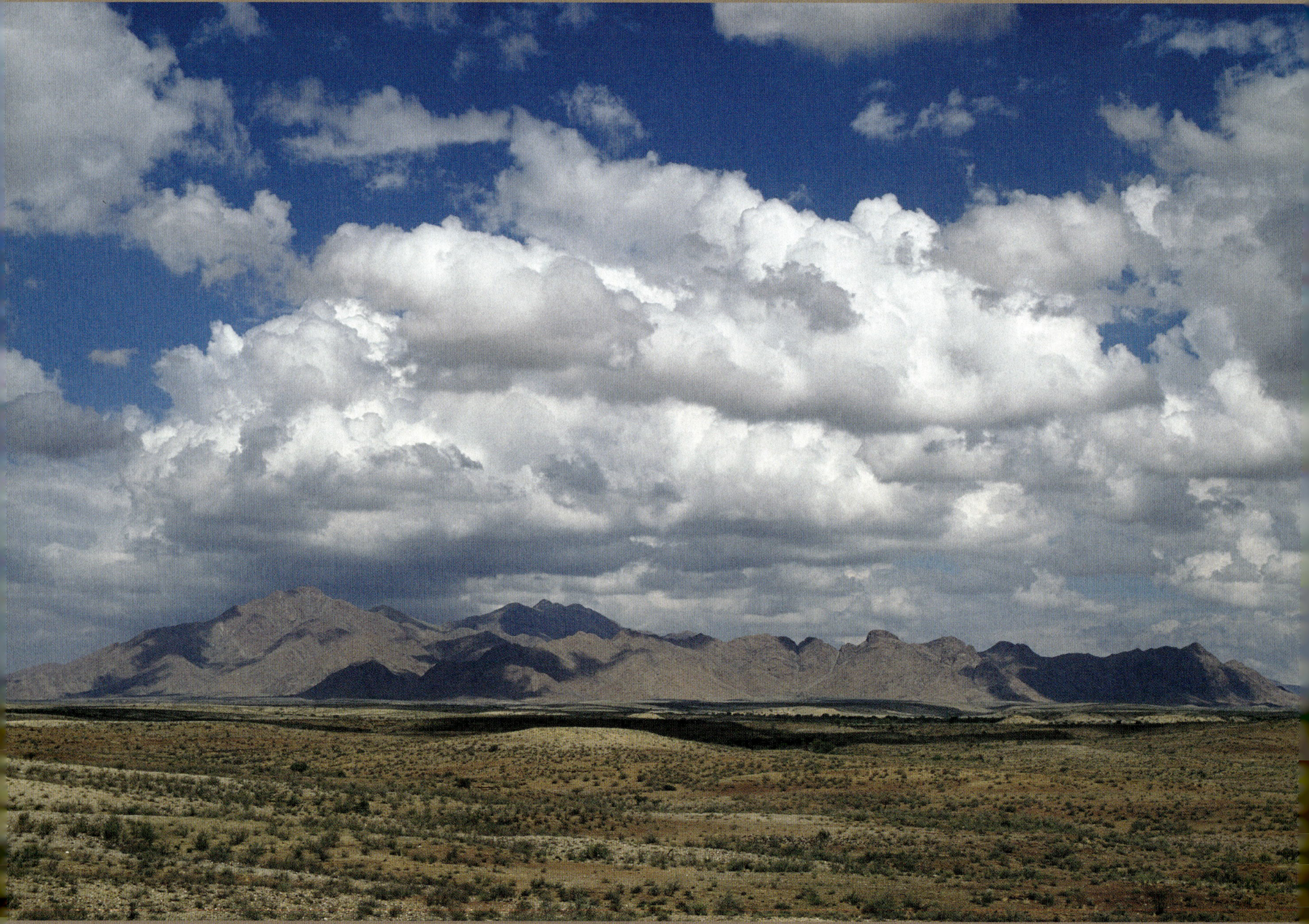

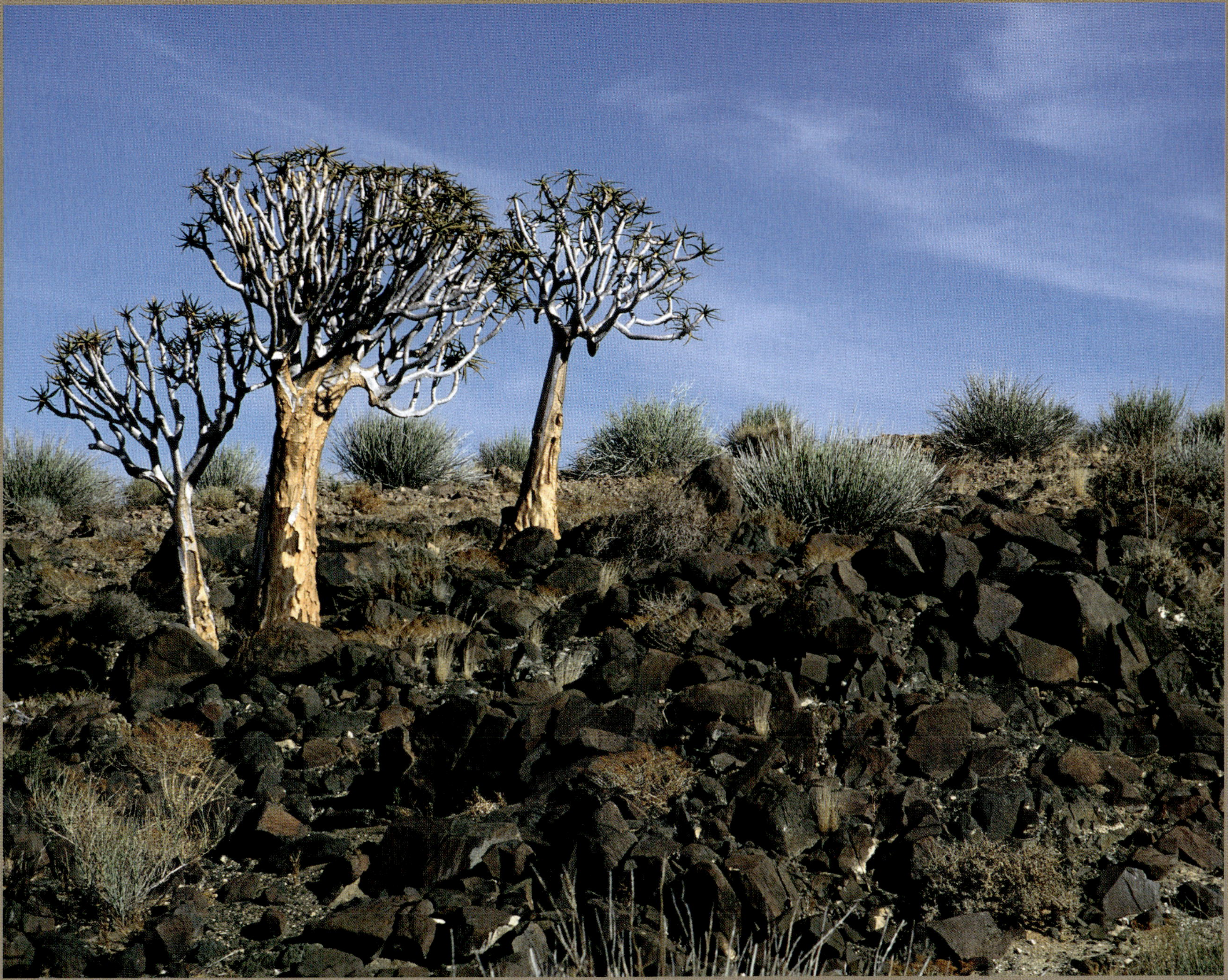

(OPPOSITE) Rostock Mountains, Namib-Naukluft Park (ABOVE) Gondwana Cañon Park, southern Namibia

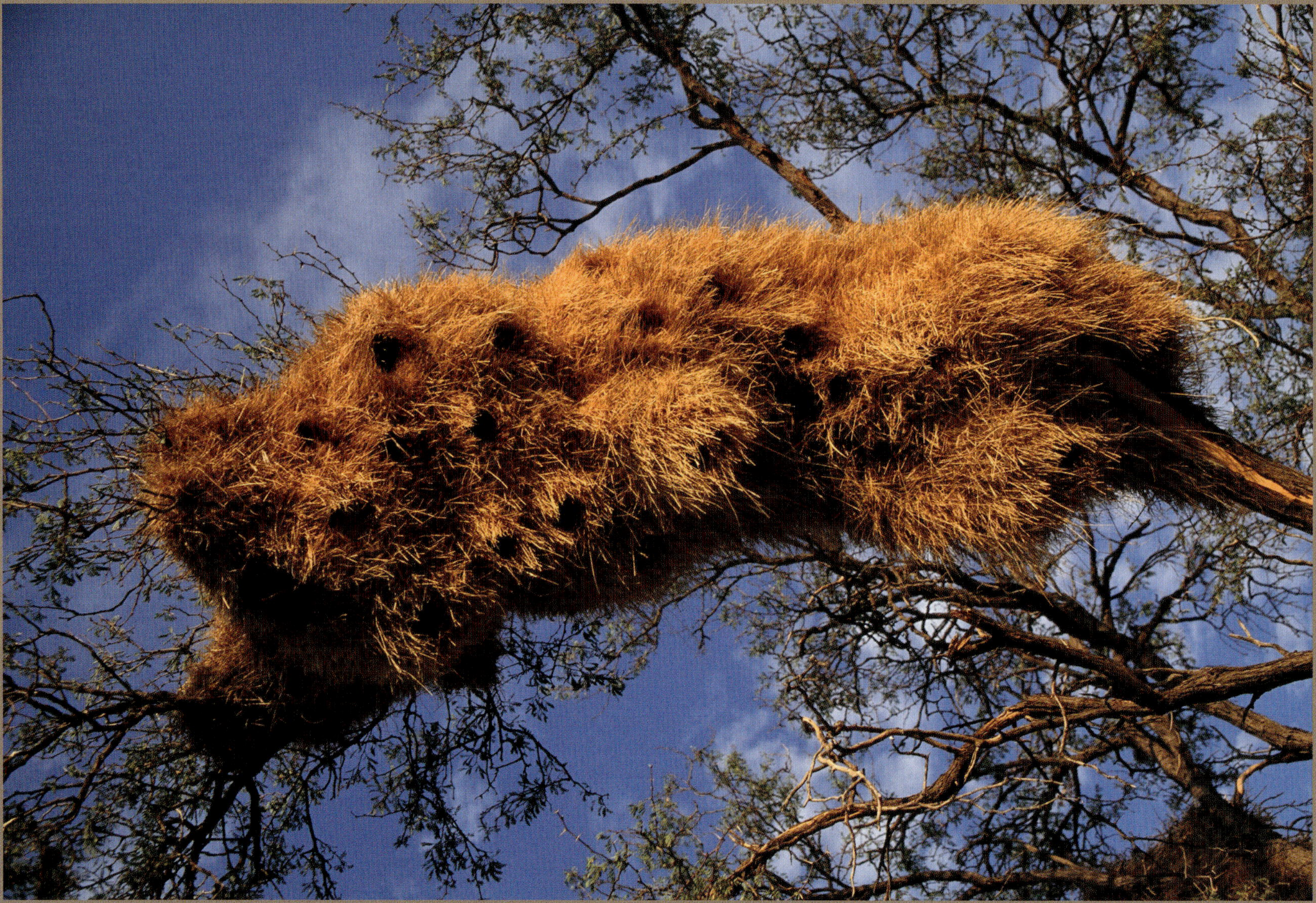

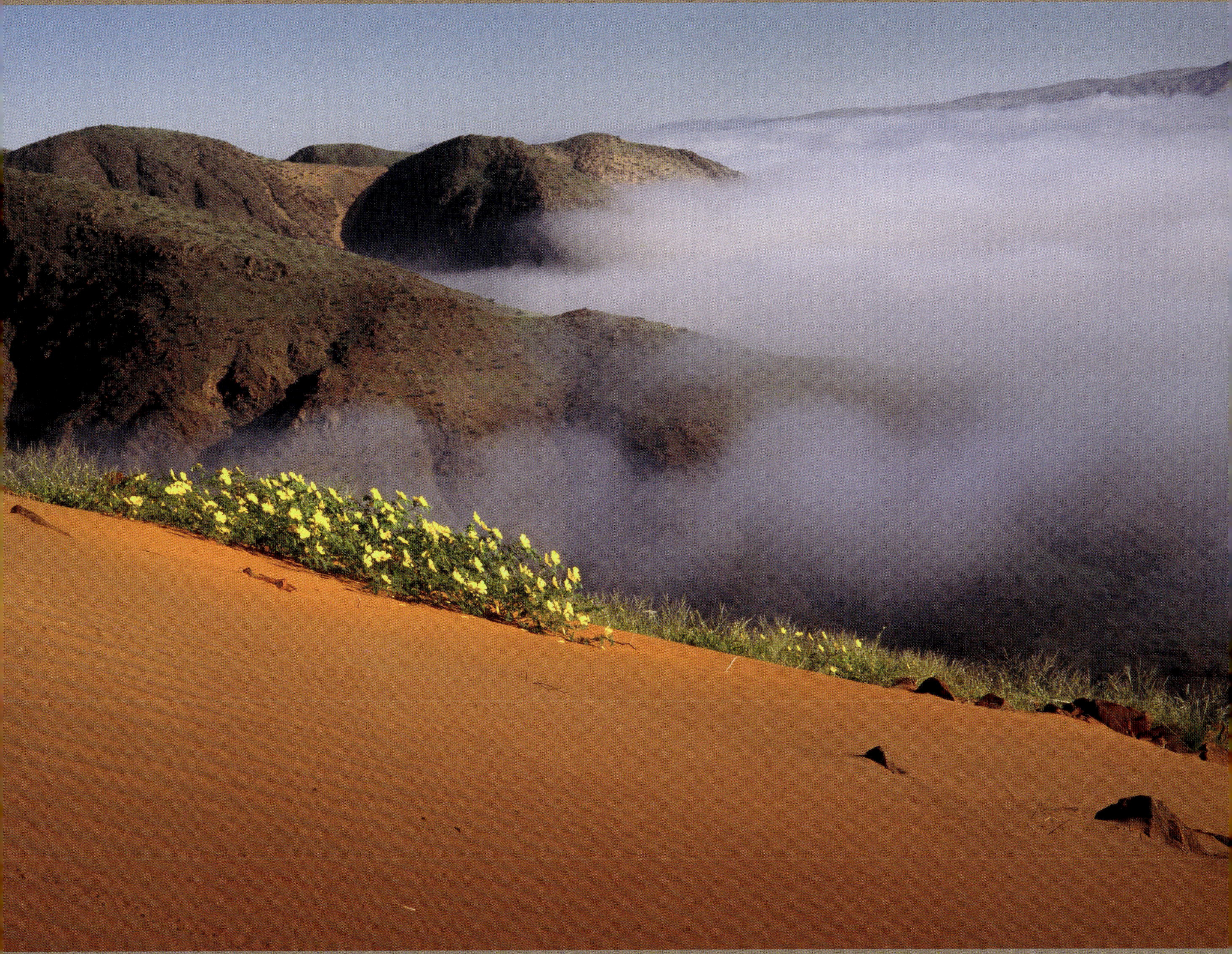

(OPPOSITE) Sociable Weavers' Nest, Namtib Biosphere Reserve (ABOVE) Morning Glory, Hartmann Valley

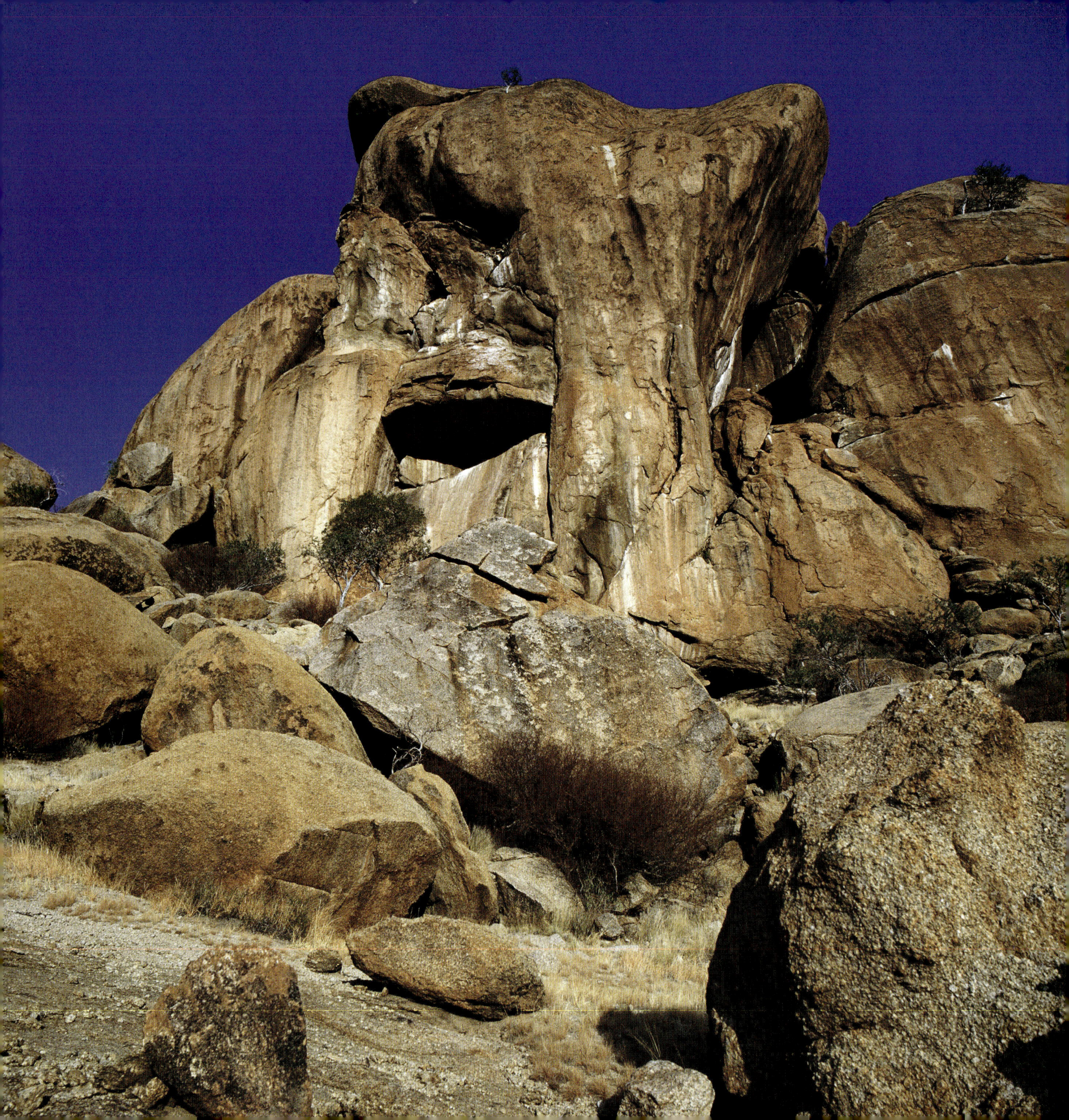

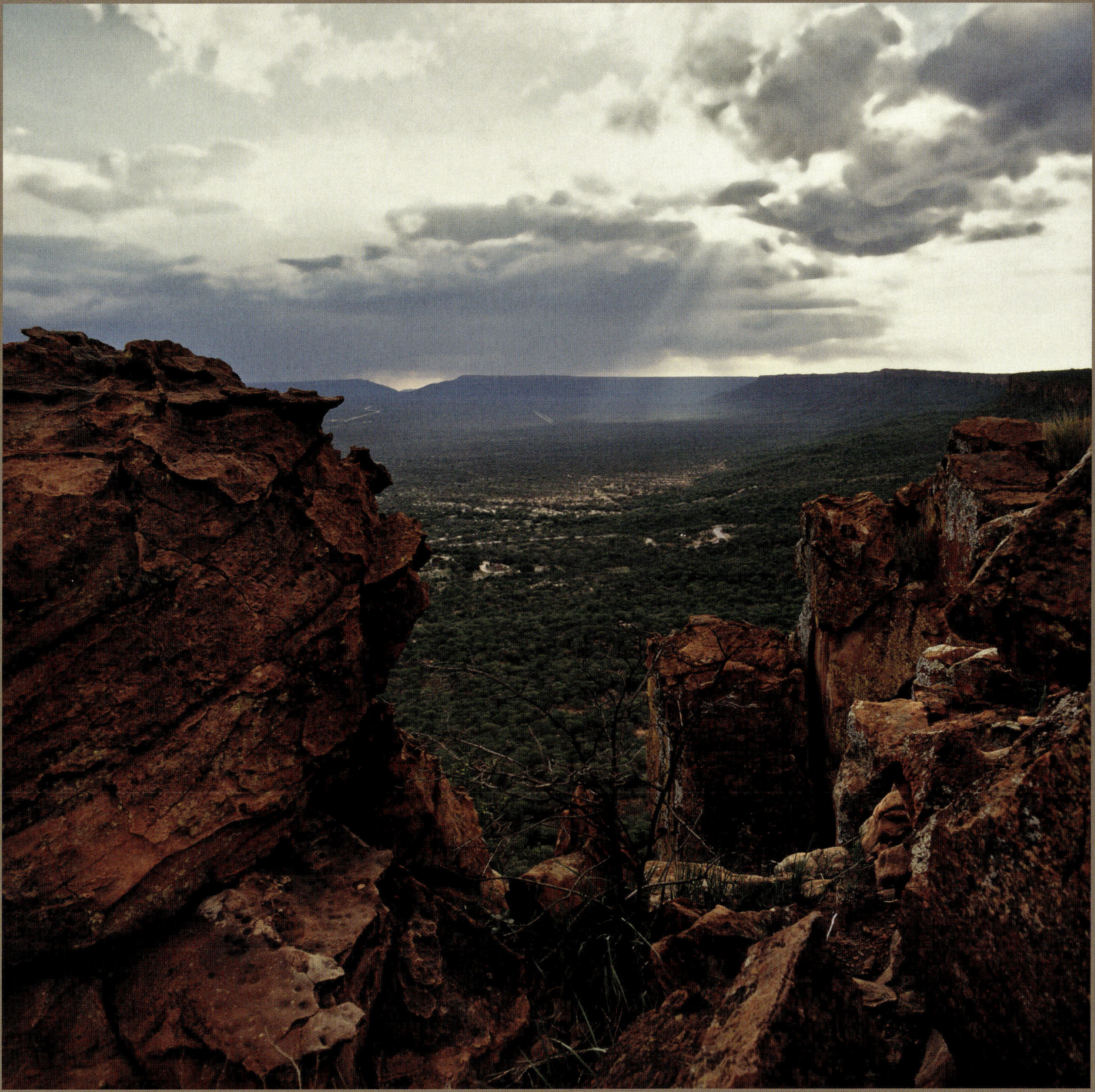

(OPPOSITE) Bull's Party, Ameib (ABOVE) Waterberg Plateau, north-eastern central Namibia

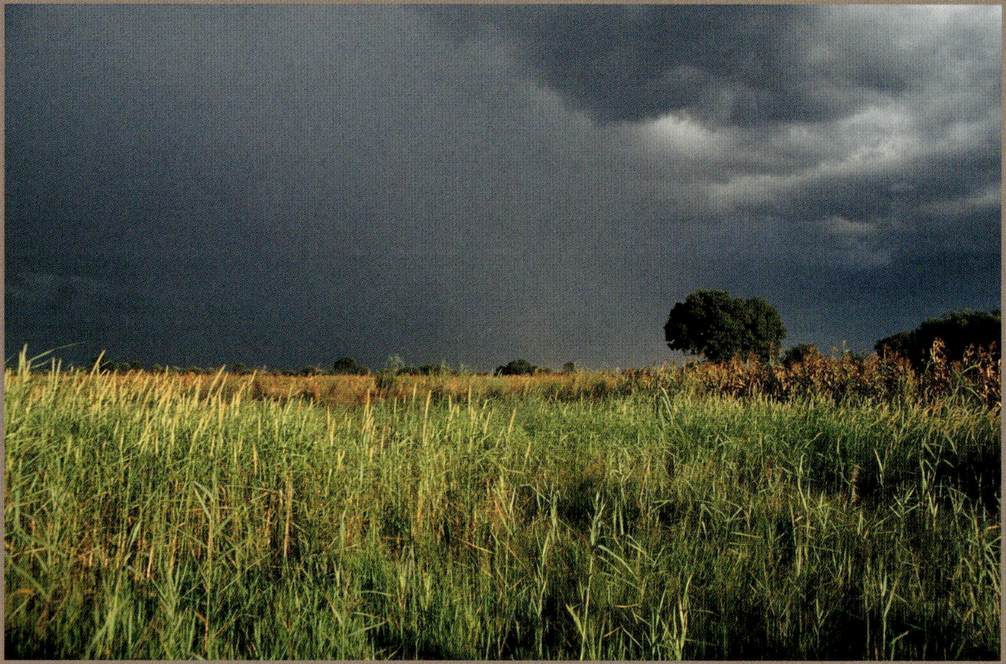

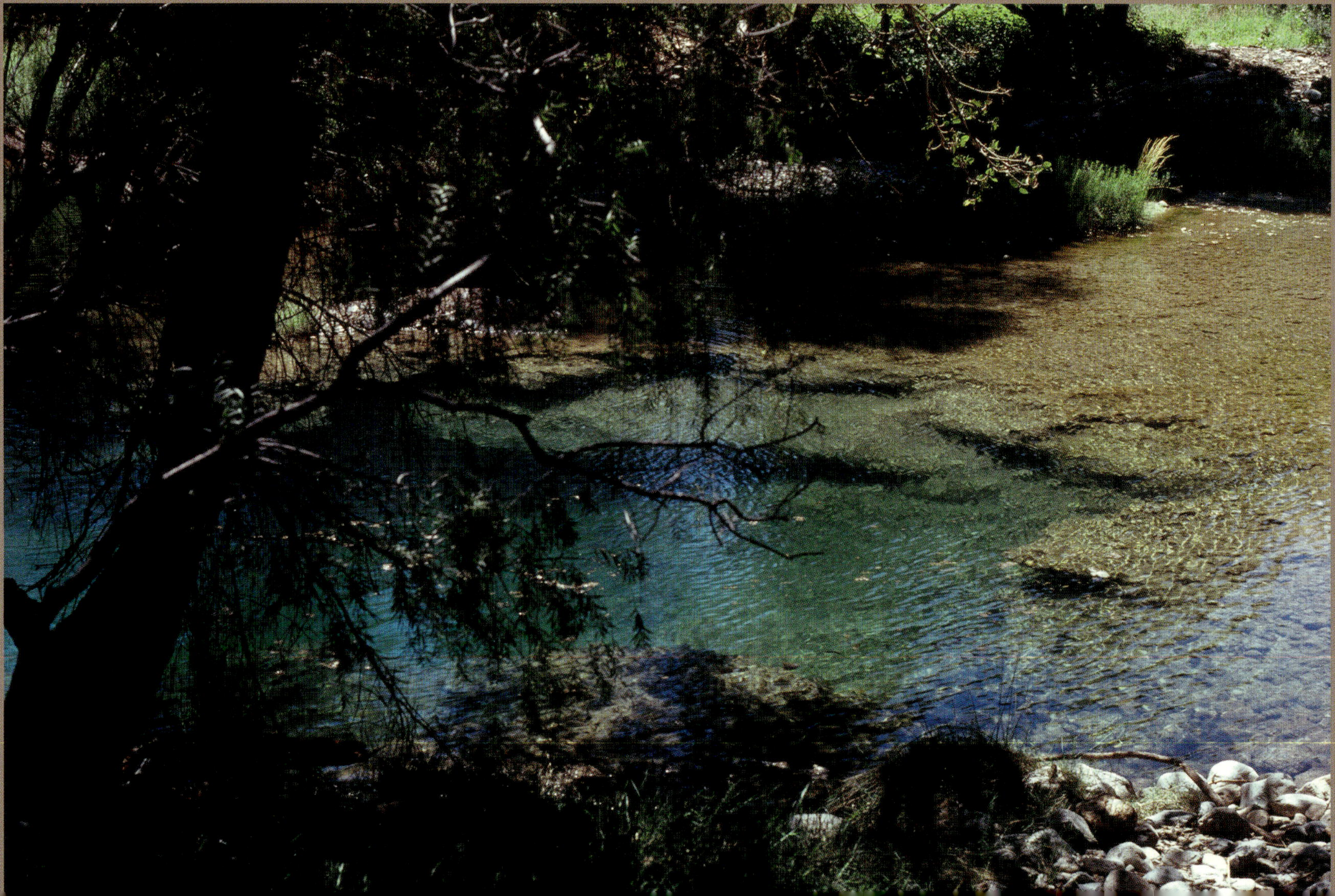

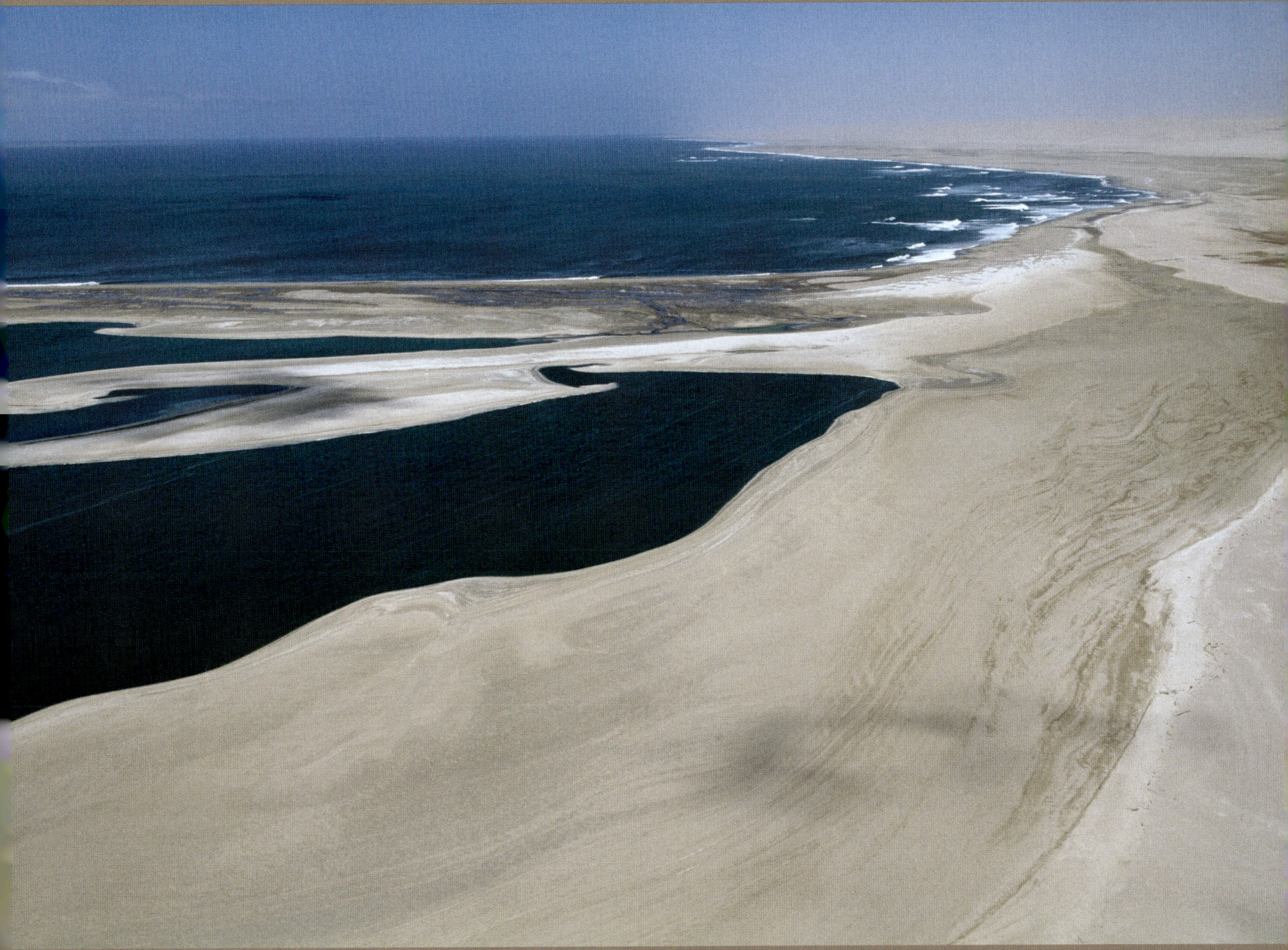

(OPPOSITE ABOVE) Mazambala Magic, East Caprivi (OPPOSITE BELOW) Plunge Pool, Naukluft Mountains
(ABOVE) Sandwich Harbour, Namib-Naukluft Park

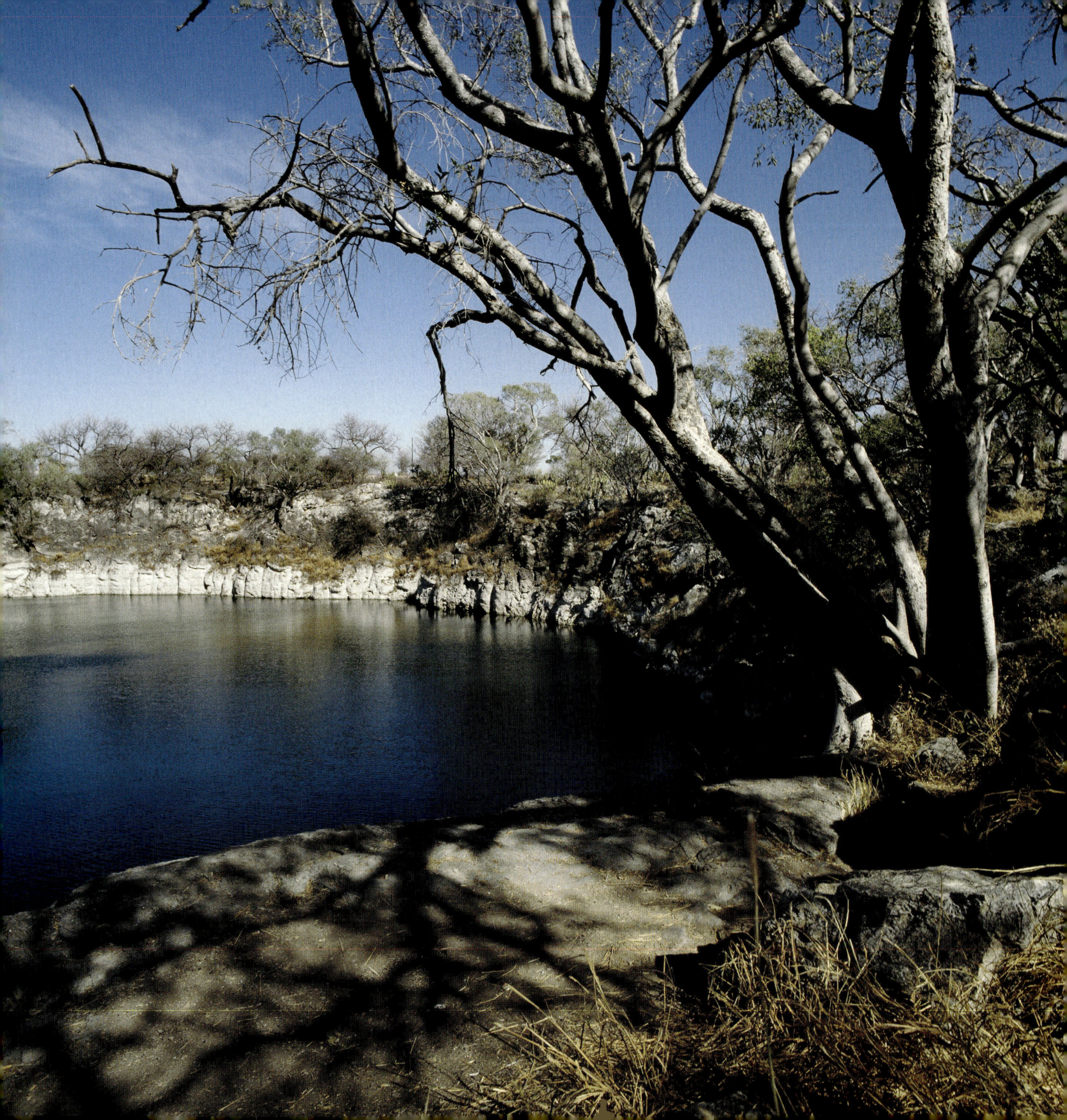

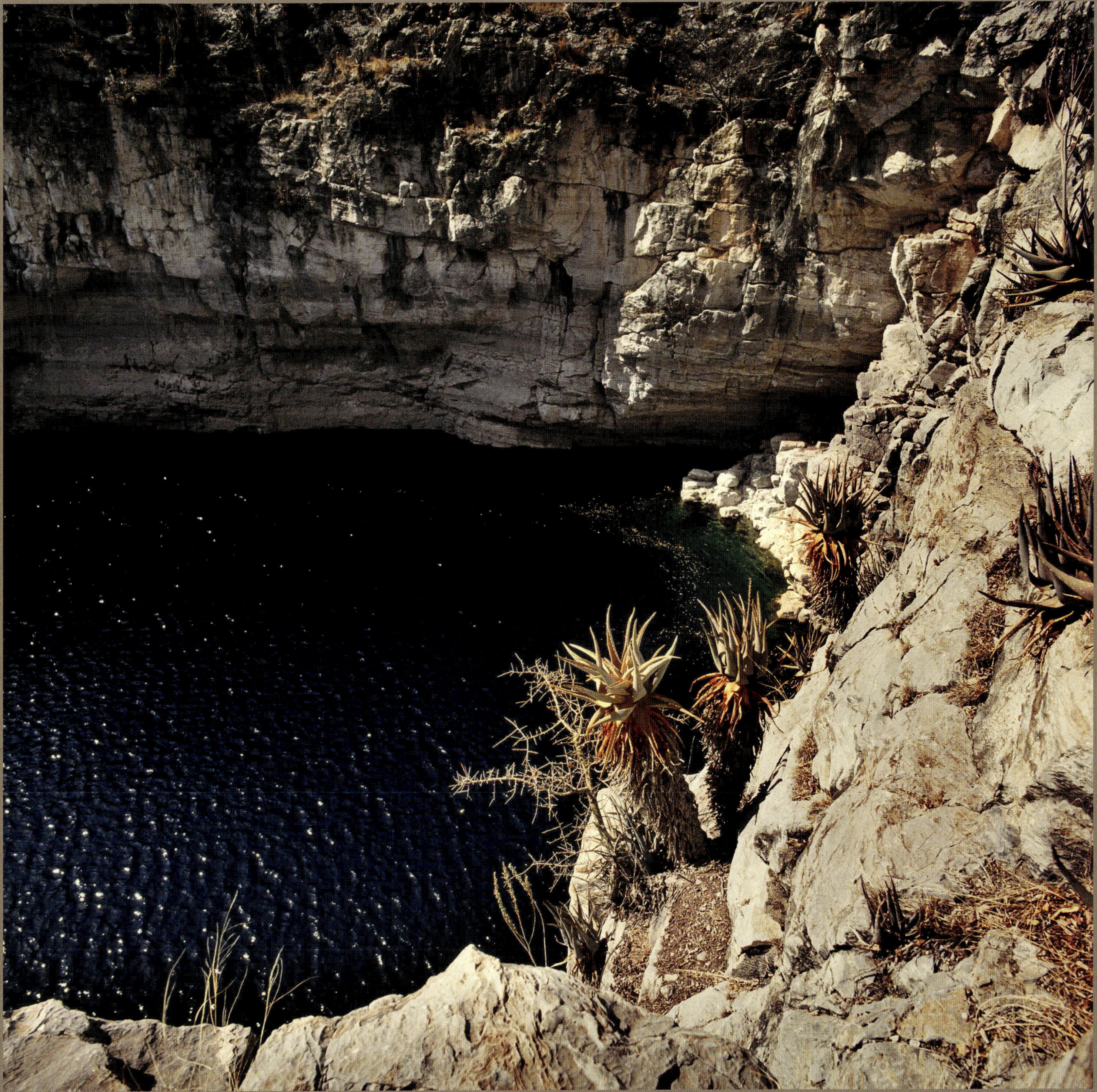

(OPPOSITE) Lake Otjikoto, northern Namibia (ABOVE) Lake Guinas, northern Namibia

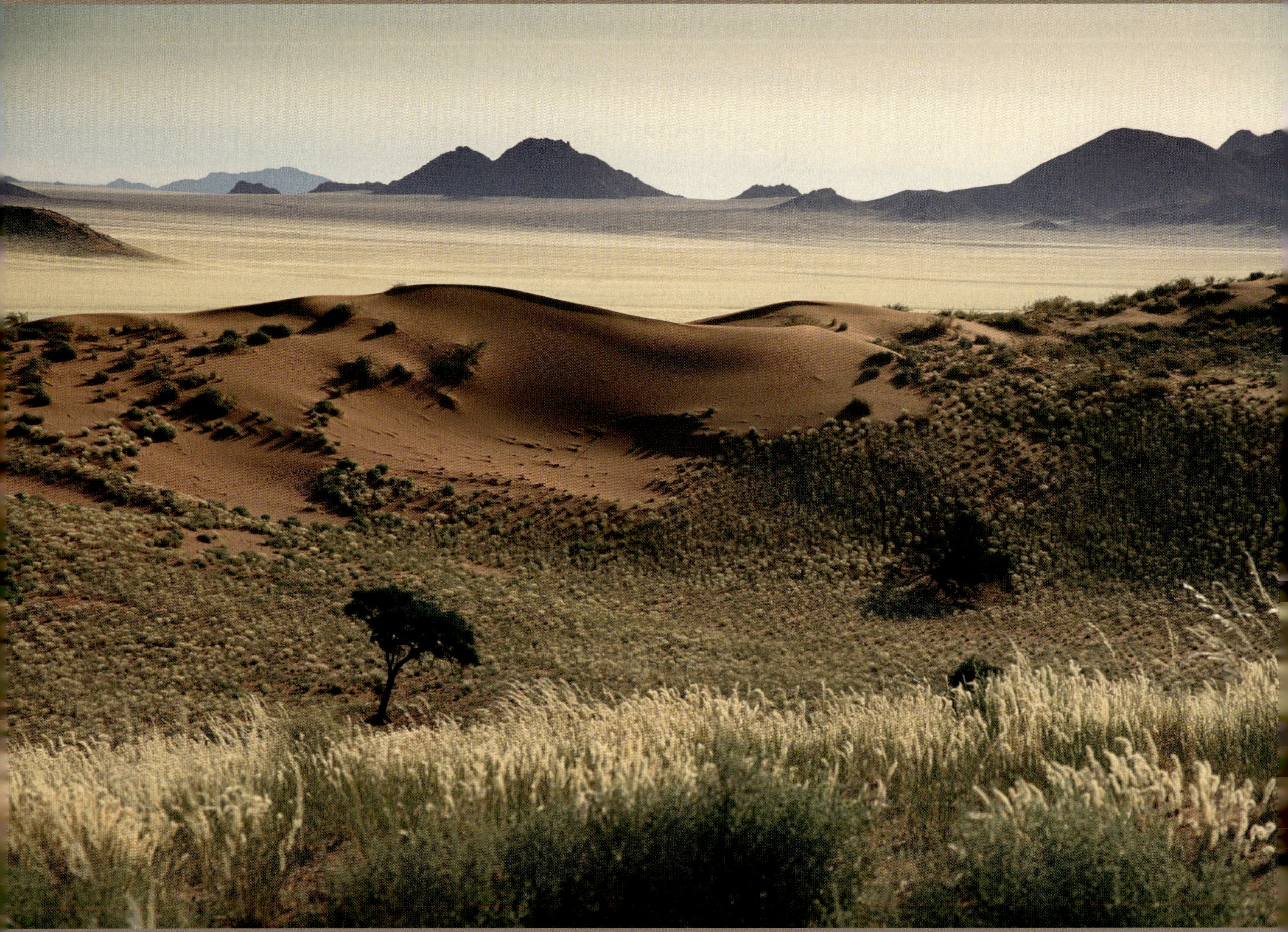

(ABOVE) Grassy Plain, NamibRand Nature Reserve

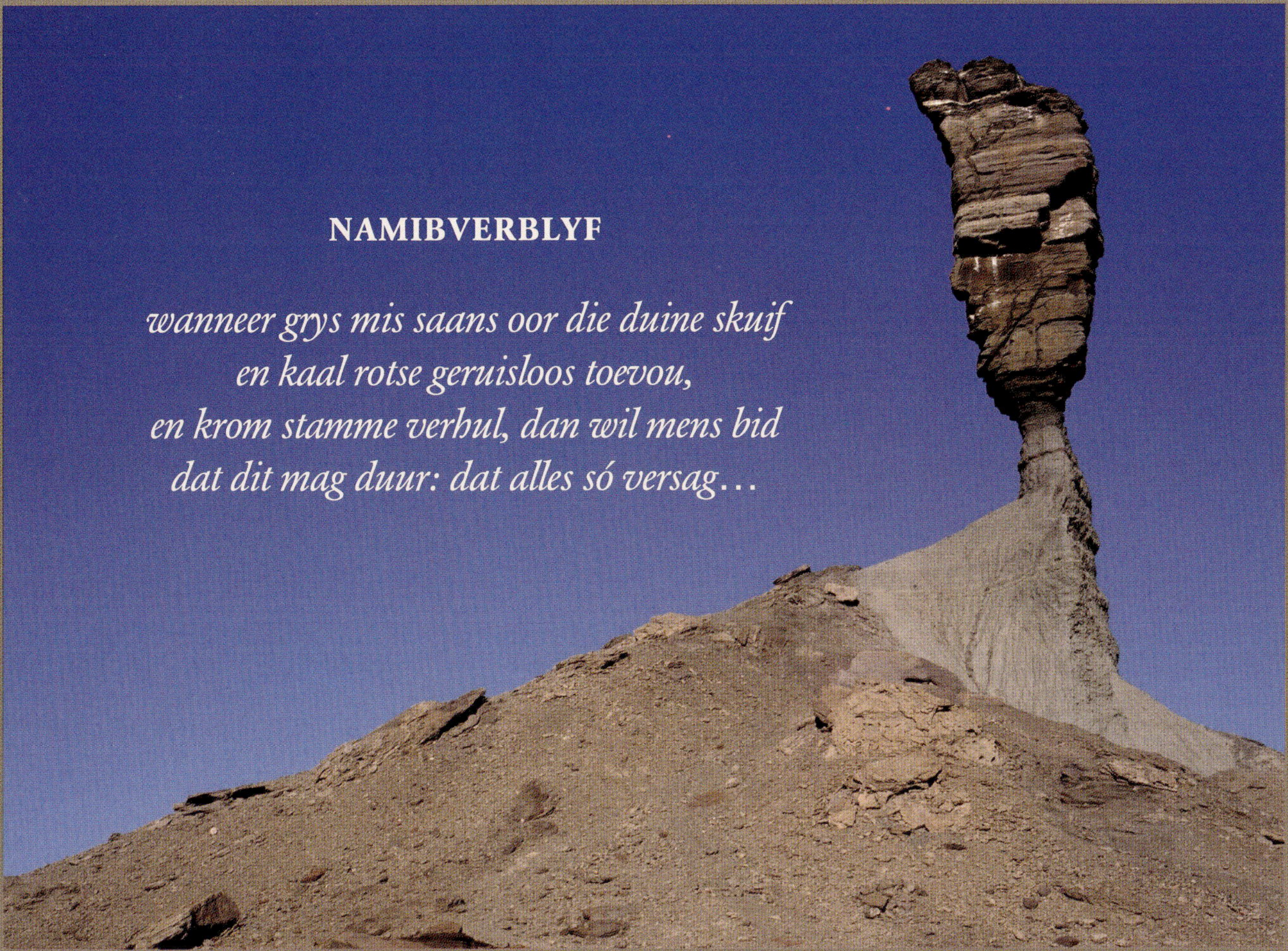

NAMIBVERBLYF

wanneer grys mis saans oor die duine skuif
en kaal rotse geruisloos toevou,
en krom stamme verhul, dan wil mens bid
dat dit mag duur: dat alles só versag…

George Weideman in *Land van sonlig en van sterre, 'n Bundel gedigte oor Namibië* saamgestel deur Daniel Hugo, Pretoria: Protea Boekhuis, 2004: 72

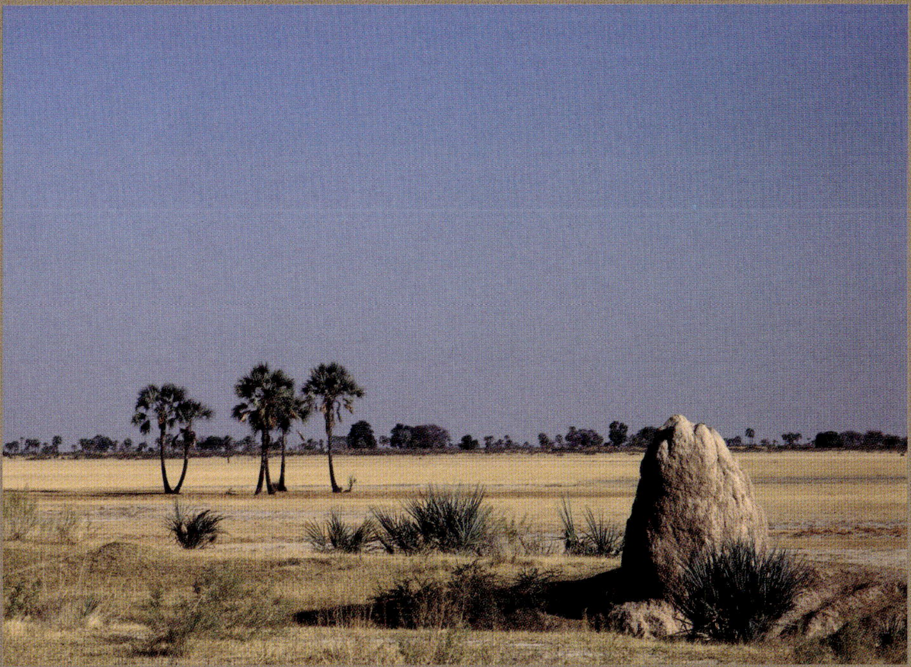

(ABOVE LEFT) Mukurob Vingerklip, southern Namibia (ABOVE RIGHT) Owambo Region, northern Namibia

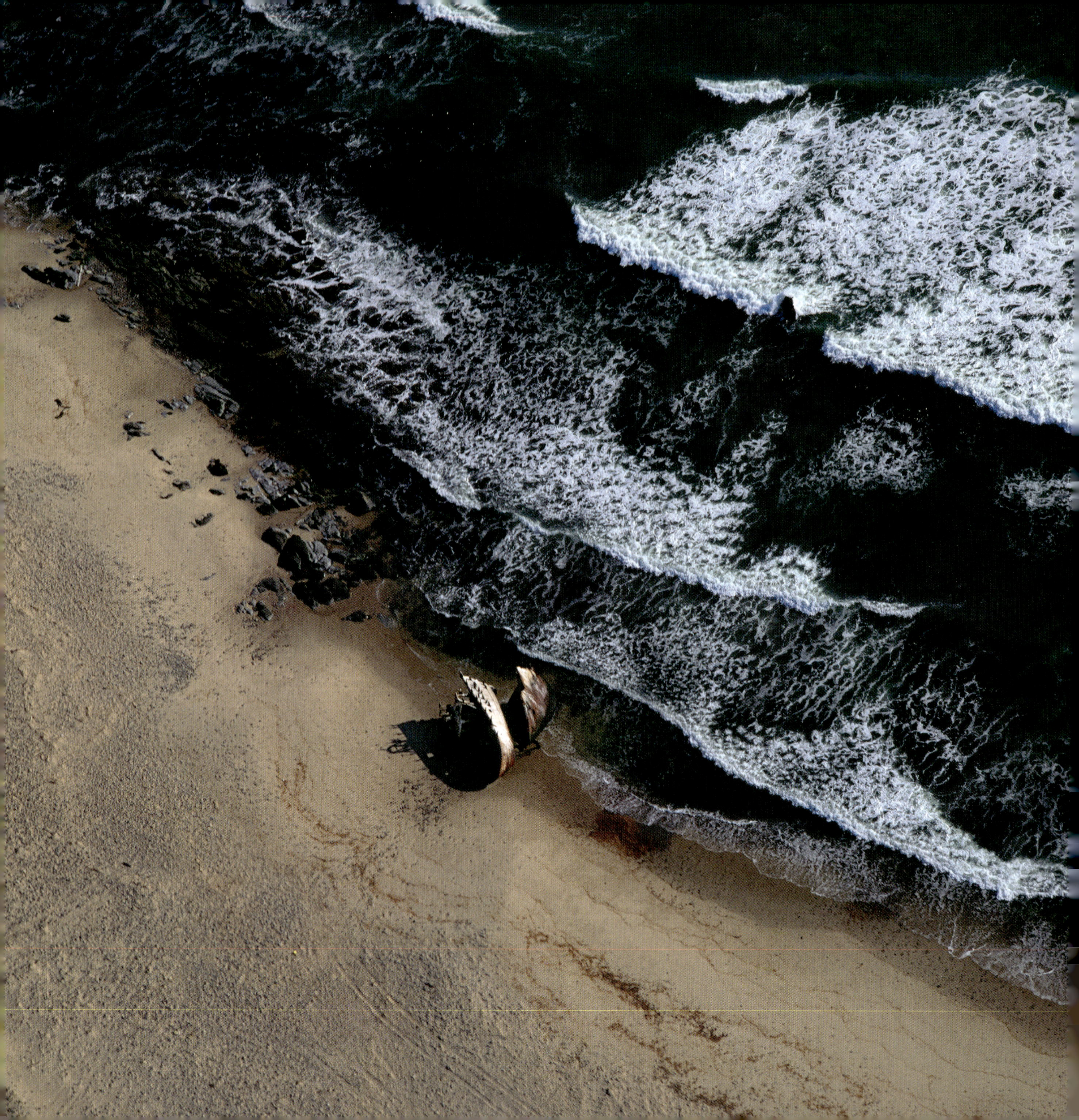

Portfolio 2

SKELETON COAST CLASSICS

My first visit to the Skeleton Coast was in October 1977 as journalist/photographer for the Department of Nature Conservation and Tourism. My boss, Director Bernabé de la Bat, had instructed me to write an article on the wilderness section of the Skeleton Coast Park for the 1978 *SWA Annual*. It was on this assignment that I met Louw Schoeman, who became my husband some years later. His enthusiasm for the area was infectious and from the outset he aroused my interest in its long-term conservation.

On that first visit I was bowled over by the photographic potential of the Skeleton Coast and its hinterland, Kaokoland and Damaraland. The sand seas of ivory-coloured dunes, the deep canyons, extensive gravel plains, wide horizons, diversity of colour, texture and form, and the ever-changing moods created by light and shadow, presented endless possibilities. Moreover, climatic conditions in this volatile region are unpredictable and change rapidly, making a scene that one minute has profile, dimension and contrast, flat and colourless the next.

Thus all too often the "ultimate image" remained elusive, bringing to mind the maxim: the best pictures are the ones we never take.

Over the next 16 years I assembled an extensive library of images on the many facets of the Skeleton Coast – from the geomorphology, flora and fauna to the shipwrecks and mining paraphernalia left by countless prospectors, miners and fortune hunters. I wrote numerous articles on the conservation and wilderness aspects of the region, a key theme being the necessity in this day and age to preserve pristine and uninhabited areas "...where the earth and its community of life are untrammelled by man, where man himself is a visitor who does not remain". These endeavours culminated in the publication of the first edition of my book *Skeleton Coast*.

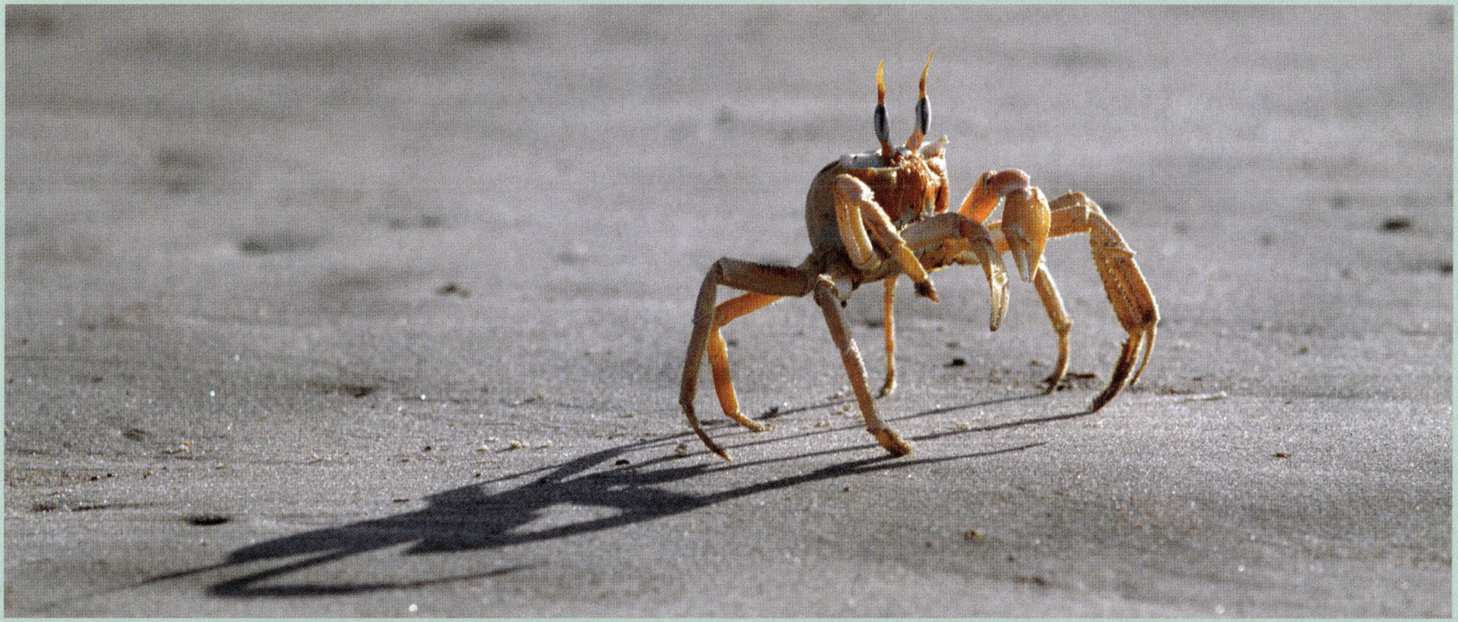

(OPPOSITE) Skeleton Coast wreck (ABOVE) Ghost Crab

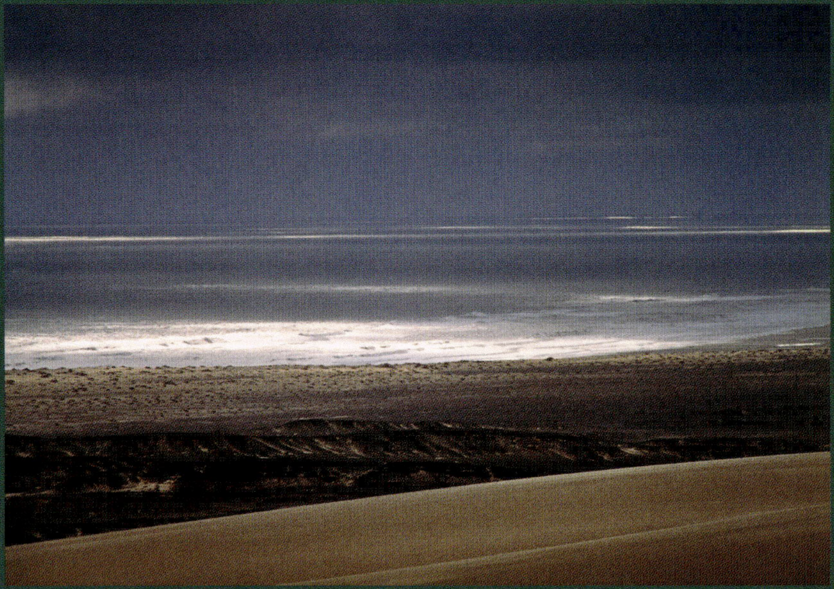

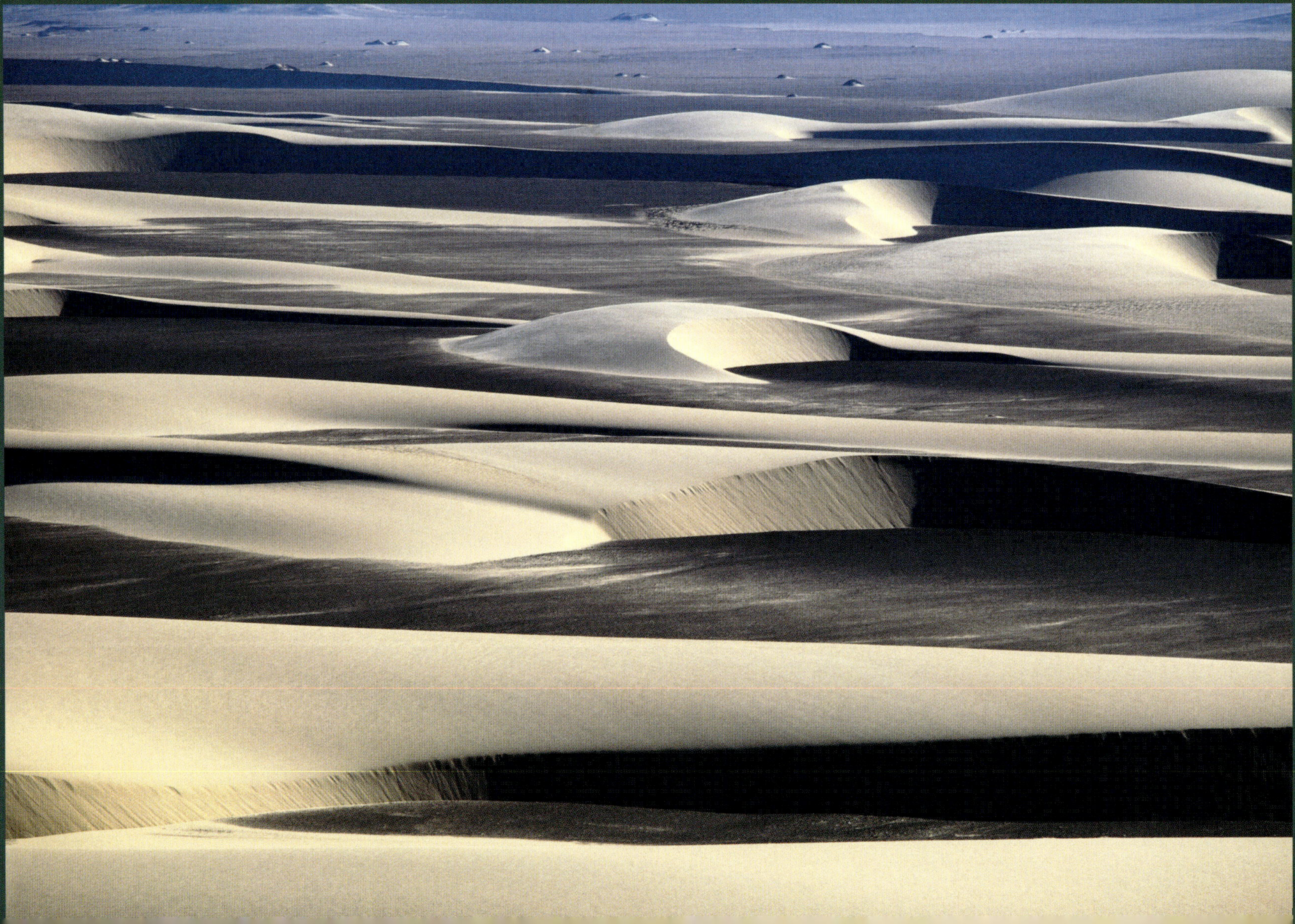

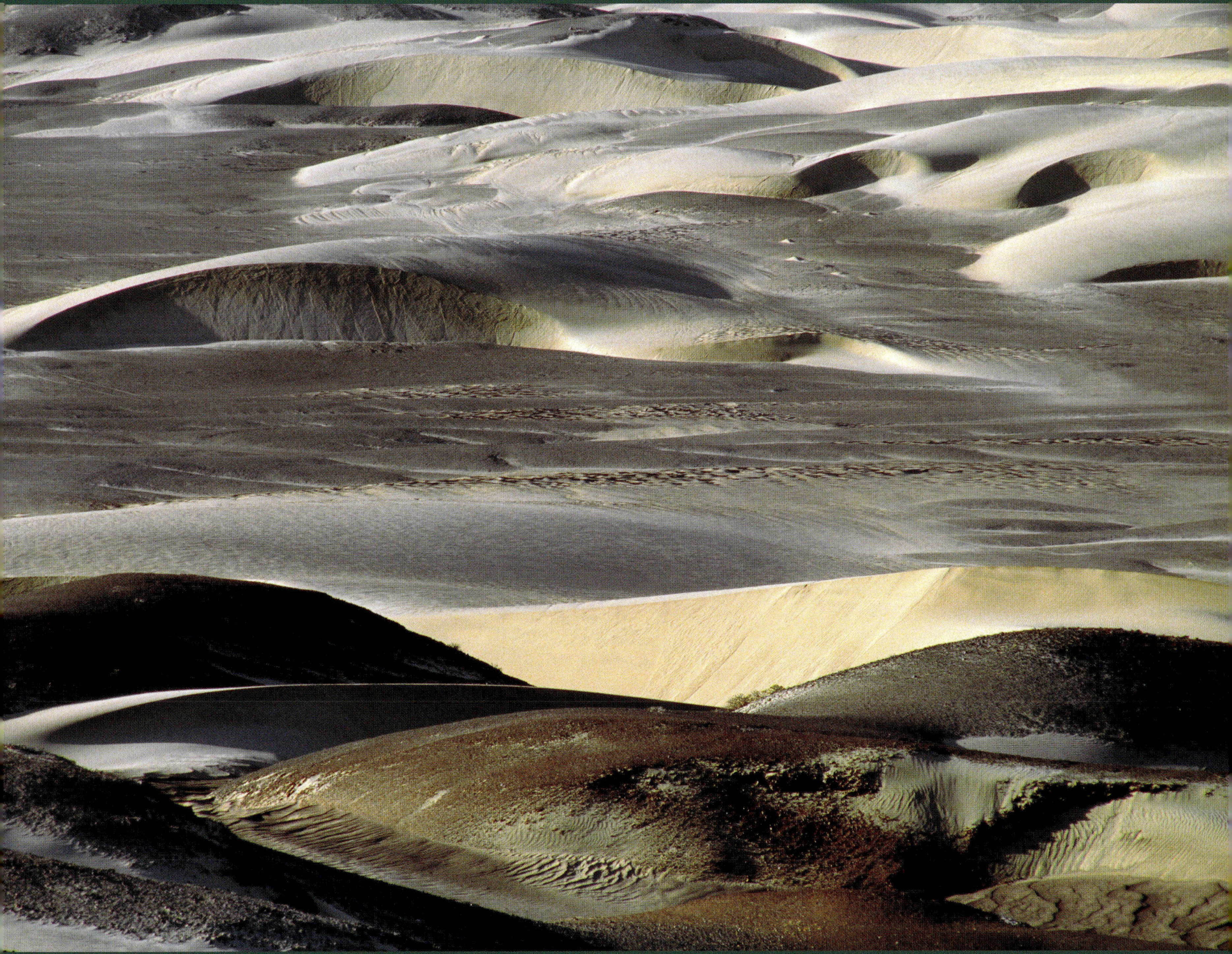

(OPPOSITE ABOVE) Silver Sea (OPPOSITE BELOW) Dune Strata, morning light (ABOVE) Golden Dunes

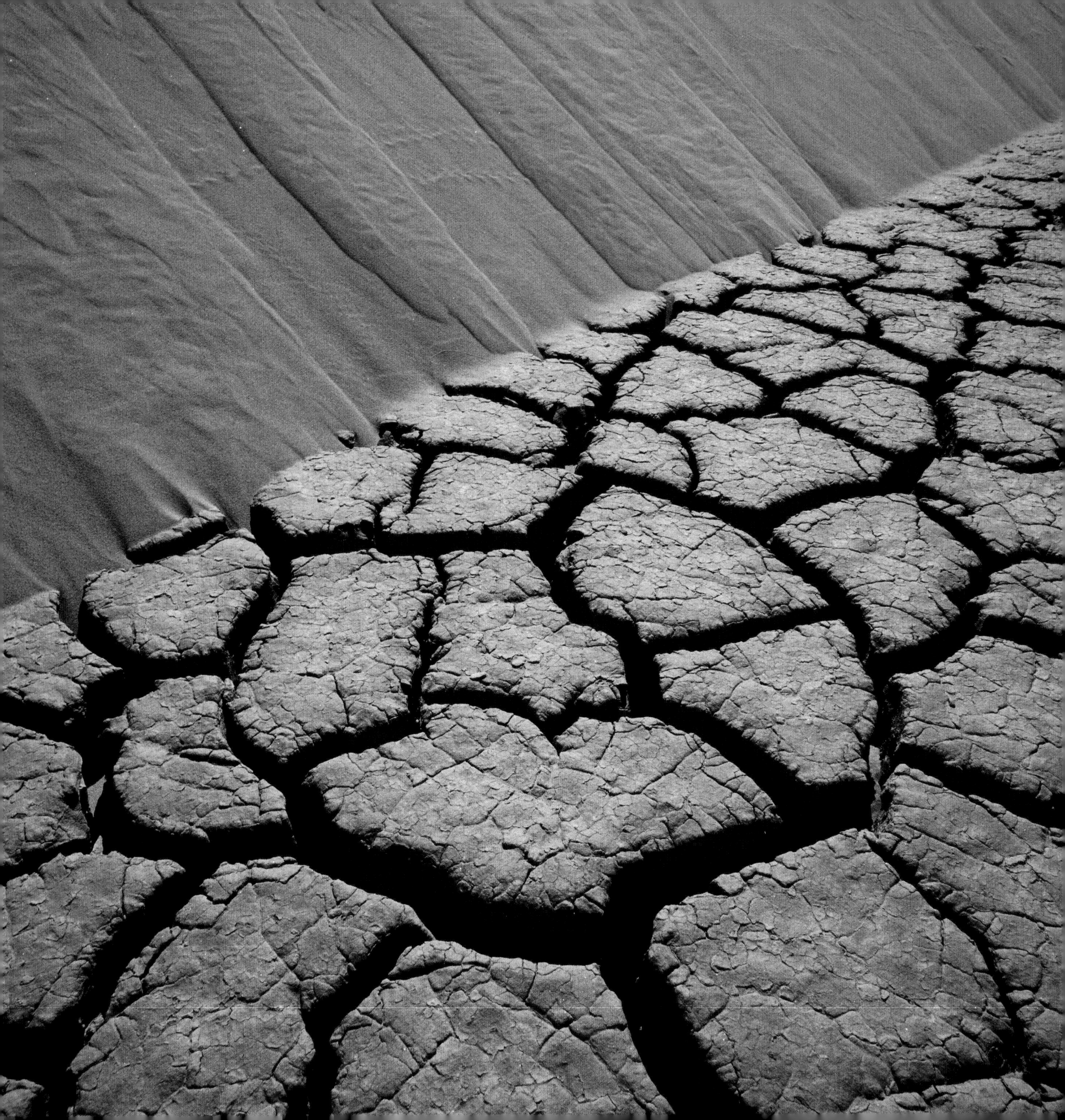

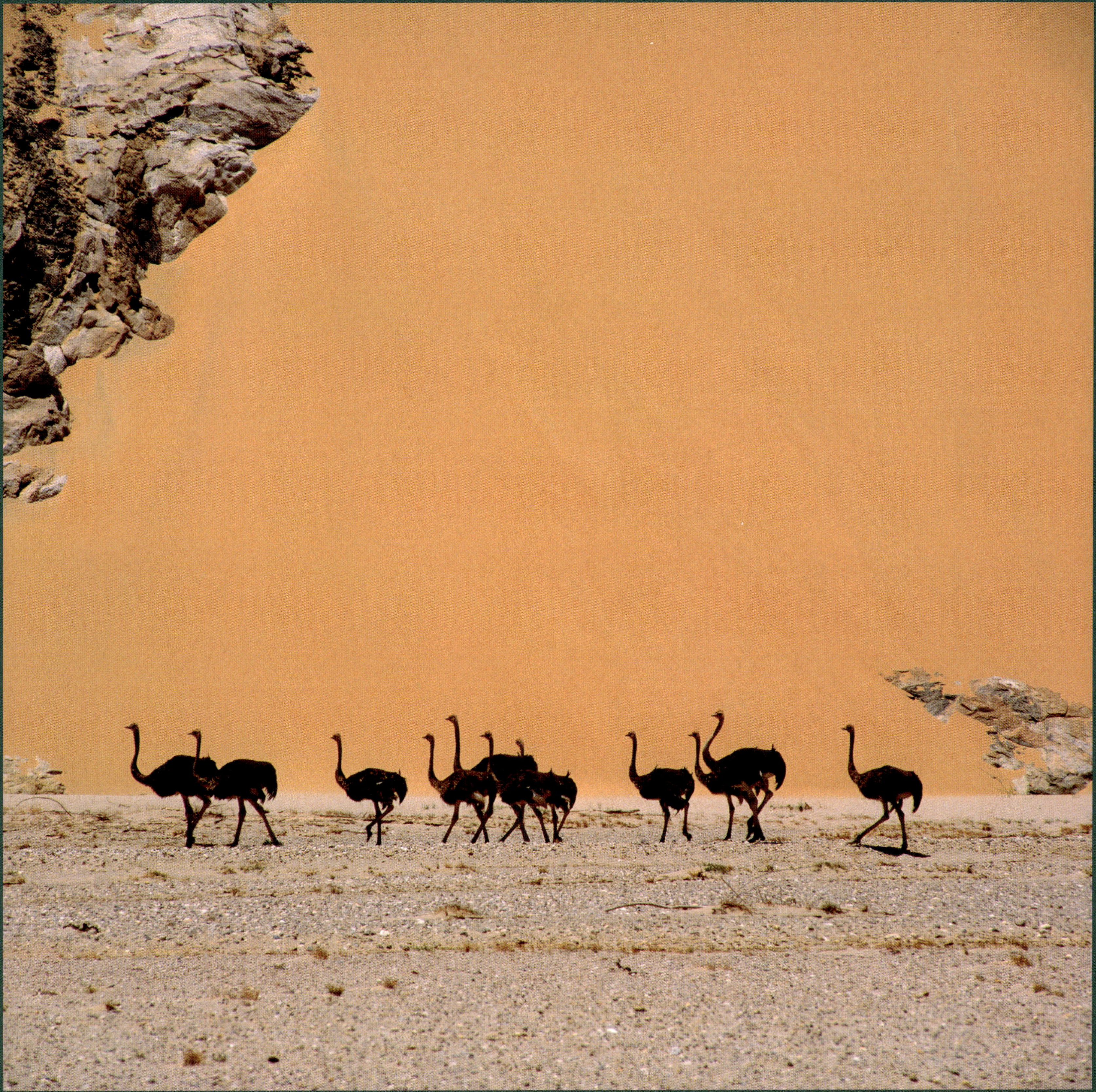

(OPPOSITE) Cracked Mud (ABOVE) Ostrich in the Hoarusib Canyon

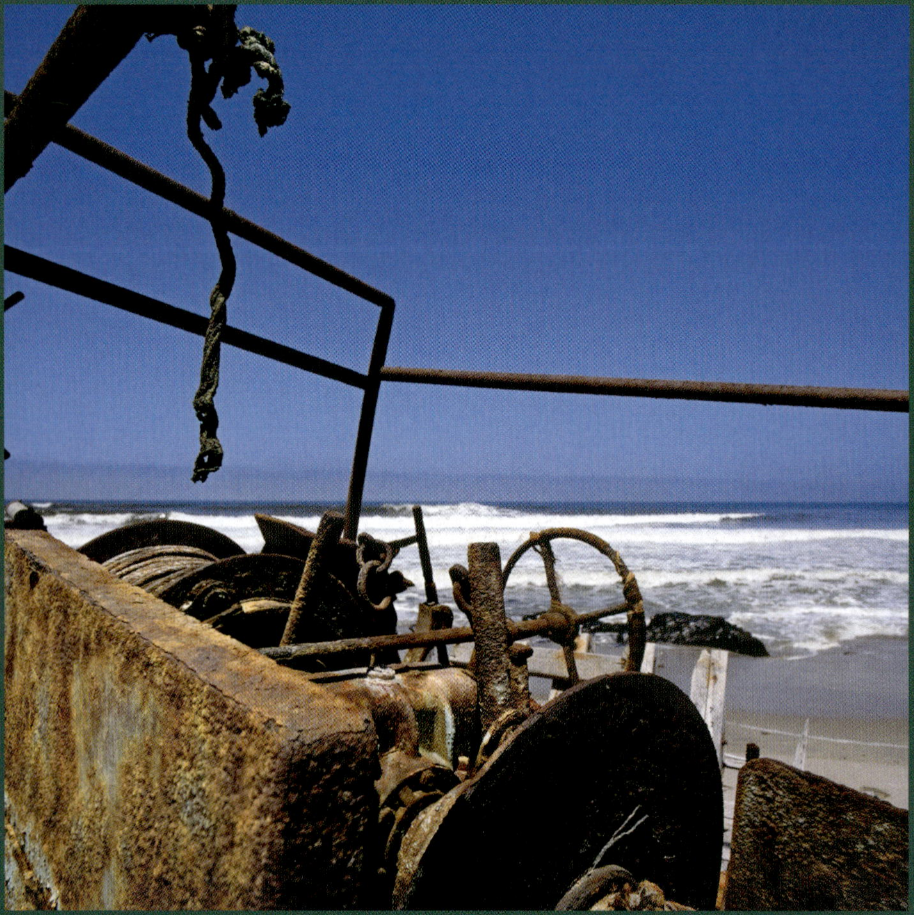

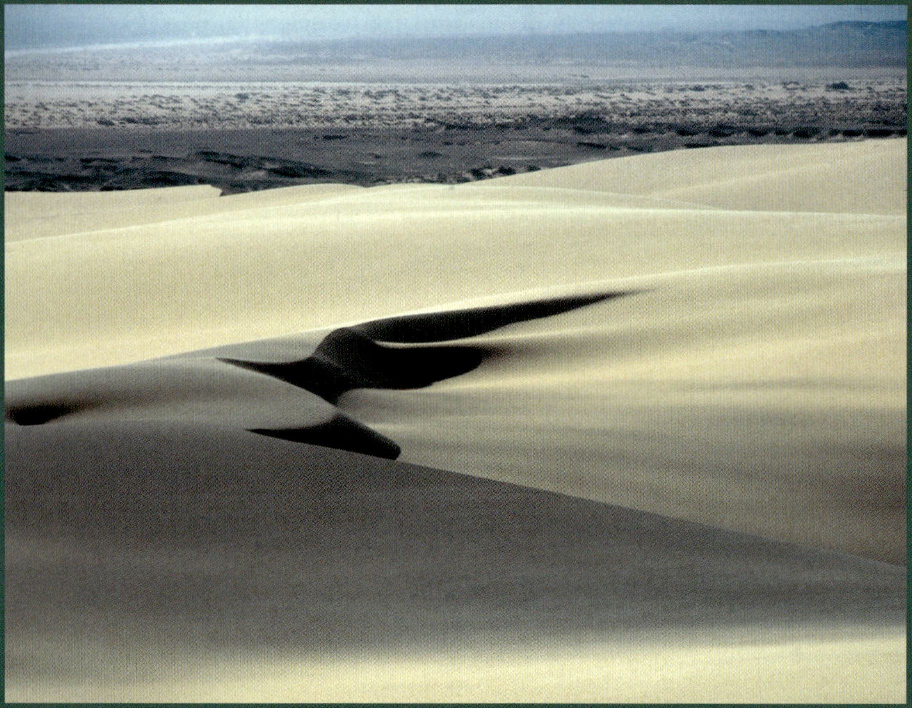

LUGFOTO

(Skedelkus, Namibië)

met gevlekte oë
sweef ek navigerend
oor jou uitgestrekte lyf
totdat in spieëlings
jou relief verteder
tot handgeskaapte duintjies
wat breekwater
teen die skedels
in die spergebied kon lê

Kobus Lombard, *Tussen wysvinger en duim*,
Pretoria: Protea Boekhuis, 2005: 59

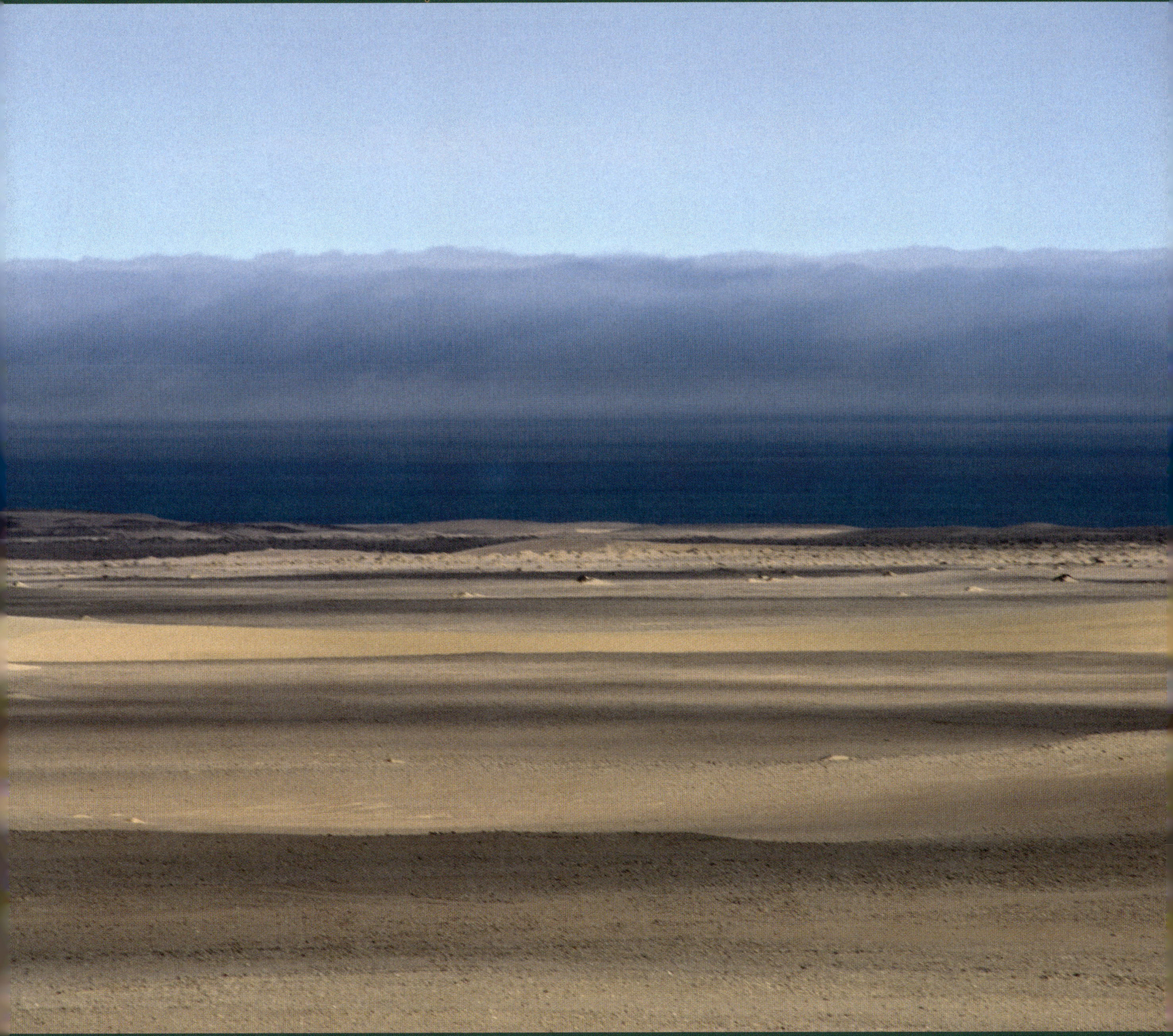

(OPPOSITE ABOVE) Wreck of the *Benguela Eagle* (OPPOSITE BELOW) Versace Dunes (ABOVE) Coastal Mist

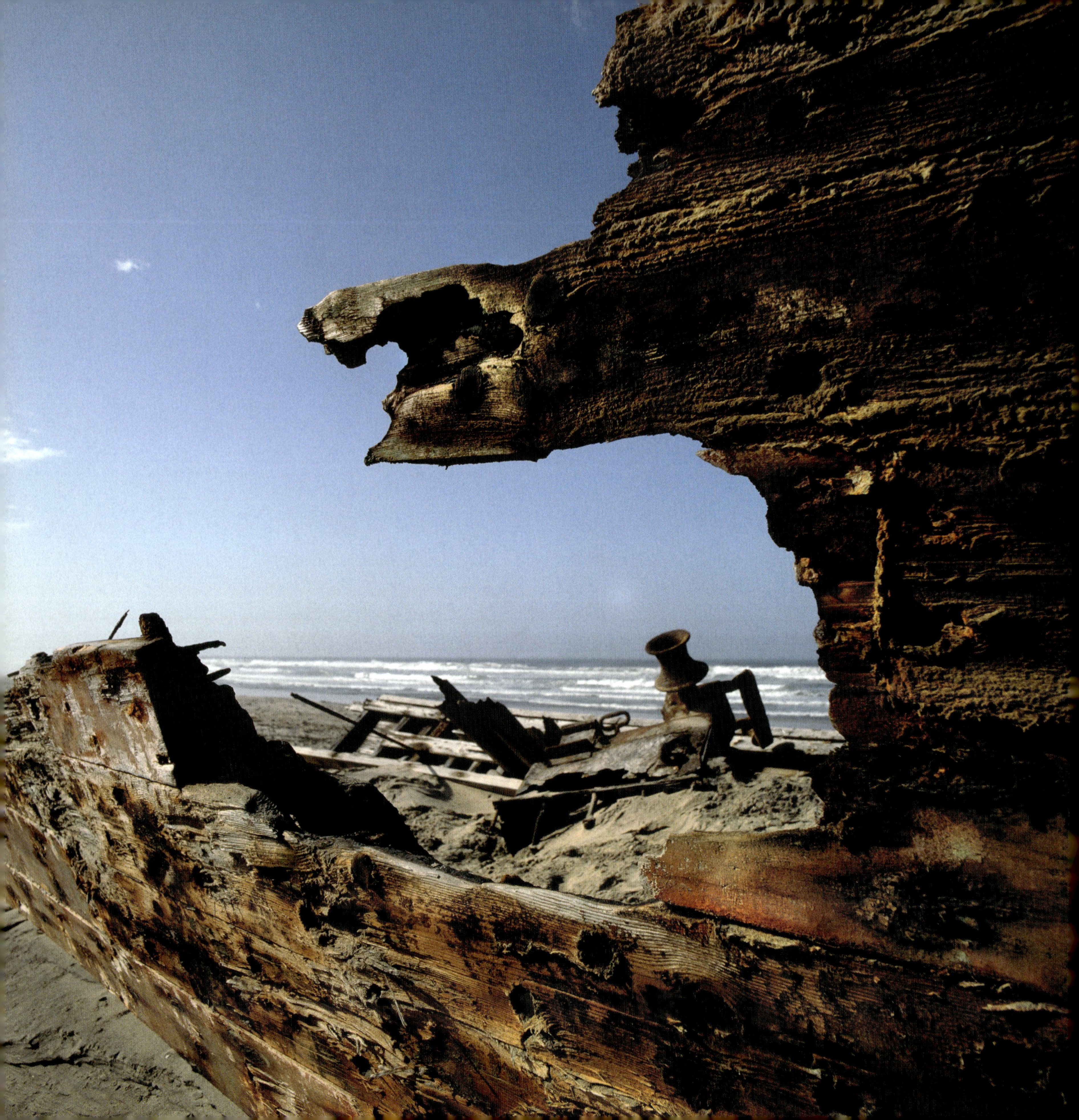

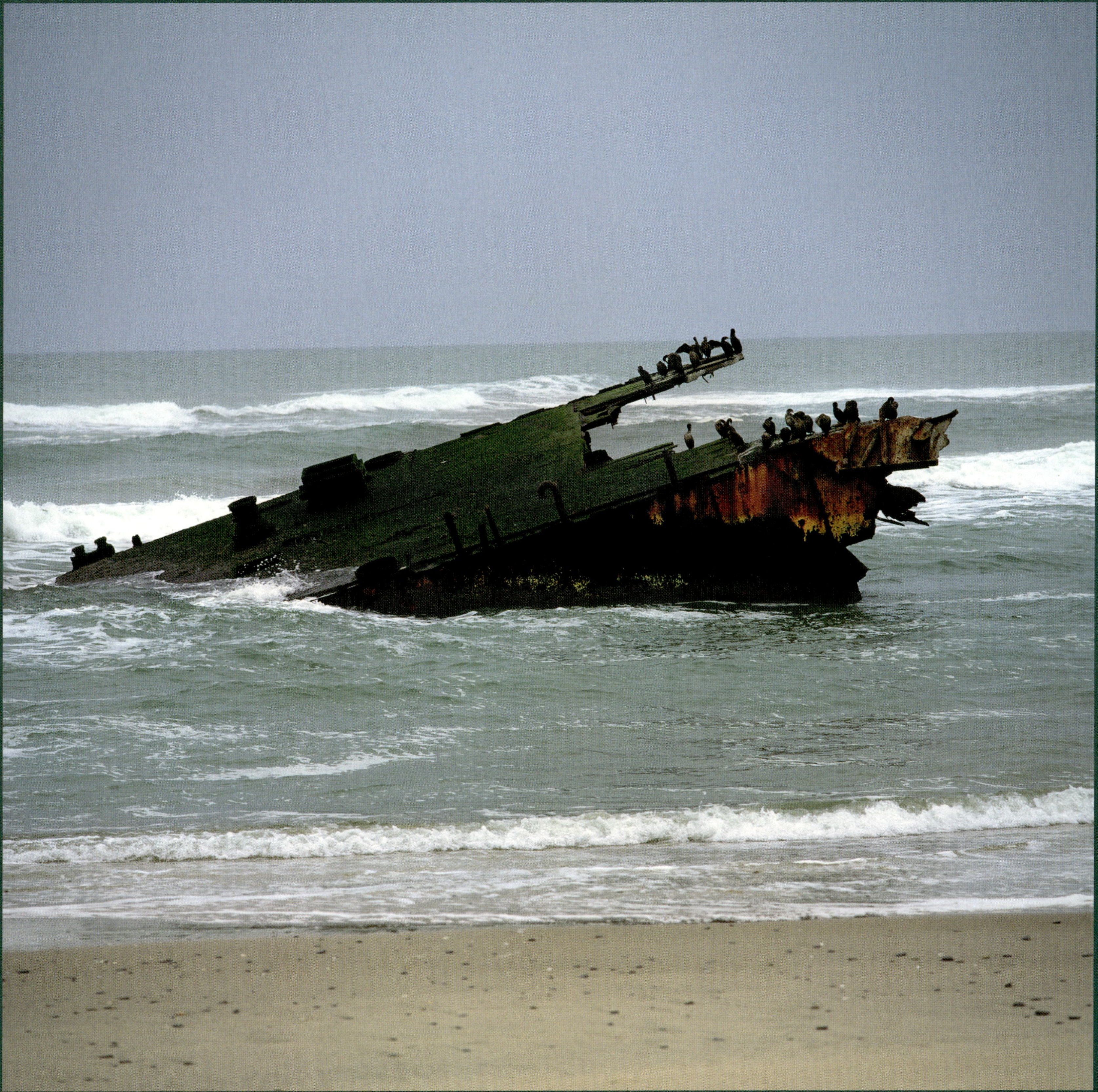

(OPPOSITE) Wreck of the *Karimona* (ABOVE) Wreck of the *Kaio Maru*

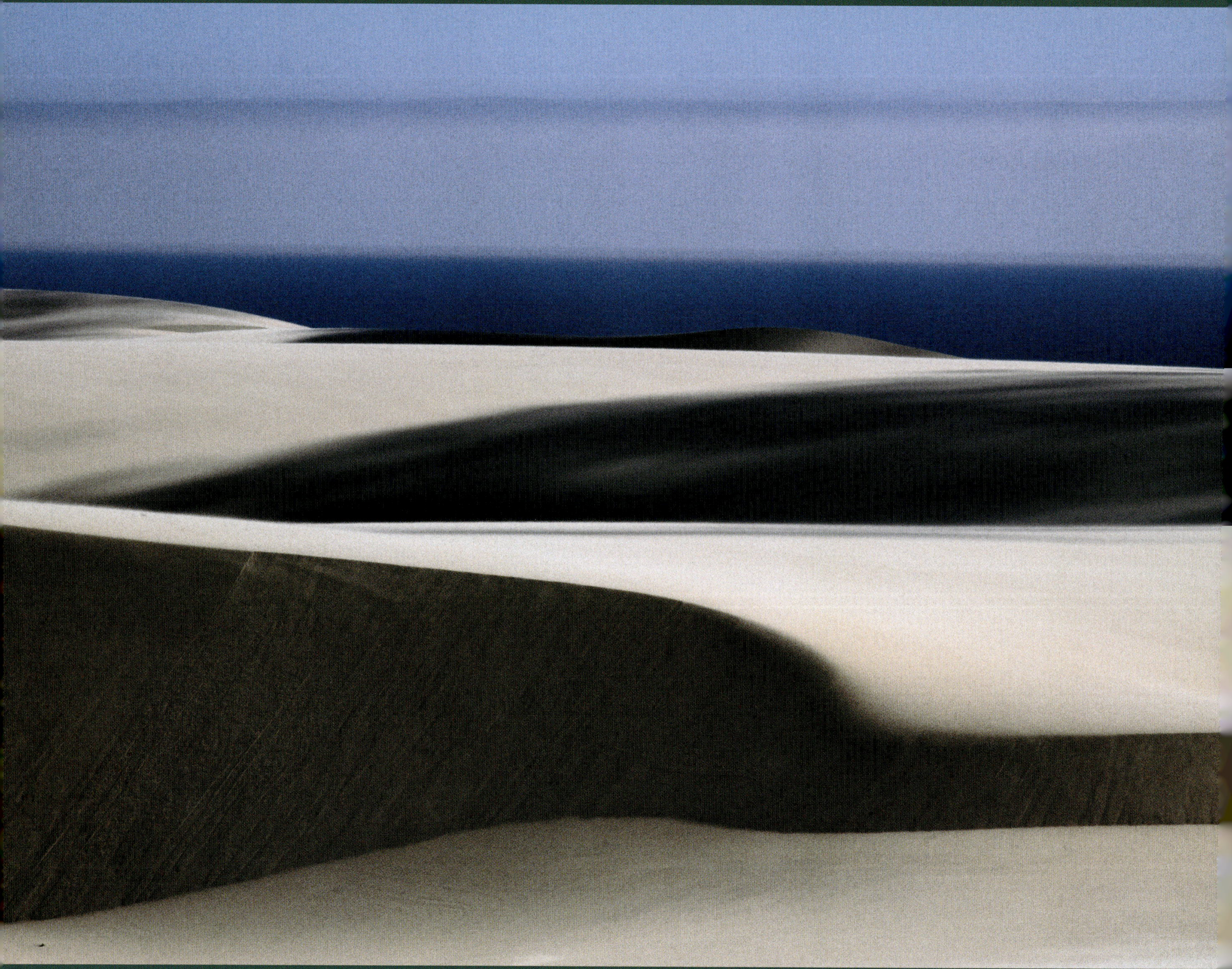

"Mit dem Finden von Wasser steht und fällt alles."

Thomas Dressler, Bilder Namibias. Roggebaai, Cape Town: Sunbird Publishers, 2000

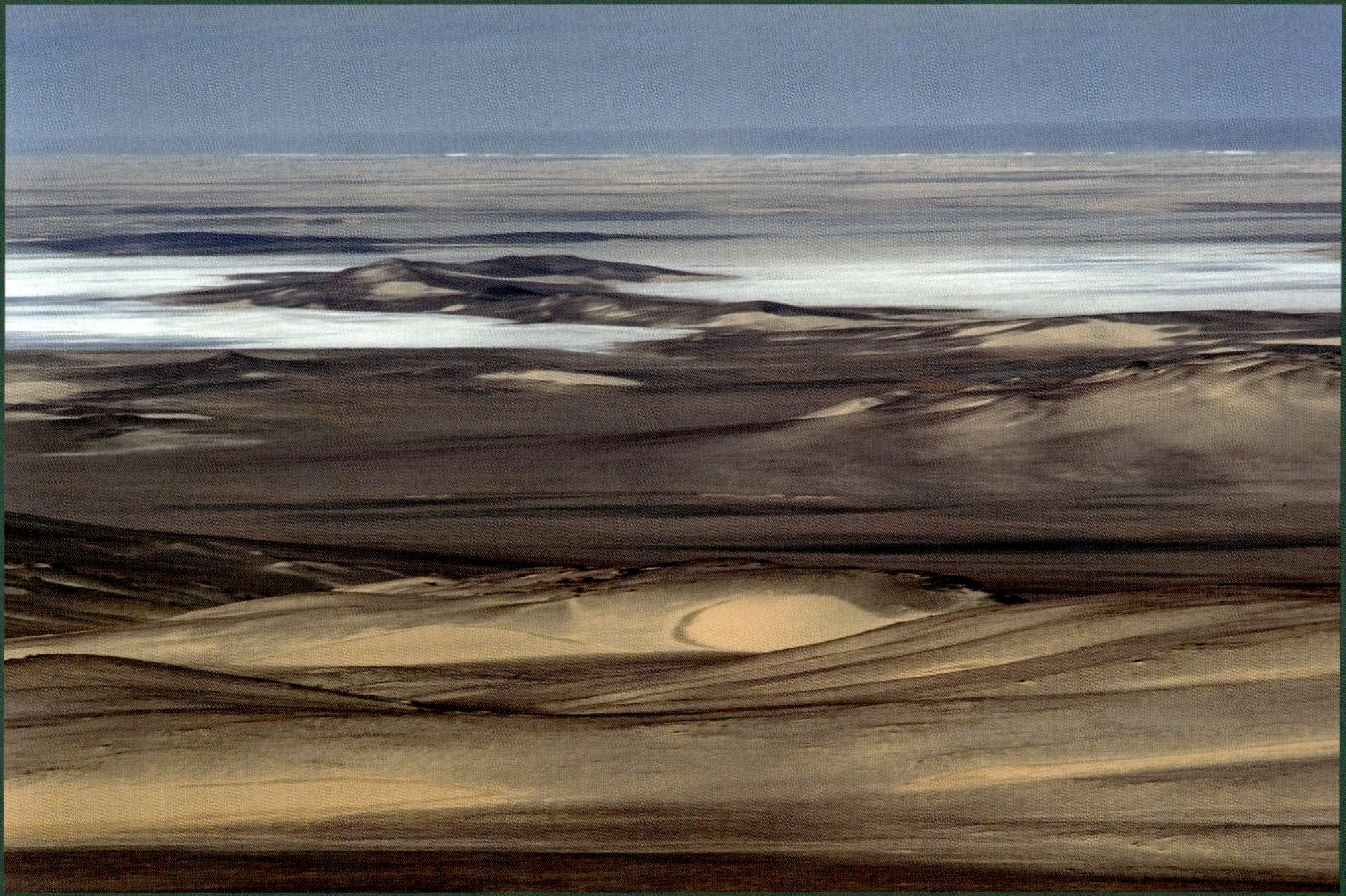

(OPPOSITE) Dune Shadows (ABOVE) Cape Frio Saltpan

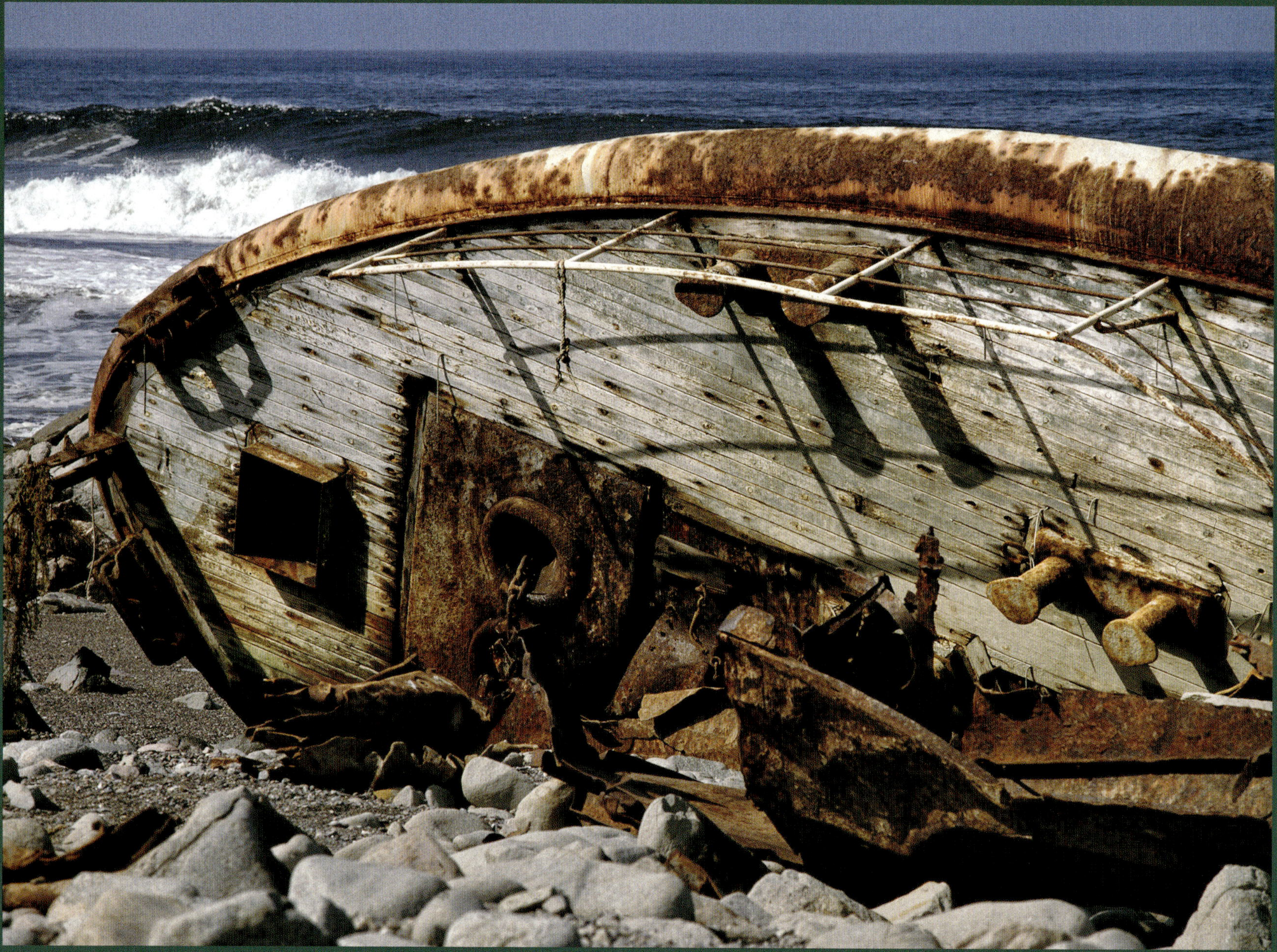

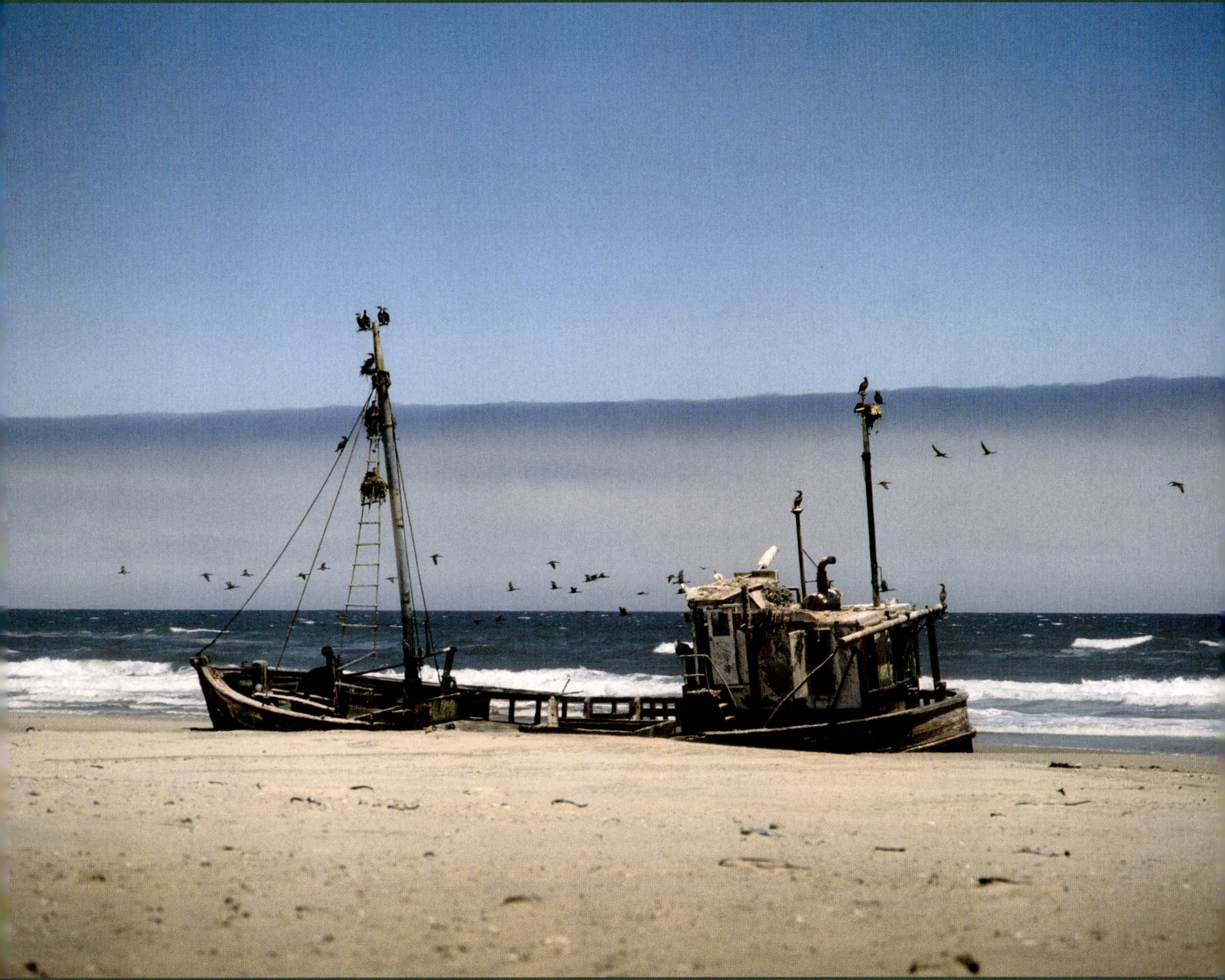

(OPPOSITE) Hull of the *Suiderkus* (ABOVE) Wreck of the *Montrose*

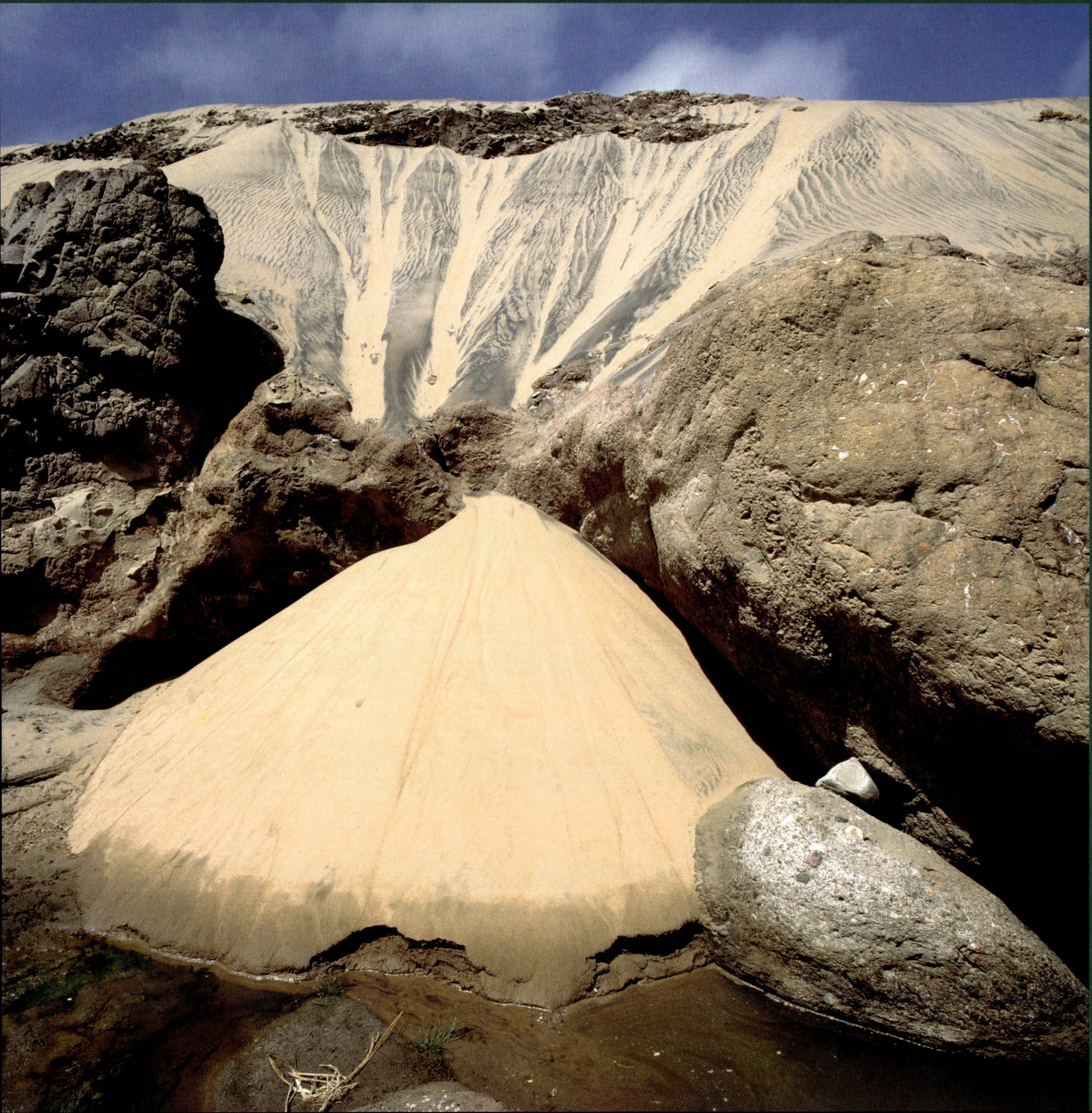

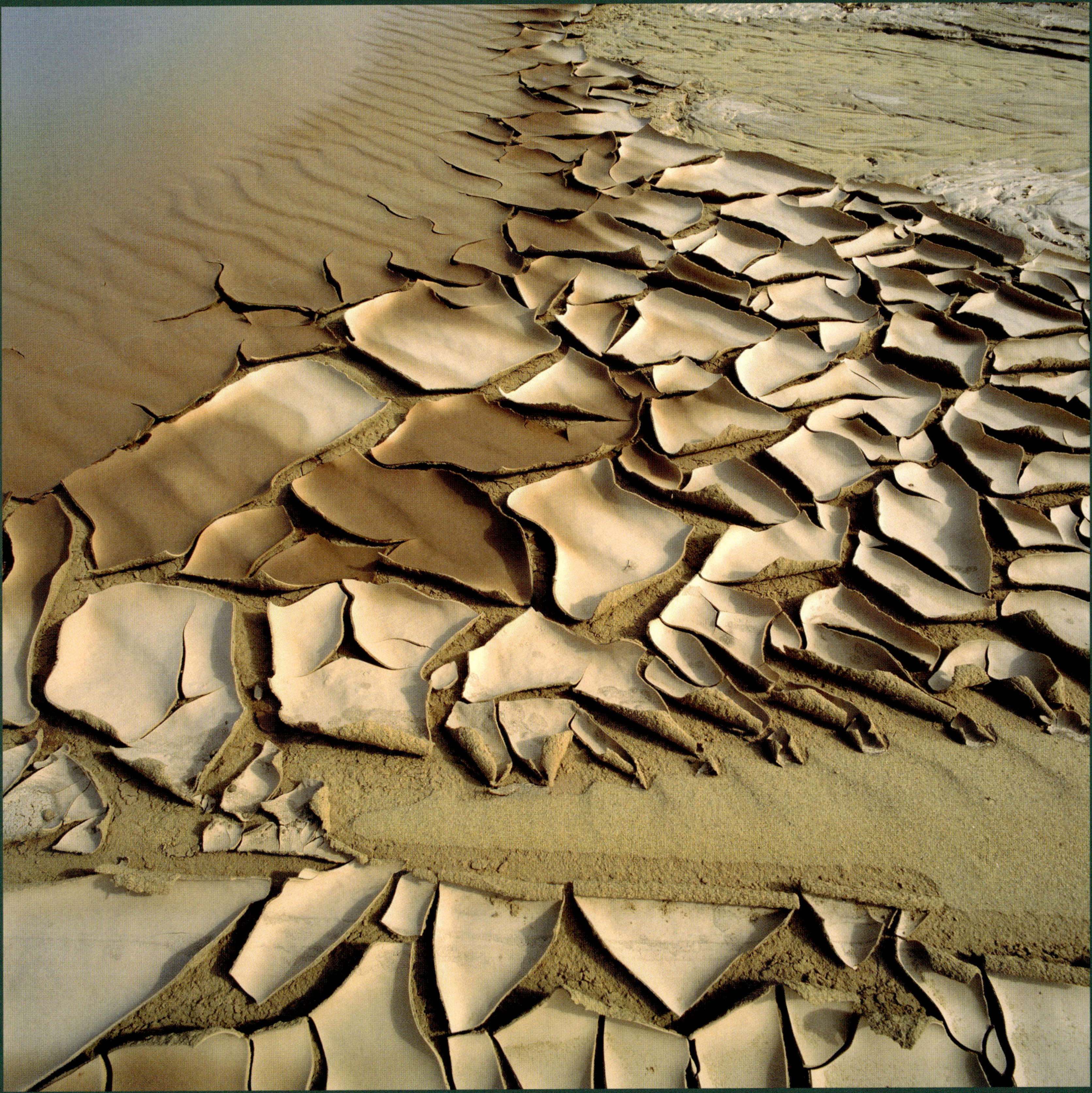

(OPPOSITE) Khumib Spring (ABOVE) Sechomib Silt

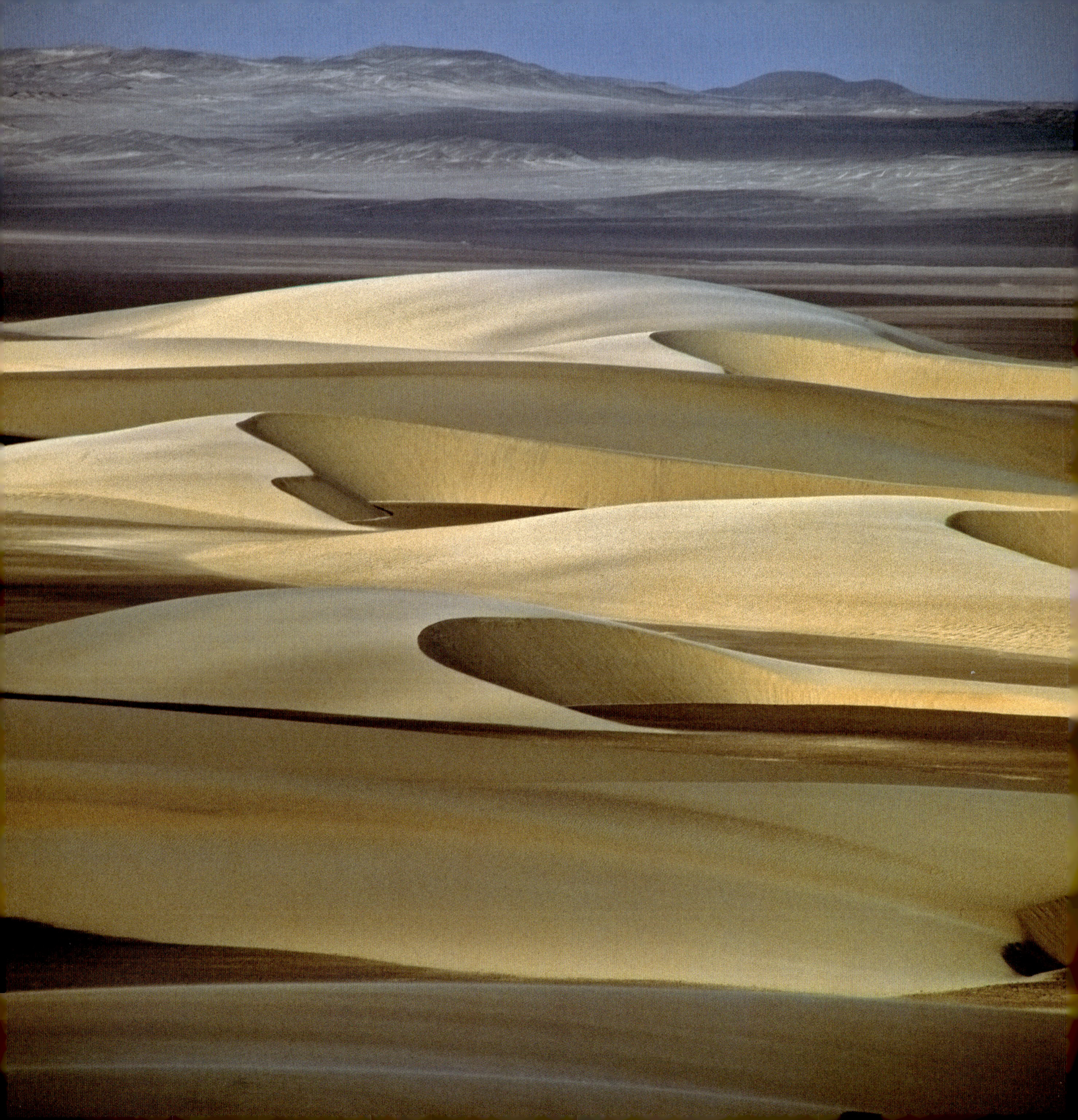

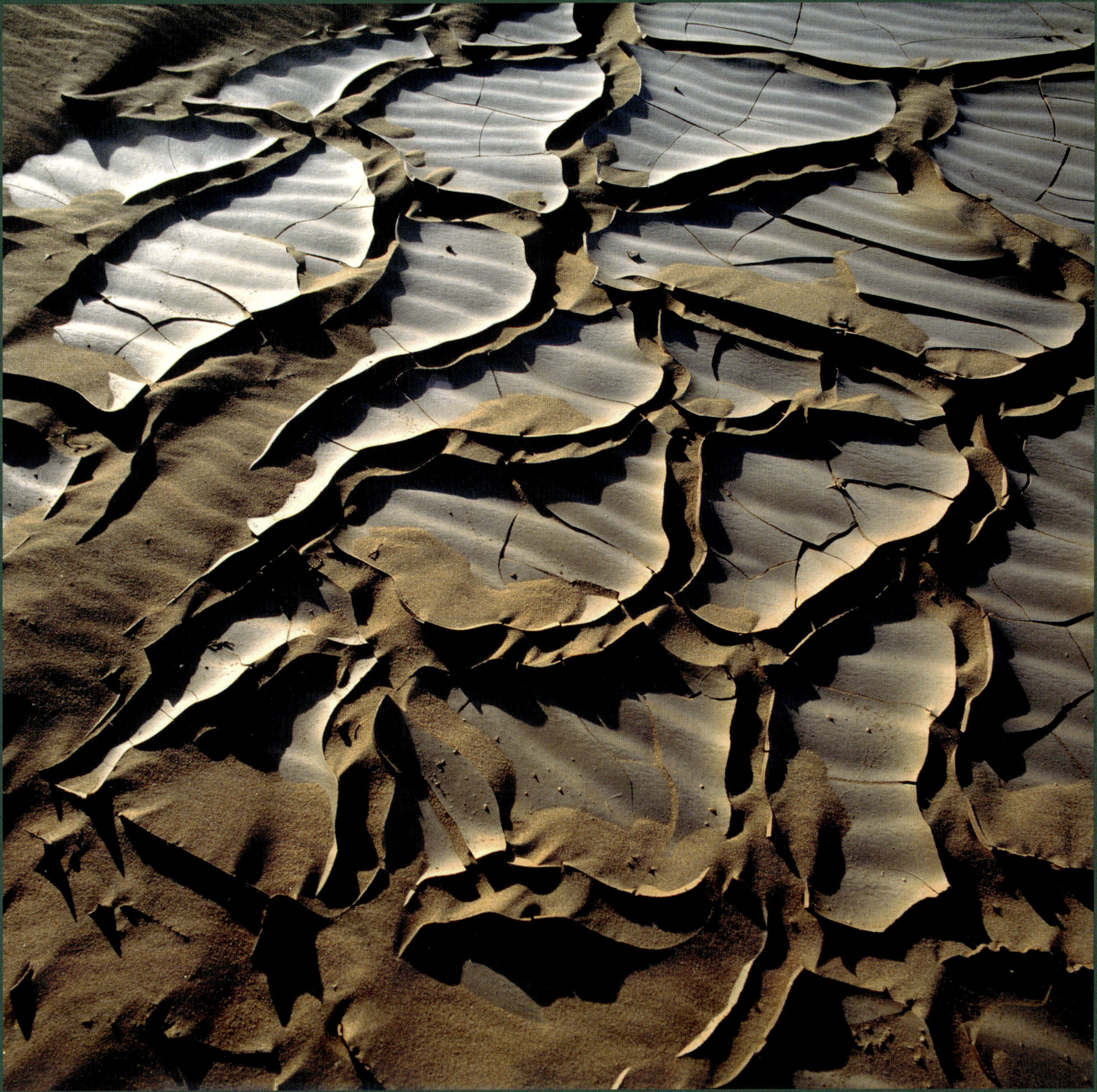

(OPPOSITE) Dune Strata, evening light (ABOVE) Nadas River Ripples

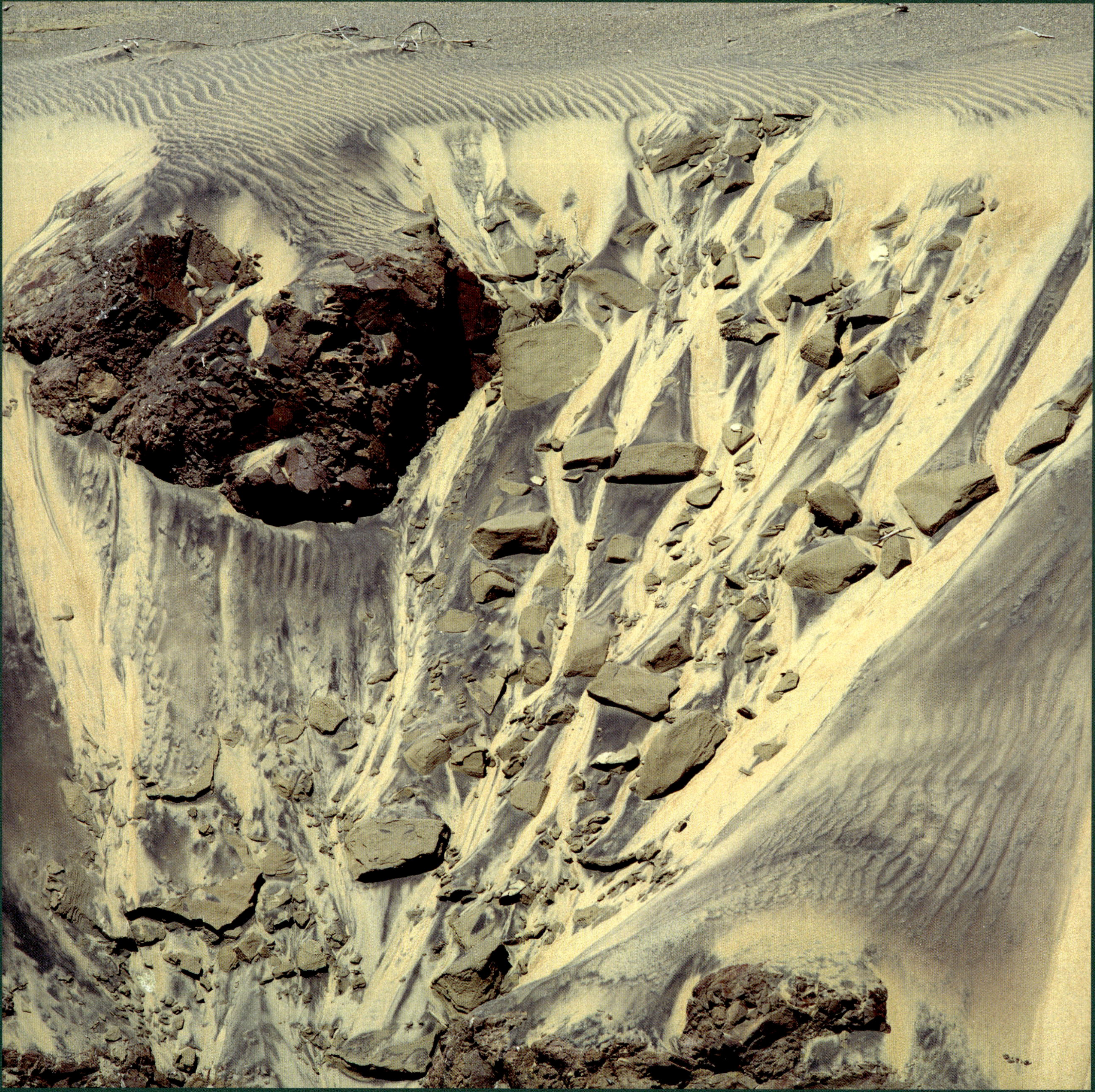

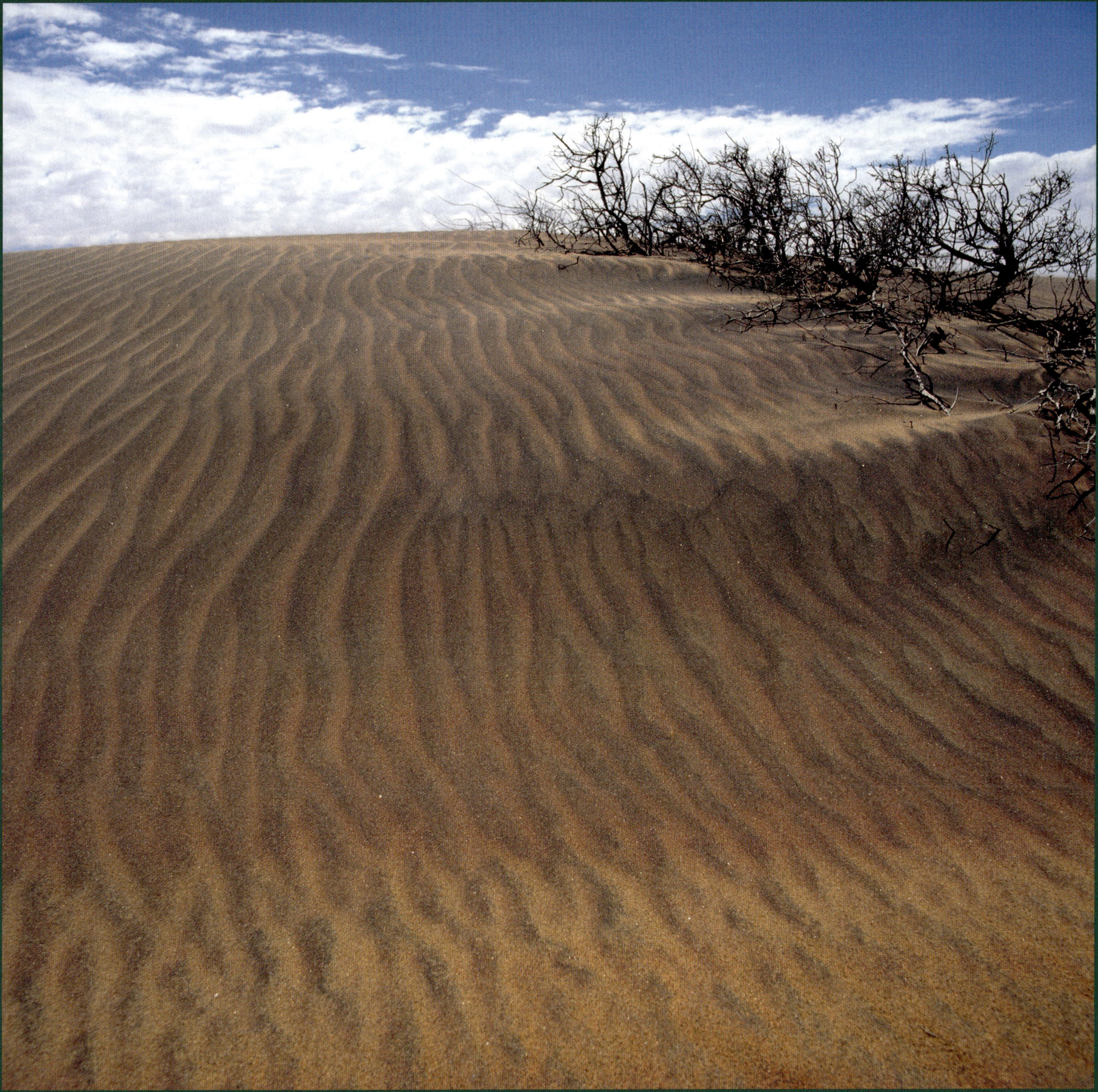

(OPPOSITE) Khumib Wall (ABOVE) Garnet Dune

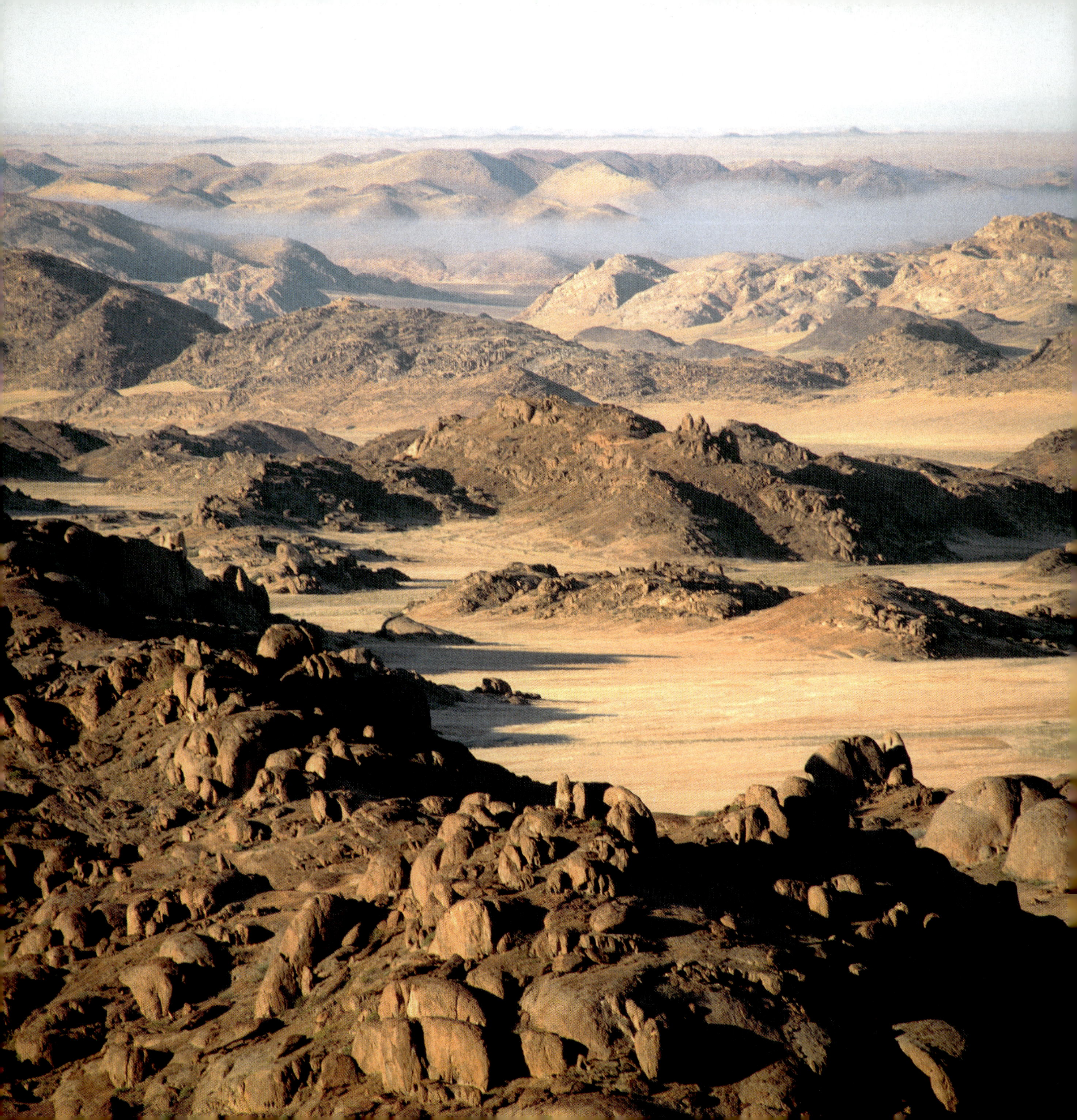

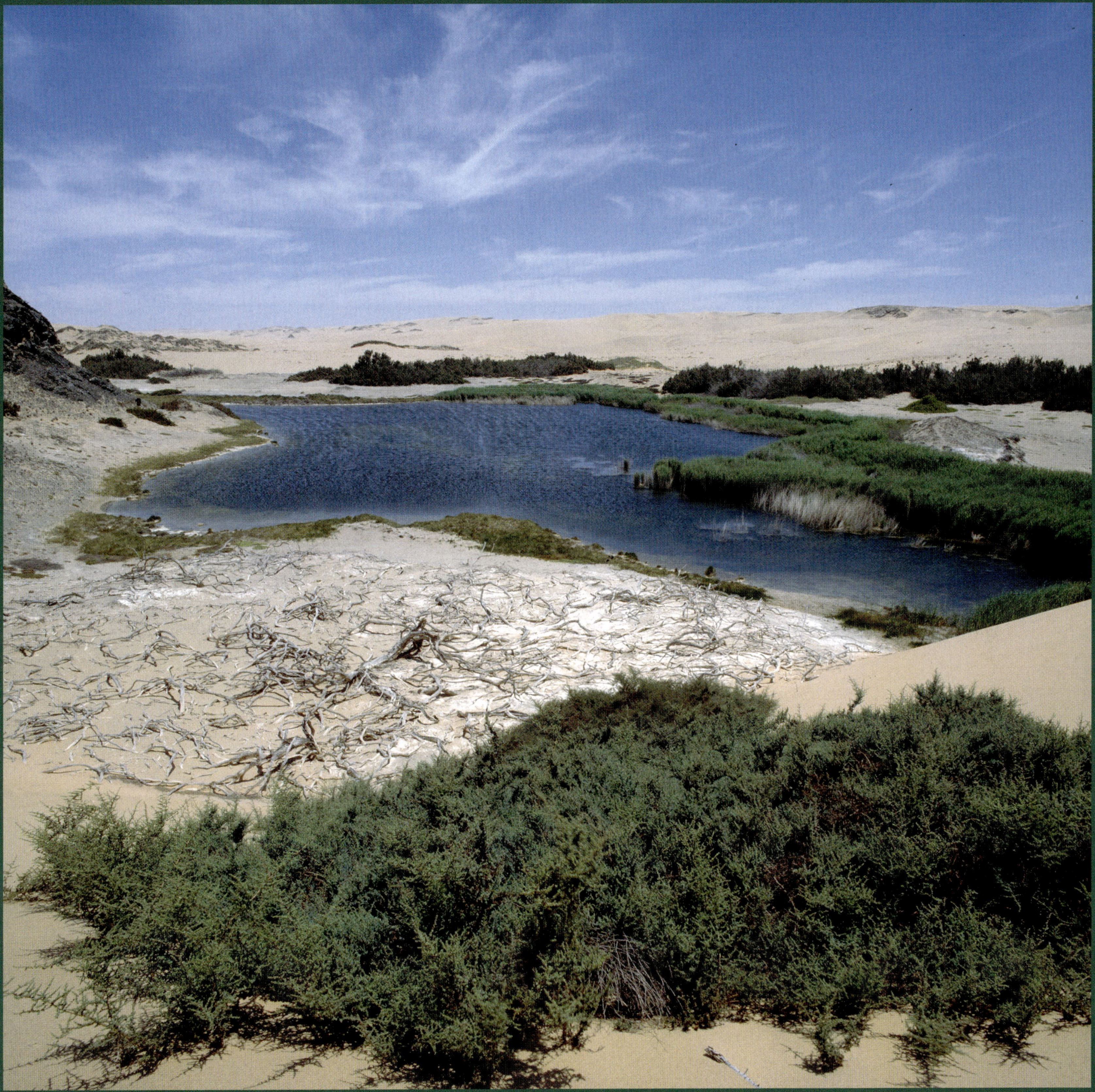

(OPPOSITE) Rocky Mountains (ABOVE) Auses Waterhole

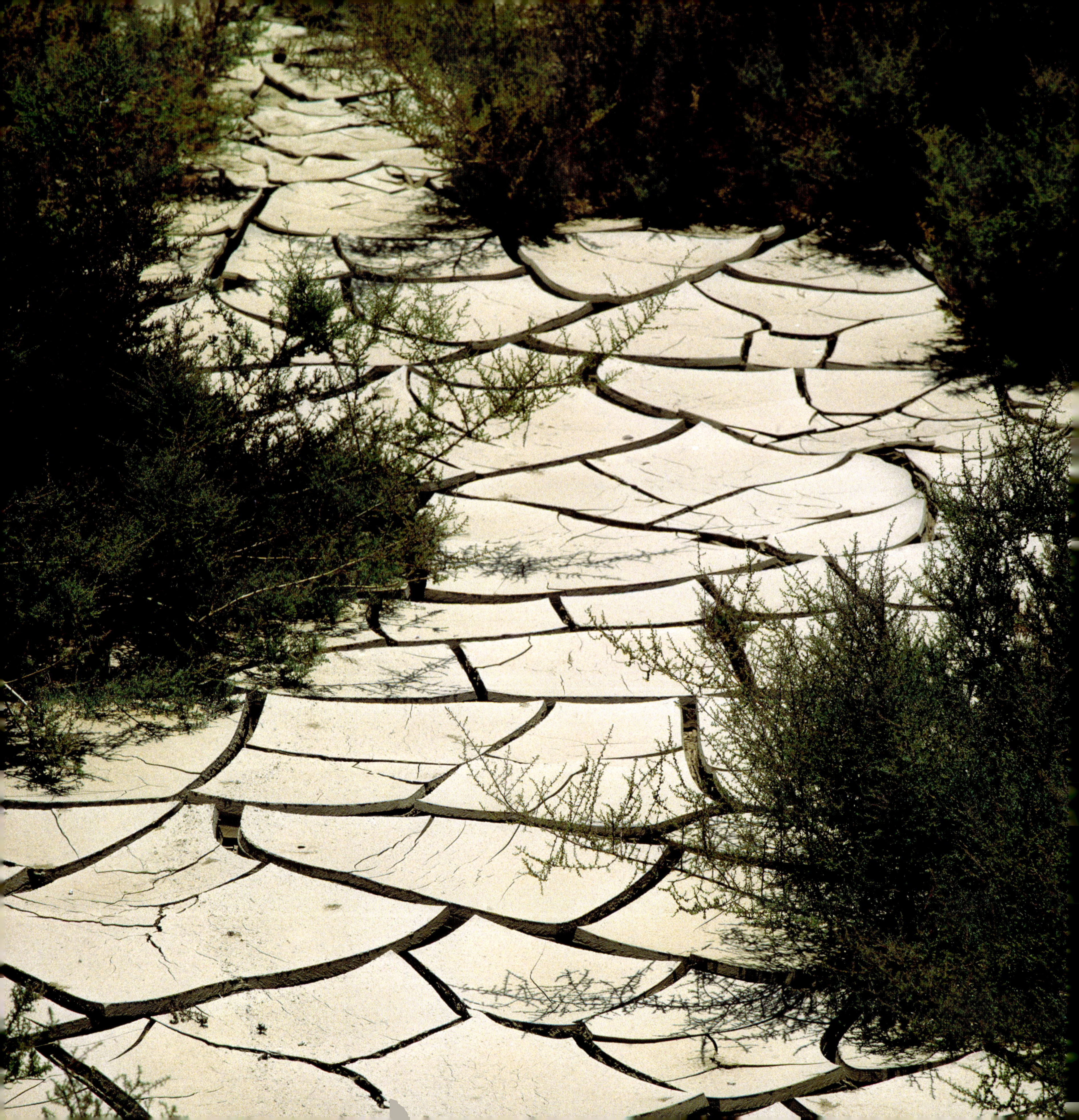

"The gods must have created my land with a purpose
to give colonial conquerors a fatal dose
if along the Skeleton Coast they dared to pose
for a portrait or grow a multi-coloured rose
here they died of thirst or bled through the nose
thus, just make an attempt and we'll ceaselessly oppose."

First stanza from the poem 'Desert Sandwich' by Mvula ya Nangolo, published in *Thoughts from Exile*, Windhoek: Longman Namibia, 1991: 9

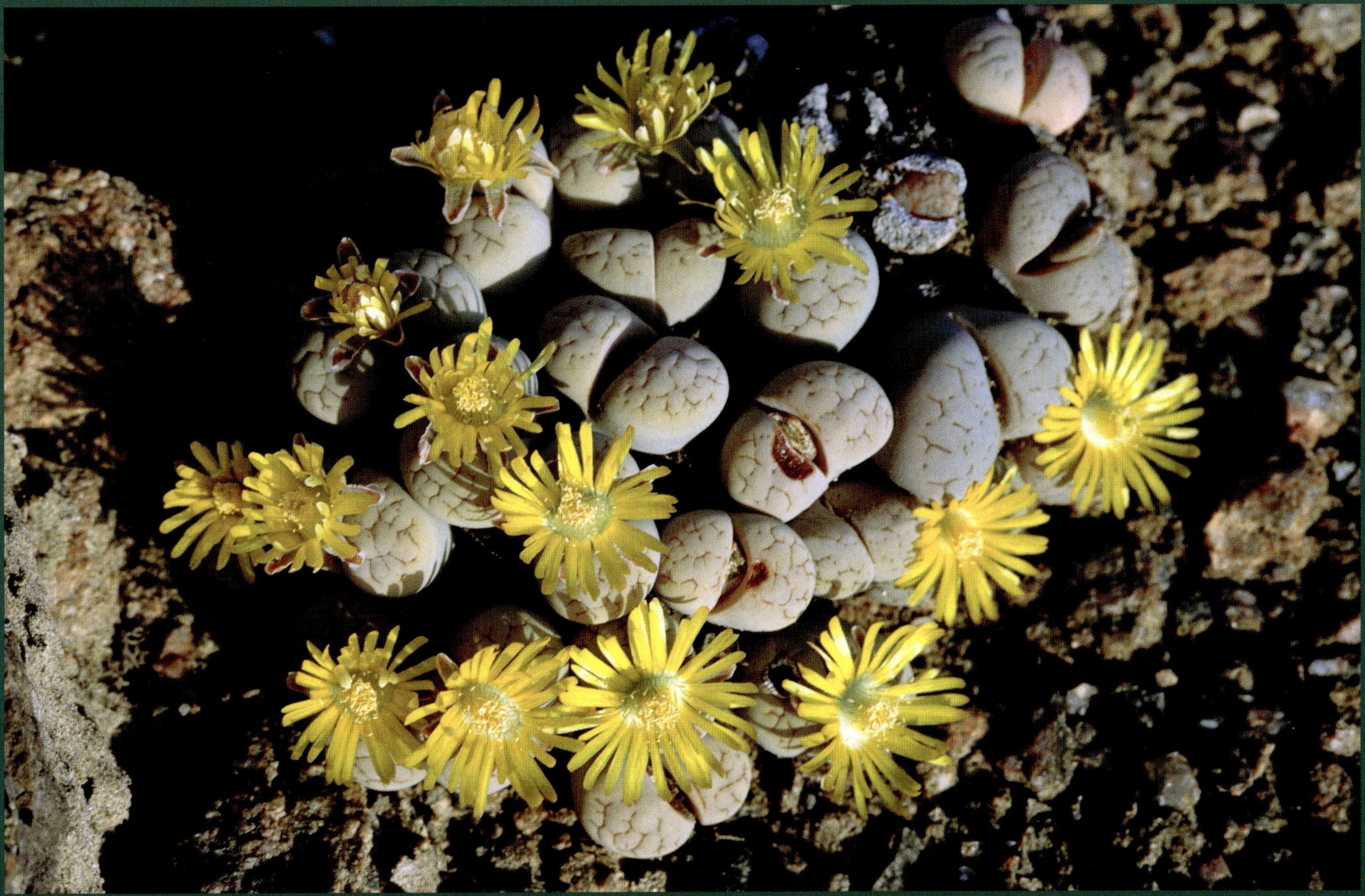

(OPPOSITE) Crazy Paving (ABOVE) Flowering Stones

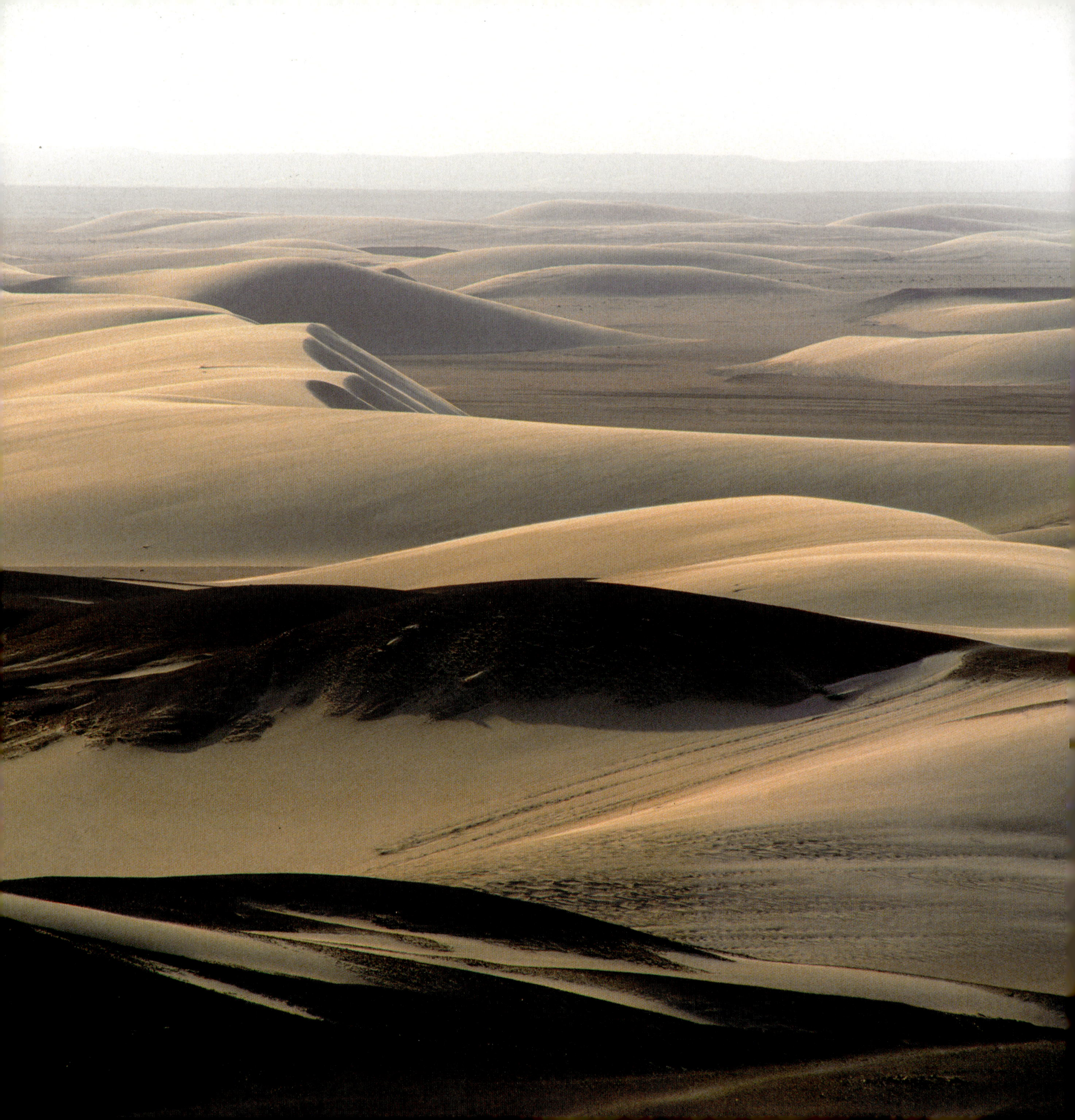

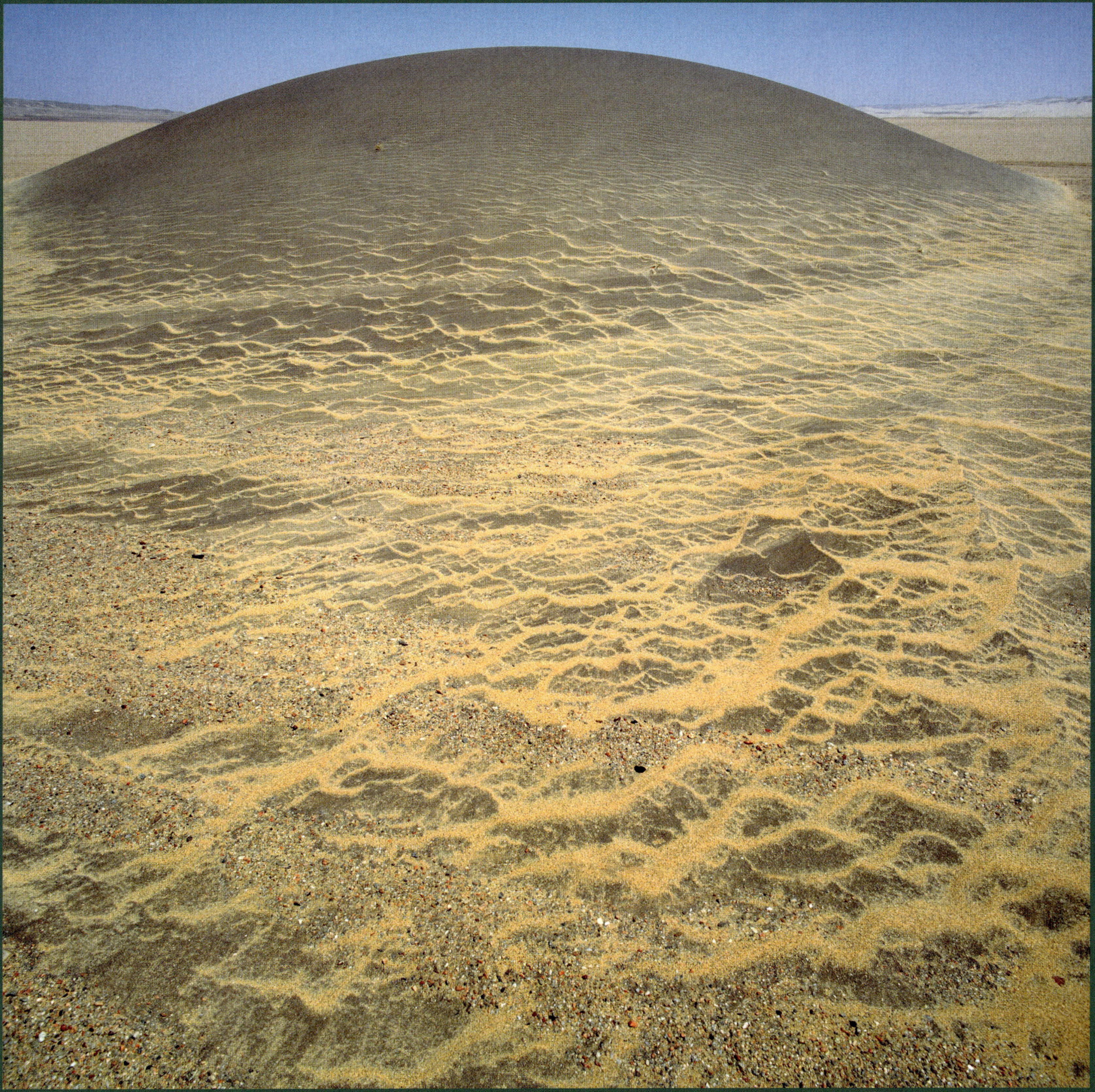

(OPPOSITE) Dune Panorama, north of Sarusas (ABOVE) Dune

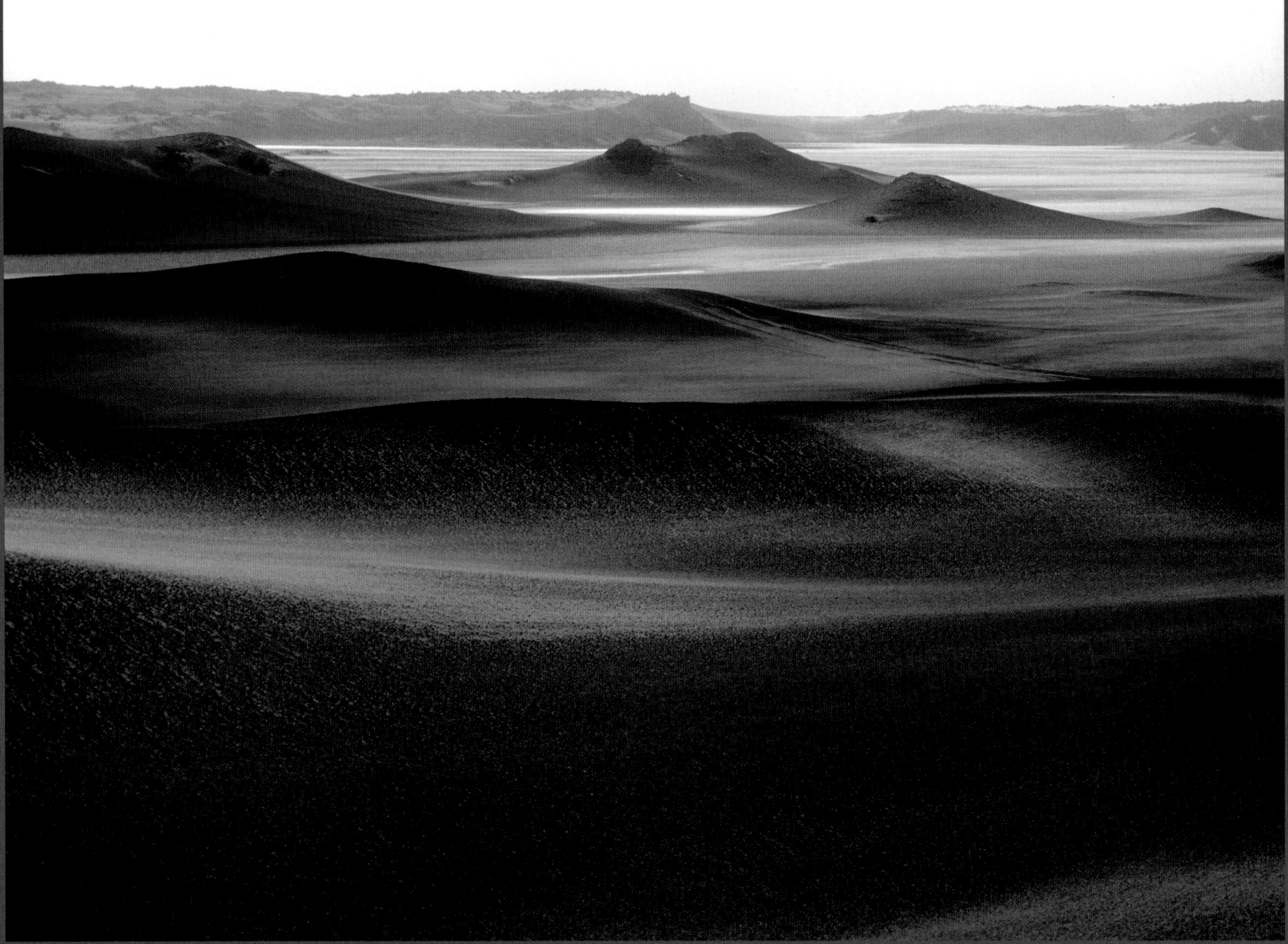

Mariners call it "Skeleton Coast" and dread it.
Treasure seekers know it as "The Coast of Diamonds and Death".

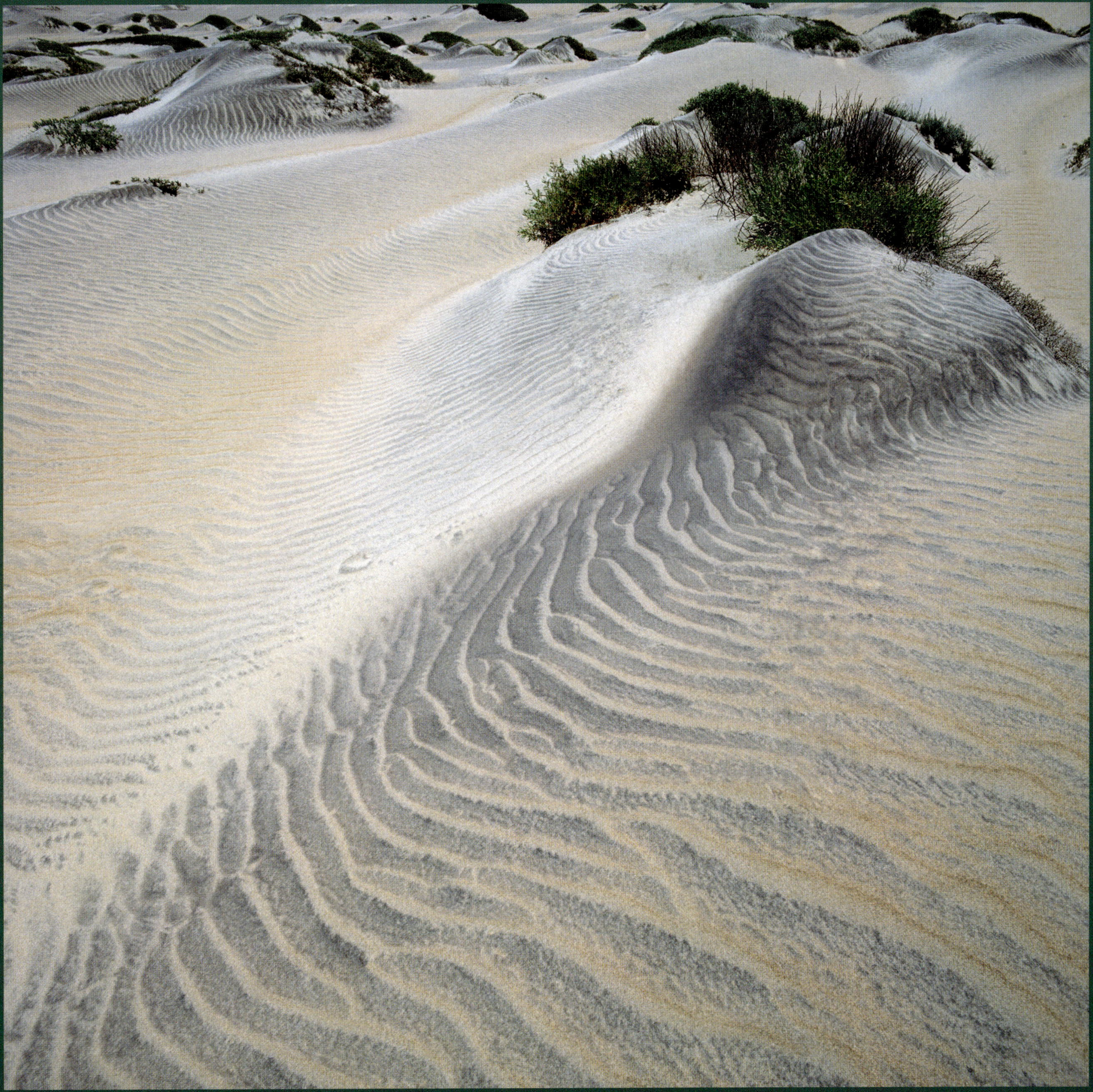

(OPPOSITE) Agate Mountain Salt Pan (ABOVE) Zebra Dune

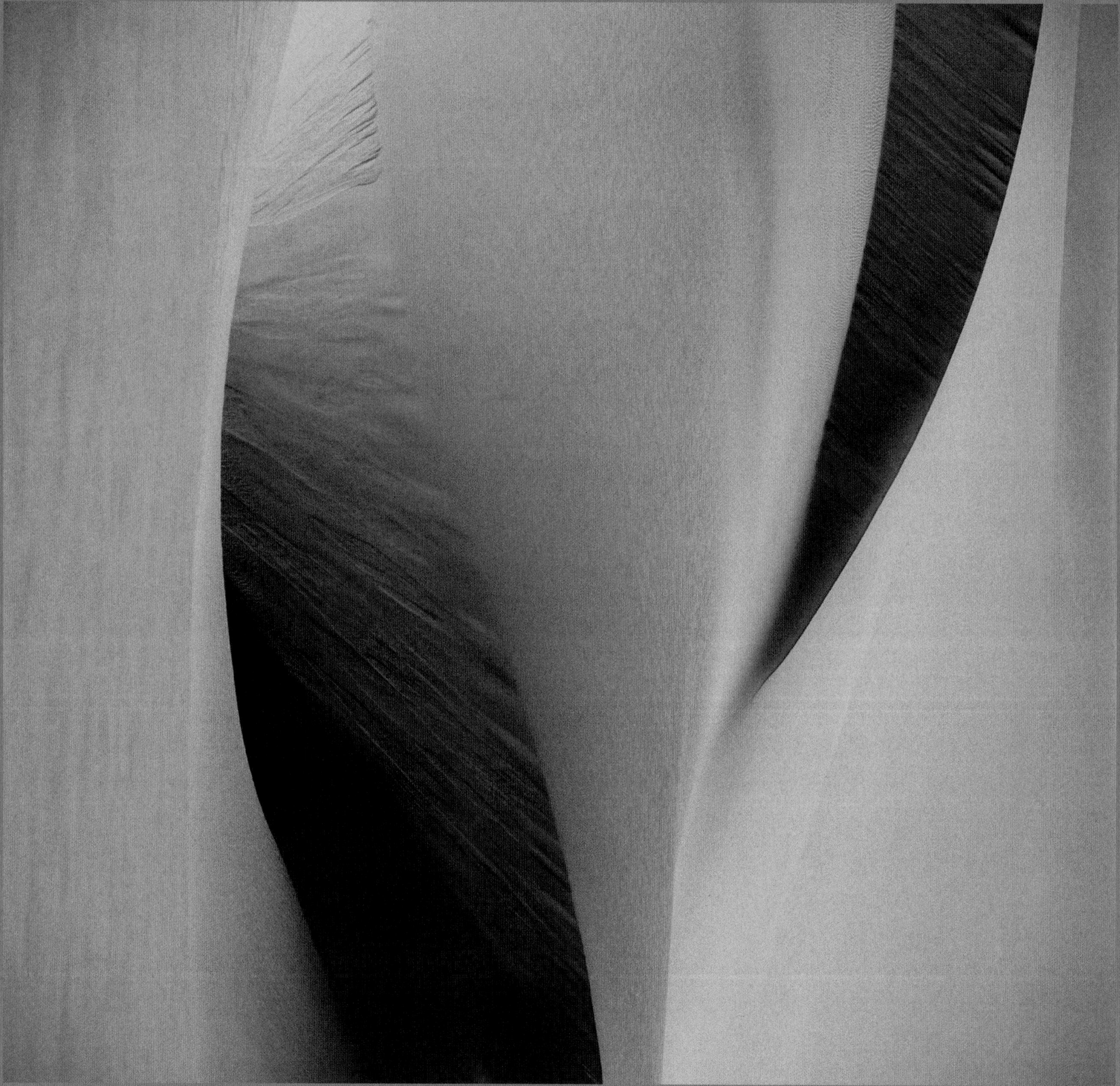

Pregnant Sand The warm hues and clean lines of desert sand reflect the simplicity and down-to-earth lifestyle of the Nama people, the only true descendants of the Khoekhoe in Namibia.

Portfolio 3
ELEVEN

The *Eleven FotoFashionFusion* project was a collaboration between myself and Namibian fashion designer Melanie Harteveld Becker as a follow-up to our previous undertaking, *The Five Seasons*, also an integration of photographic images with fashion design. Both these projects were launched with a fashion show and exhibition in the National Art Gallery of Namibia in Windhoek.

Our challenge was to devise a theme that was equally colourful and open to interpretation as *The Five Seasons*, but had subject matter to which Namibians could relate more readily. We came up with a winning formula. While the theme of our first project was universal, the theme of *Eleven* would go to the very roots of the country. It would highlight those elements – the natural environment and the people – that define the Namibia of today. Hence *Eleven*'s close-up textural images of the land portray the environmental roots of the country's eleven population groups through the elements of sand, rock, water, cloud and sky.

The title image of the *Eleven* portfolio, *Vertical Reflection*, was chosen to reflect the colours of Namibia's savannahs, veld flowers, indigenous fruits and veld fires, the textures and movement of the dunes, the vibrancy of the growing season, the diversity and complex structure of the country's geomorphological components, and the composite nature of the Namibian people.

A further objective of the *Eleven* project was to give credence to the premise that not only is fashion art, but that it is a living, vibrant, expressive and valid form of art that fulfils one of art's most important functions, namely to uplift and transport the viewer.

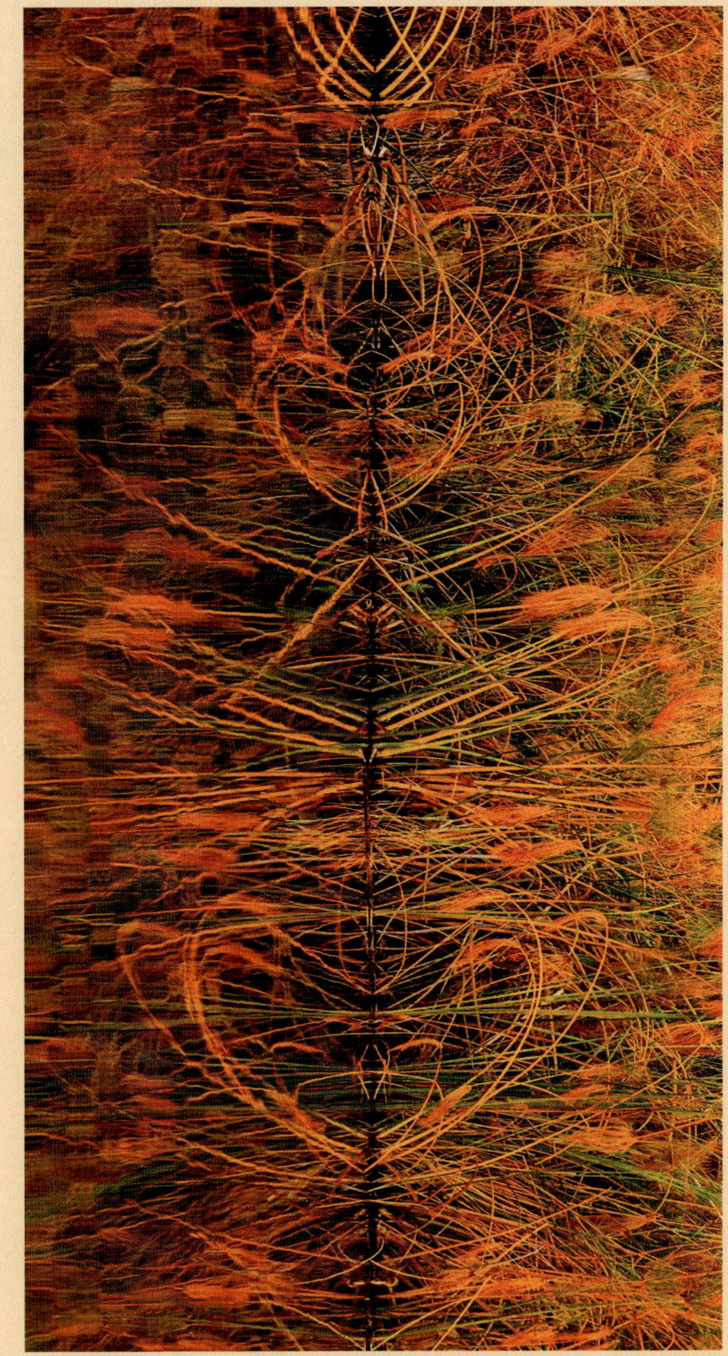

Vertical Reflection Portrays the seasons, the line down the middle fusing rather than dividing image and mirror image, the graphic lines and patterns symbolising a synthesis of photography, fashion, music, dance and song.

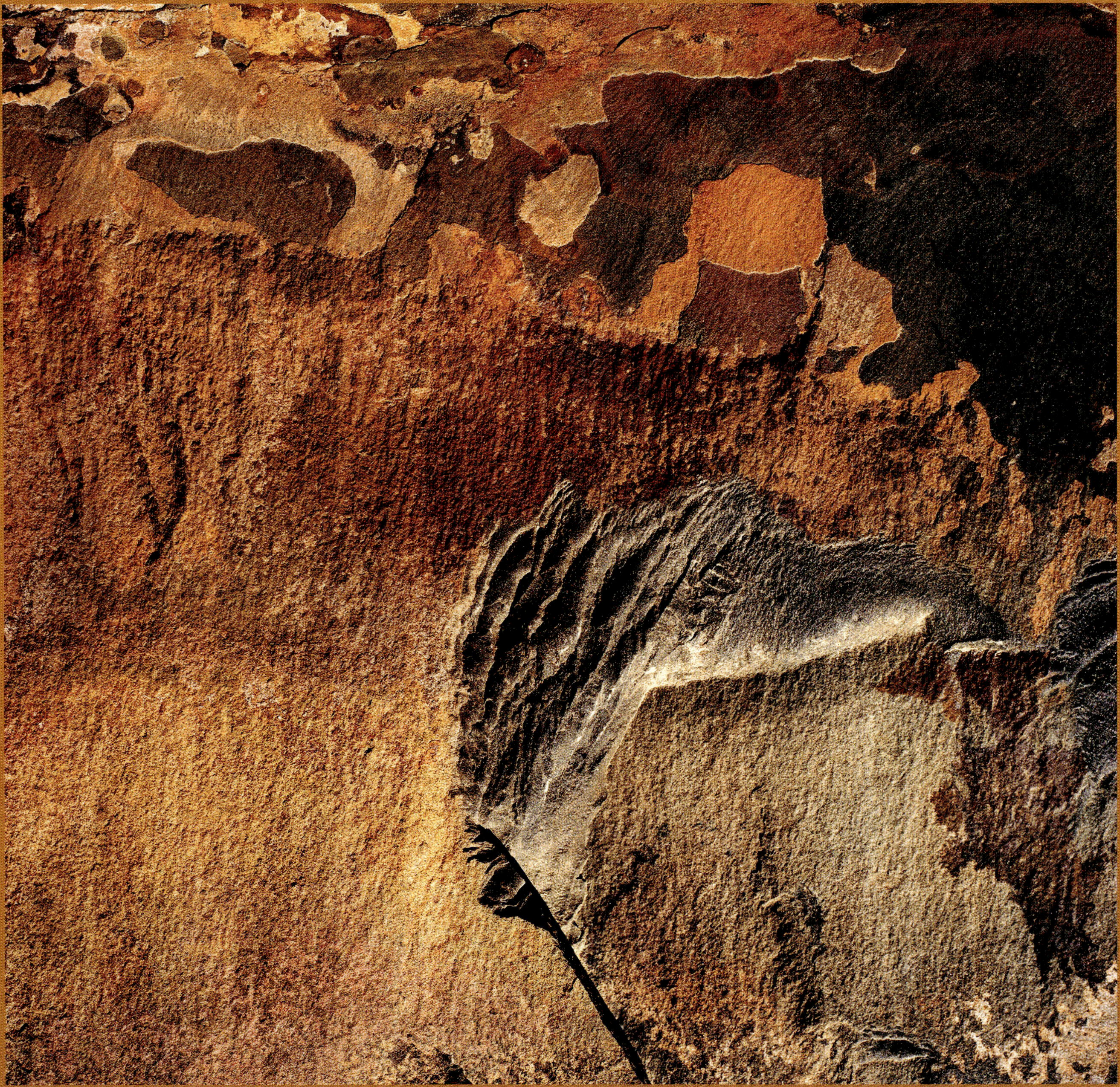

Rock Diva The rock surface mirrors the rugged landscape of Damaraland, home of the Damara people, the vibrant colours suggesting the volcanic forces that shaped the land many aeons ago.

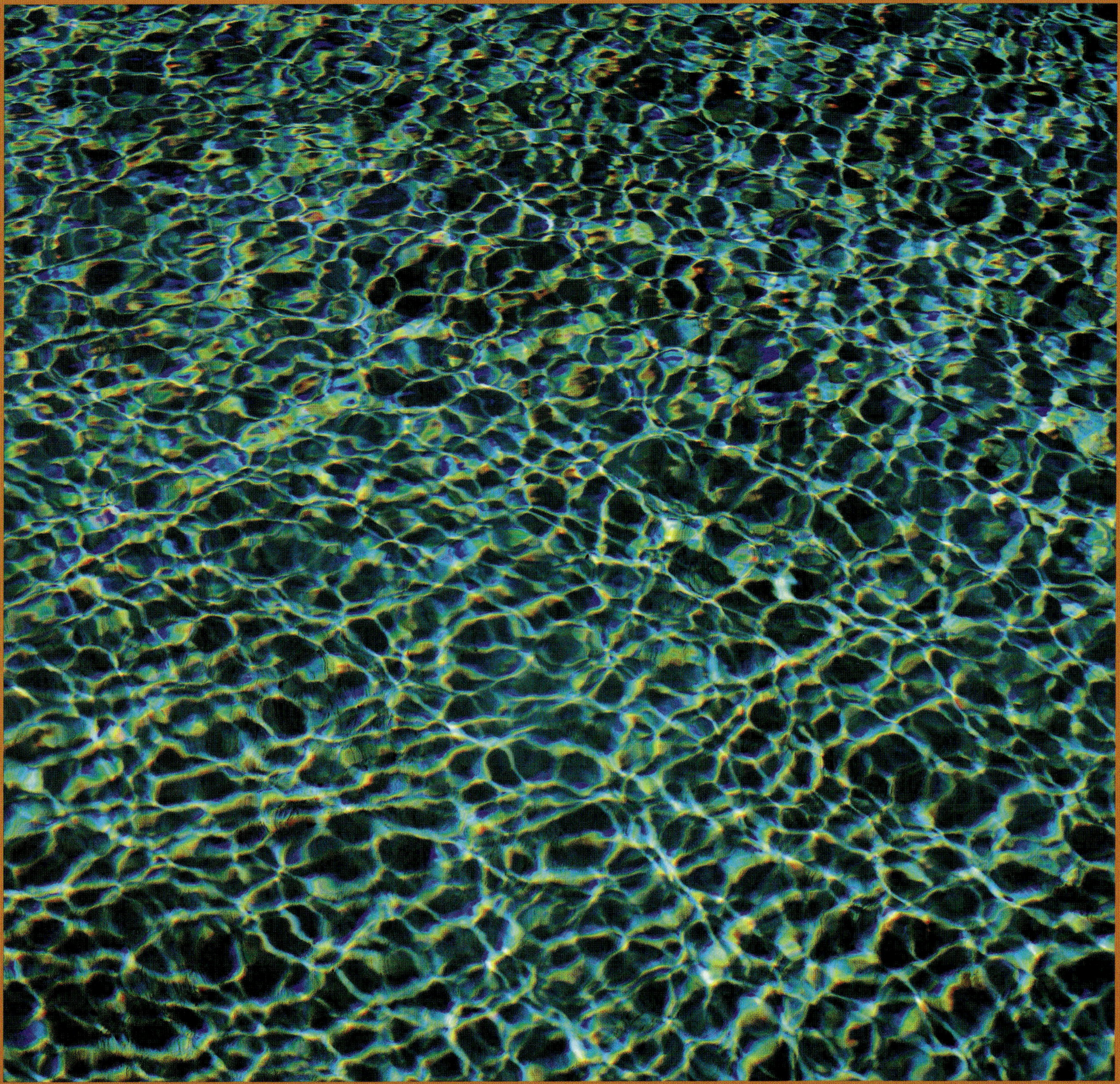

Marble Mosaic The image reflects the bubbling water of the hot-water springs at Rehoboth, where some ninety Baster families, moving from the Cape through southern Namibia, settled in 1870.

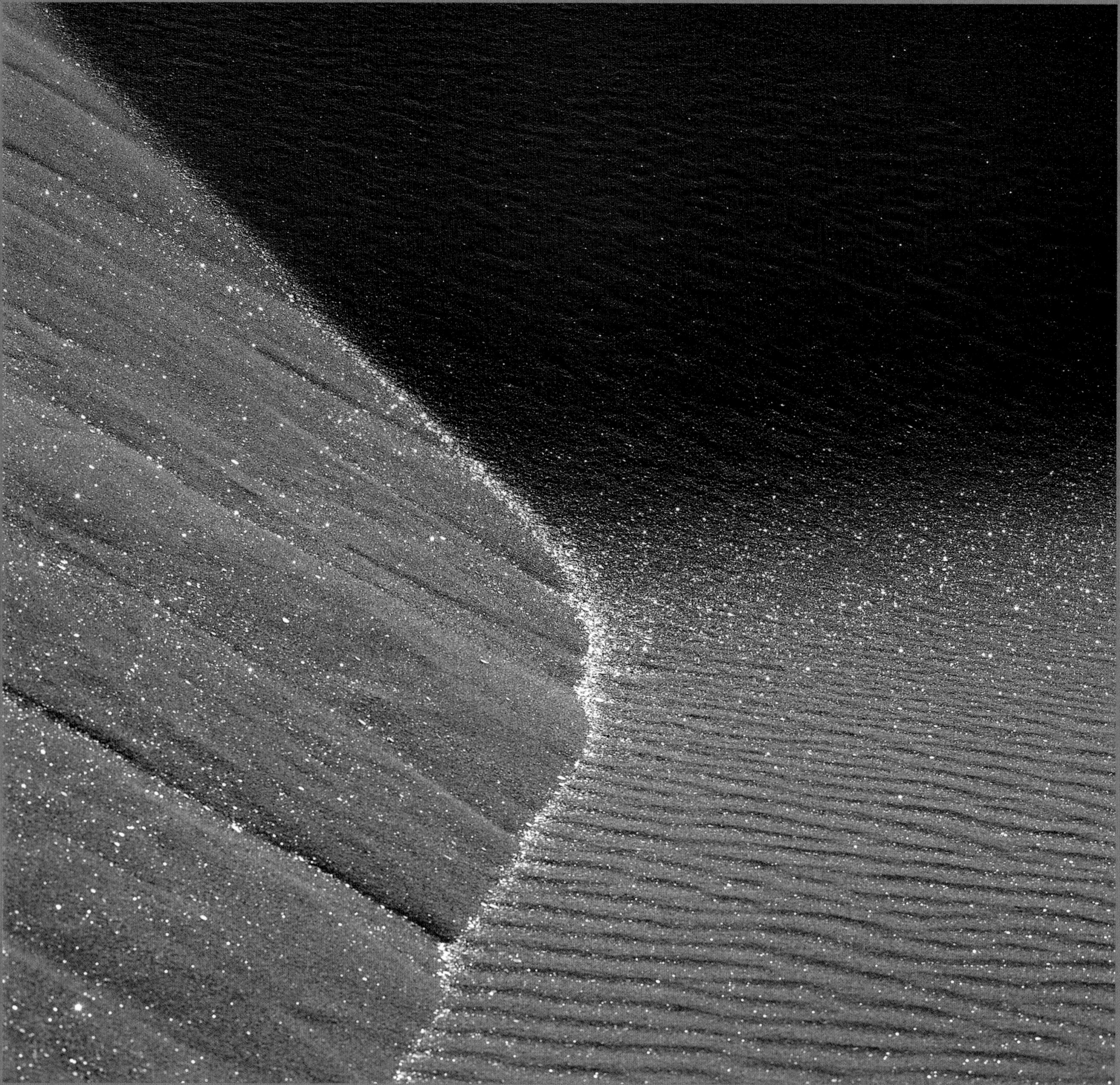

Sperrgebiet Sparkle Early pioneers of European descent started settling in Namibia in the 1800s. The mica flakes in the image symbolise the diamonds they found and mined in the shifting sands of the Namib.

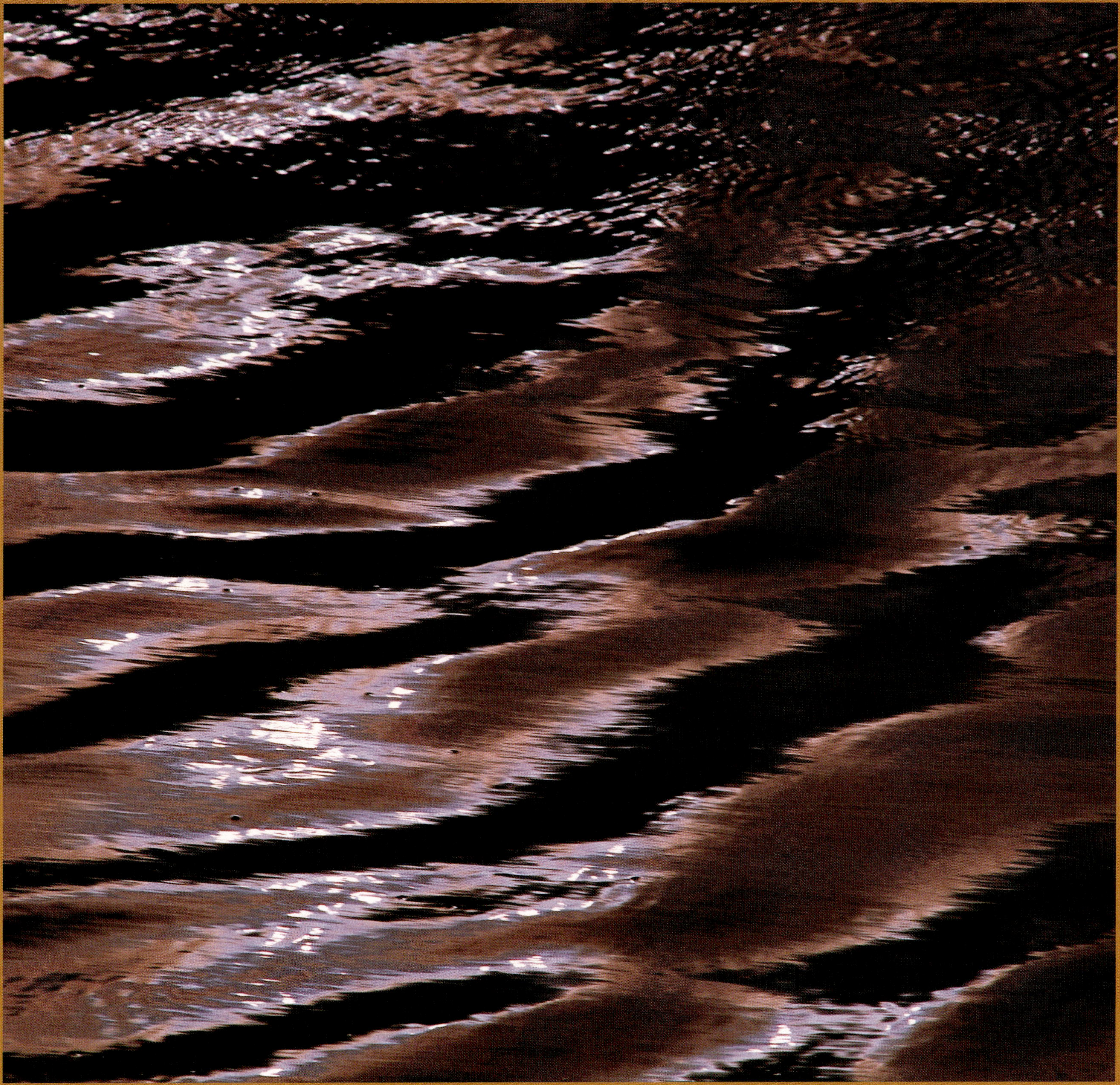

Liquid Sky Most Caprivians make their living on the banks of the Zambezi, Kwando, Linyanti and Chobe rivers. The image reflects the hues and patterns of the dark backwaters of the Caprivi Region.

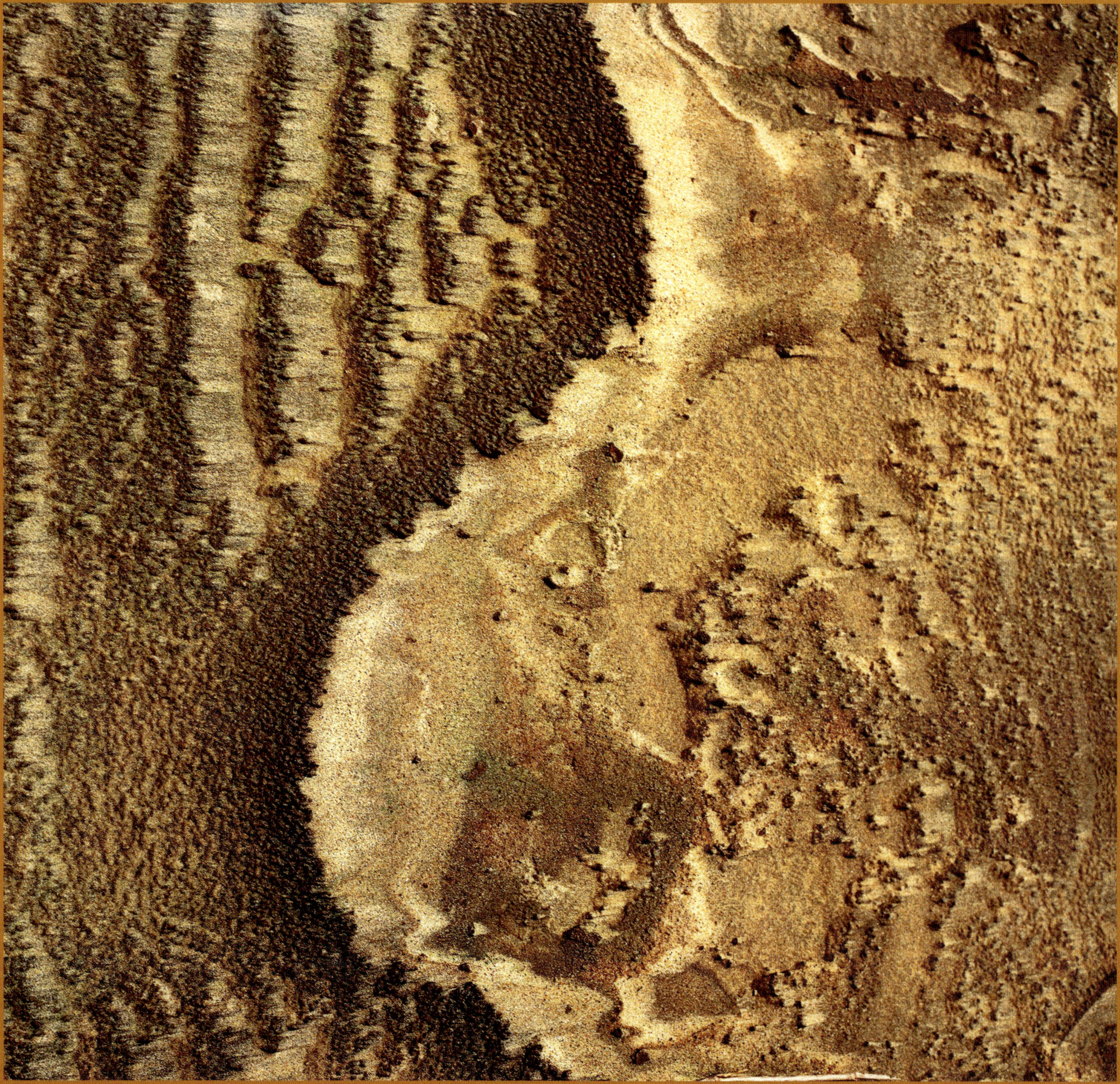

Lace Agate The snake-like shape simulates the gradual southern migration of the Herero from a legendary African marshland of water and reeds known as Roruu, to settle in Namibia in about 1550.

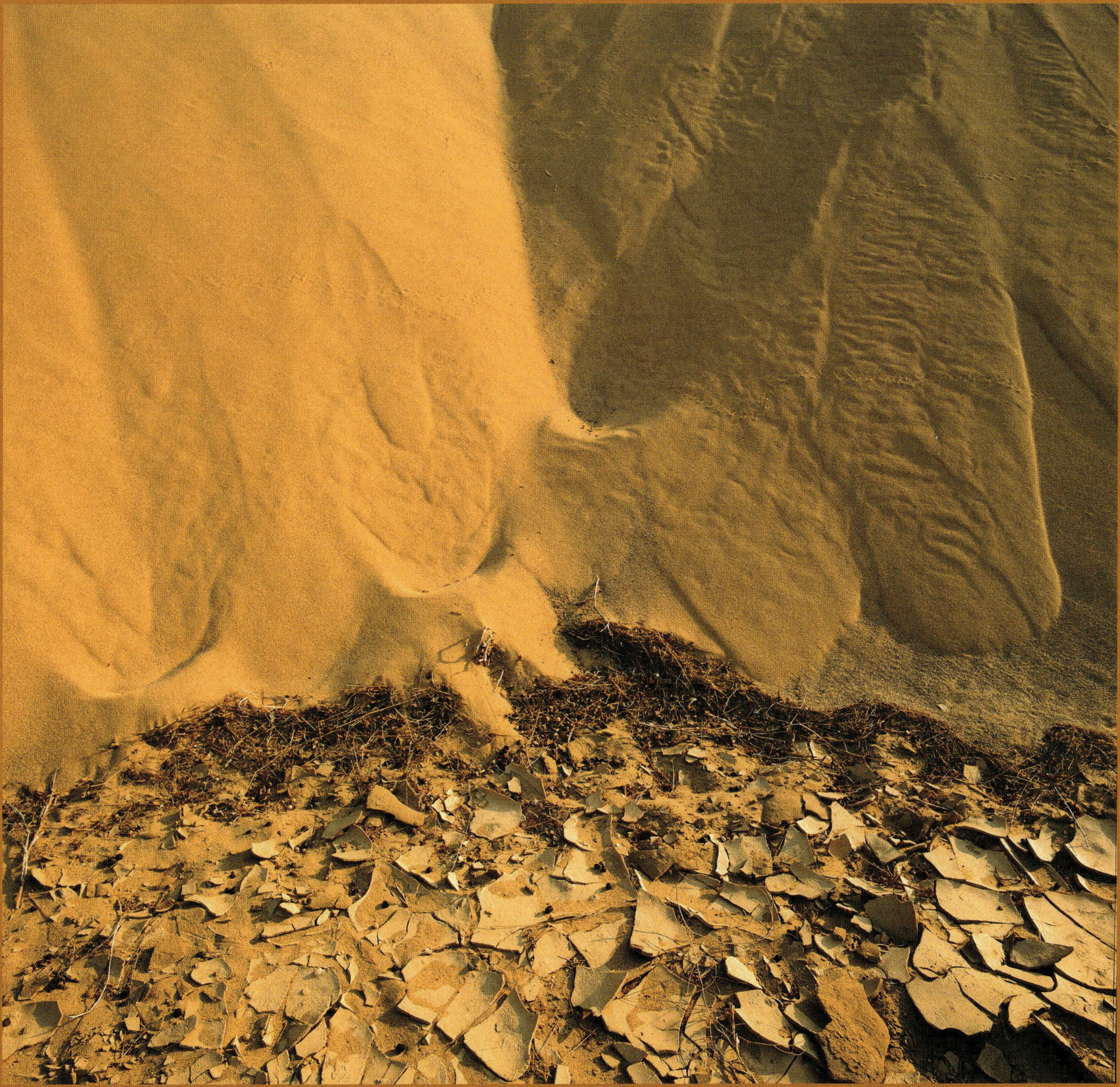

Textured Trinity The three components of Namibia's Tswana, who embarked on a Thirstland trek through Botswana to settle in Namibia, are reflected in the three dimensions of this image.

Desert Disk Descended from the Khoisan, the San are the earliest known inhabitants of Namibia. There is a high degree of mysticism in their culture, expressed here symbolically as a sun or moon.

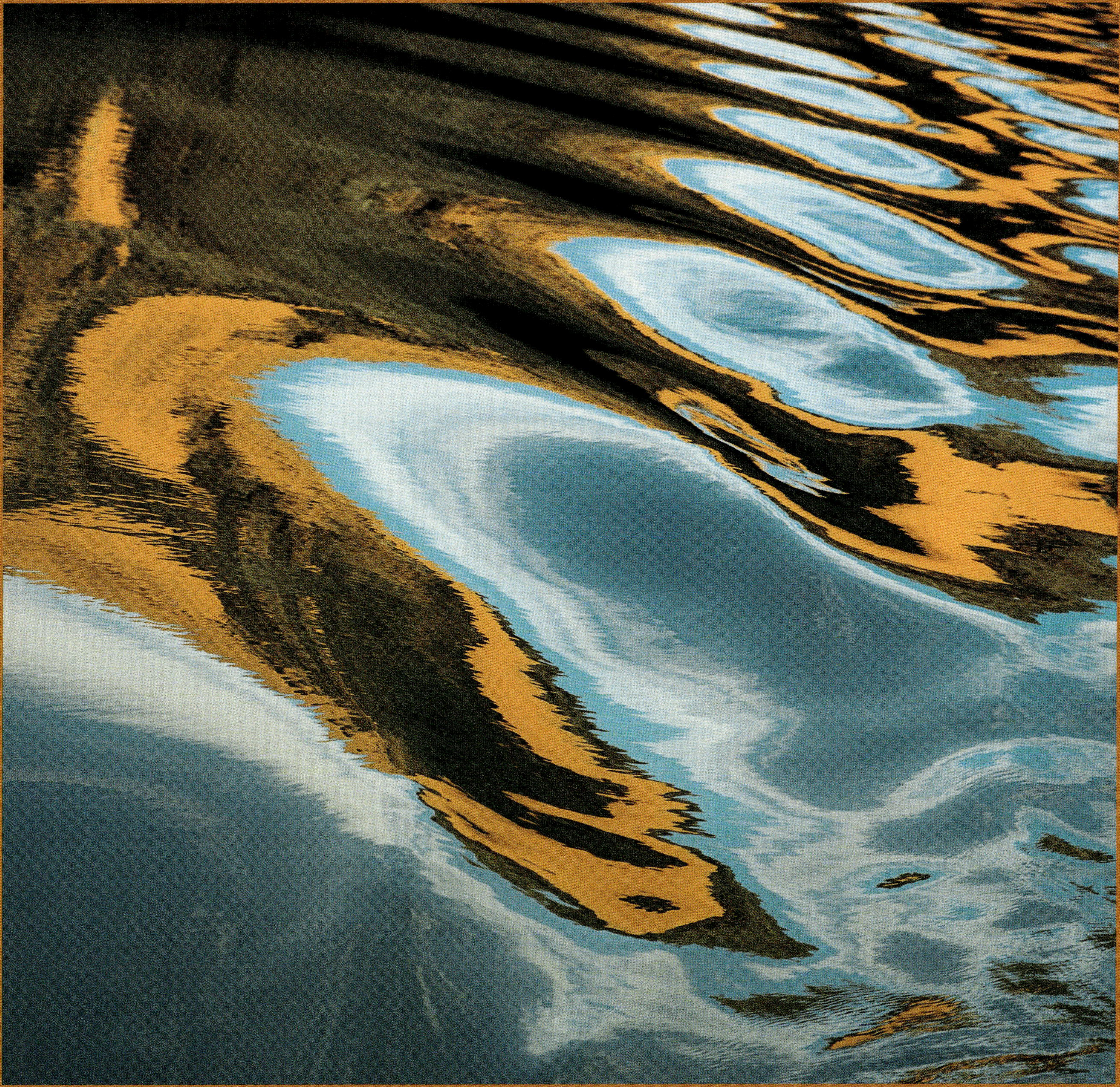

Oshana Silk During the rainy season life on the vast plains of the four Owambo regions in northern Namibia depends on the efundja, the floods that feed the flat, shallow depressions called oshanas.

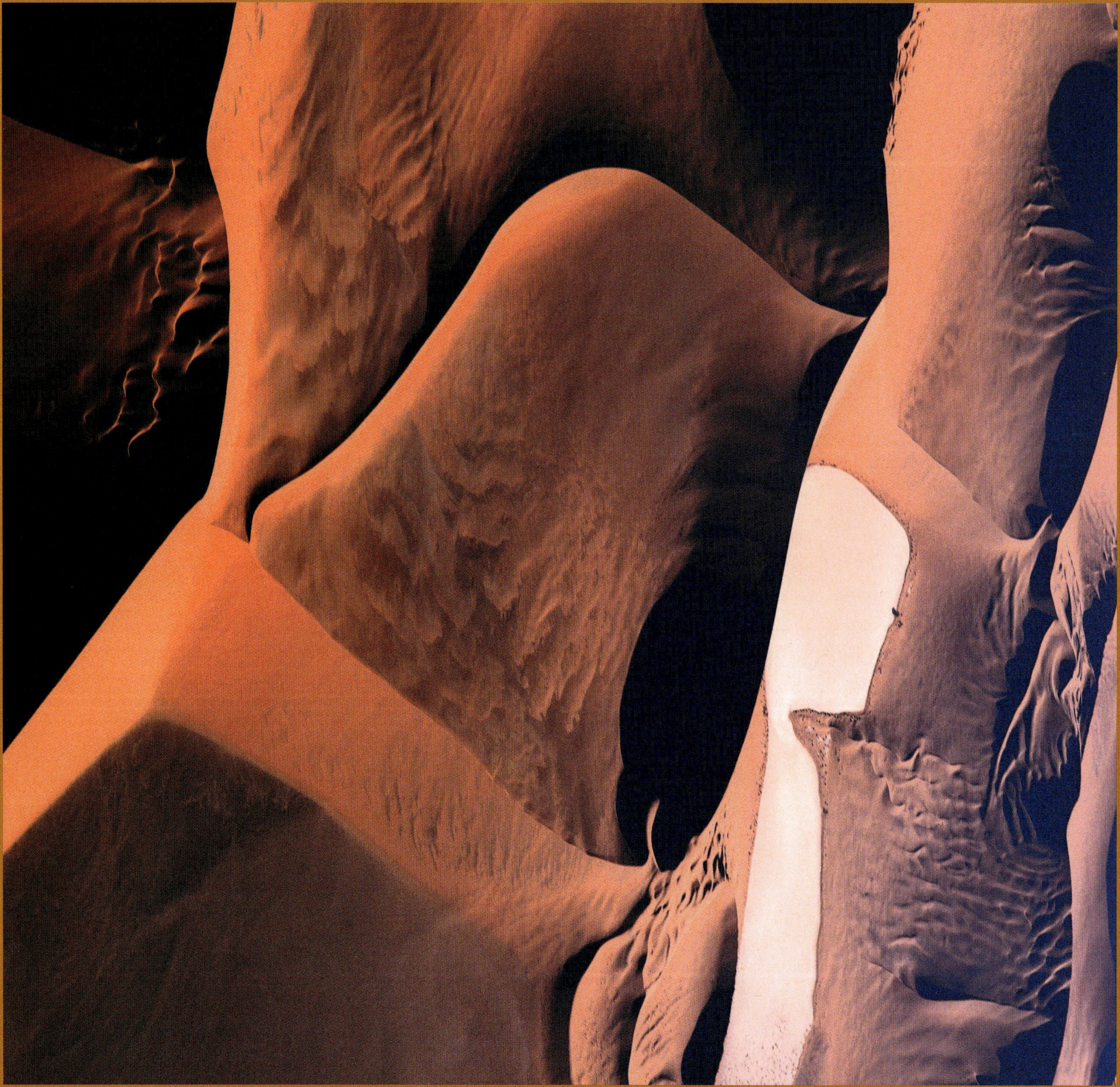

Shades of Velvet The curves and contours in this aerial view of Sossusvlei suggest the playfulness and dance associated with Namibia's Coloureds, descendants of South Africa's Cape Coloureds.

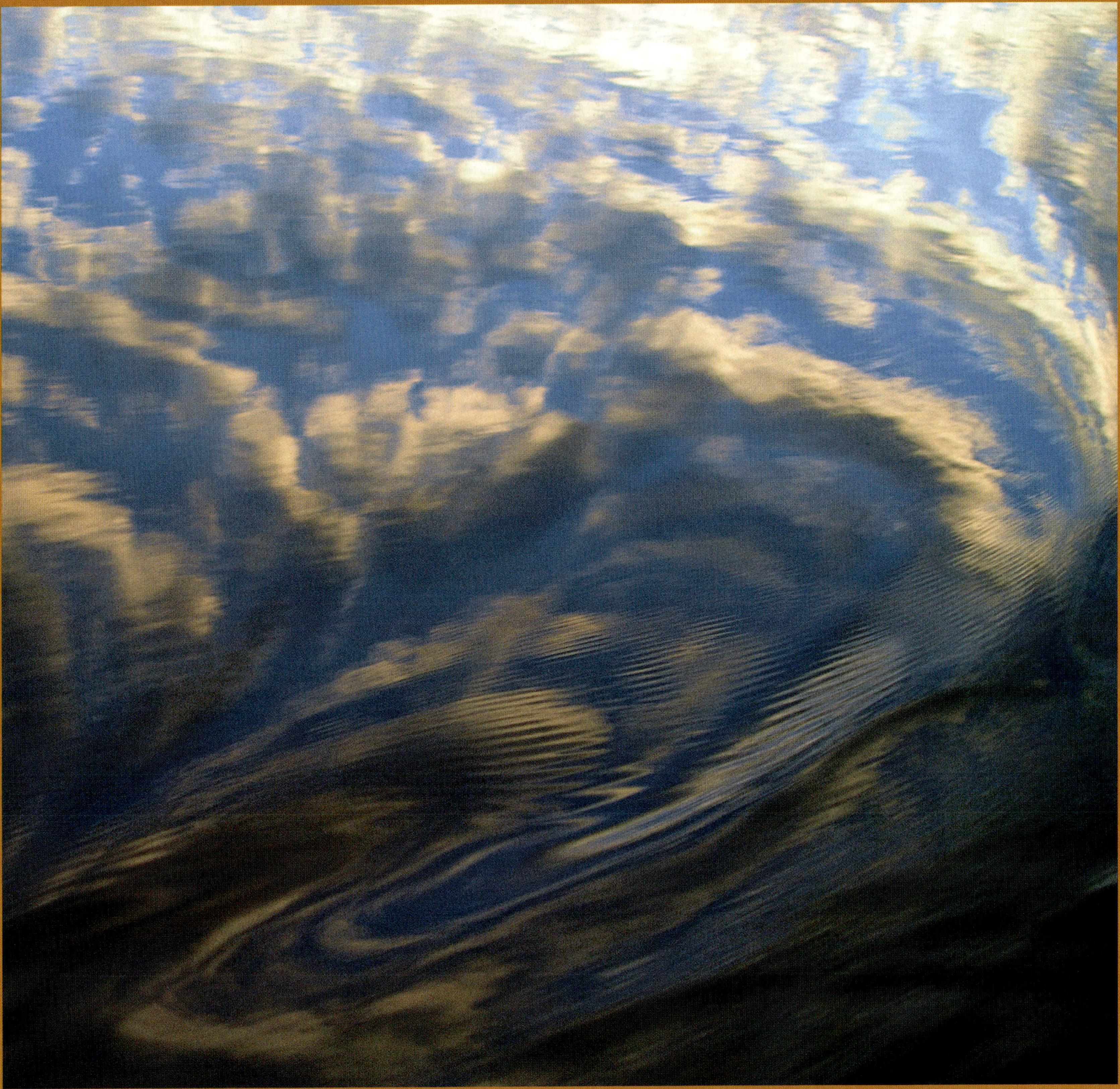

Water Taffeta Reflected clouds suggest the rural lifestyle of the Kavangos, who make a living on the banks of the Okavango River, the border between Namibia and Angola for some 400 kilometres.

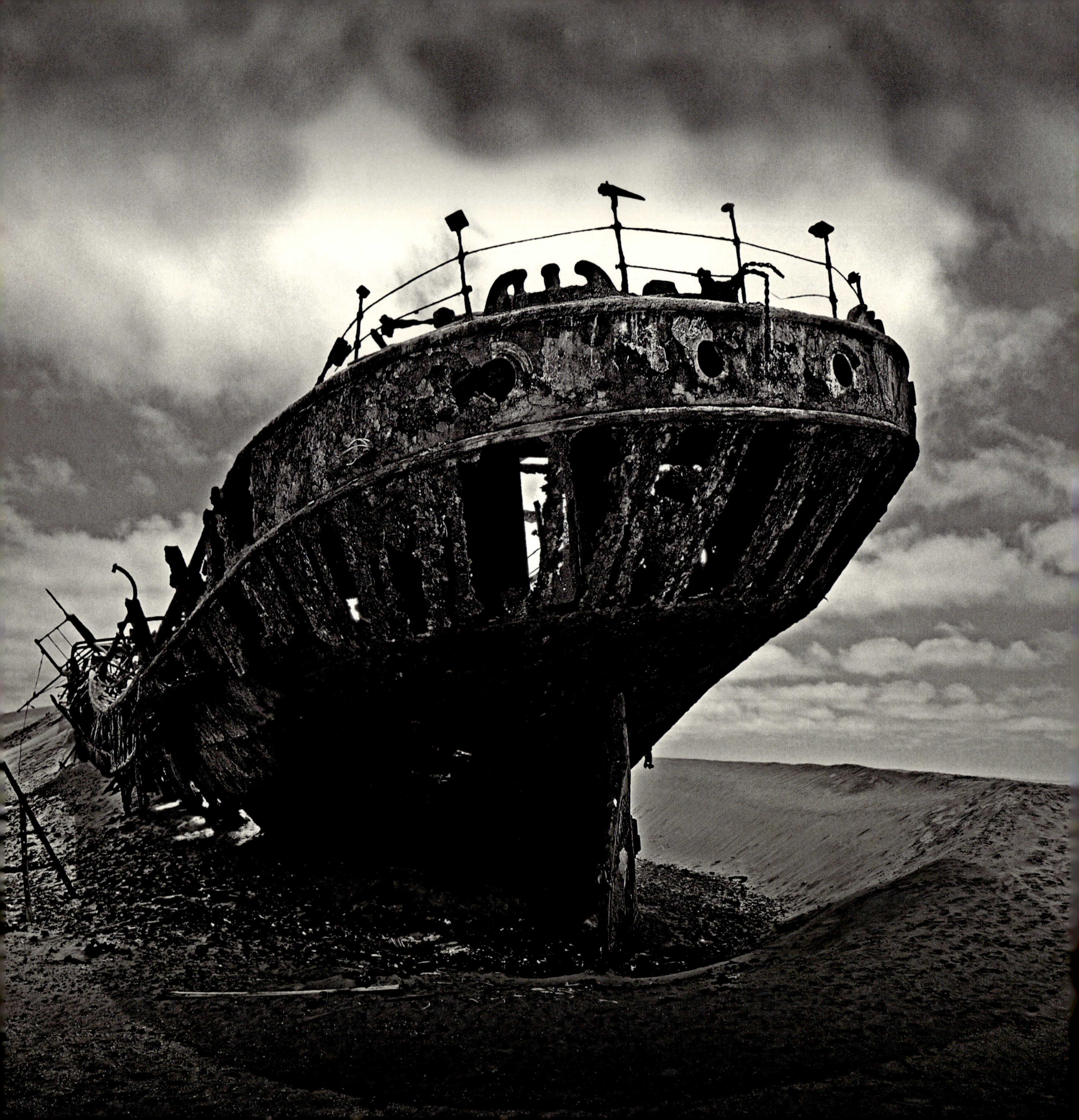

Portfolio 4

PRESENCE OF THE PAST

Developing the *Presence of the Past* portfolio has been one of my most exhilarating photographic journeys to date. It depicts artefacts left by man in the Namib Desert and other arid regions of Namibia, and was instigated by my late husband Louw one day when we were driving along the gravel road from Keetmanshoop to Lüderitz, and he spotted the Buchholtzbrunn ruin in the distance.

As we drove closer, my heart started thumping and my photographic instincts switched into alpha mode. The ruin framed by two quiver trees asked, if not demanded, to be photographed, and the imperative was to do it in black and white. We spent many hours there, with me changing backs and loading film at speed, and Louw, as was his wont, scouting the surroundings for further possibilities. Soon after that trip, the road we had travelled that day was superseded by the current tarred road, so we had happened on the incomparable Buchholtzbrunn just in time.

We became captivated by the theme. Whenever we had the opportunity, we explored Namibia's back roads, scouring the landscape for "presence of the past". When Louw returned to Windhoek in an empty aircraft after dropping tourists off in the Skeleton Coast or Kunene environs, he would "hunt" for deserted mines and other such relics from the air. When he located subject matter he thought had potential, we would fly or drive there to take a closer look.

These historical remnants had all the graphic qualities and staying power a photographer could wish for. Whether it was the ruin of a dwelling, a deserted mine, a shipwreck, or the remains of a vehicle, they emanated an air of sadness, despair and decay – of hopes that had been dashed, efforts squandered, dreams that had turned to dust – all of which added to their photo-worthiness.

The 30 images presented in this portfolio have been reproduced in split-tone from black-and-white negatives by fine-art printer Andreas Kahlau of Silvertone International in Johannesburg.

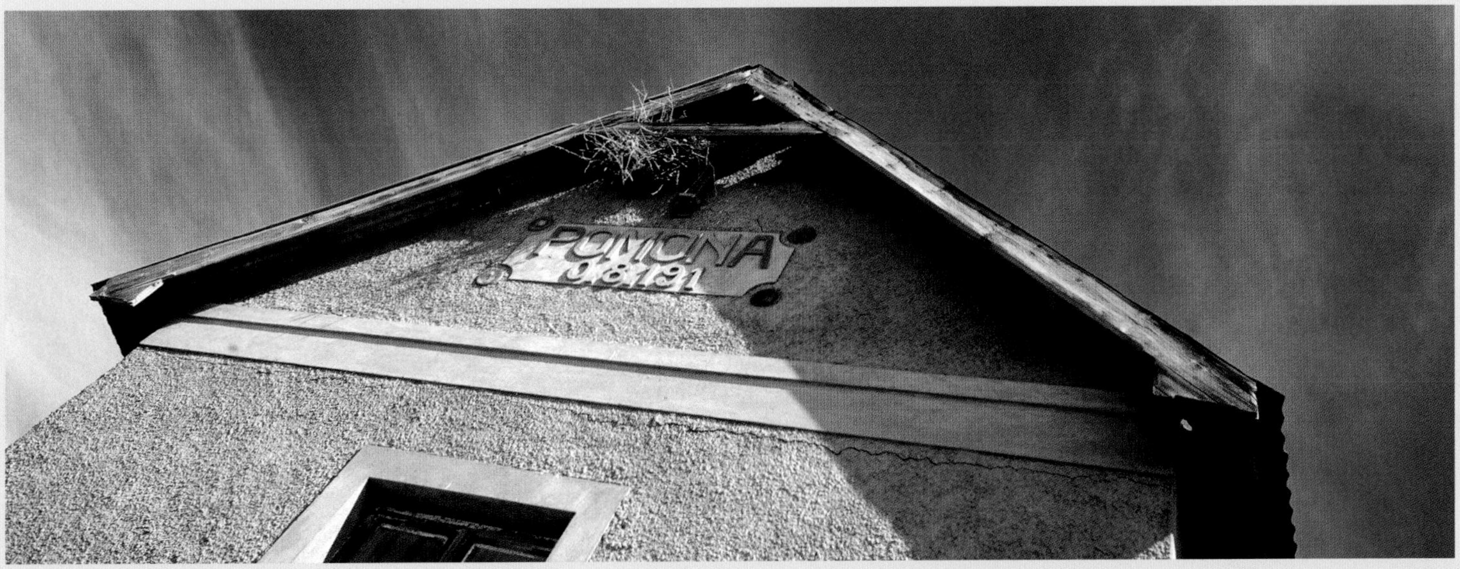

(OPPOSITE) Wreck of the *Eduard Bohlen* (ABOVE) Pomona

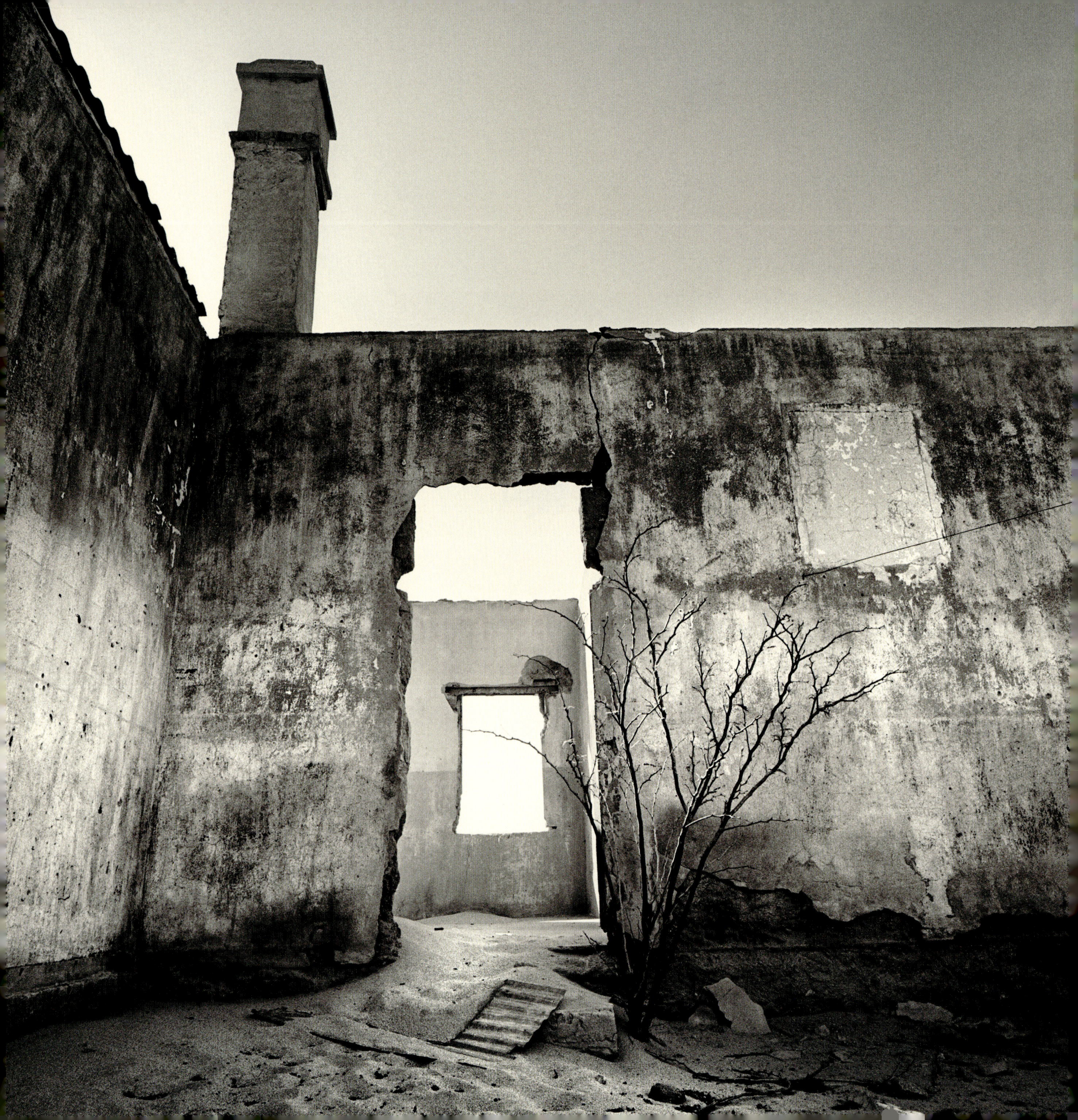

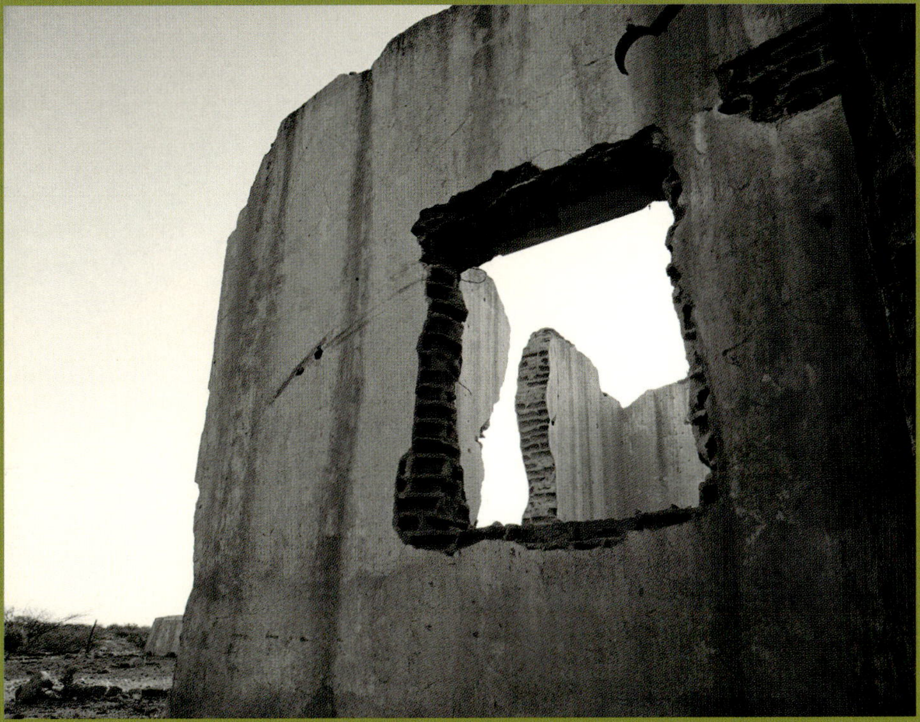

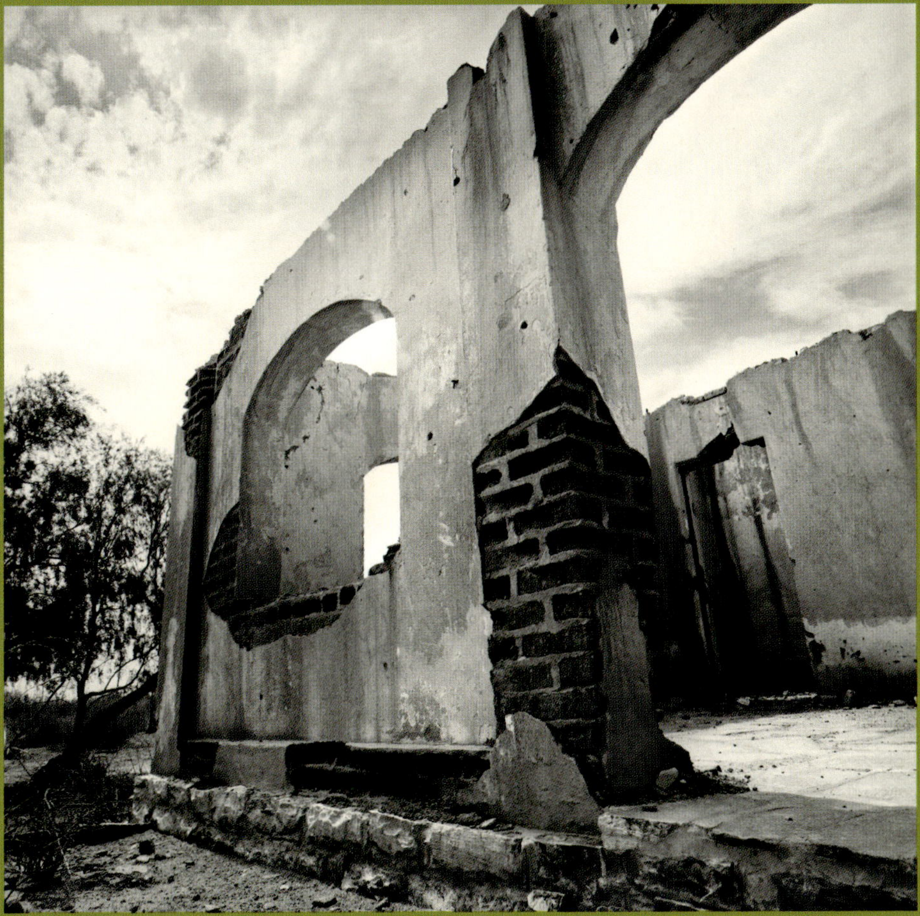

Weissenfels

NAMIBIA

Wild west land,
holster in the hip of Africa,
strung on the studded belt of Capricorn.

the sun lassoos the rain
tugged from the barebacked land.
the rocks crack in pistol shots.

yet on a sparse frontier,
crossed freely, are
the cattle of the heart.

Dorian Haarhof, published in *Flamingo*,
Vol. 4, Number 40, October 1992: 29

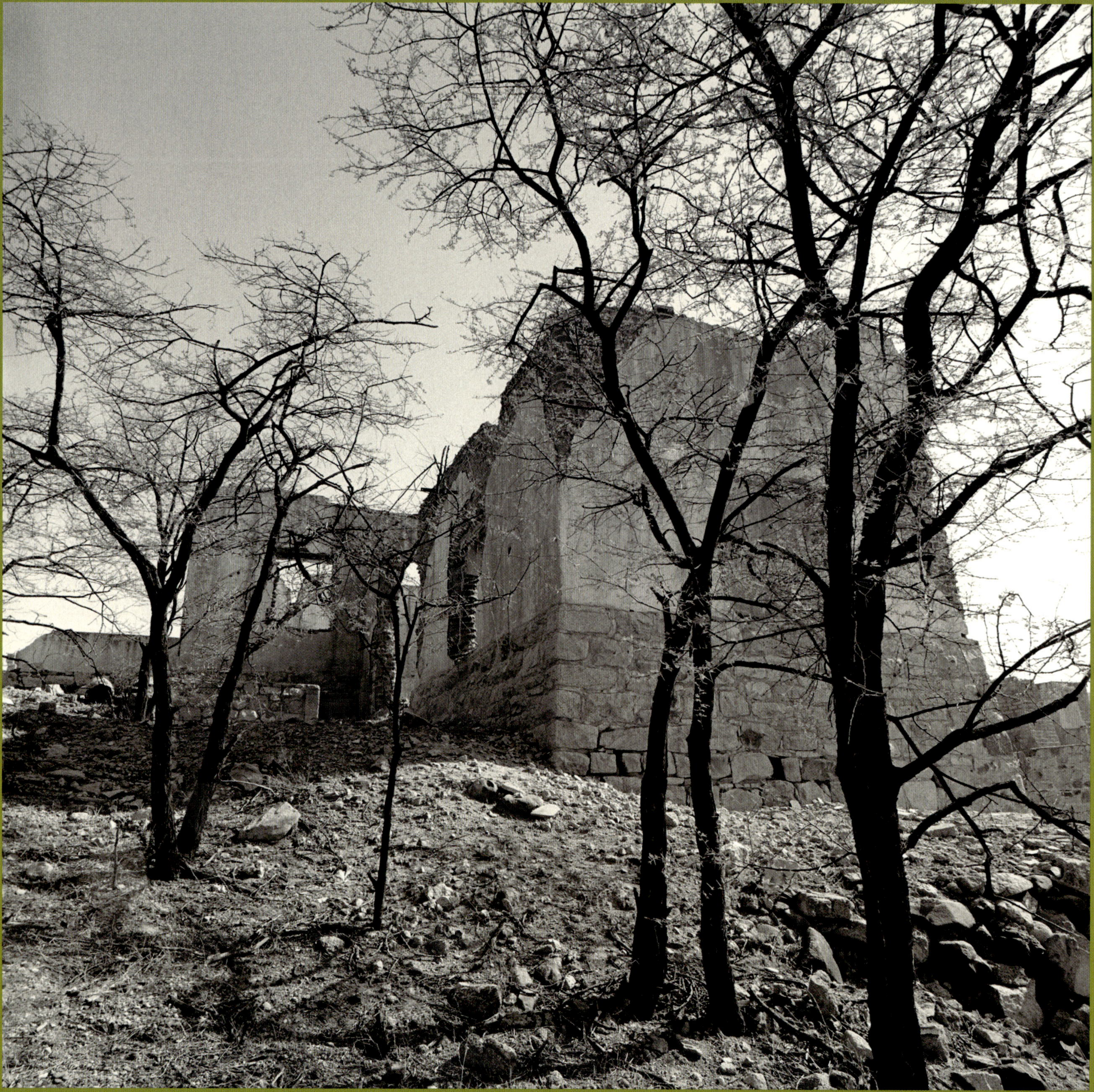

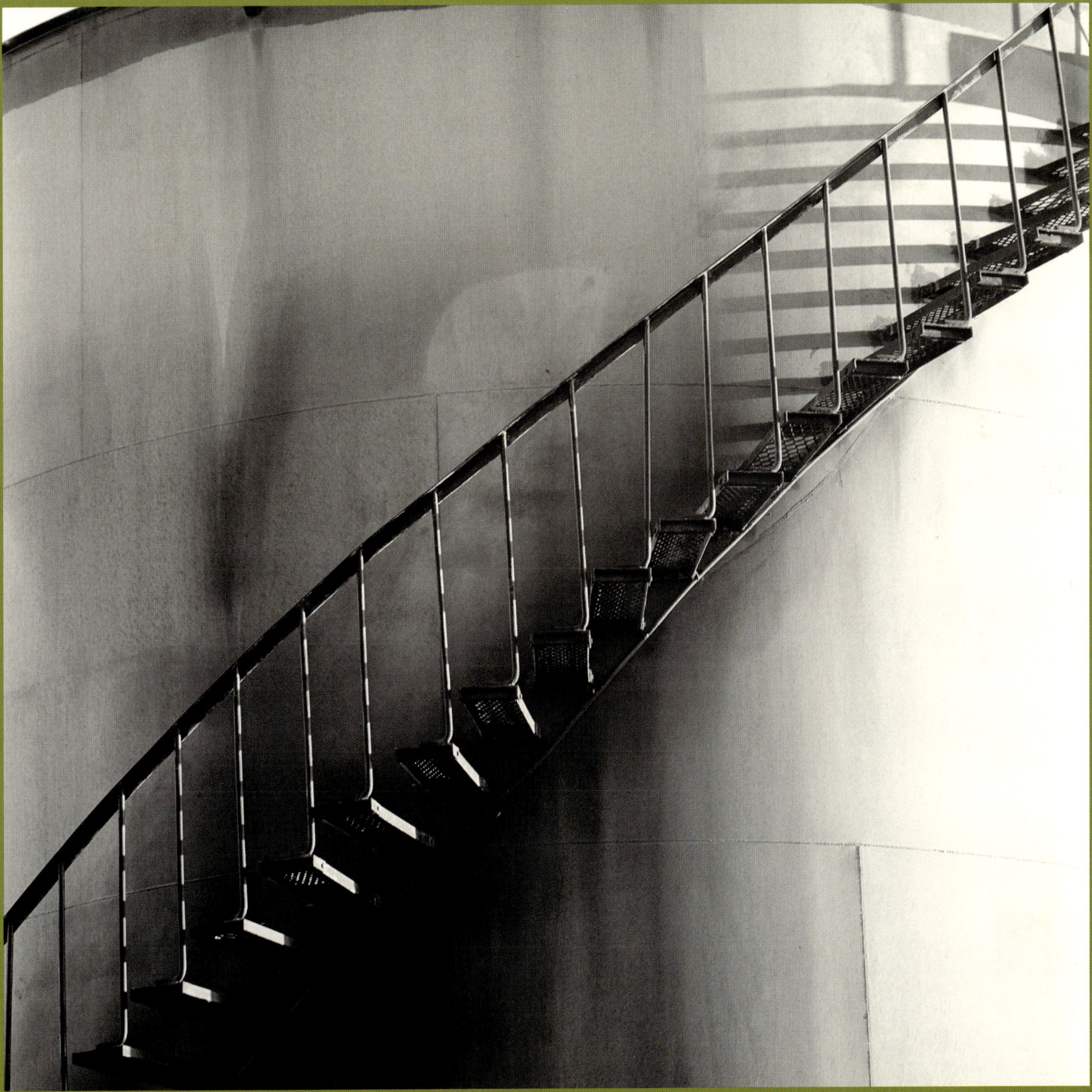

(OPPOSITE) Futura Tin (ABOVE) Spiral

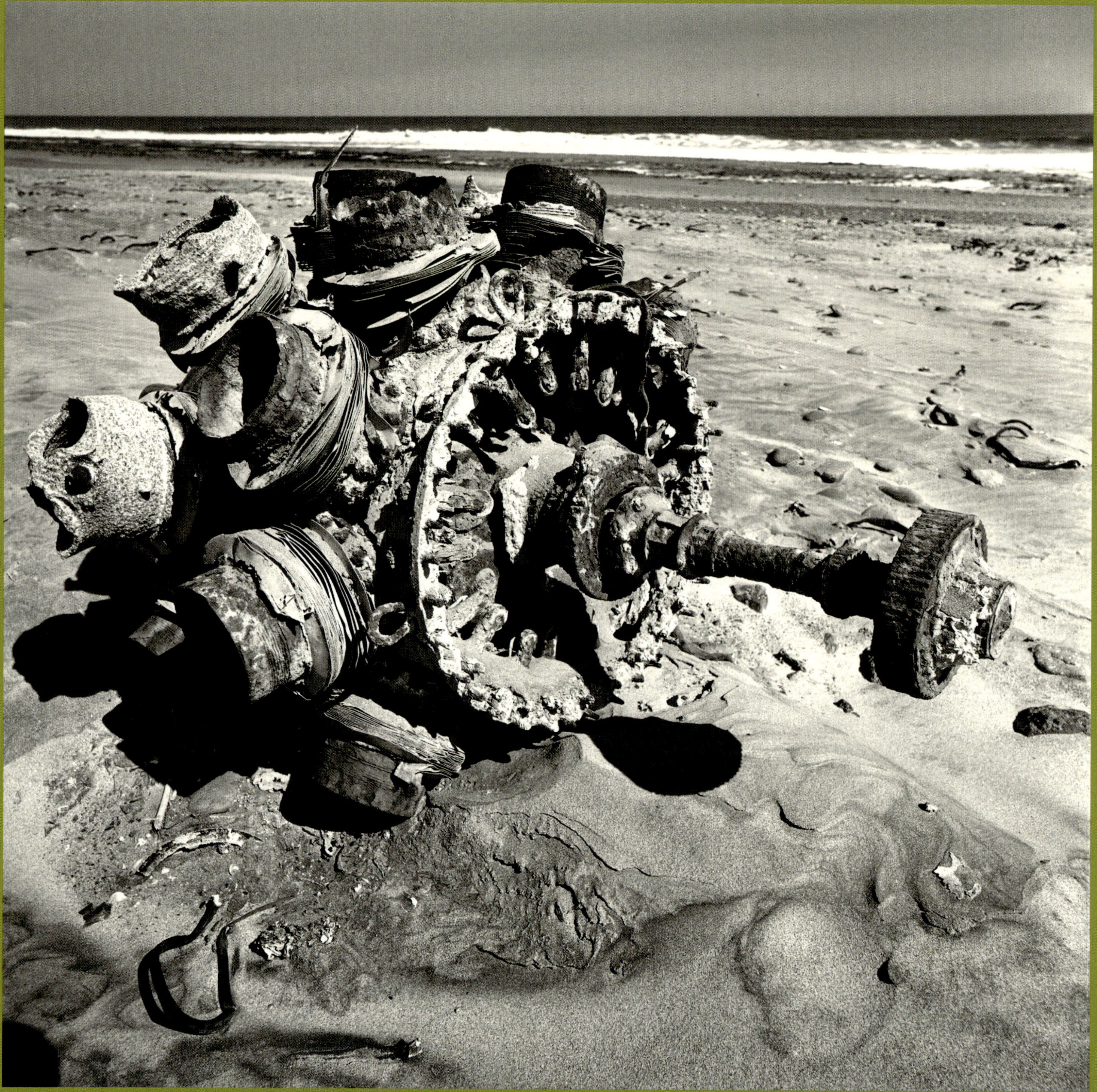

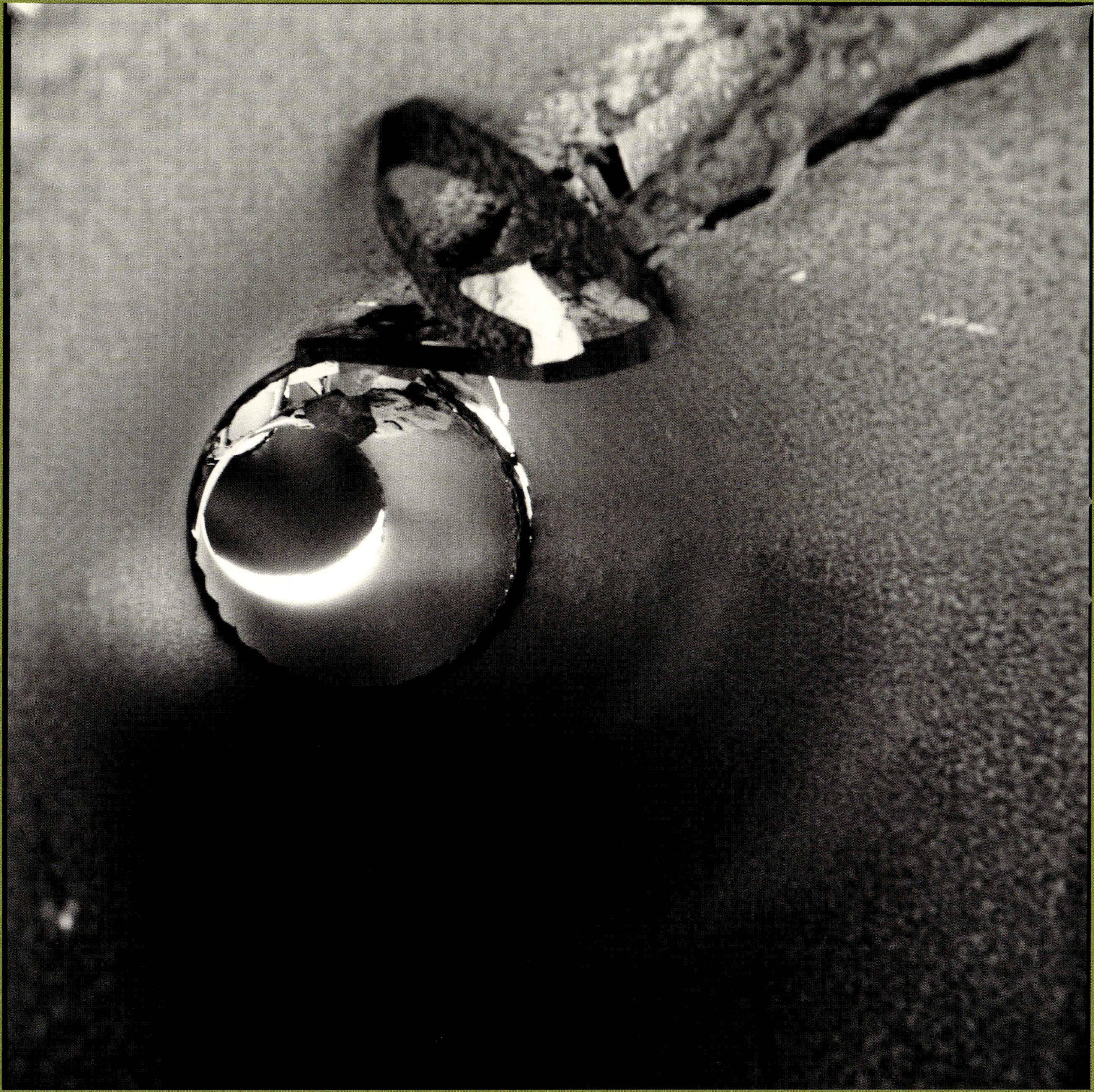

(OPPOSITE) Ventura Bomber (ABOVE) Vortex

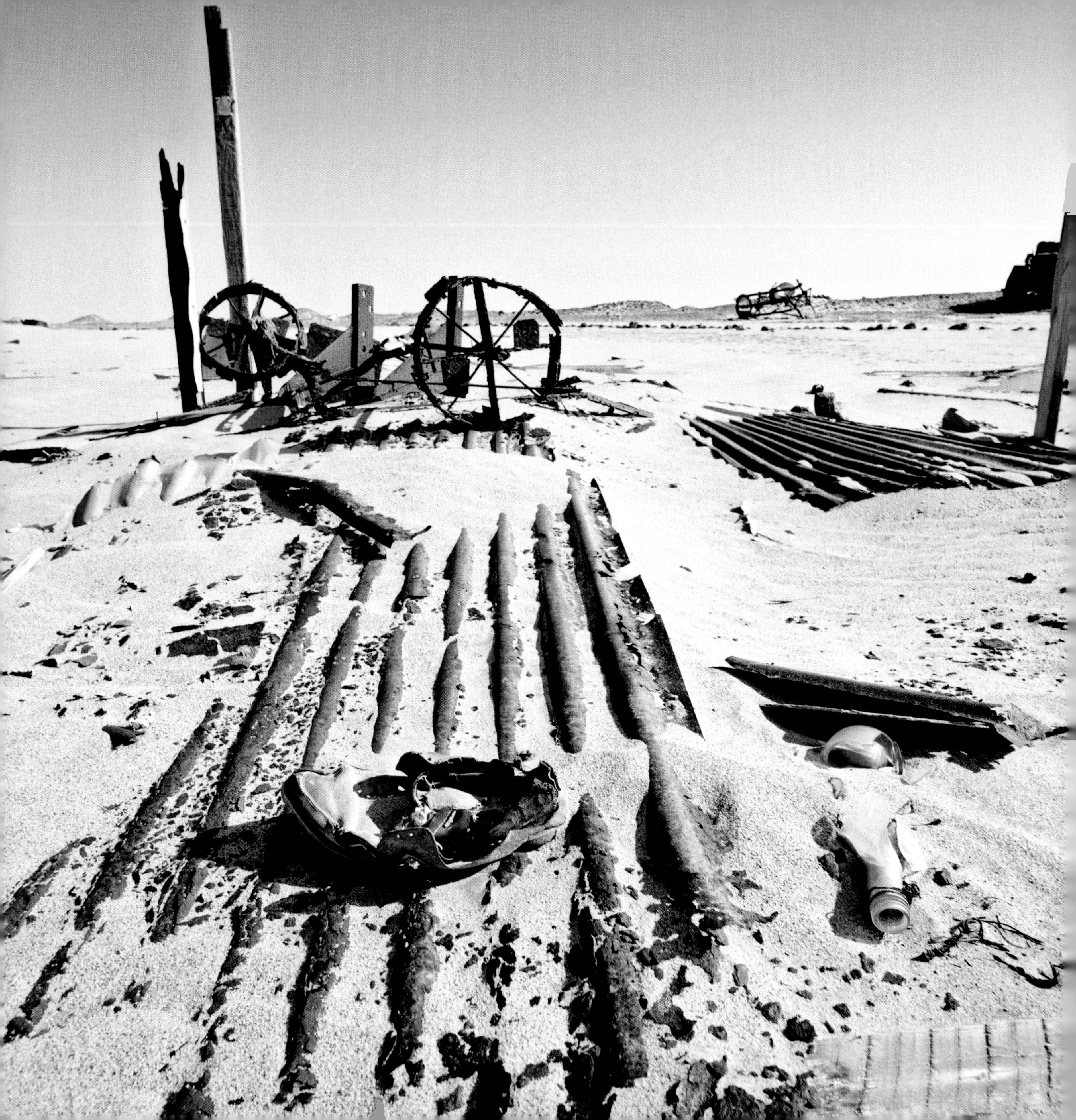

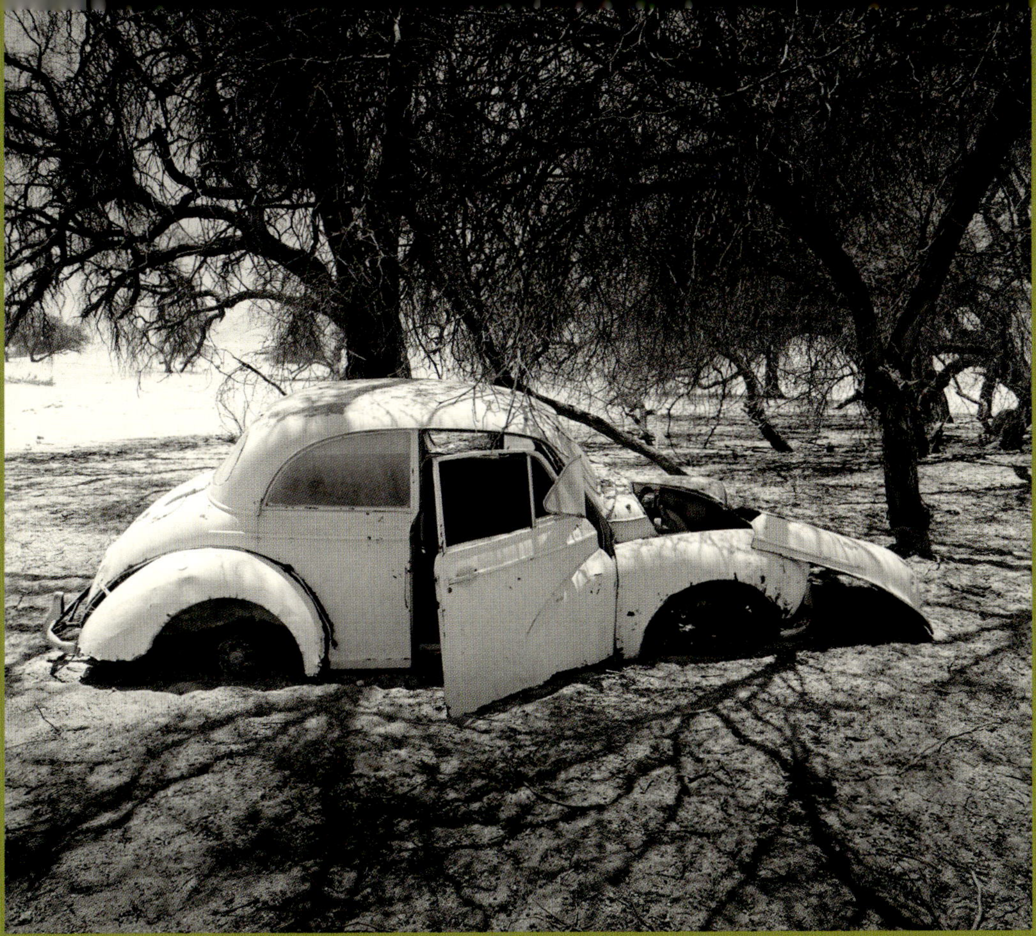

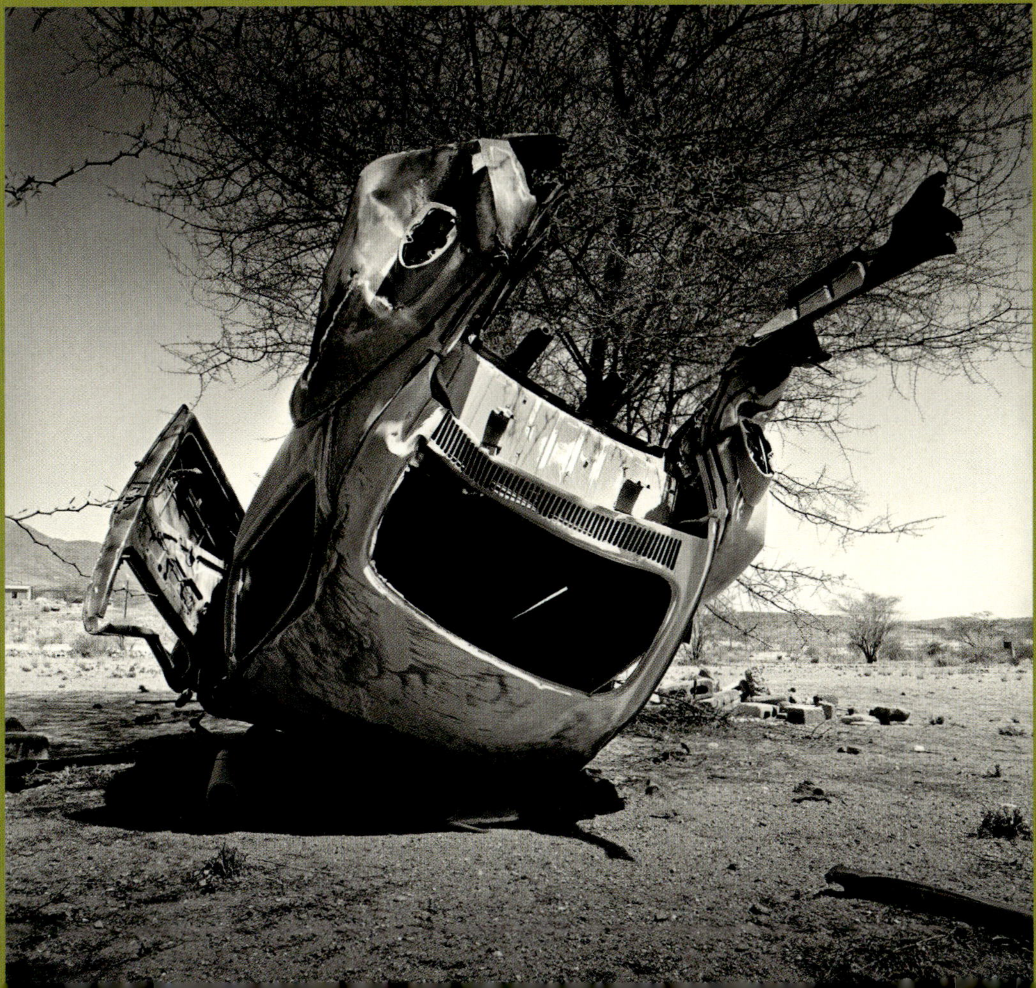

(OPPOSITE) Westies Mine, Skeleton Coast Park
(TOP) Sundowner (BOTTOM) Bottoms Up

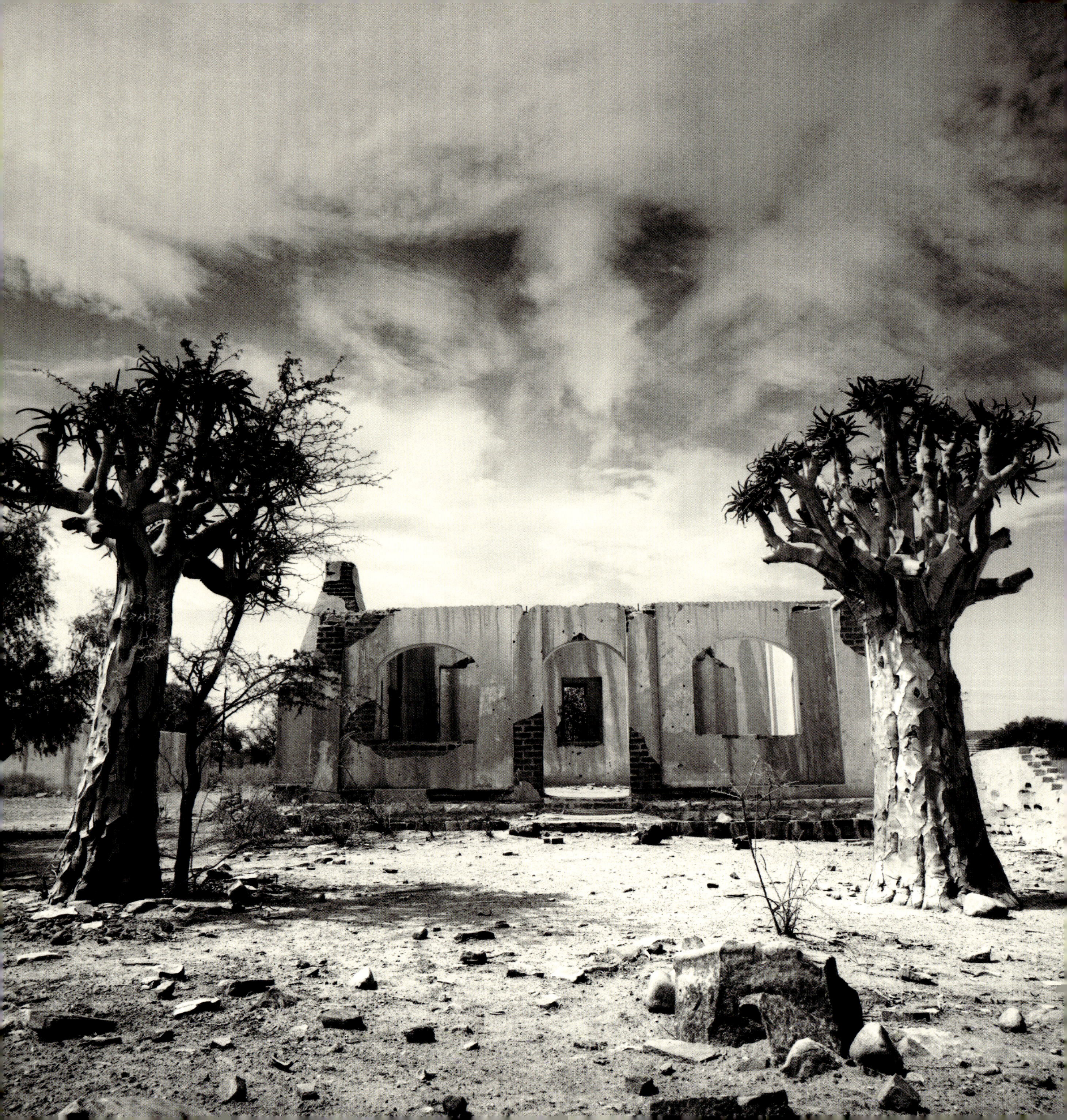

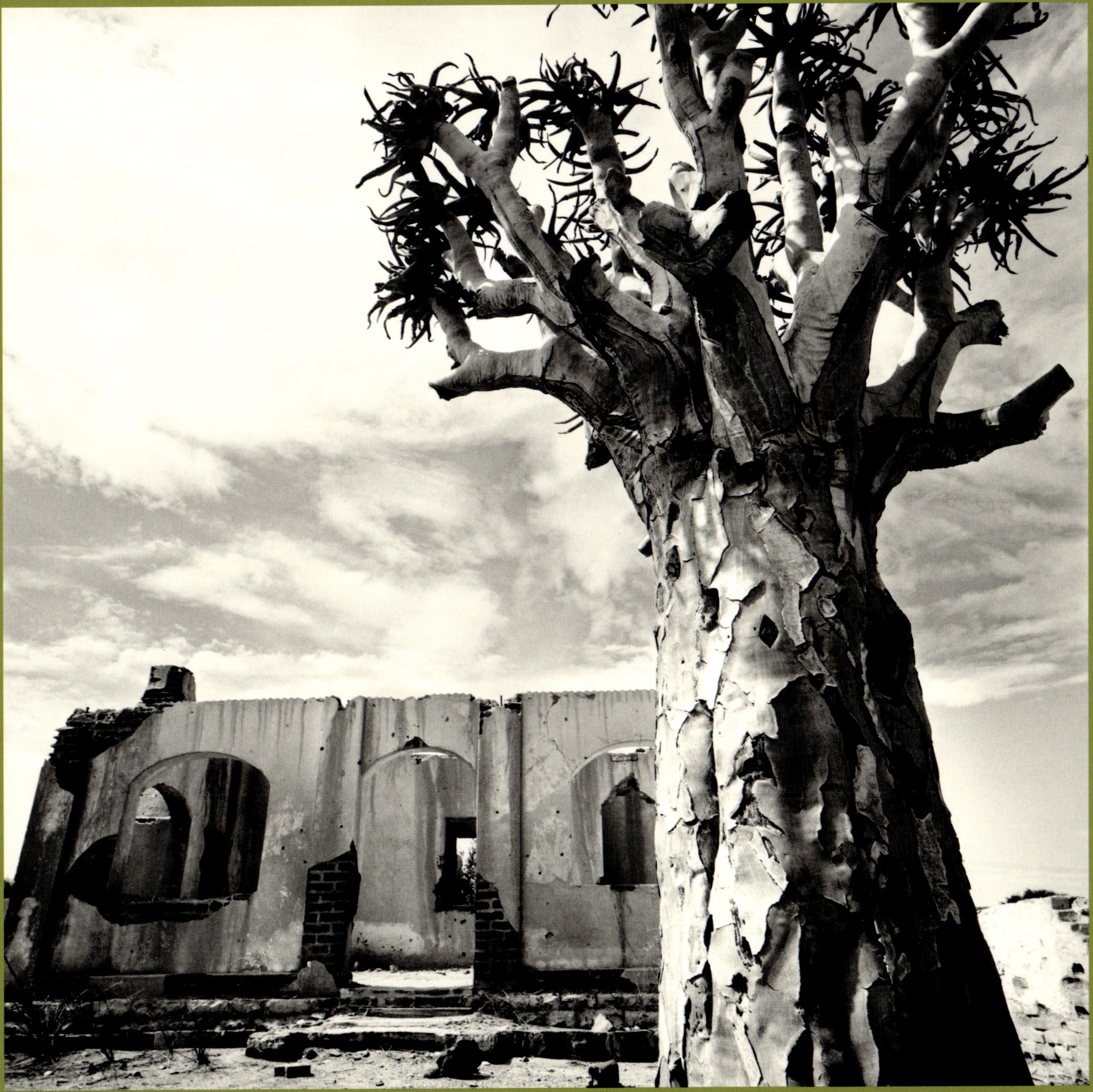

Buchholtzbrunn

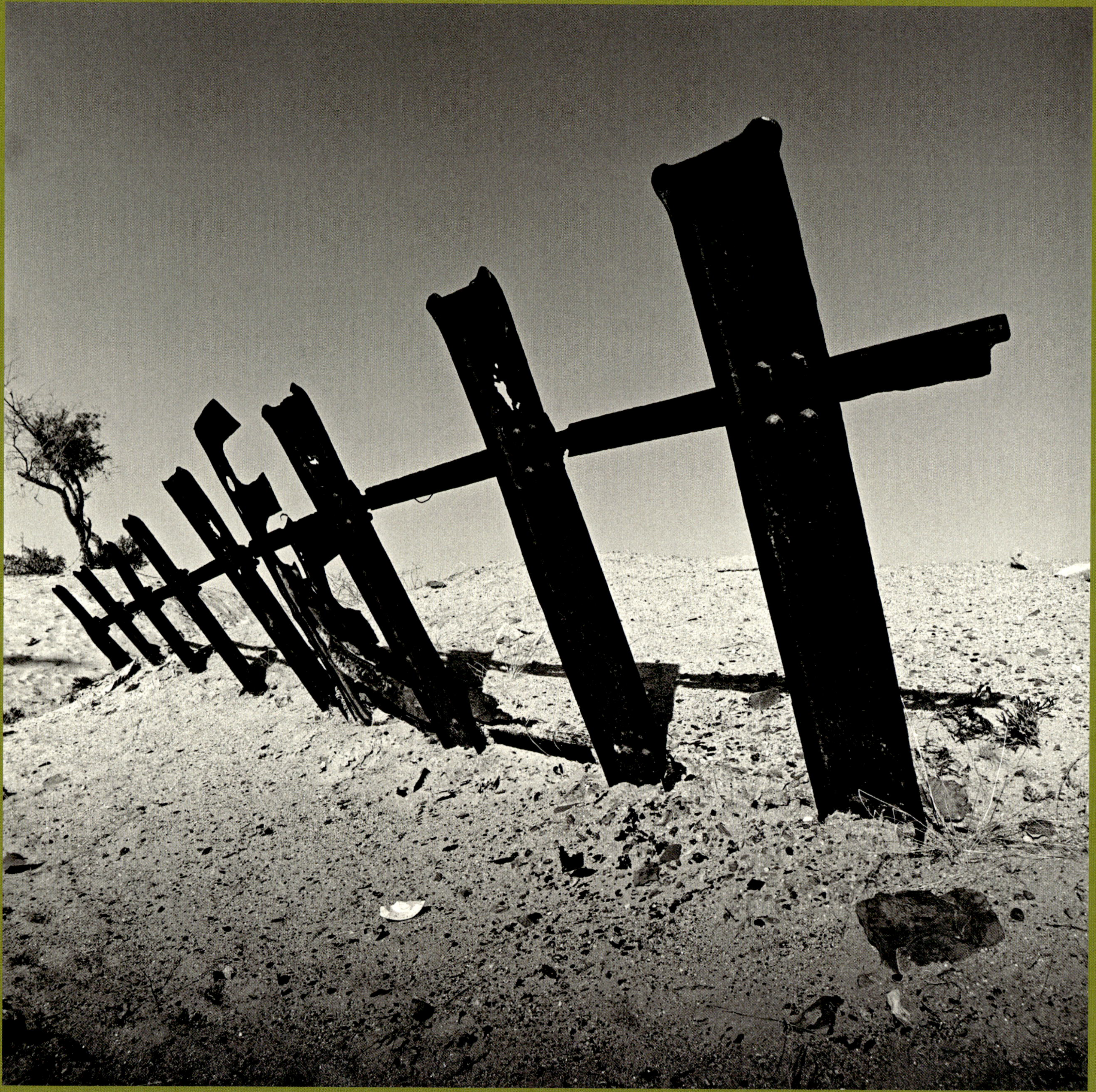

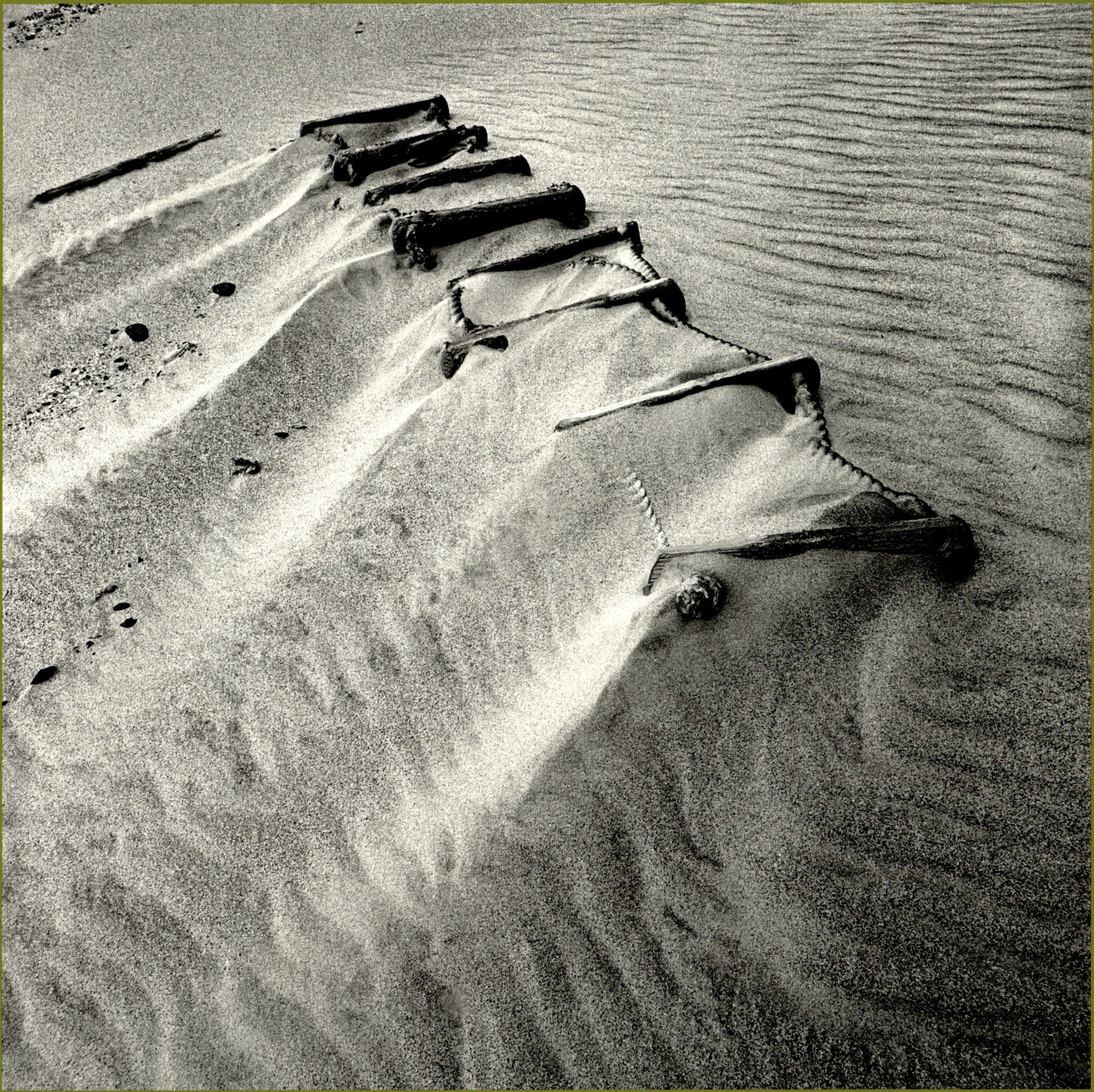

(OPPOSITE) End of the Line (ABOVE) Ladder to Nowhere

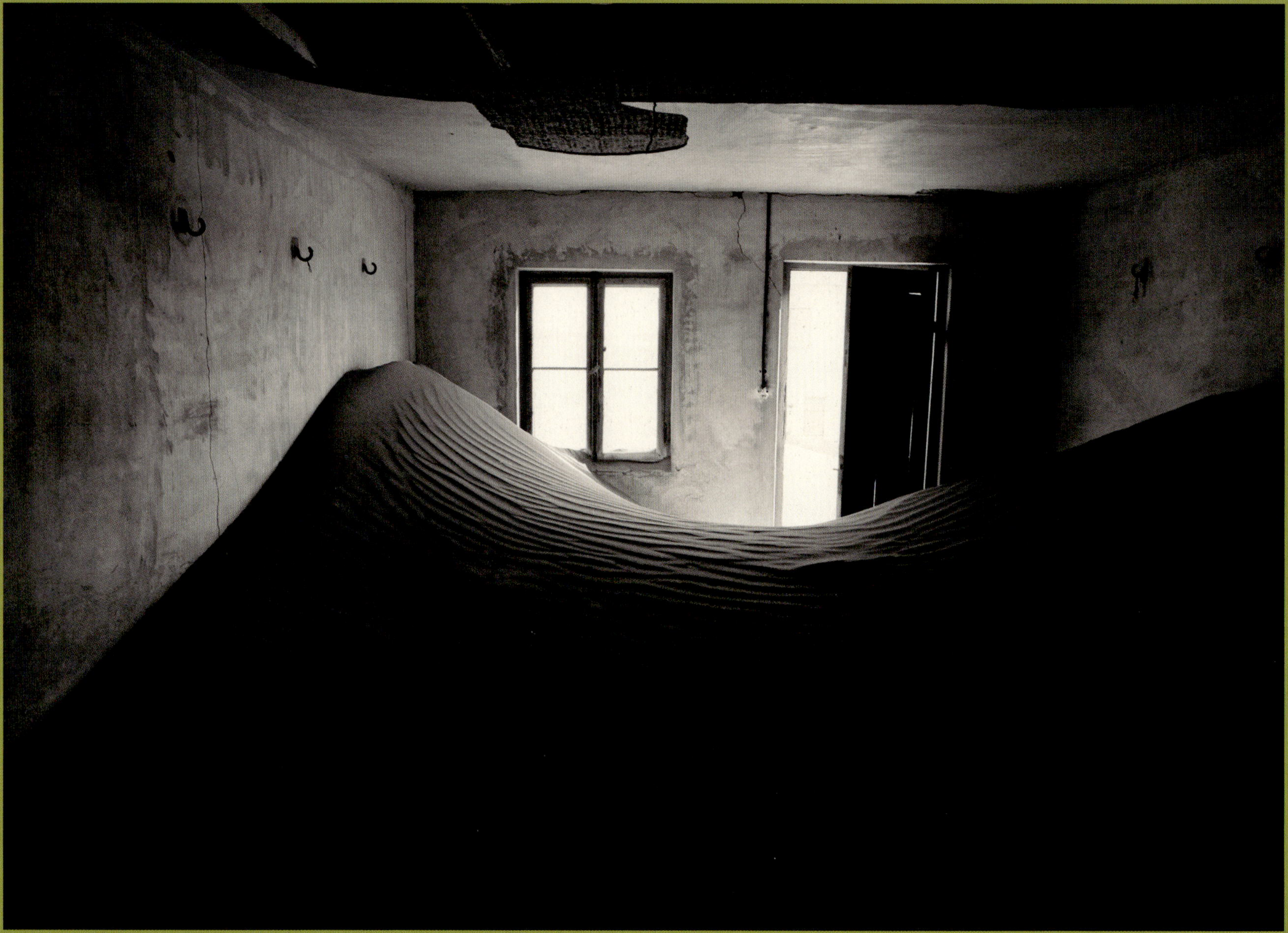

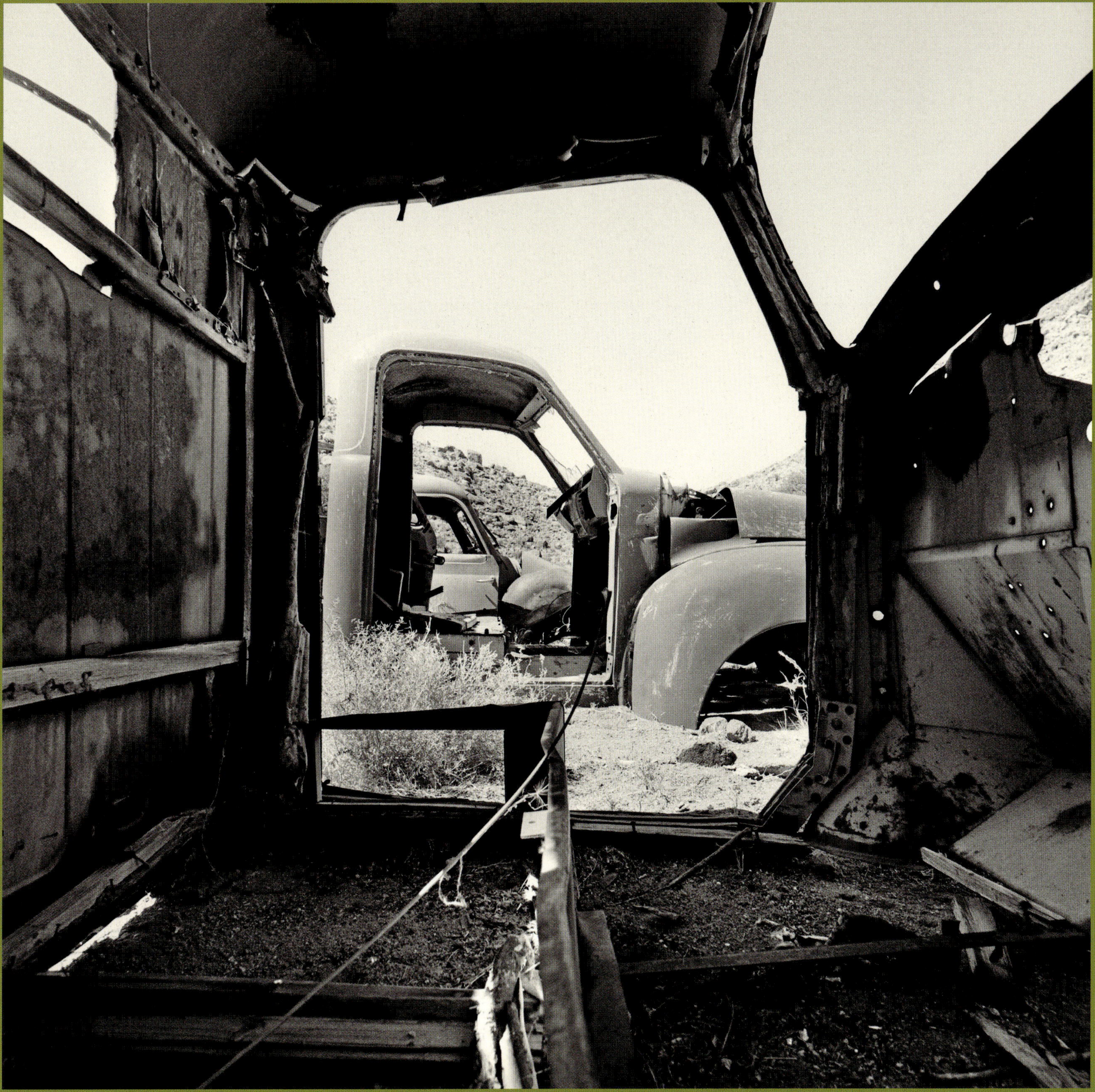

(OPPOSITE) Kolmanskop Interior (ABOVE) Karuschka

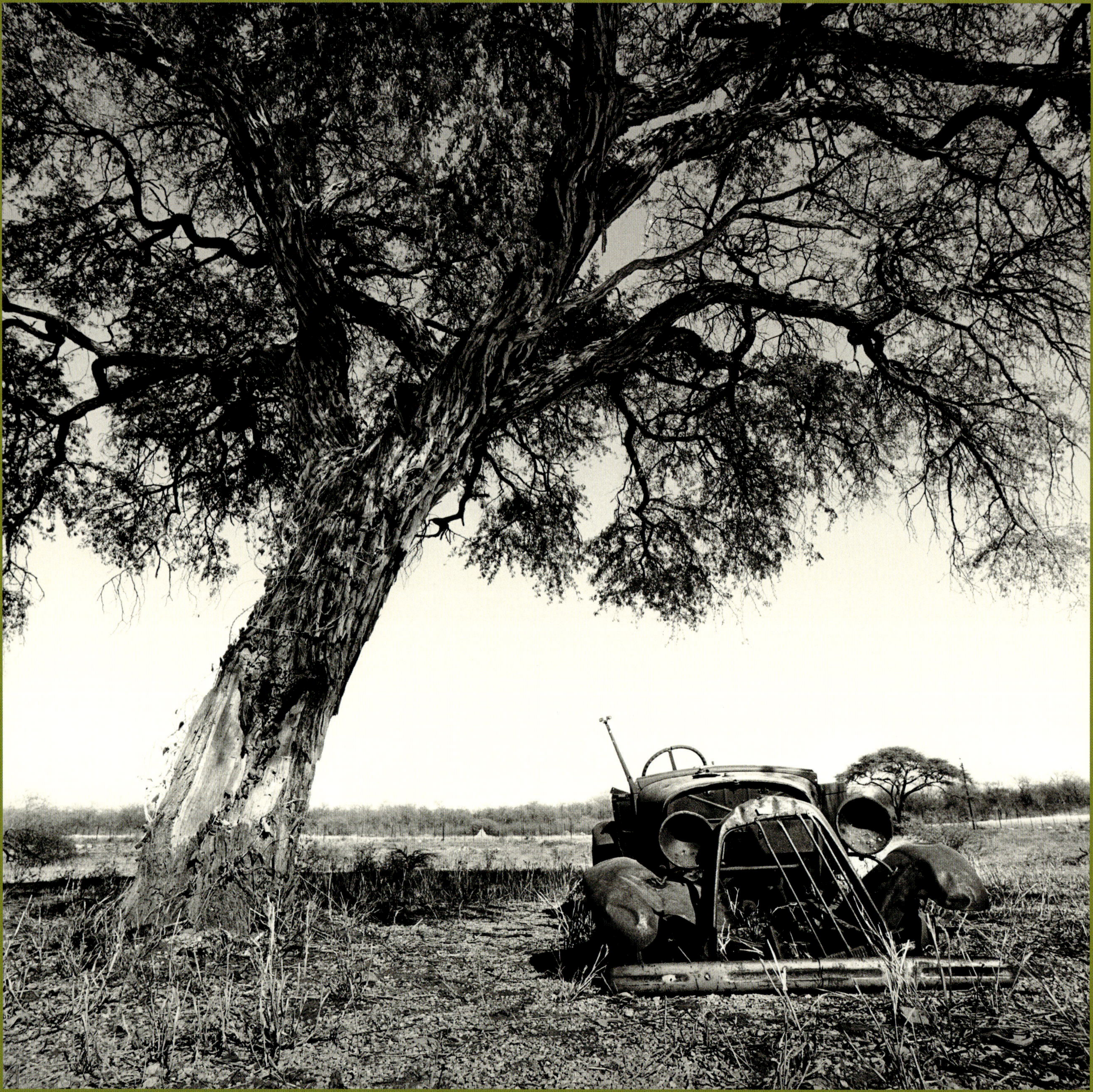

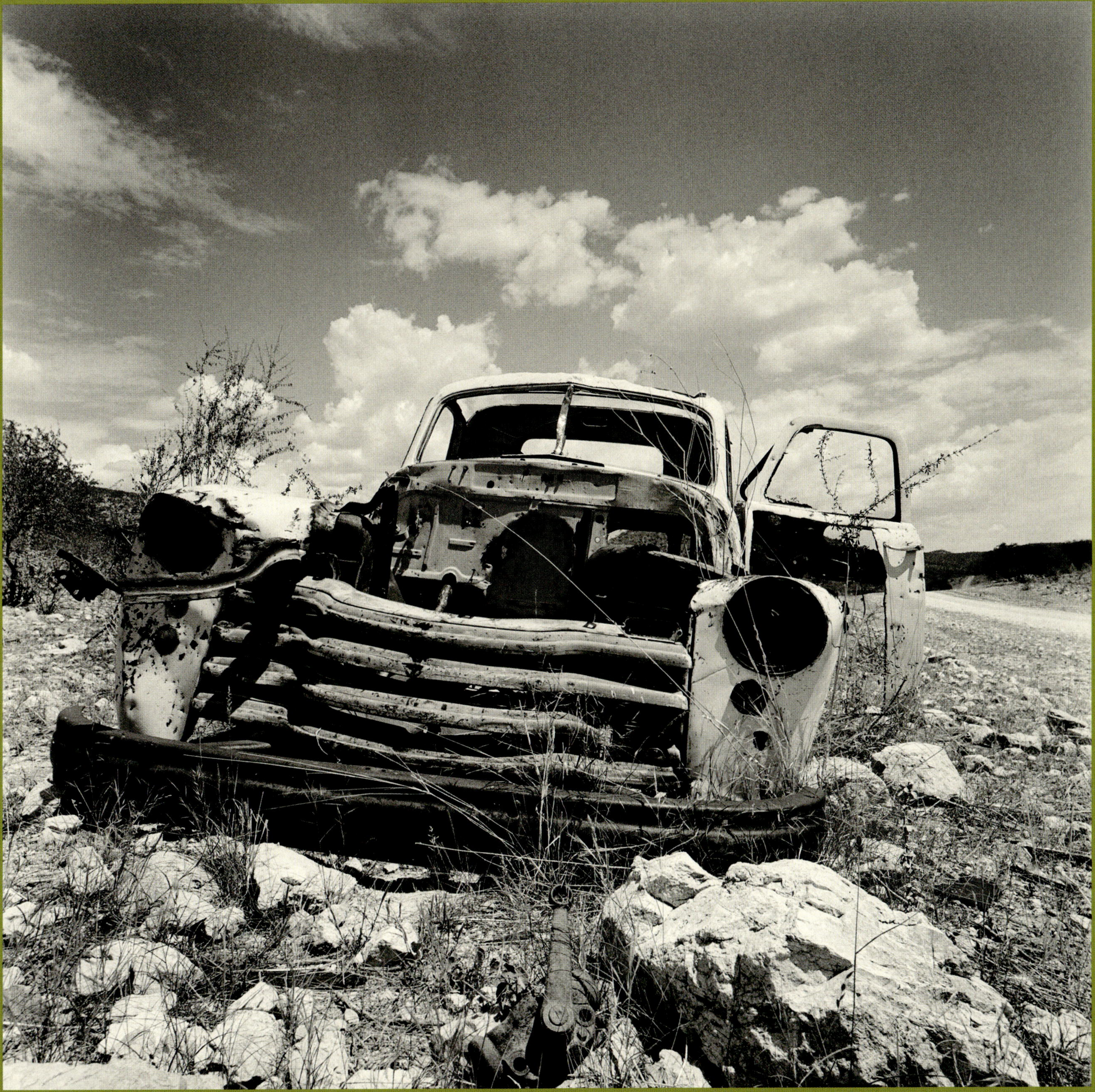

(OPPOSITE) Etosha Overland (ABOVE) End of the Road

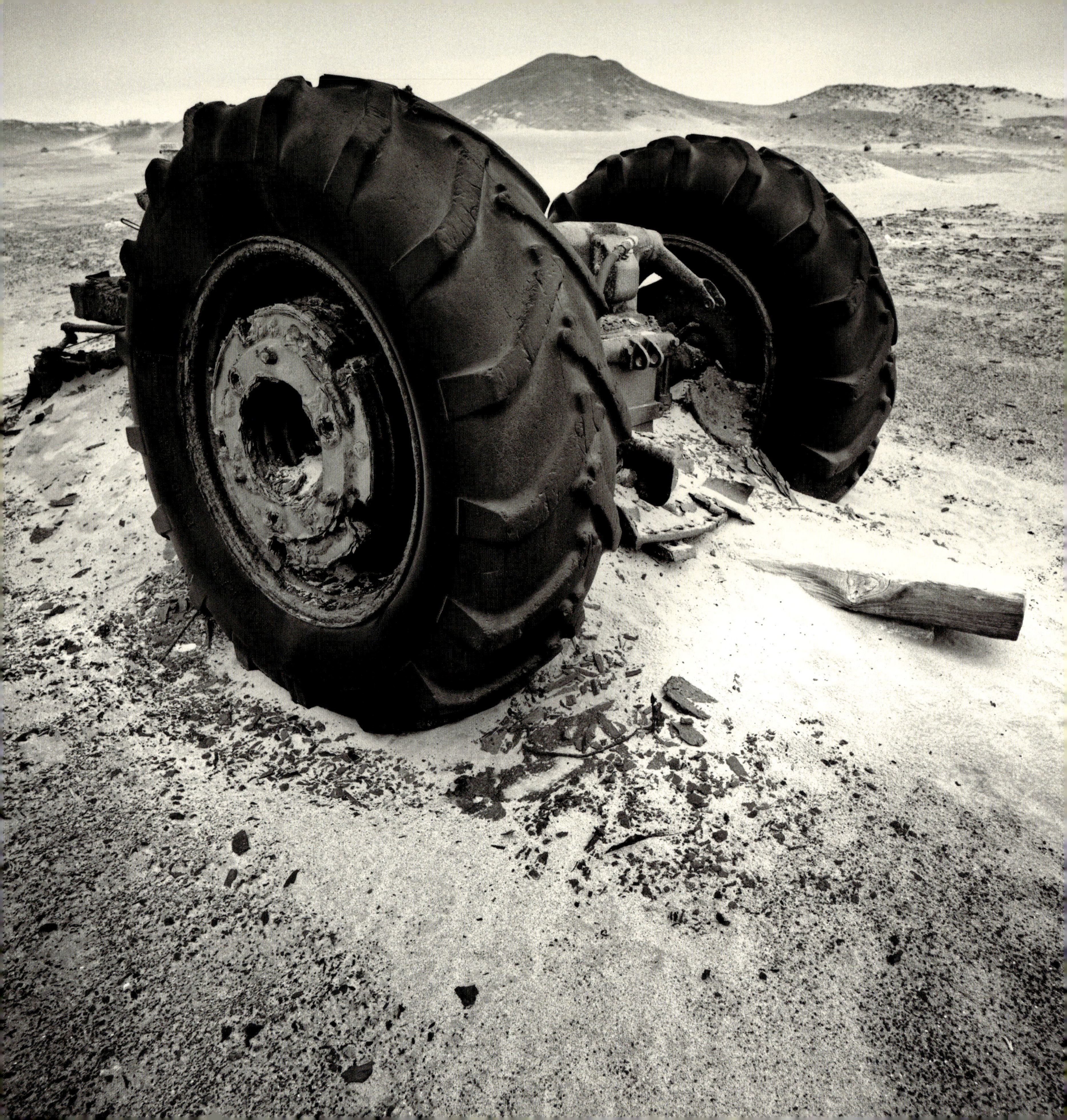

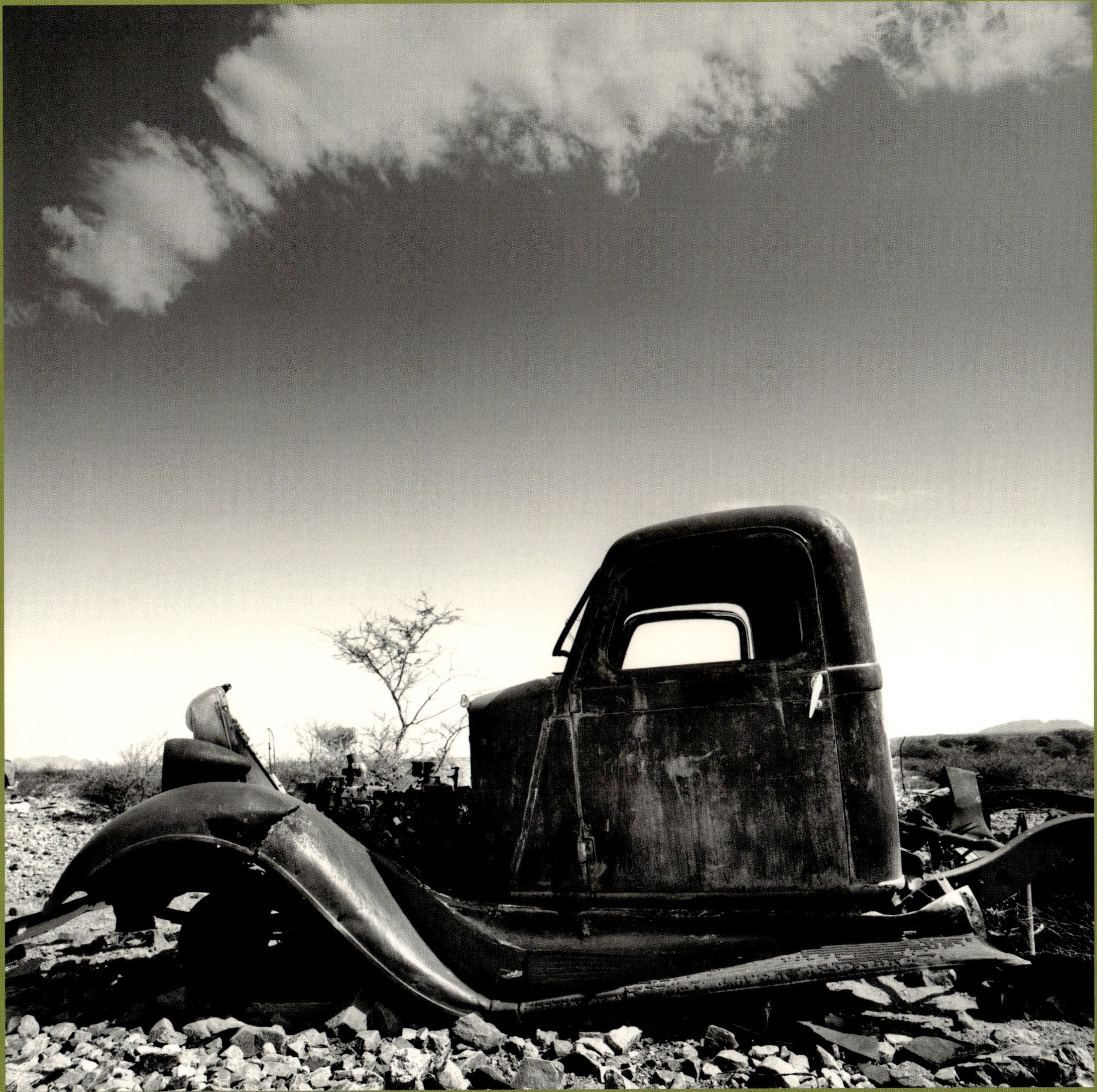

(OPPOSITE) Tyre Traction (ABOVE) Damaraland Dodge

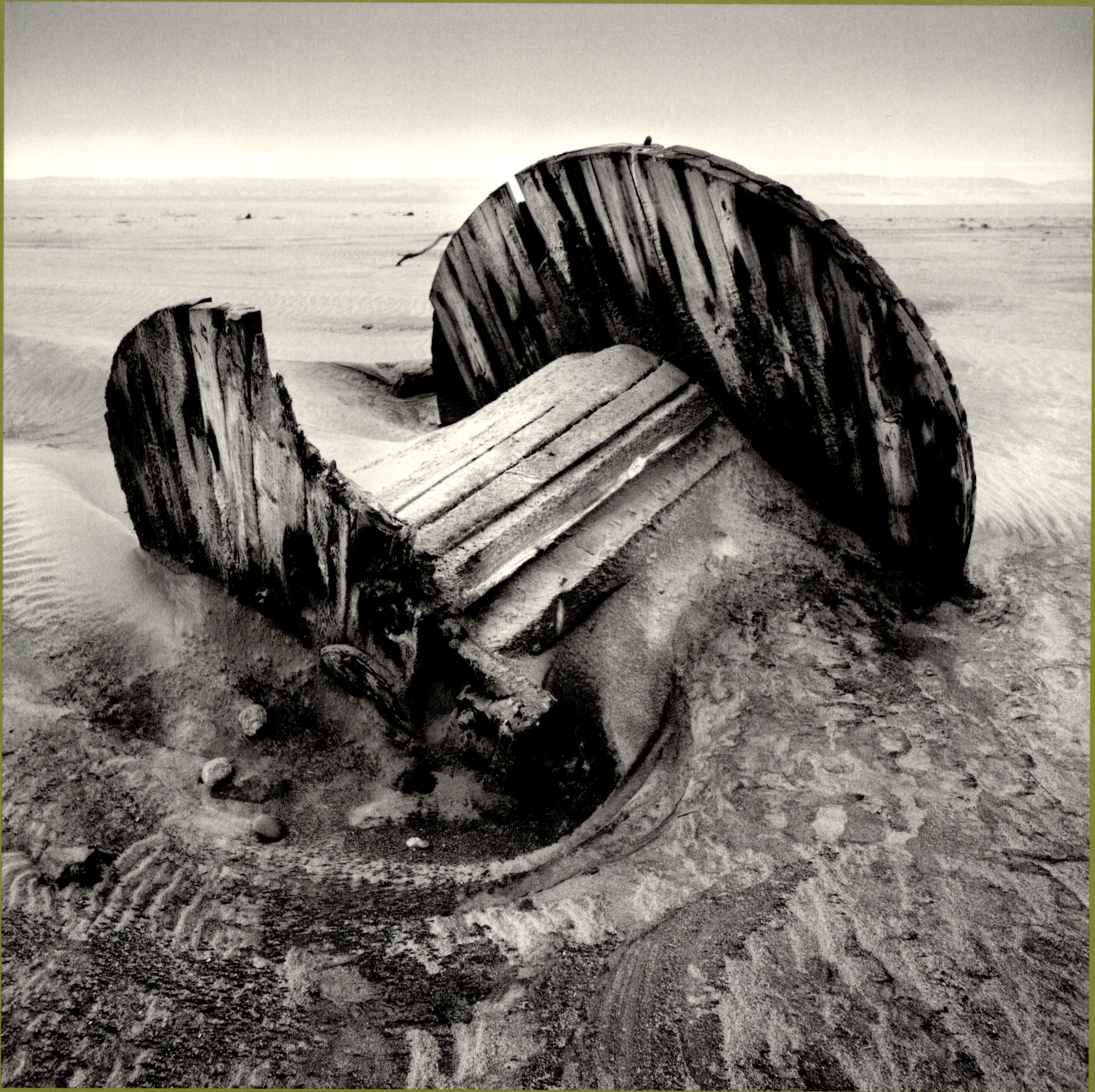

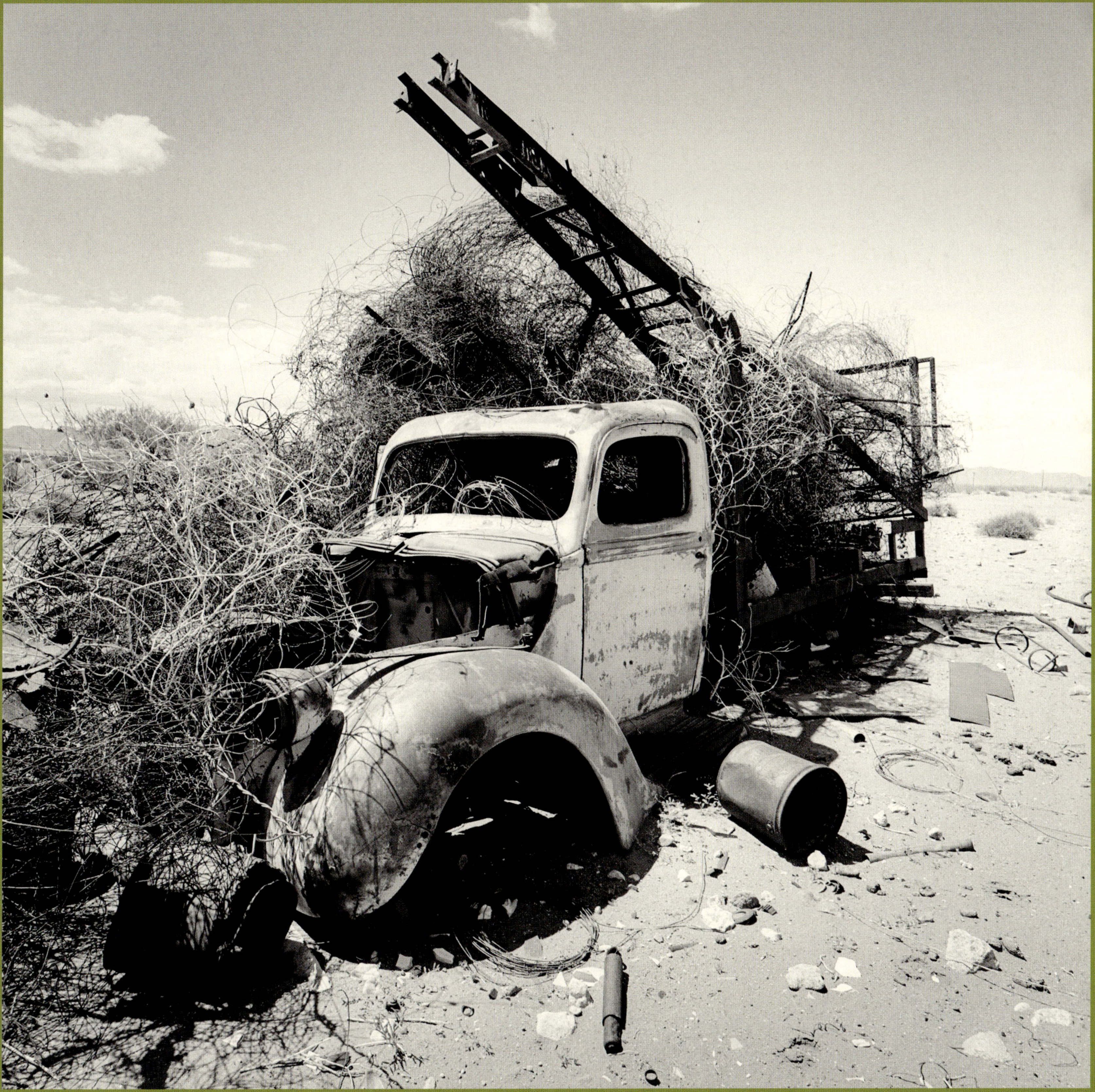

(OPPOSITE) Sand Drift (ABOVE) The Last Load

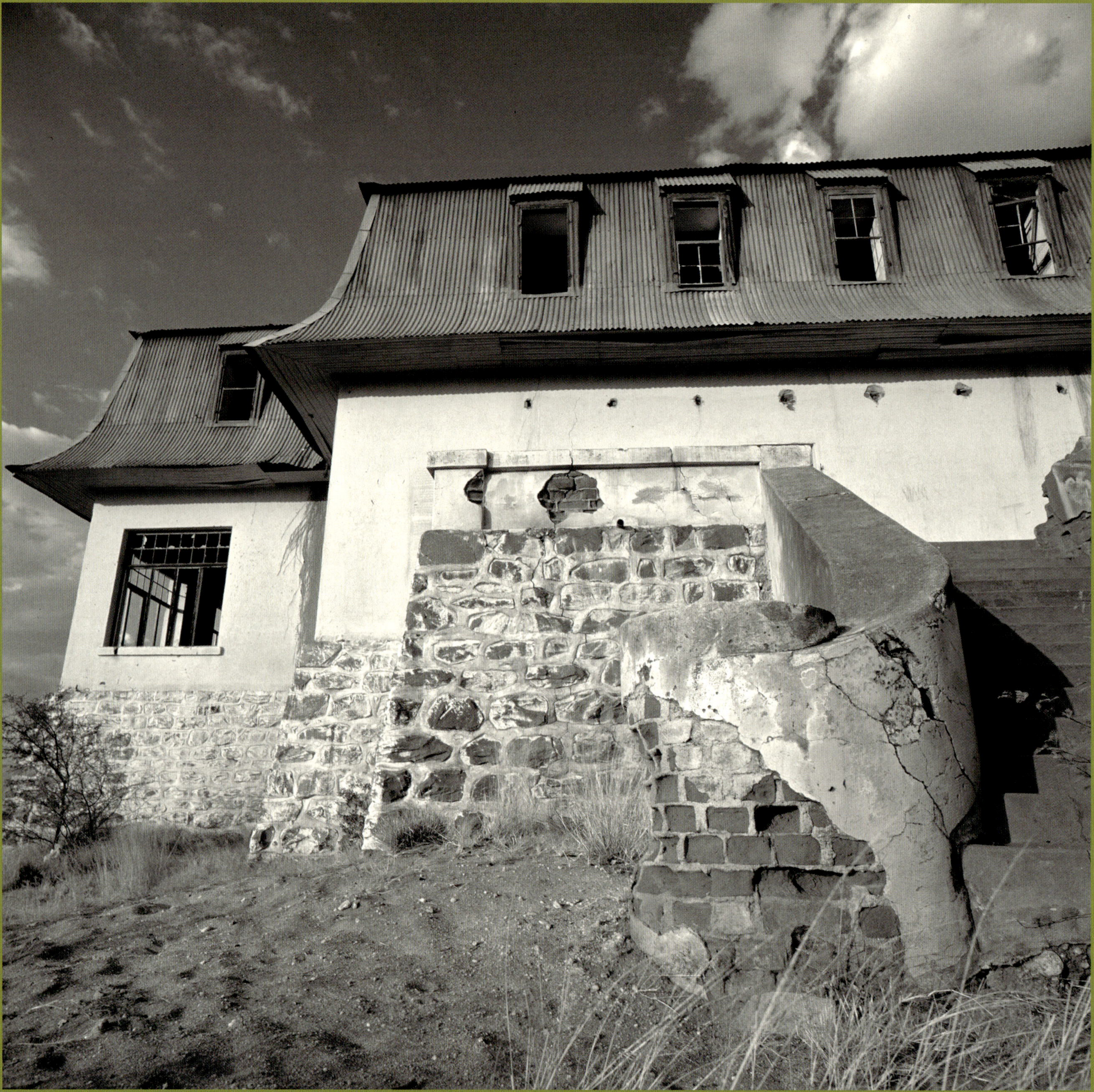

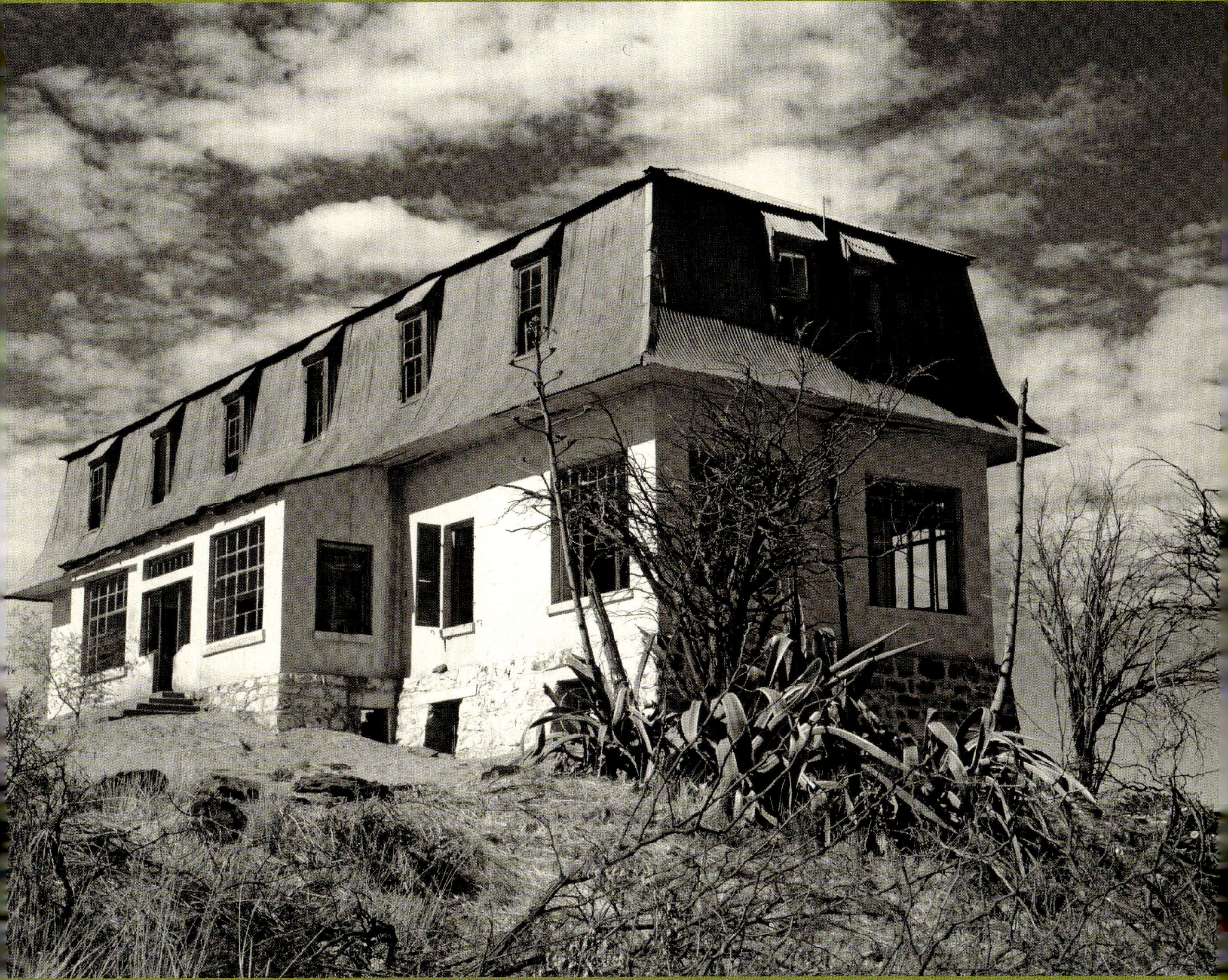

Liebig House

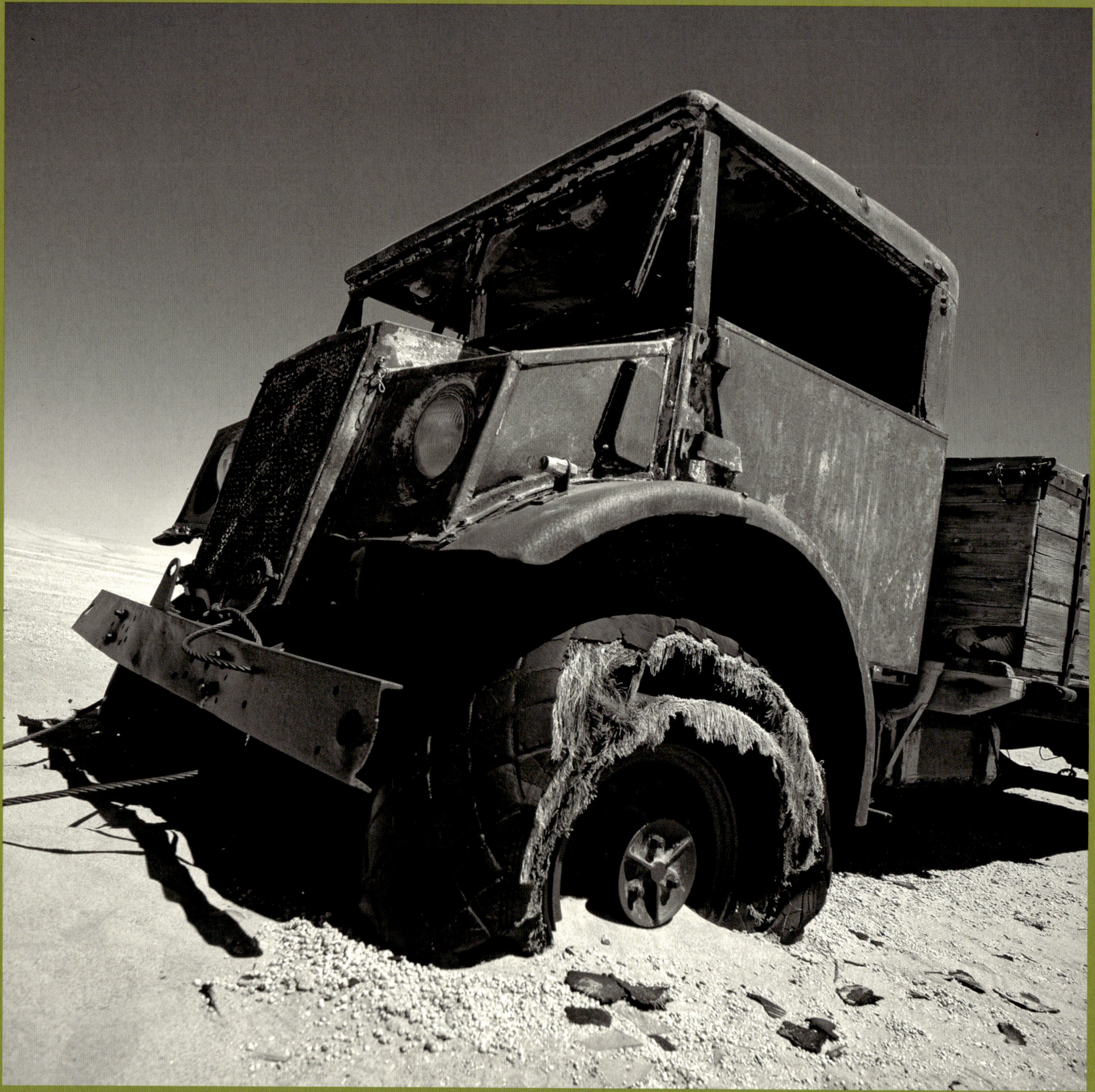

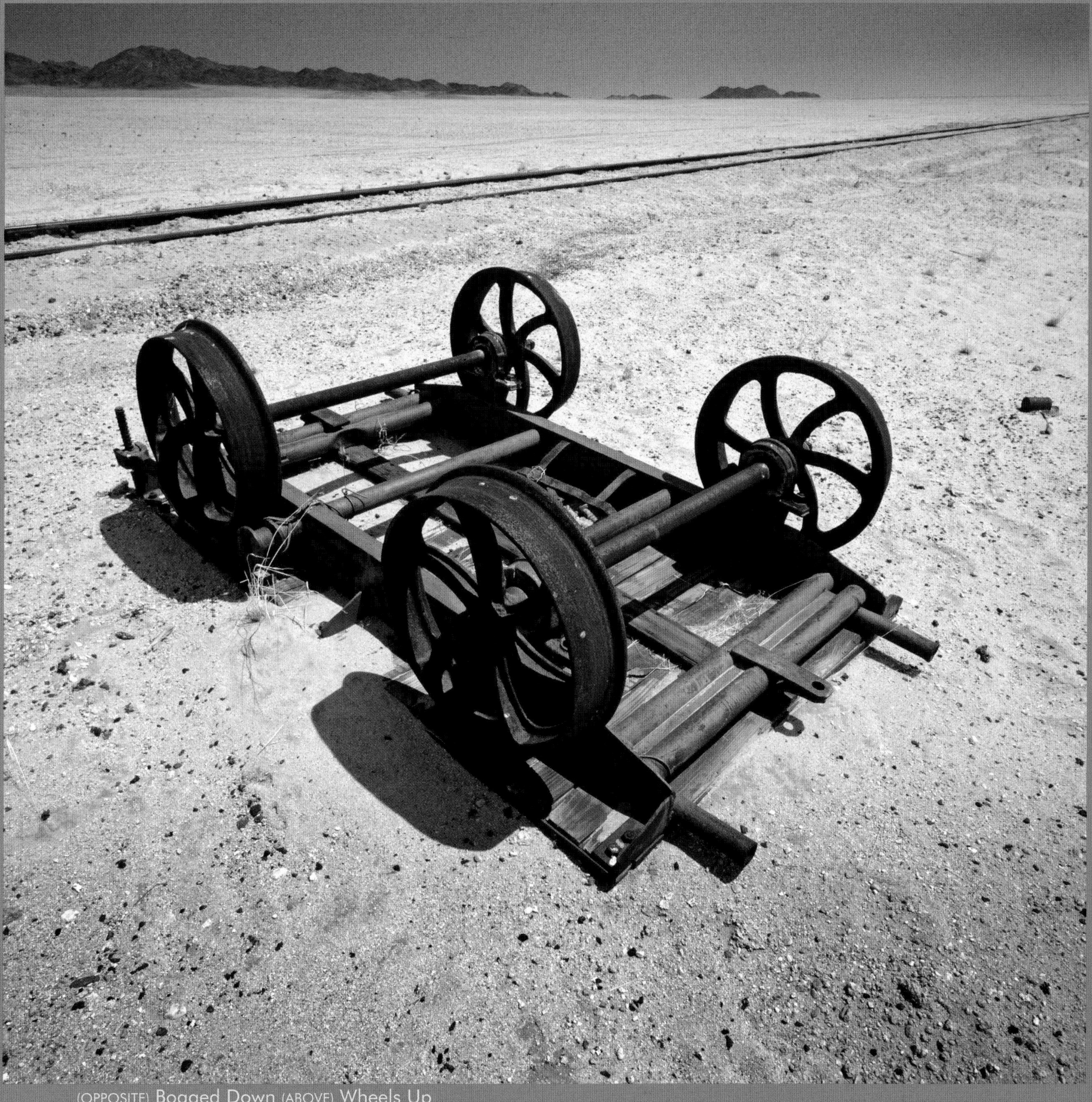

(OPPOSITE) Bogged Down (ABOVE) Wheels Up

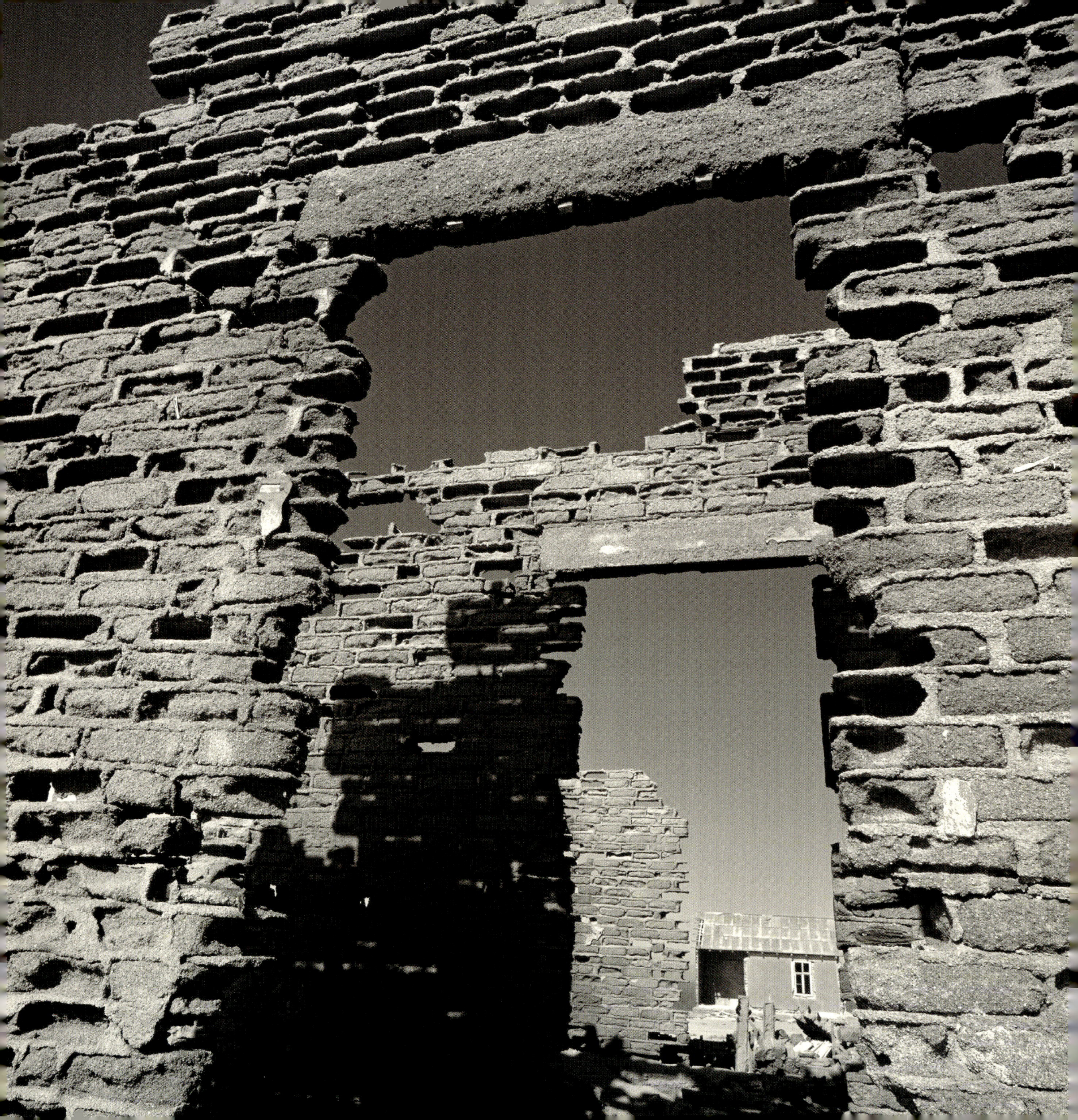

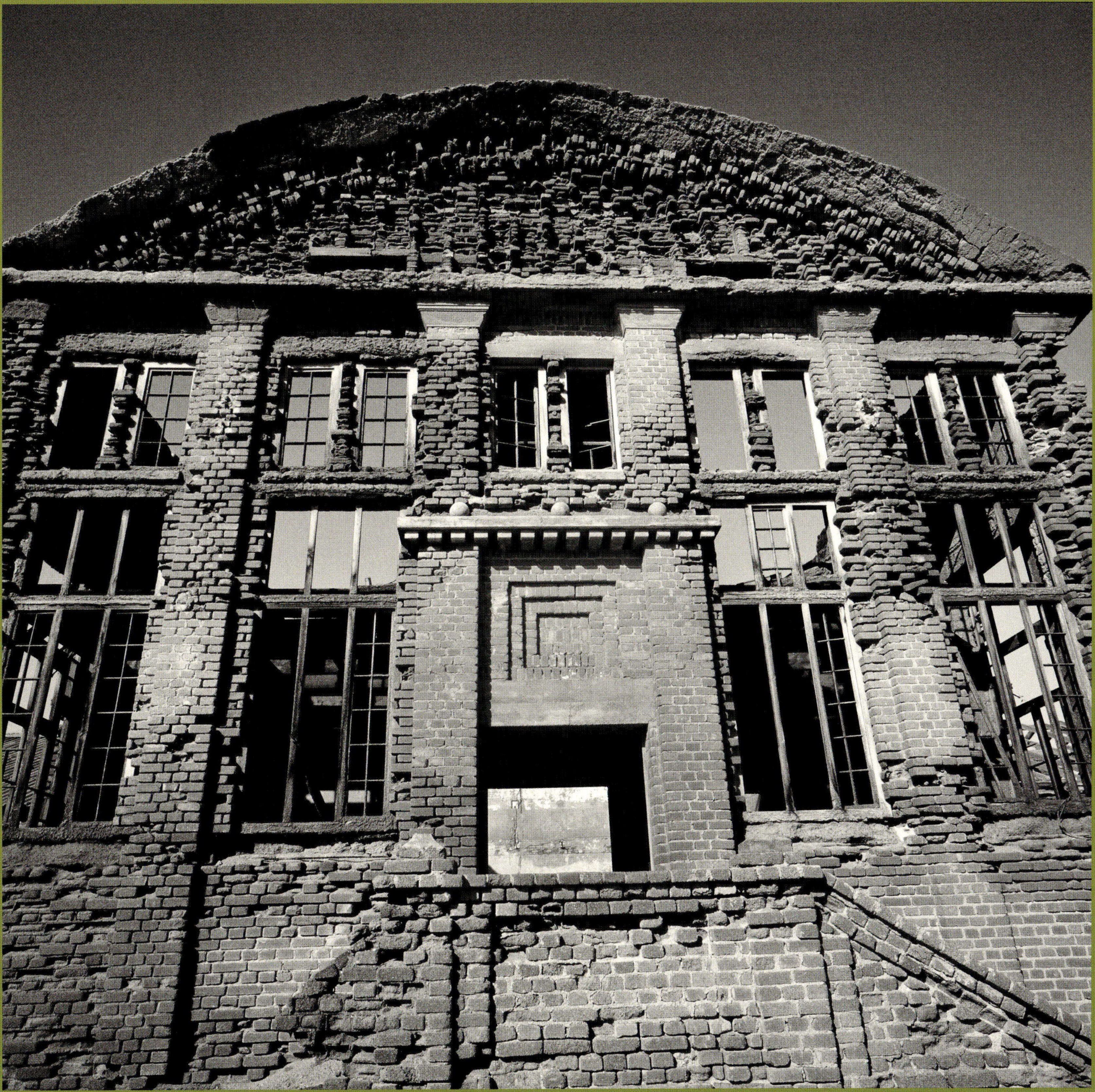

Elizabeth Bay

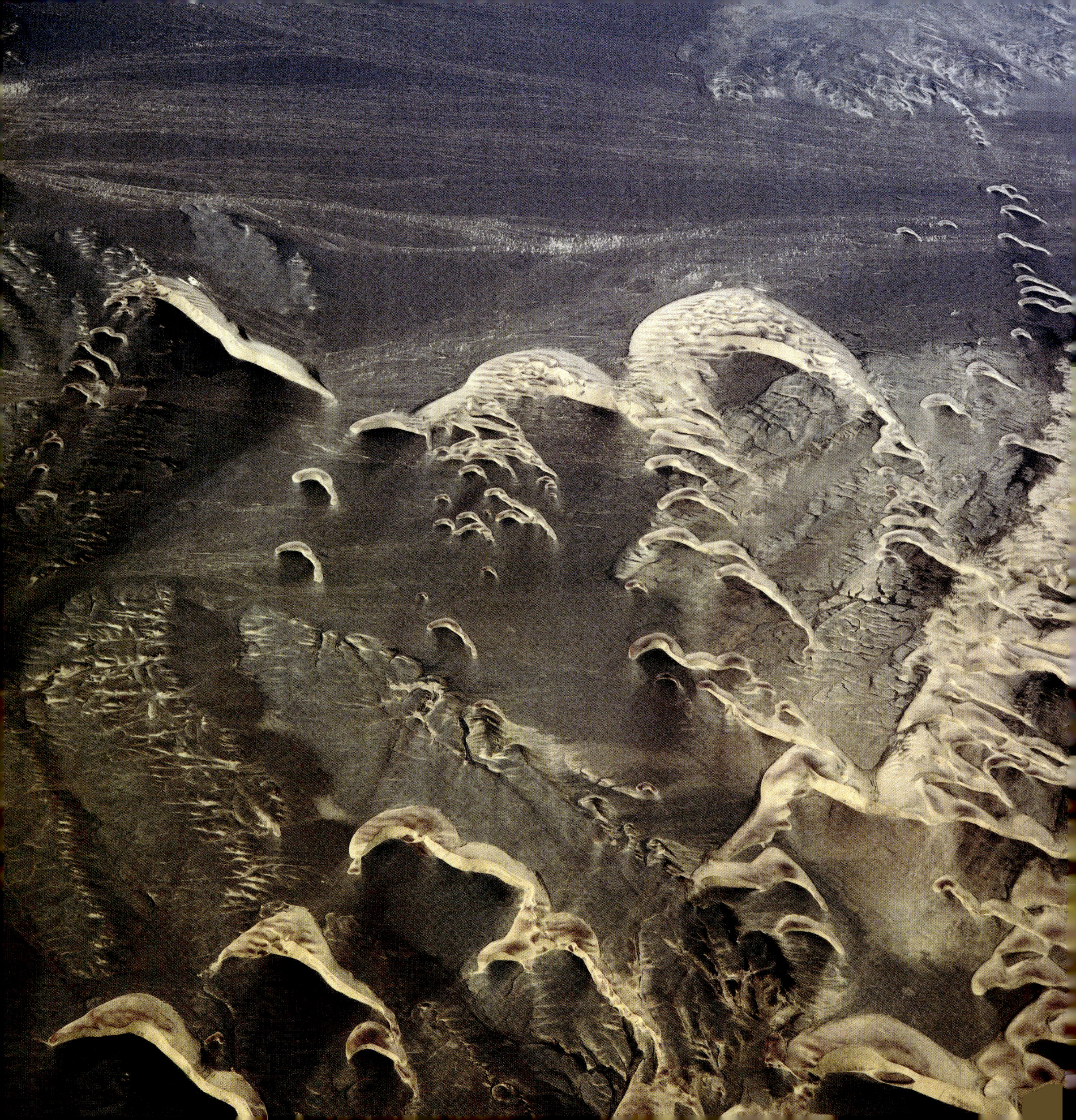

Portfolio 5

NAMIB FROM THE AIR

Selecting the images for this portfolio presented a considerable challenge, as I had released the shutter of my sturdy old Hasselblad with boundless abandon when flying with Louw between his camps in the Skeleton Coast Park, Kaokoland and Damaraland, and in later years over the central and southern Namib, including the "forbidden territory" of the Sperrgebiet. To prepare for these trips, Louw would remove the door on the side of the aircraft where I would be strapped in, enabling me to lean out and angle the camera without having a window frame or part of an aircraft wing in my field of vision, and giving me, when he tilted the aircraft on its side, a full-on view of the scene below. In later years I expanded on this portfolio when flying with Bertus, his oldest, and André, second-oldest son.

It is especially the geological wonders of the Namib that come into their own as ancient landscapes when viewed from above, such as the iconic massif, the Brandberg, at 2574 metres, the highest mountain in Namibia; the Gamsberg, a conspicuous table-topped mountain in the Khomas Hochland, at the height of 2347 metres Namibia's fourth-highest mountain; the incomparable golden-yellow expanses of the Marienfluss in Kaokoland in the Kunene environs; features of the Skeleton Coast Park such as the so-called clay castles of the Hoarusib Canyon, formations of whitish-yellow sedimentary clay; the meandering barchan dunescapes between Terrace Bay and Torra Bay, their maroon-backed crescent-shaped dunes migrating north-eastwards, set off by the winding black streets of magnetite and ilmenite in between; Namibia's magical mega-feature Sossusvlei, sought after for its monumental star-shaped dunes with their deep, warm hues and gleaming white pans of desiccated cracked mud; the eerie Dead Pan dotted with ancient skeletons of camel-thorn trees; the mysteriously beautiful silver saltpan north of Lüderitz; and the awe-inspiring wreck of the *Otavi* in Spencer Bay in the Sperrgebiet.

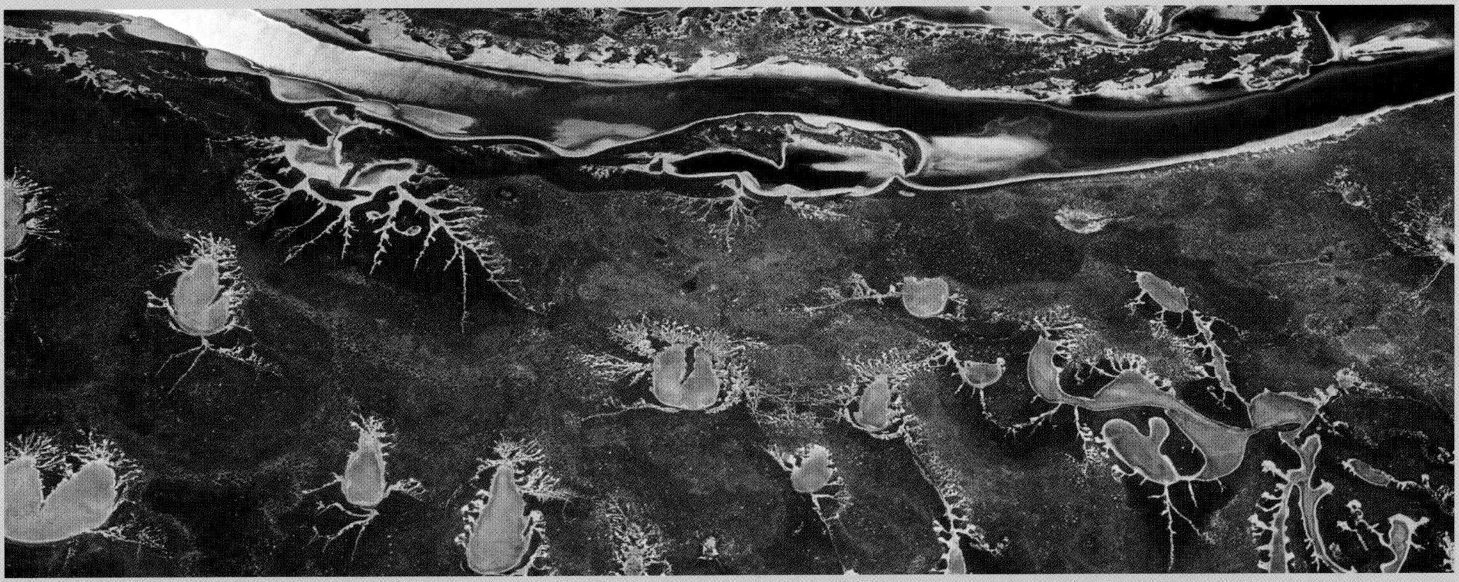

(OPPOSITE) Barchan dunes north of Lüderitz (ABOVE) Etosha Fantasy

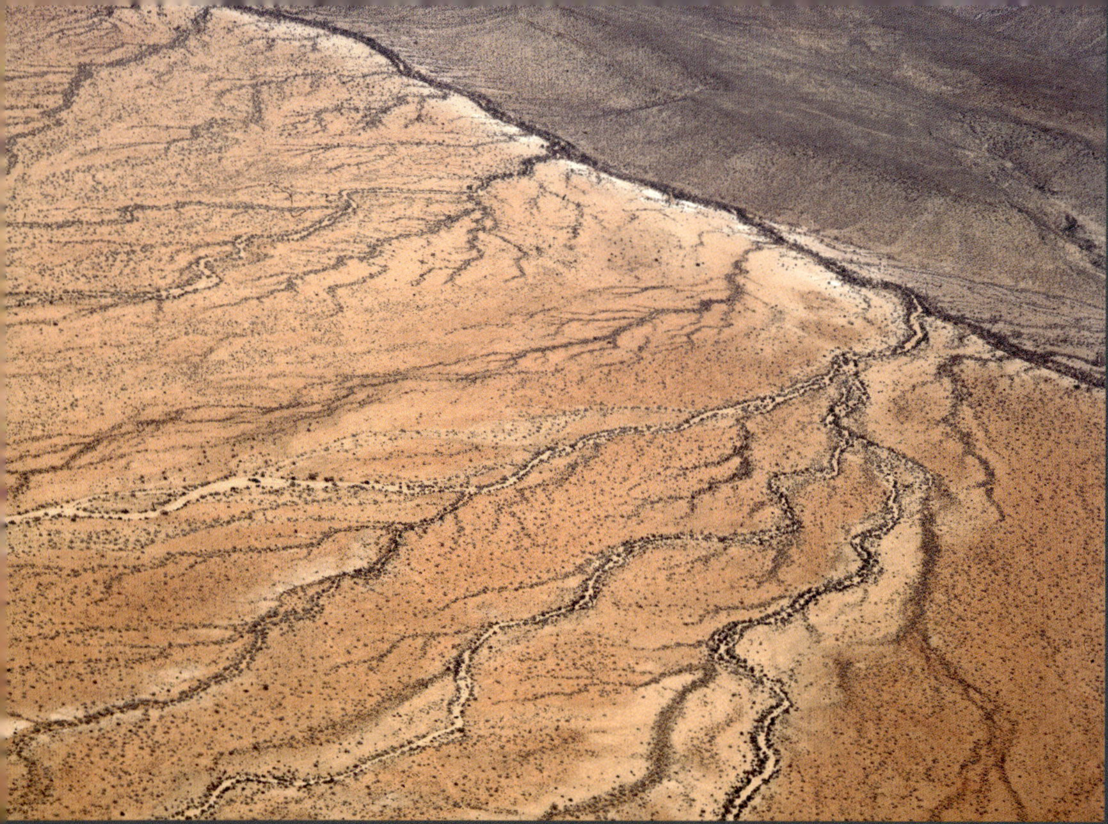

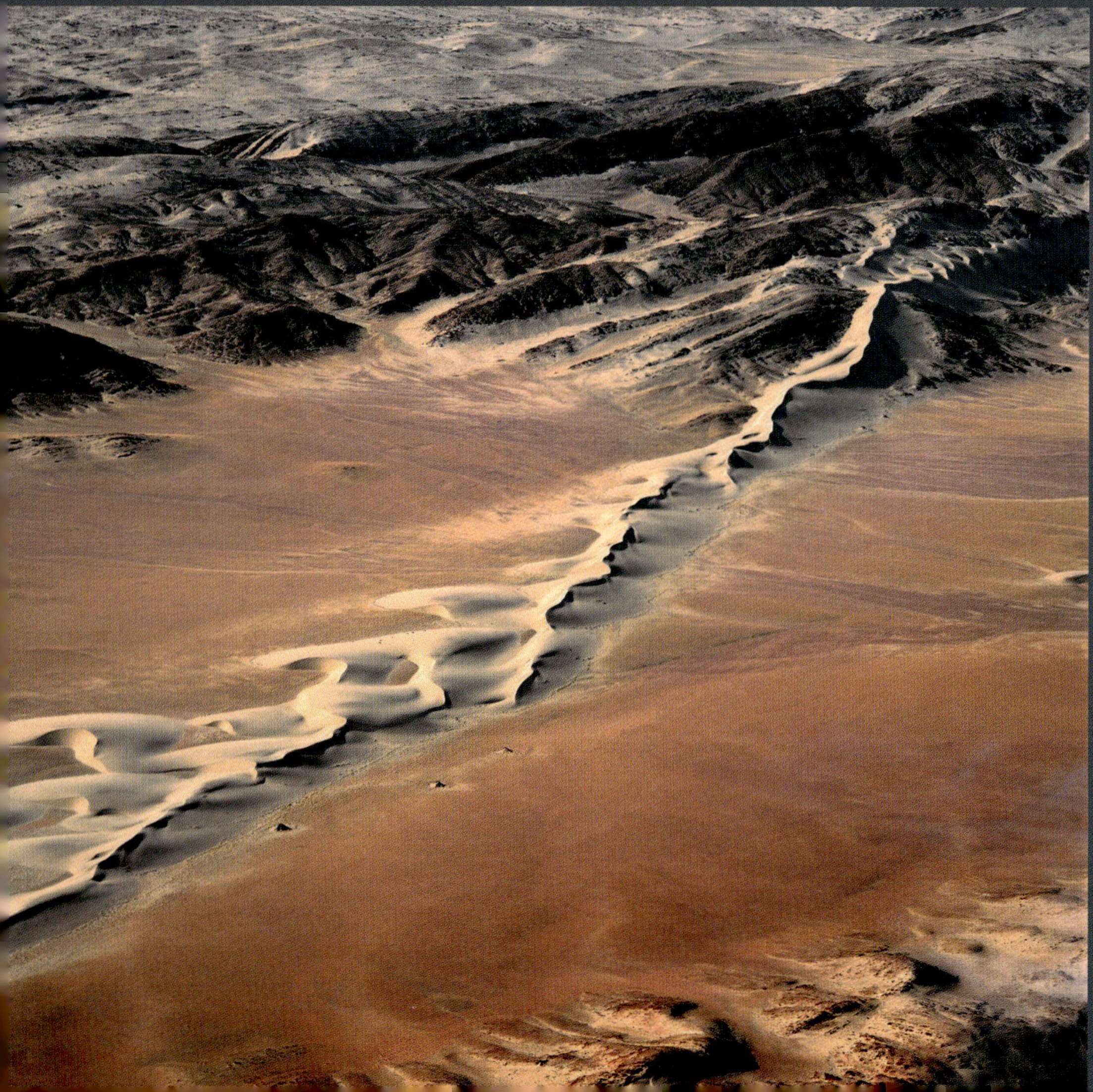

The action of the wind on these ever-shifting sands is also worthy of notice. The dry light sand is heaped up in a ridge by the first gust capable of scooping a hollow in the surface; gradually it advances like a wave of the sea with its steepest side leeward, and the sand flying from its crest seems so like the ocean spray, that the similarity is almost complete.

Thomas Baines, *Explorations in South-West Africa being an Account of a Journey in the Years 1861 and 1862 from Walvisch Bay, on the Western Coast to Lake Ngami and the Victoria Falls*, London: Longman, Green, Longman, Roberts & Green, 1864: 5

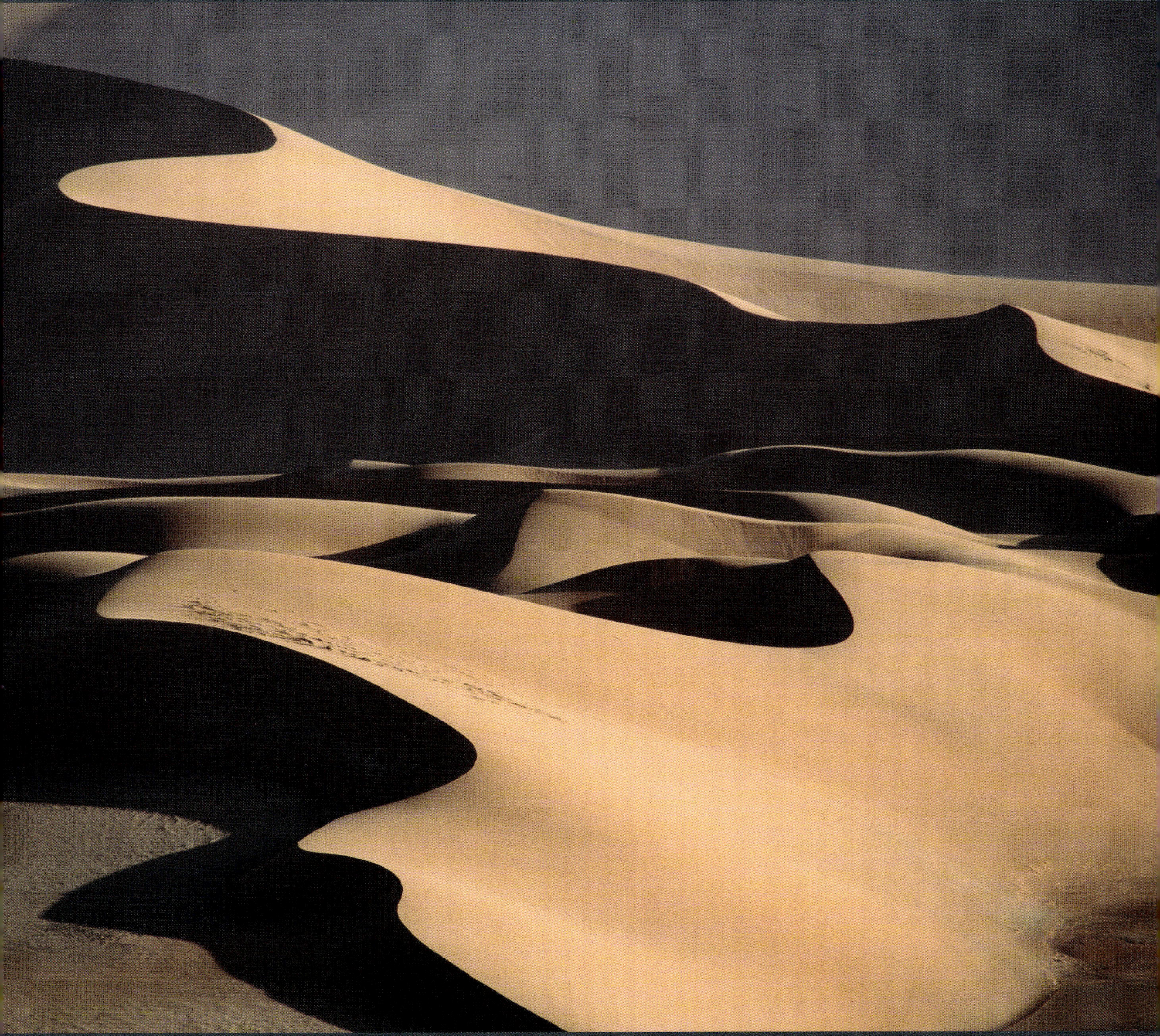

(OPPOSITE TOP) Engo Aerial (OPPOSITE BOTTOM) Engo Valley (ABOVE) Sossusvlei Dunescape

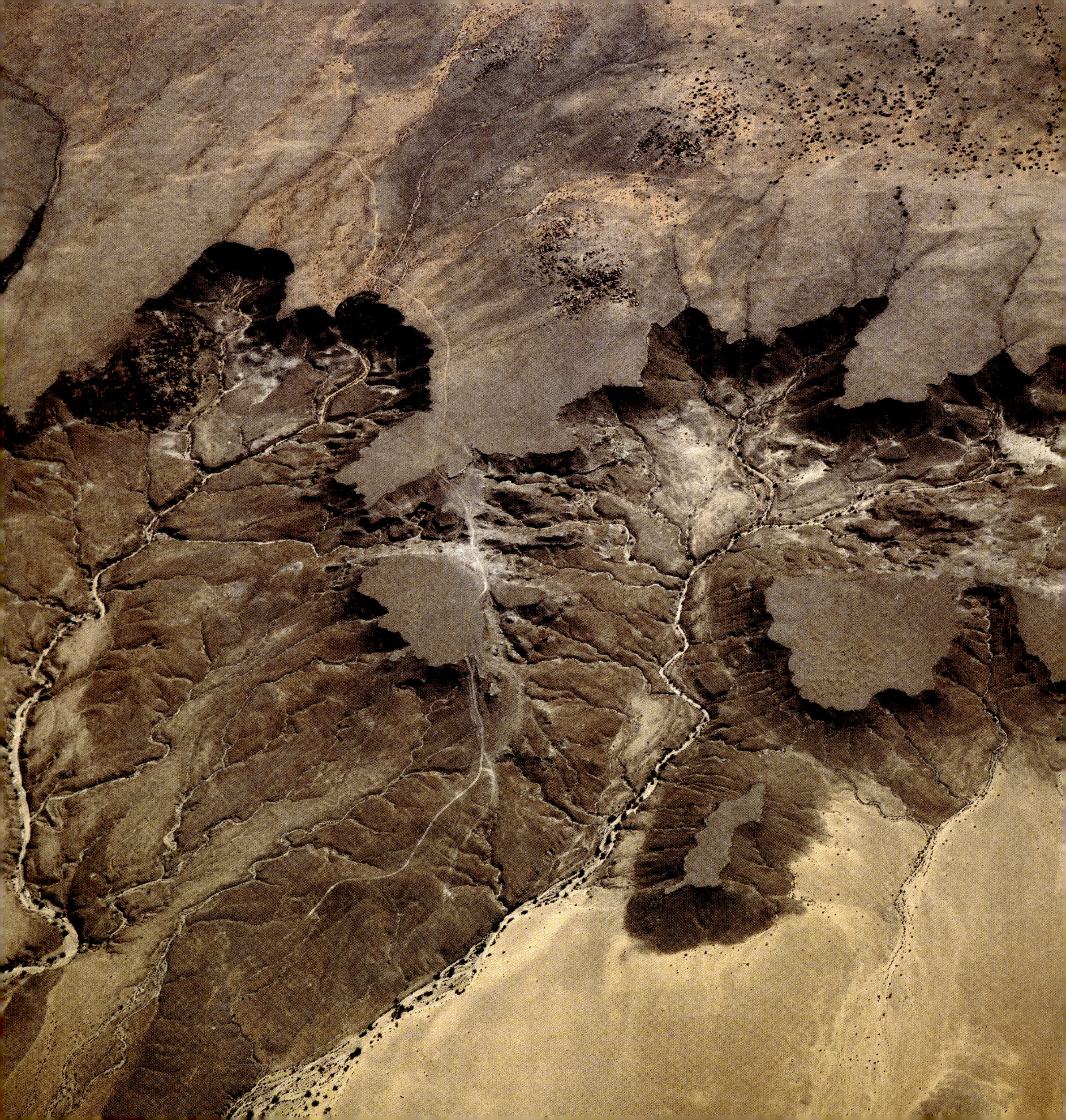

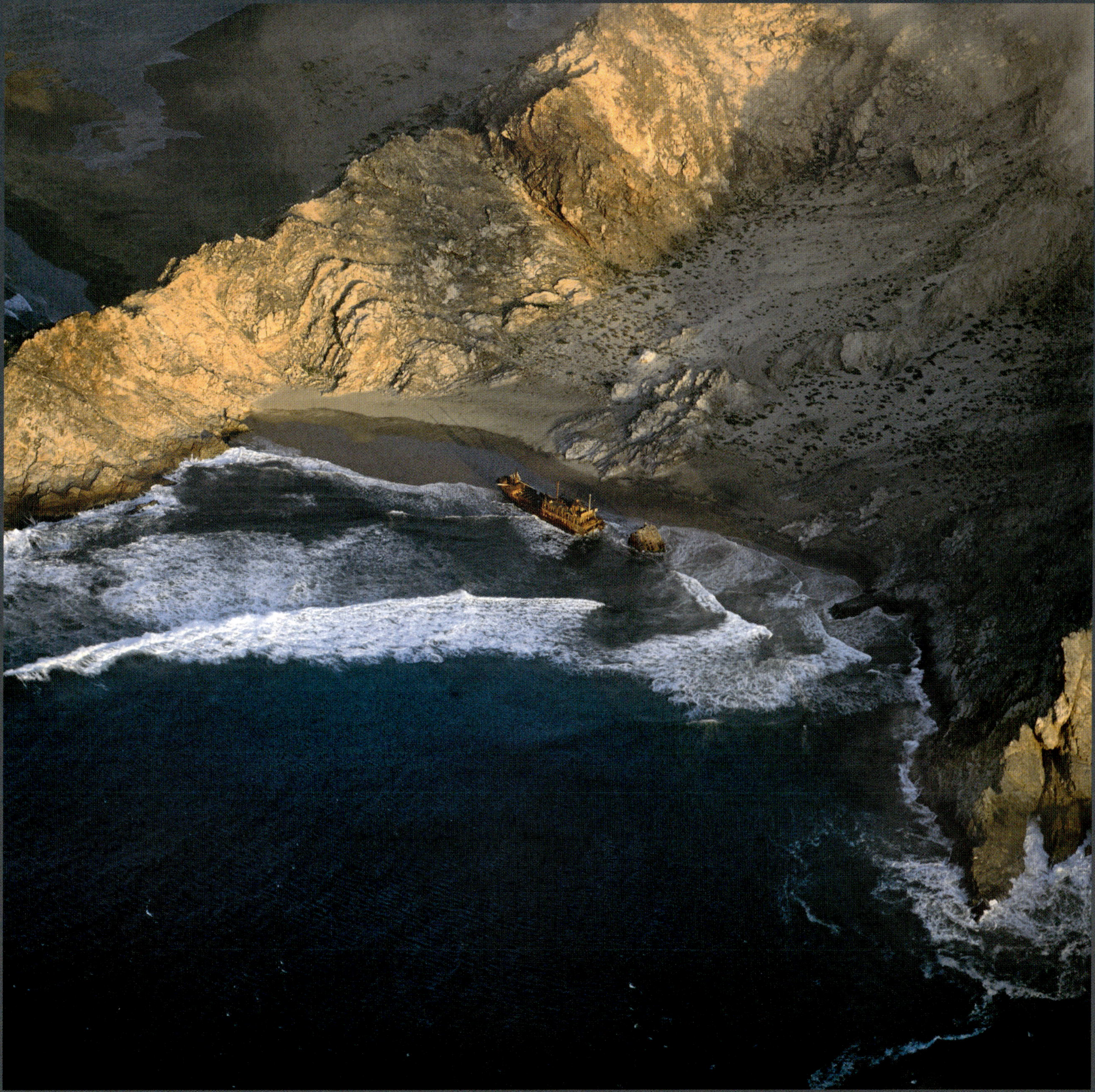

(OPPOSITE) Tablelands, northern Namibia (ABOVE) Wreck of the *Otavi*, Spencer Bay

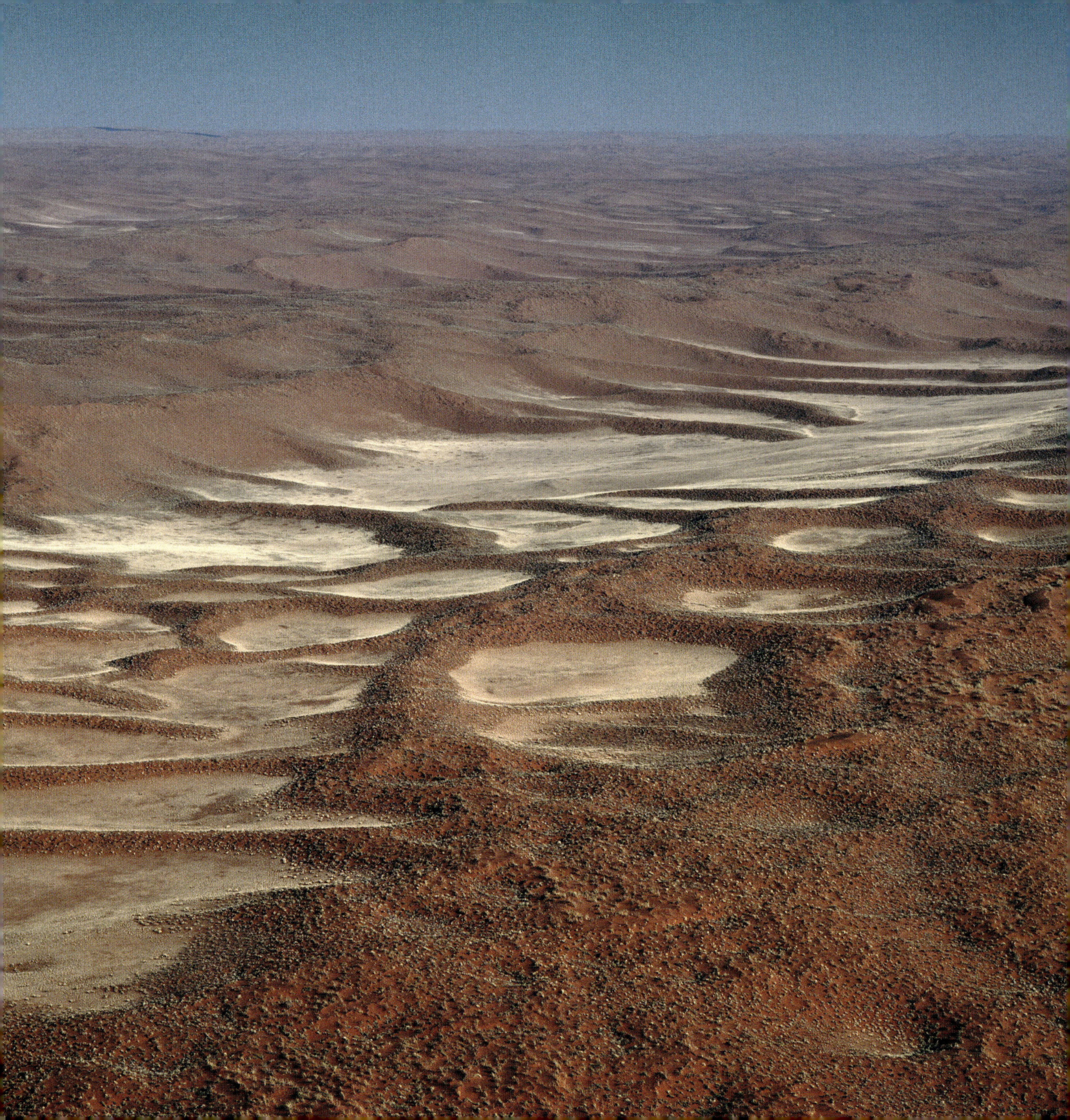

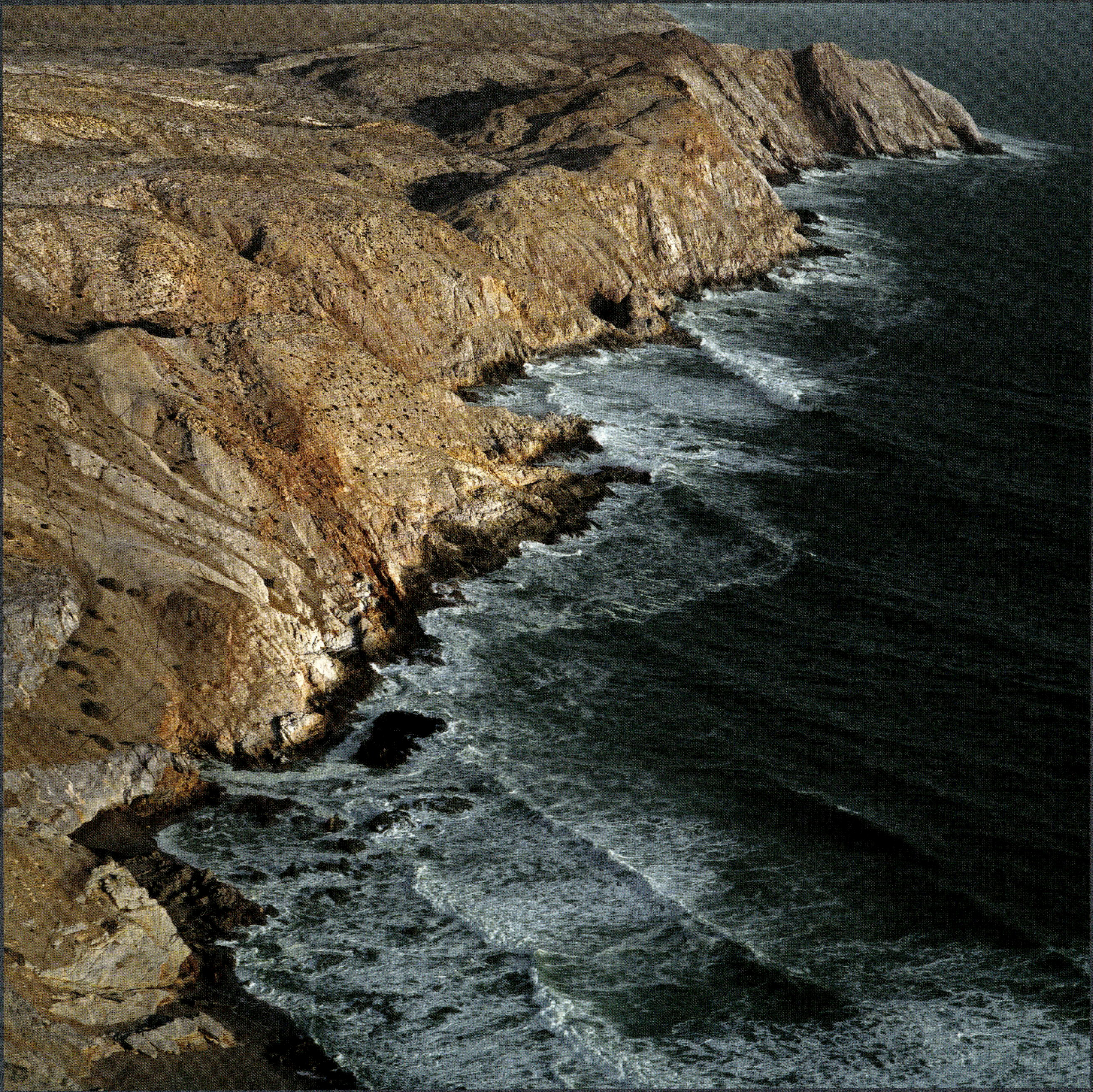

(OPPOSITE) Odondojengo Lowlands (ABOVE) Coast north of Lüderitz

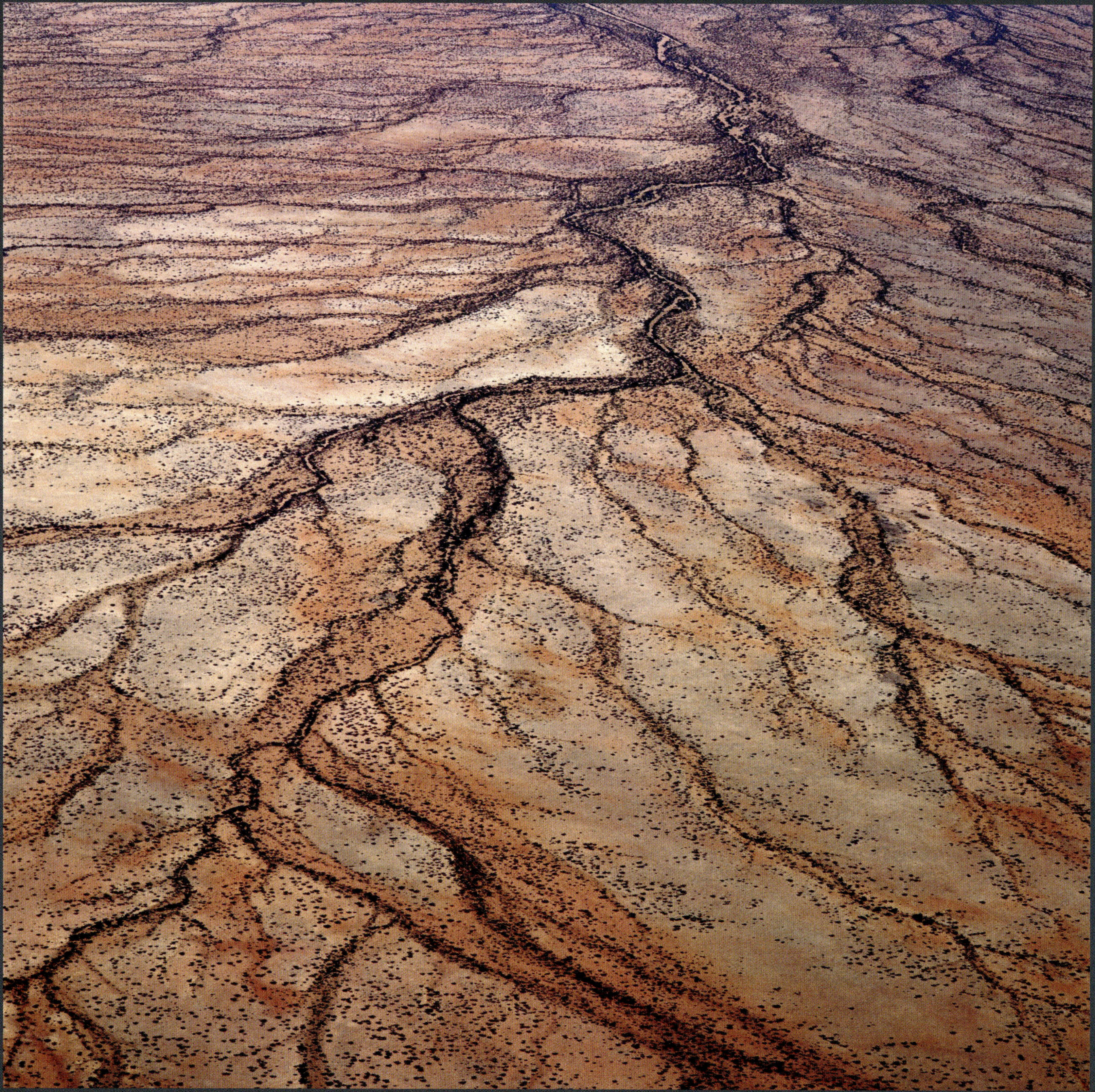

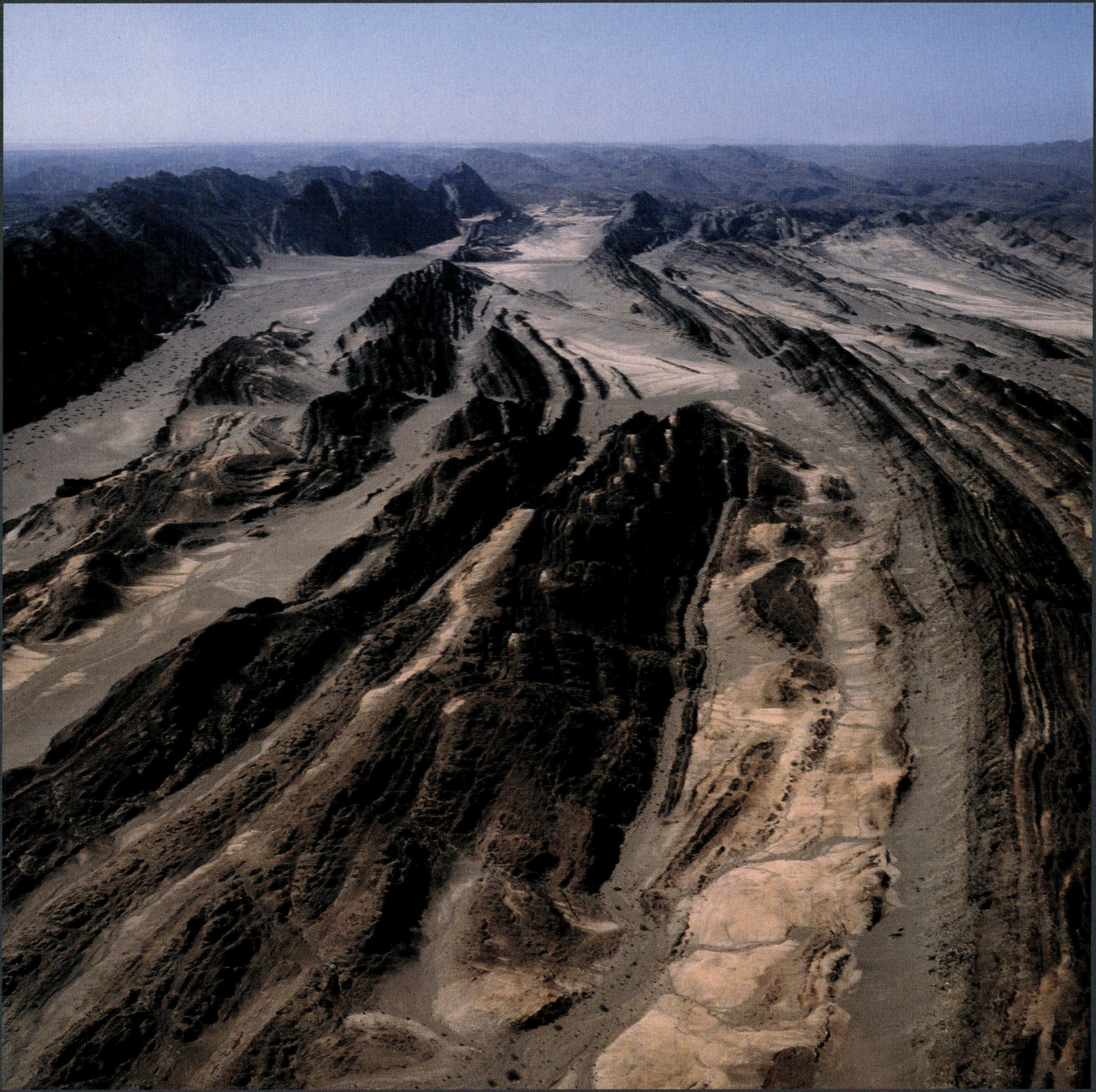

(OPPOSITE) Okonjenje Plains (ABOVE) Ugab Sediments

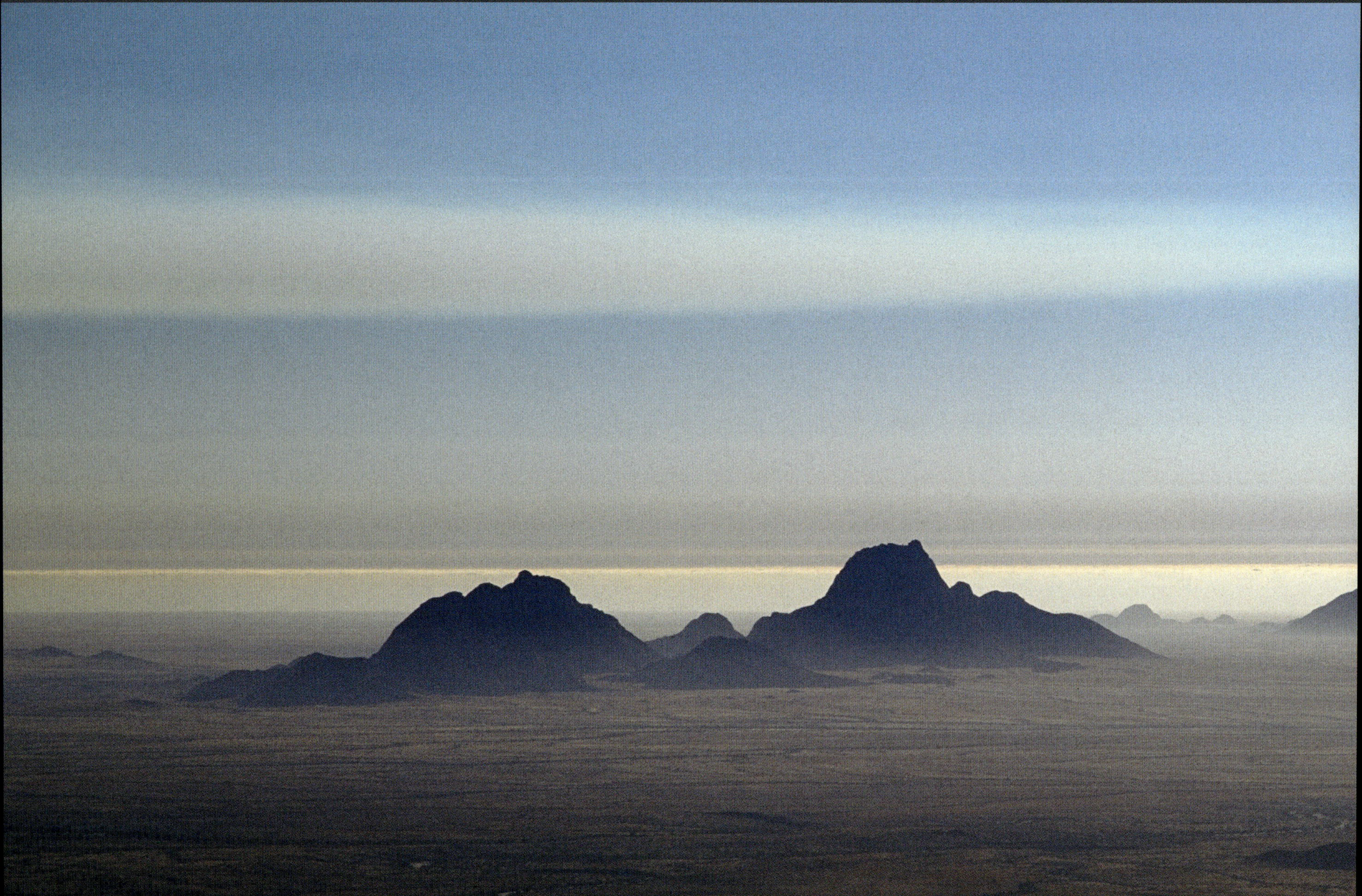

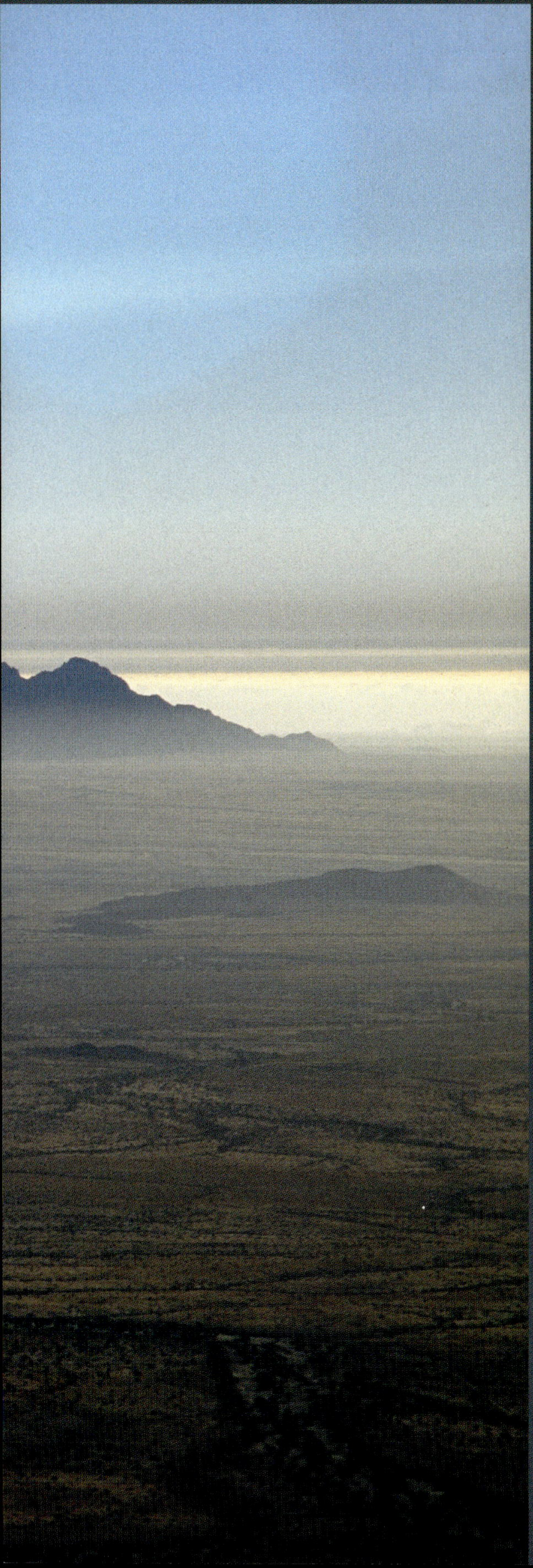

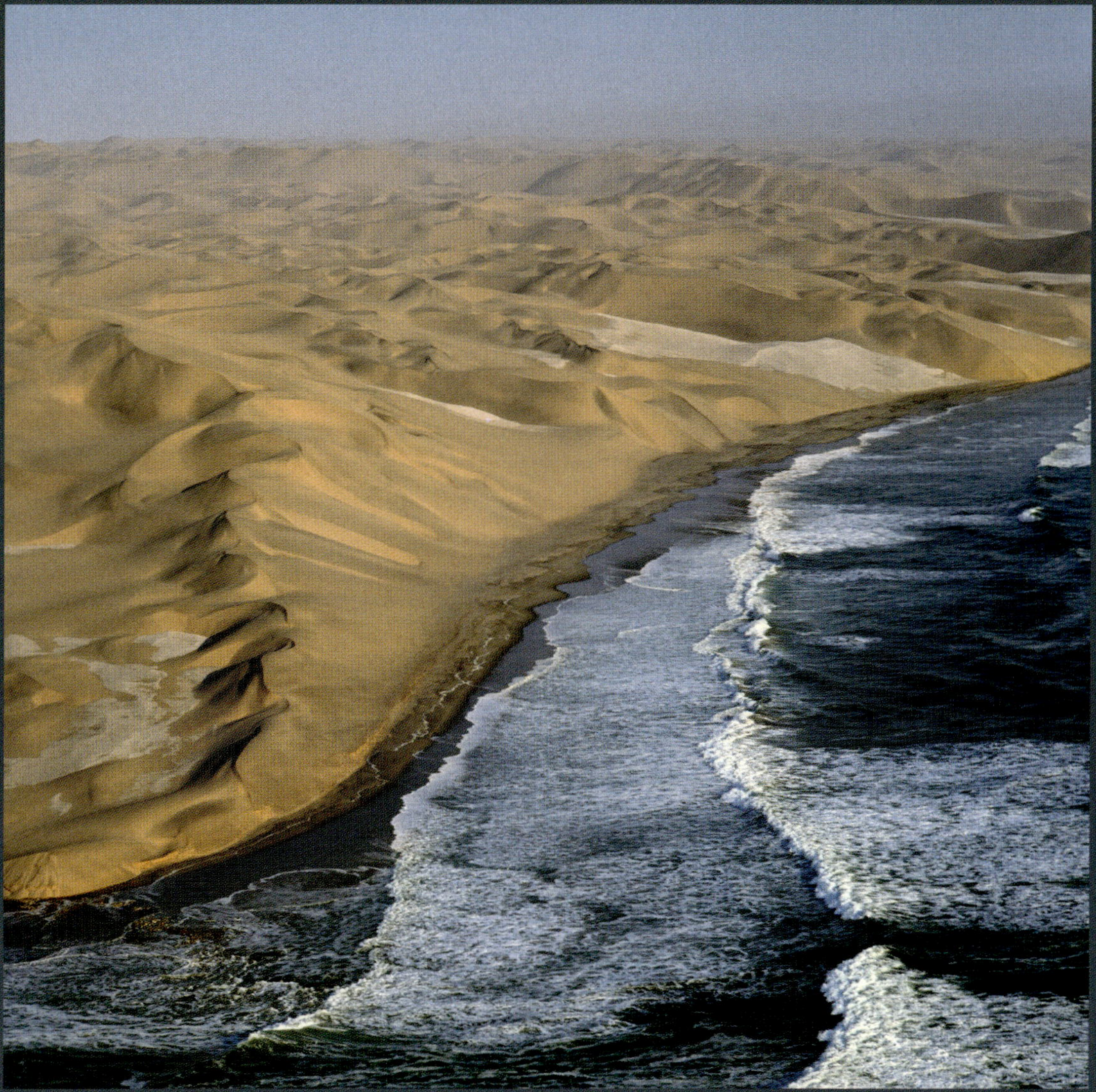

(OPPOSITE) Spitzkoppe (ABOVE) Skeleton Coast

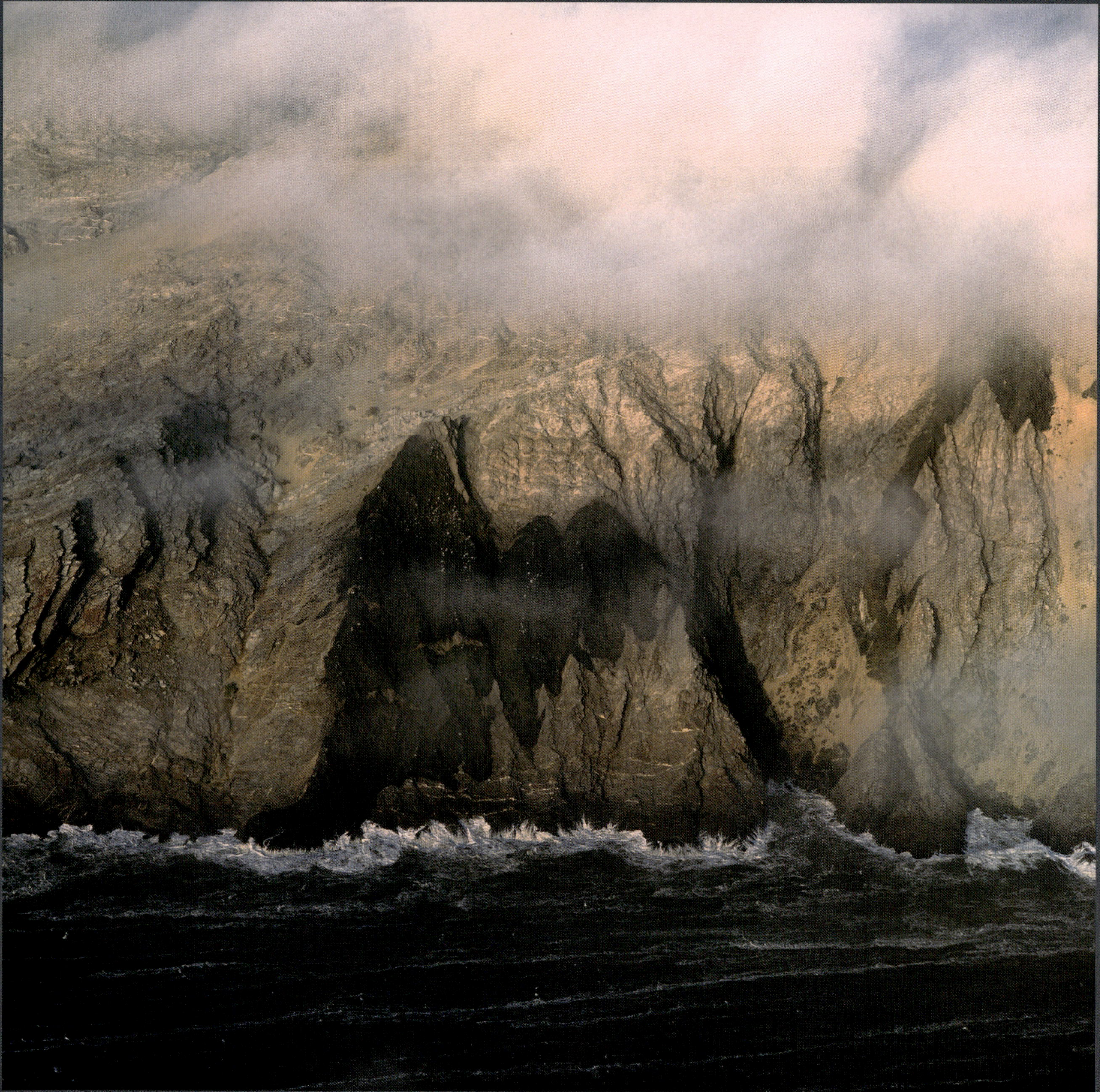

GAMSBERG

A lonely Shepherd's Tree, avatar of the gods // Marooned on a slope
As a liquid sun sets in the distant West // The land dreamlike

André du Pisani, Hornkrantz South, 2007

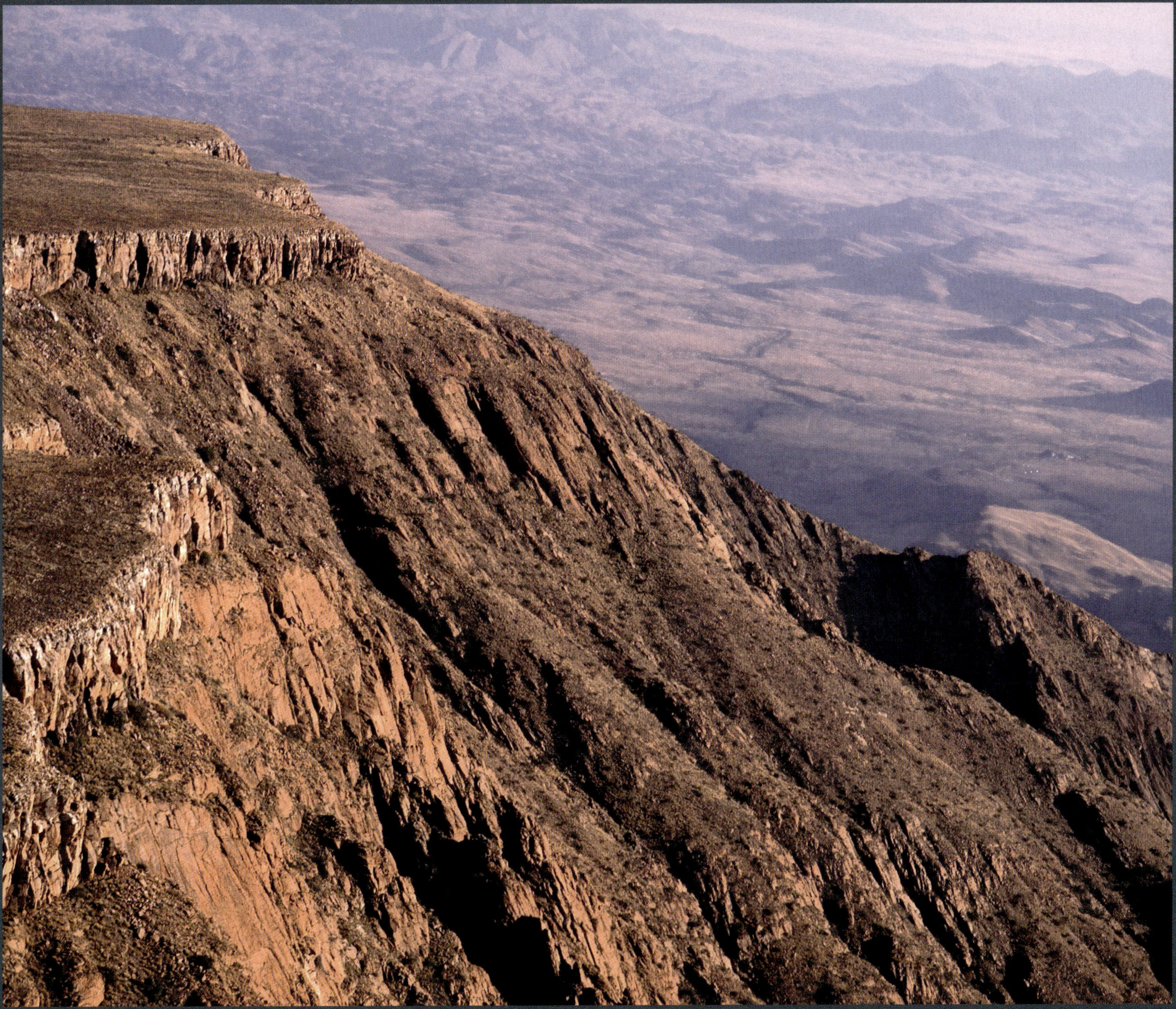

(OPPOSITE) Misty Morning, Sperrgebiet coast (ABOVE) Gamsberg Cliffs

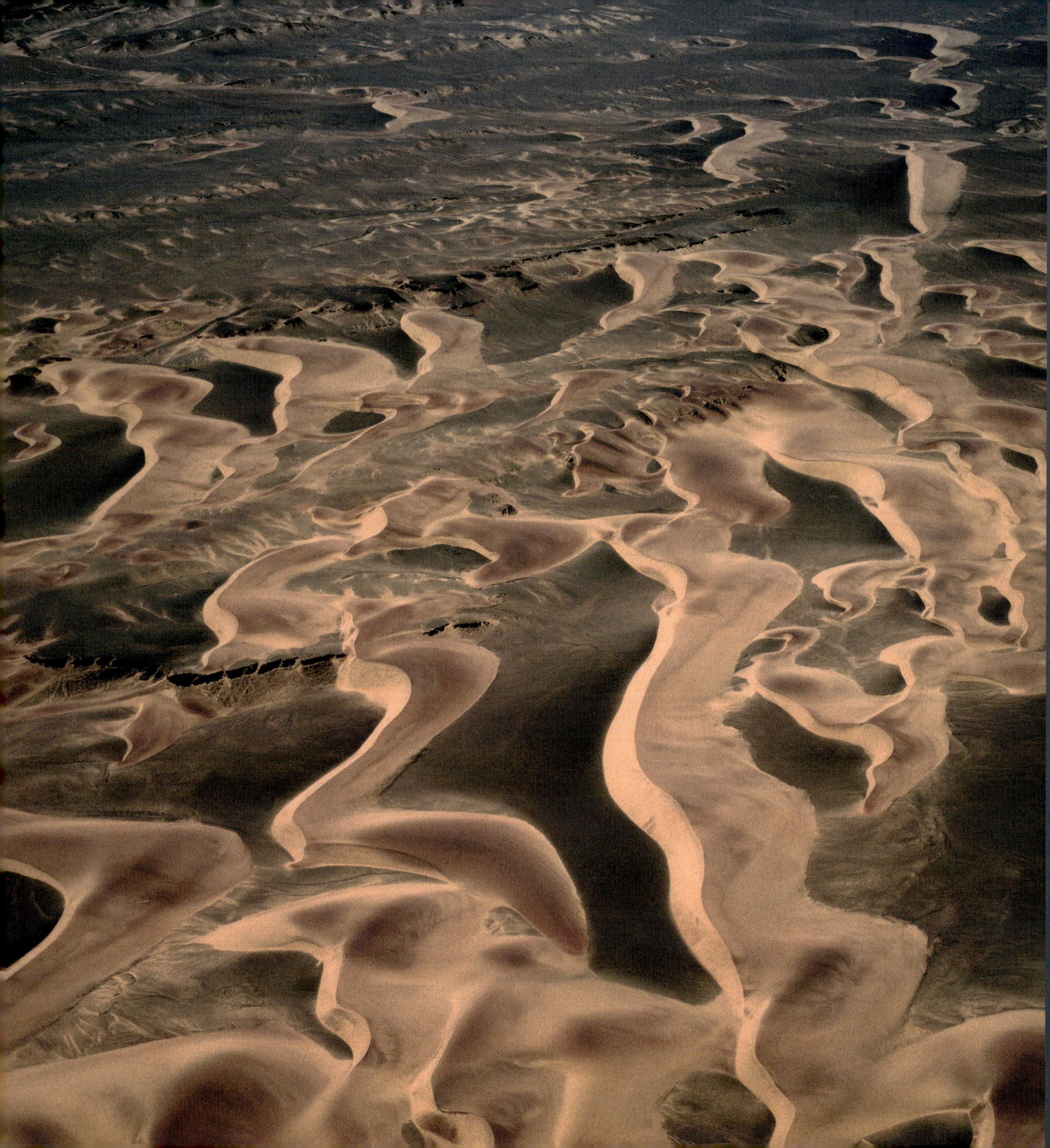

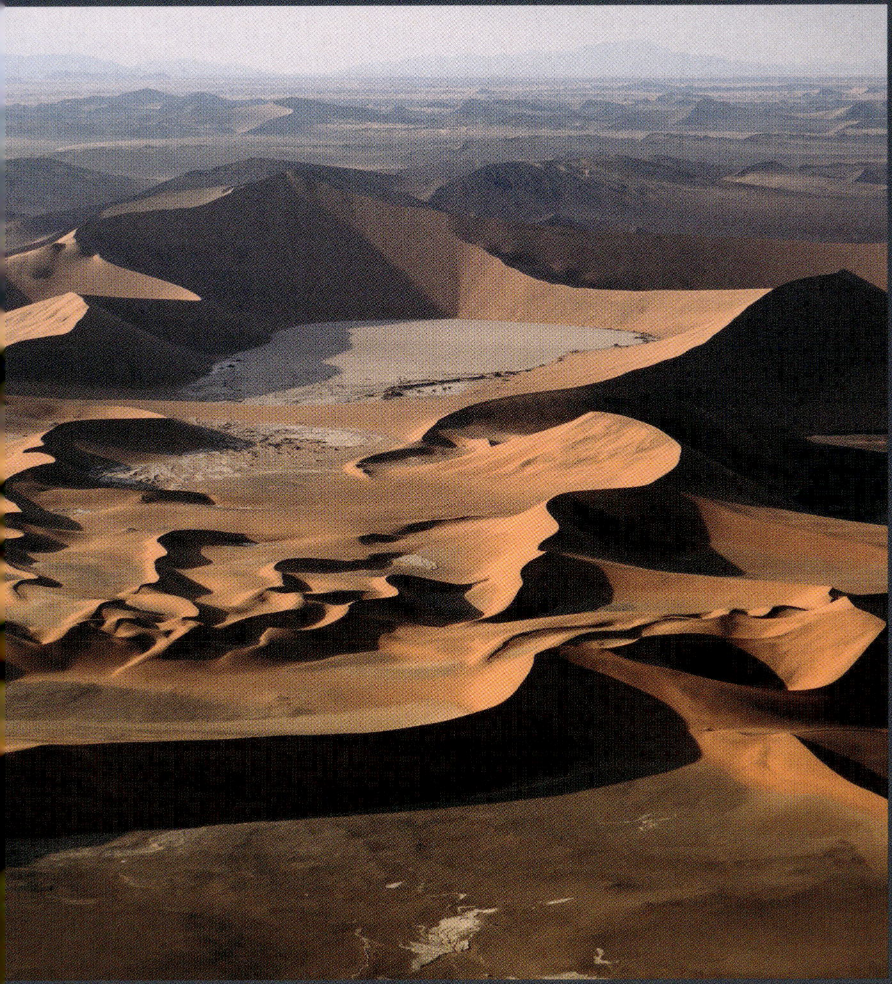

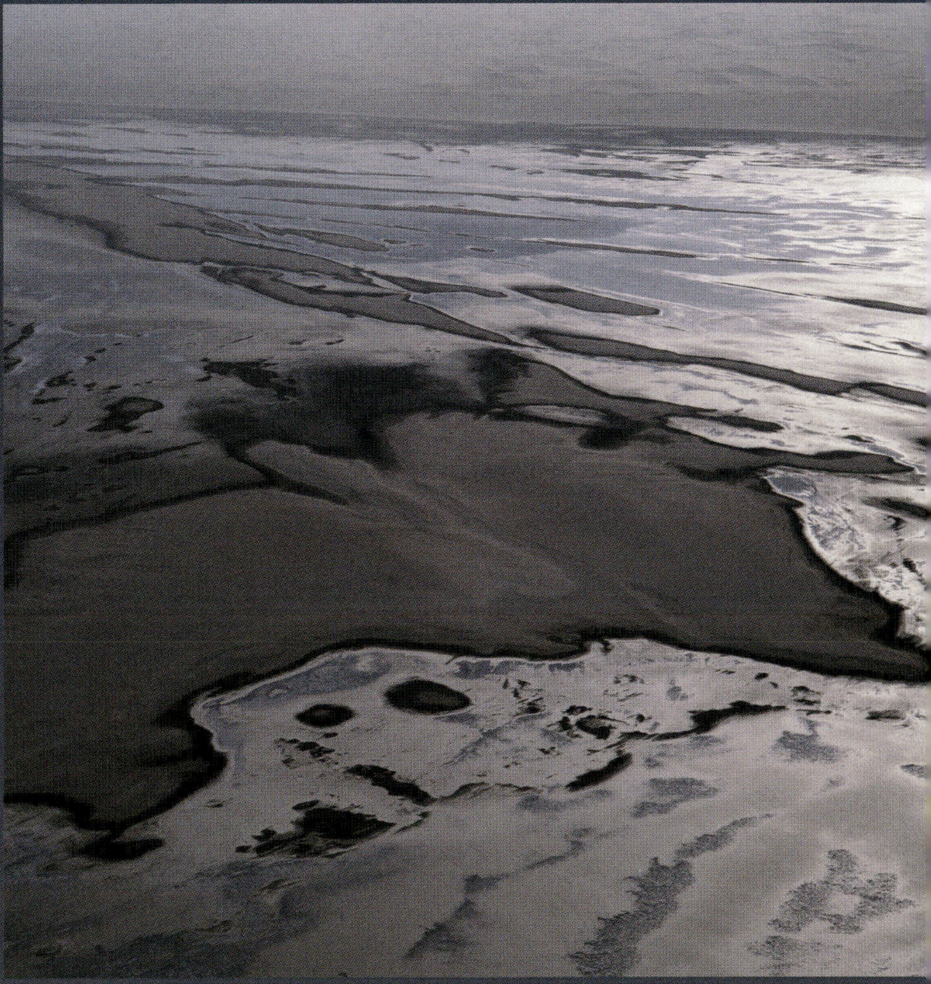

Arriving in Windhoek from London in 1974, my mother, me and my two brothers in tow, was a revelation. I remember emerging from my Oupa's winter-chilled house and standing under a flawlessly unbroken, intense blue African sky for the first time. This spiritual connection, that numinous shiver down your spine that lights up your brain, is the essence of fine art, an out-of-body experience unique to the human mind.

Dorian Cosburn, son of author

(OPPOSITE) Barchan Dunescape, between Terrace and Torra Bay

(ABOVE LEFT) Sossusvlei from the Air (ABOVE RIGHT) Silver Saltpan, north of Lüderitz

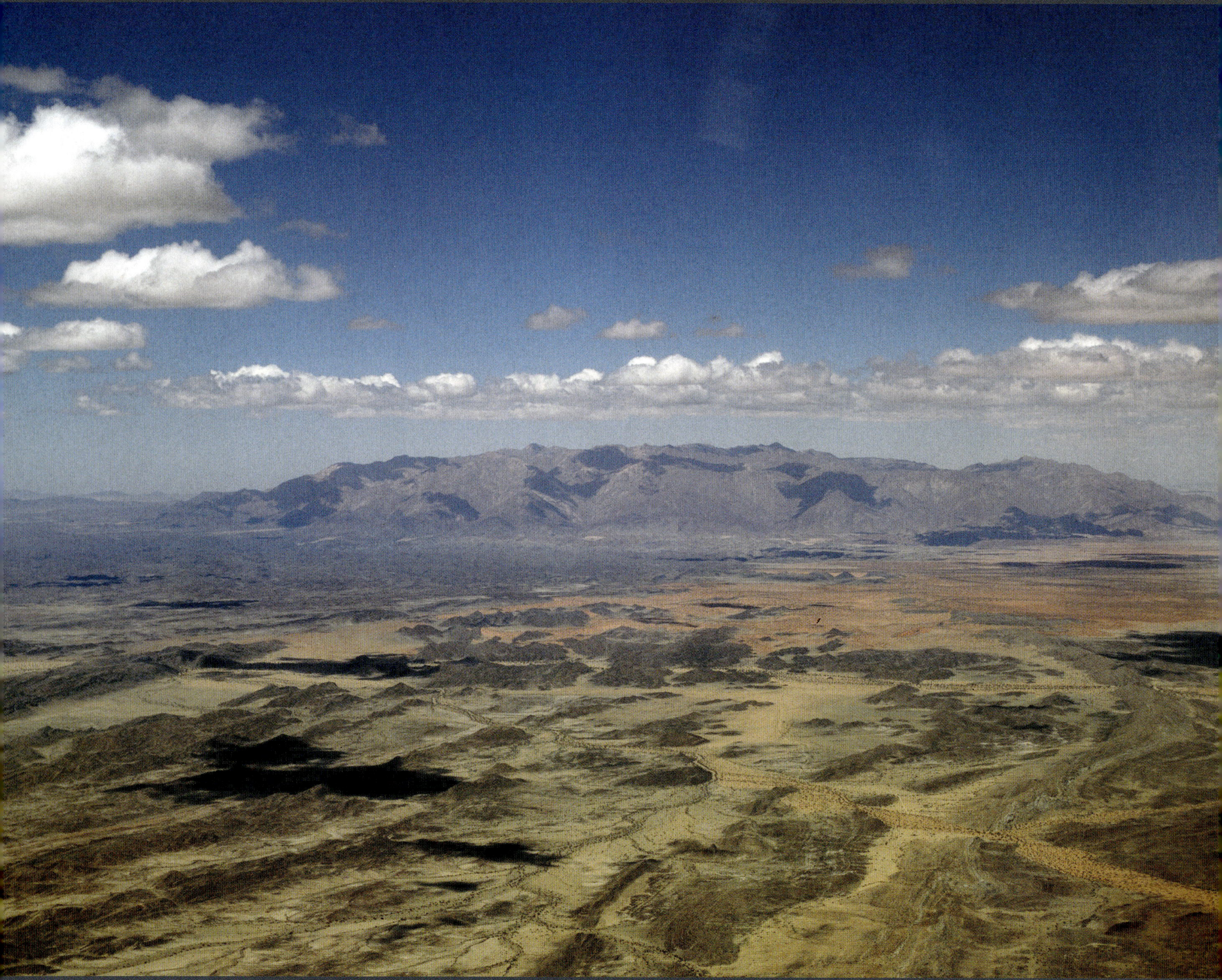

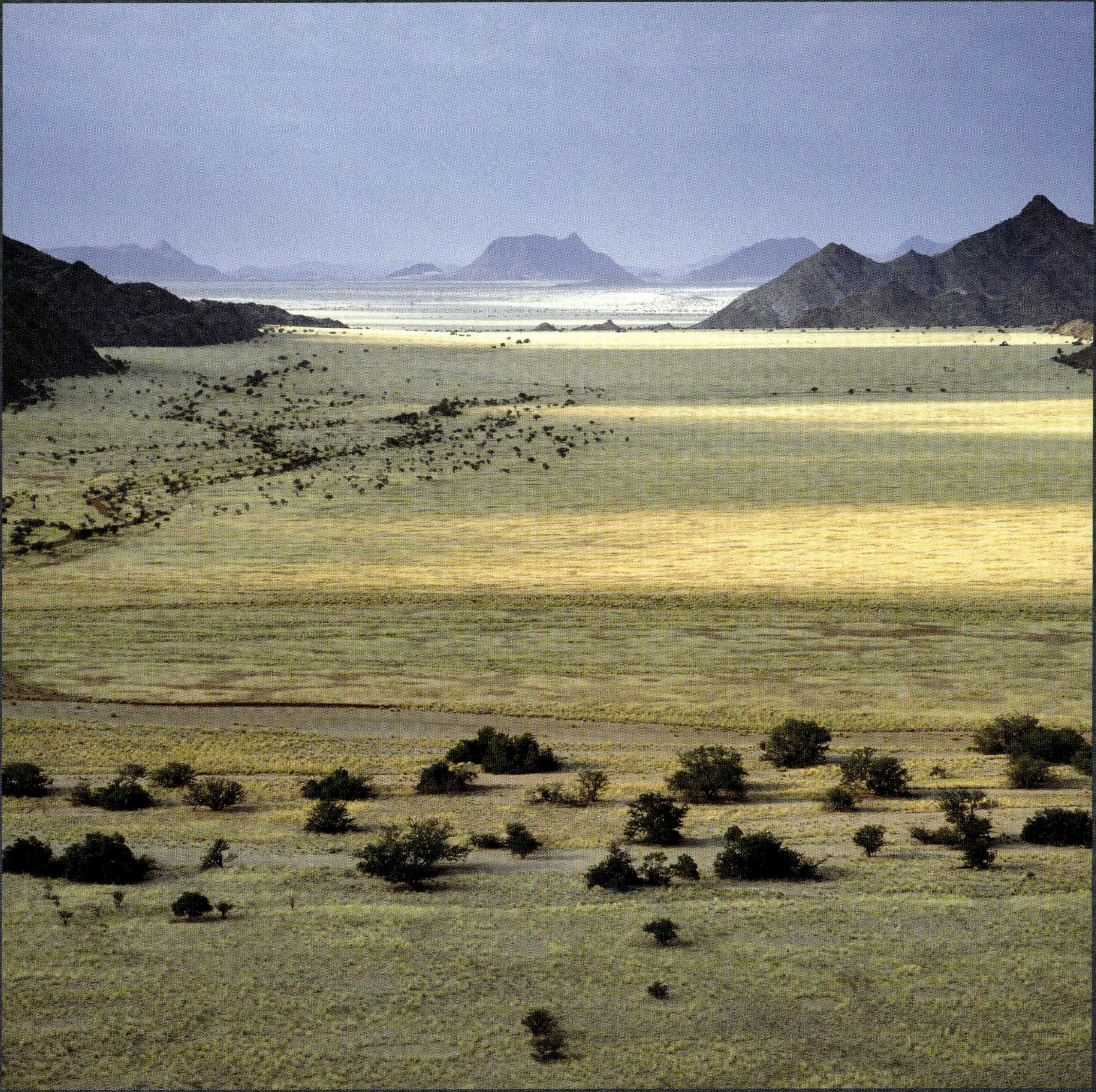

(OPPOSITE) Brandberg (ABOVE) Marienfluss

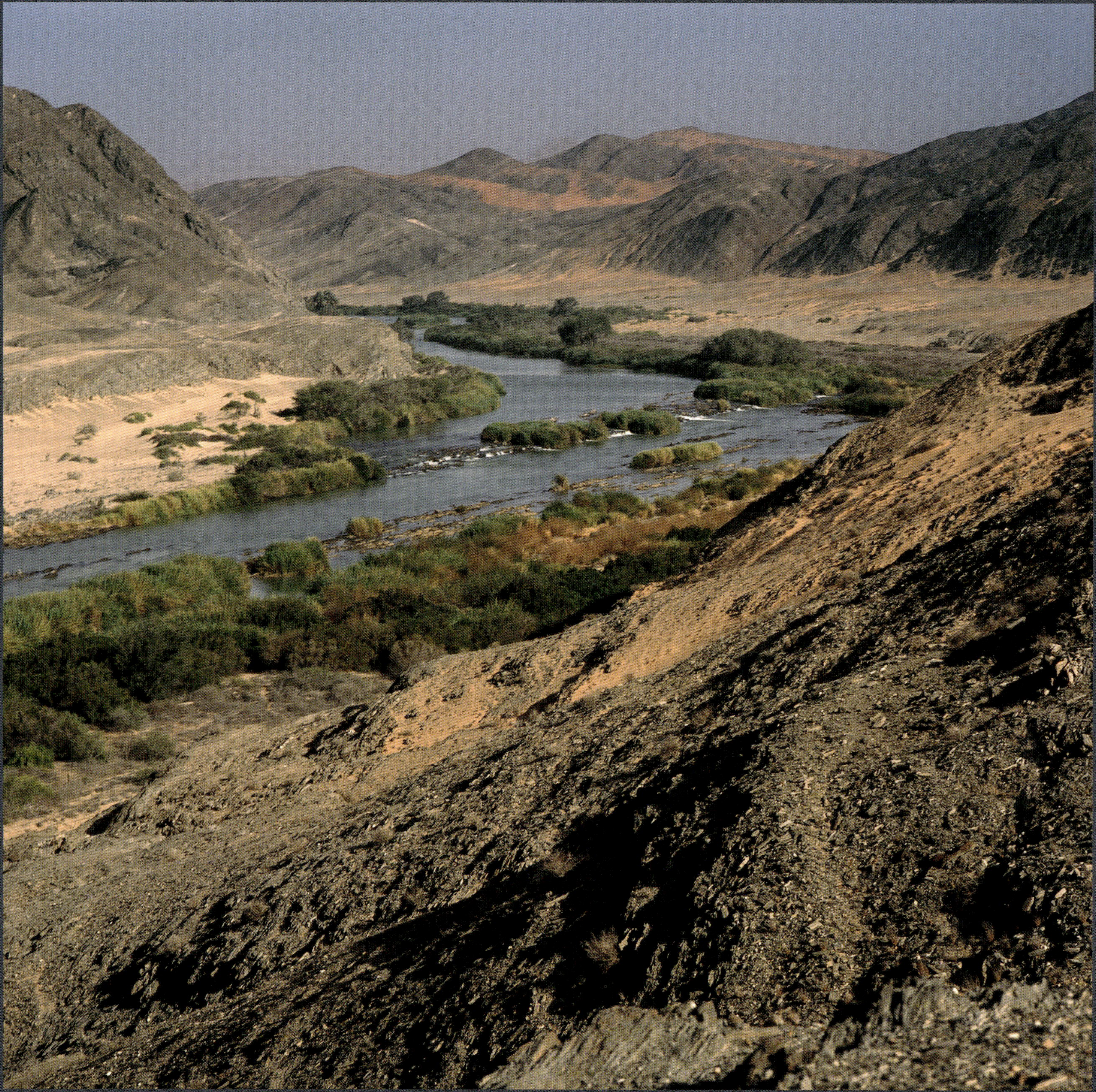

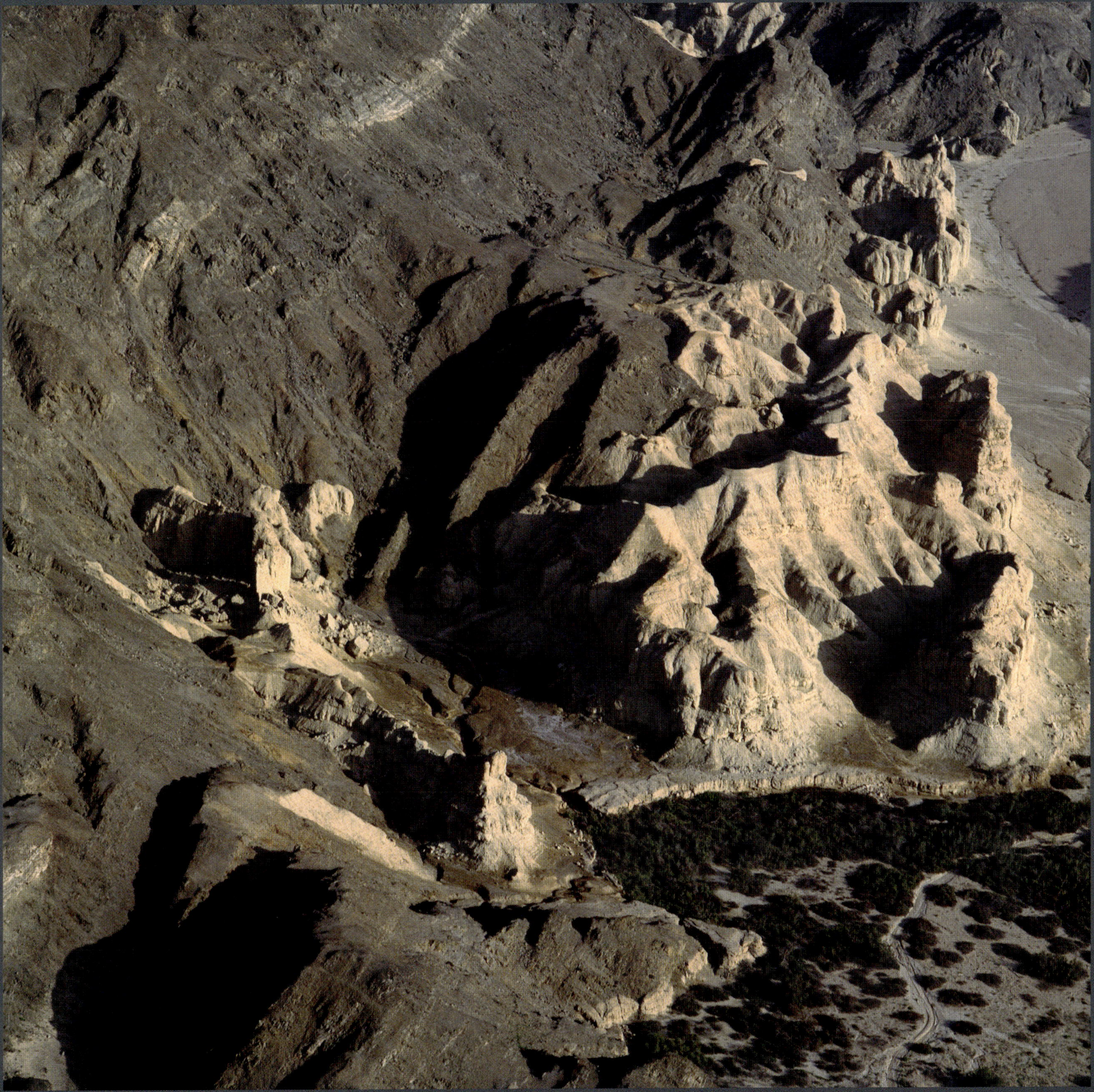

(OPPOSITE) Kunene River (ABOVE) Clay Castles of the Hoarusib

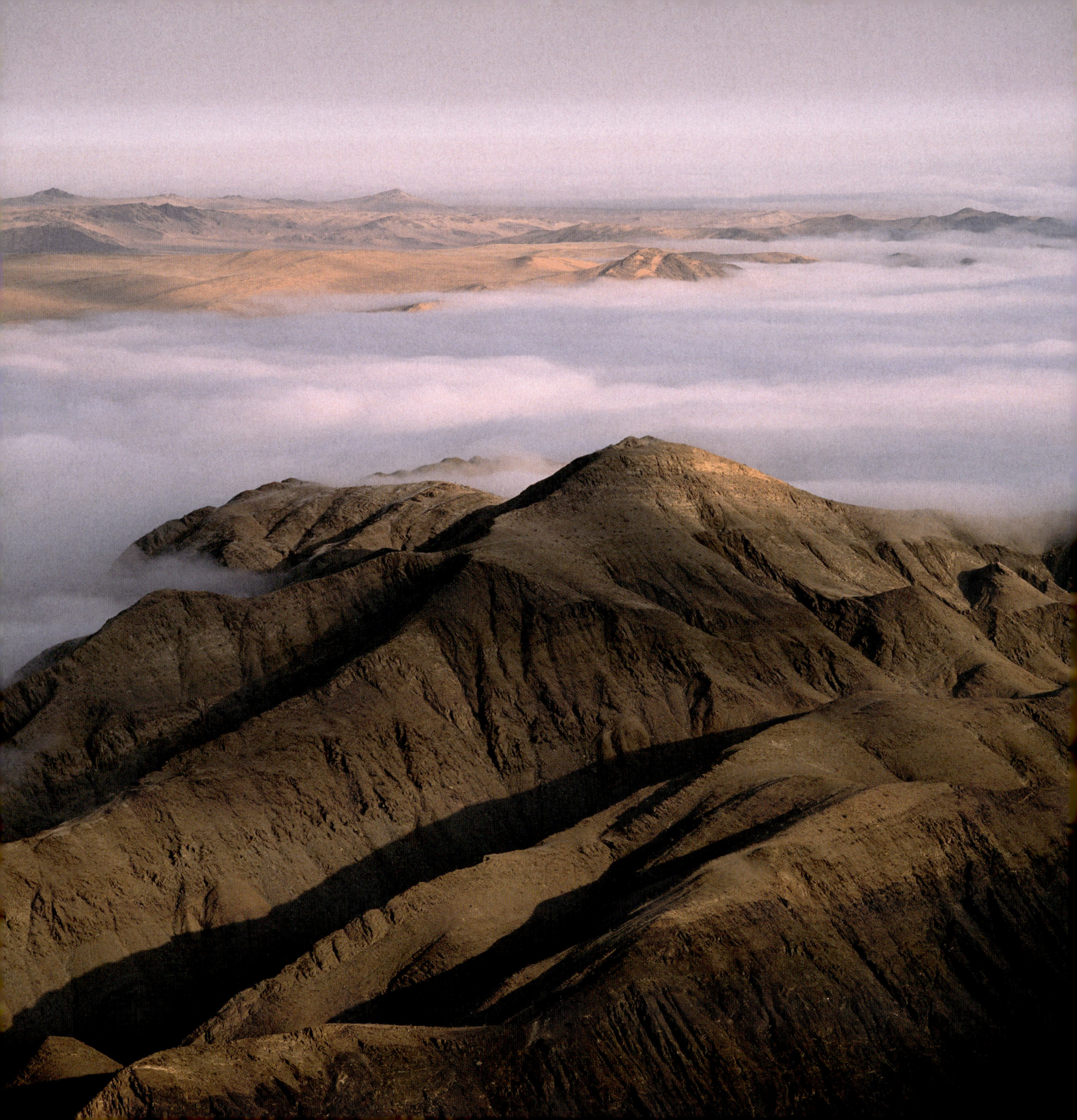

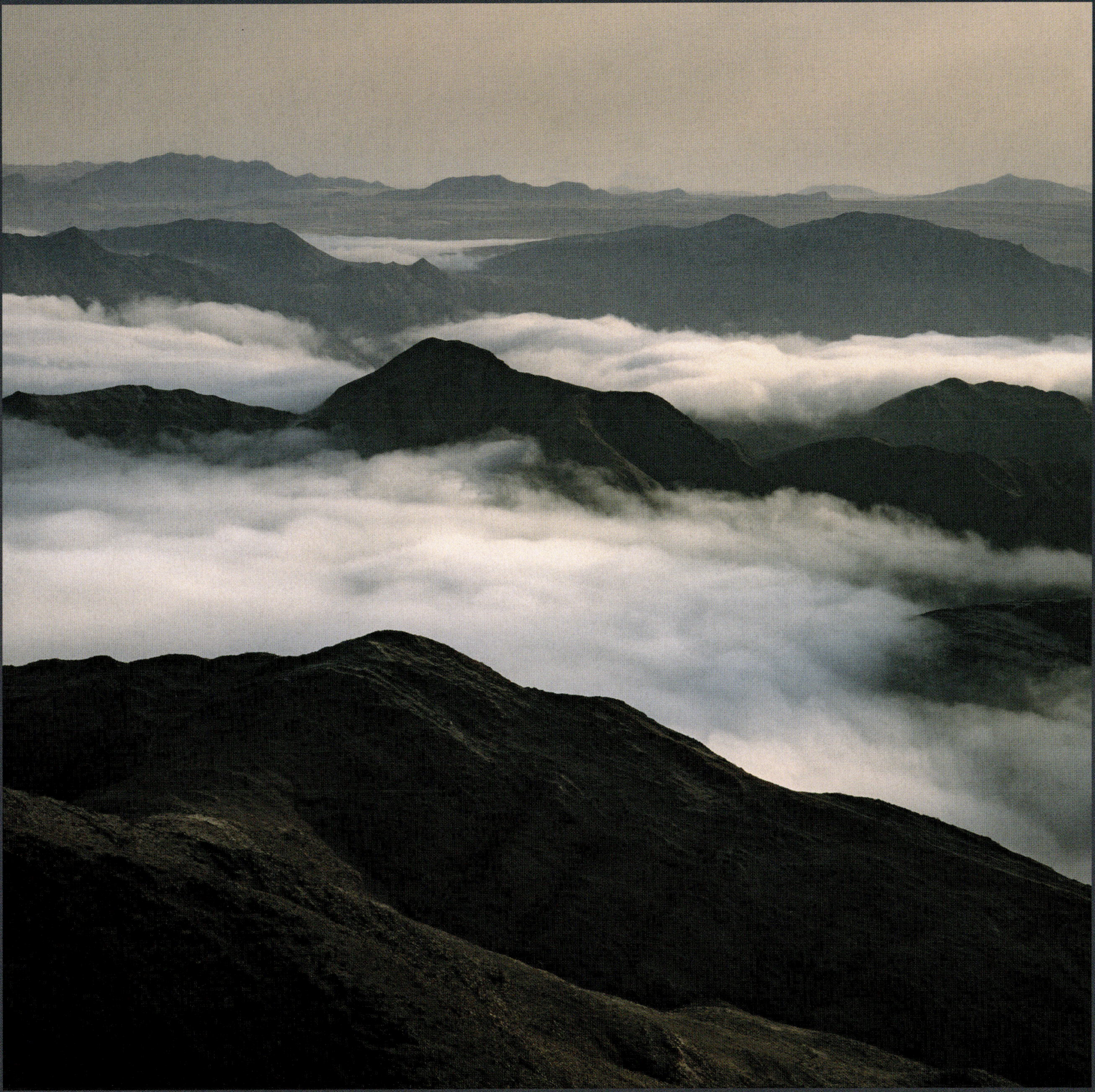

(OPPOSITE) Kunene Mist (ABOVE) Kaoko Mist

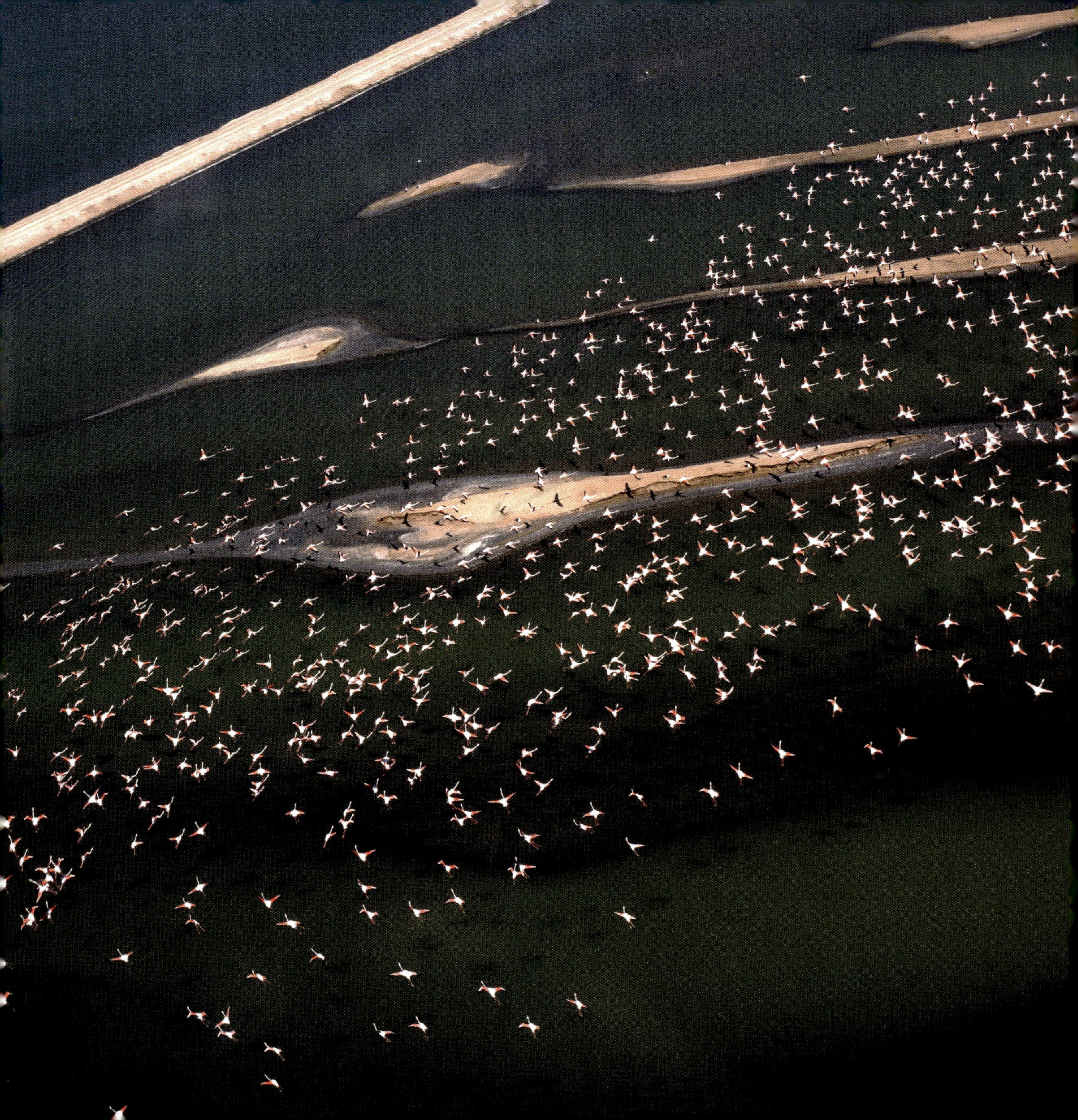

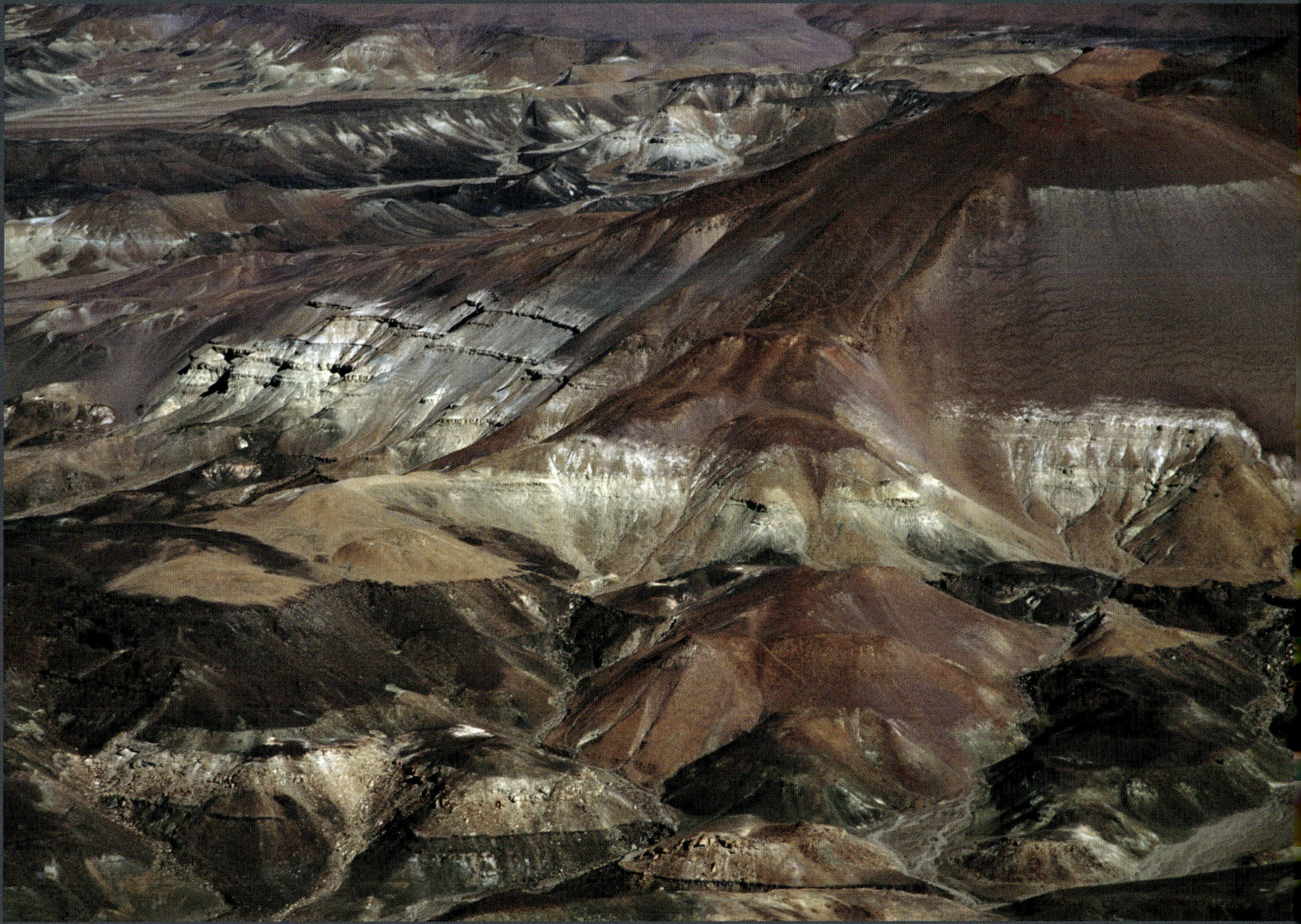

(OPPOSITE) Flamingo Flight (ABOVE) Red Mountain, Damaraland

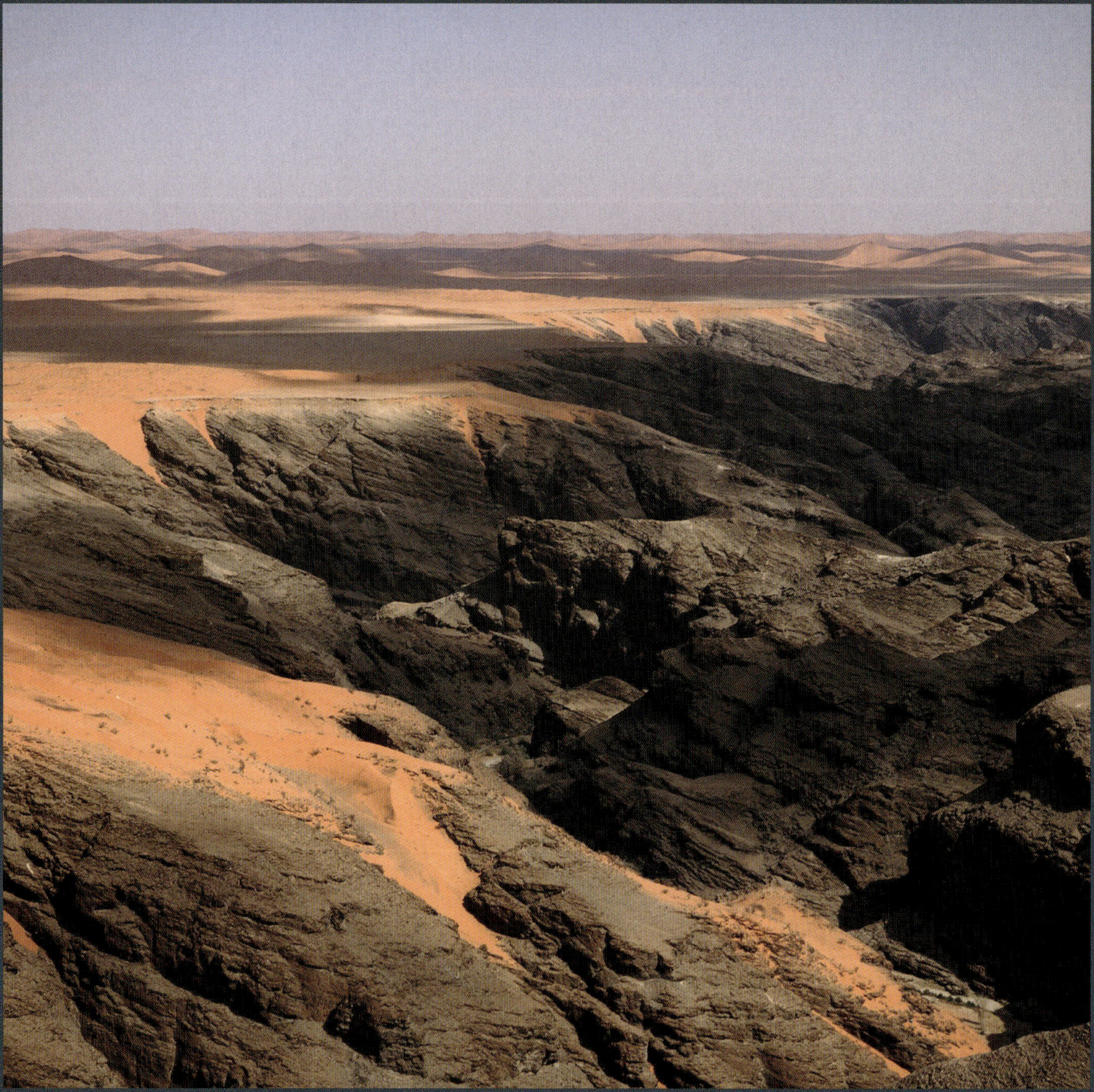

There is a stoic tenor to the landscape, to its people and its past.

Anthony Bannister & Peter Johnson, *Africa's Harsh Paradise Namibia*,
Cape Town/Johannesburg: C. Struik Publishers, 1978

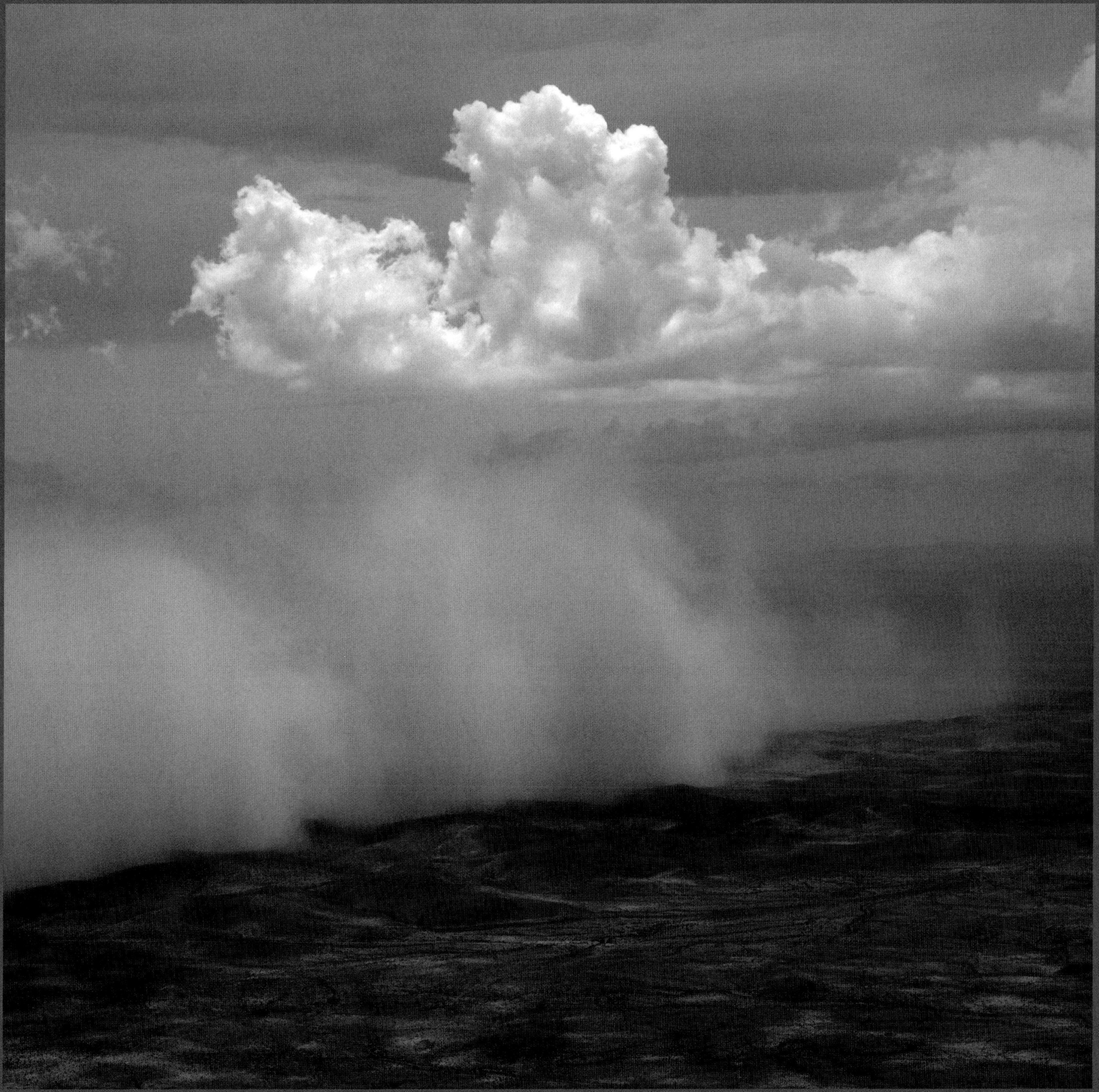

(OPPOSITE) Kuiseb Canyon (ABOVE) Dust Storm

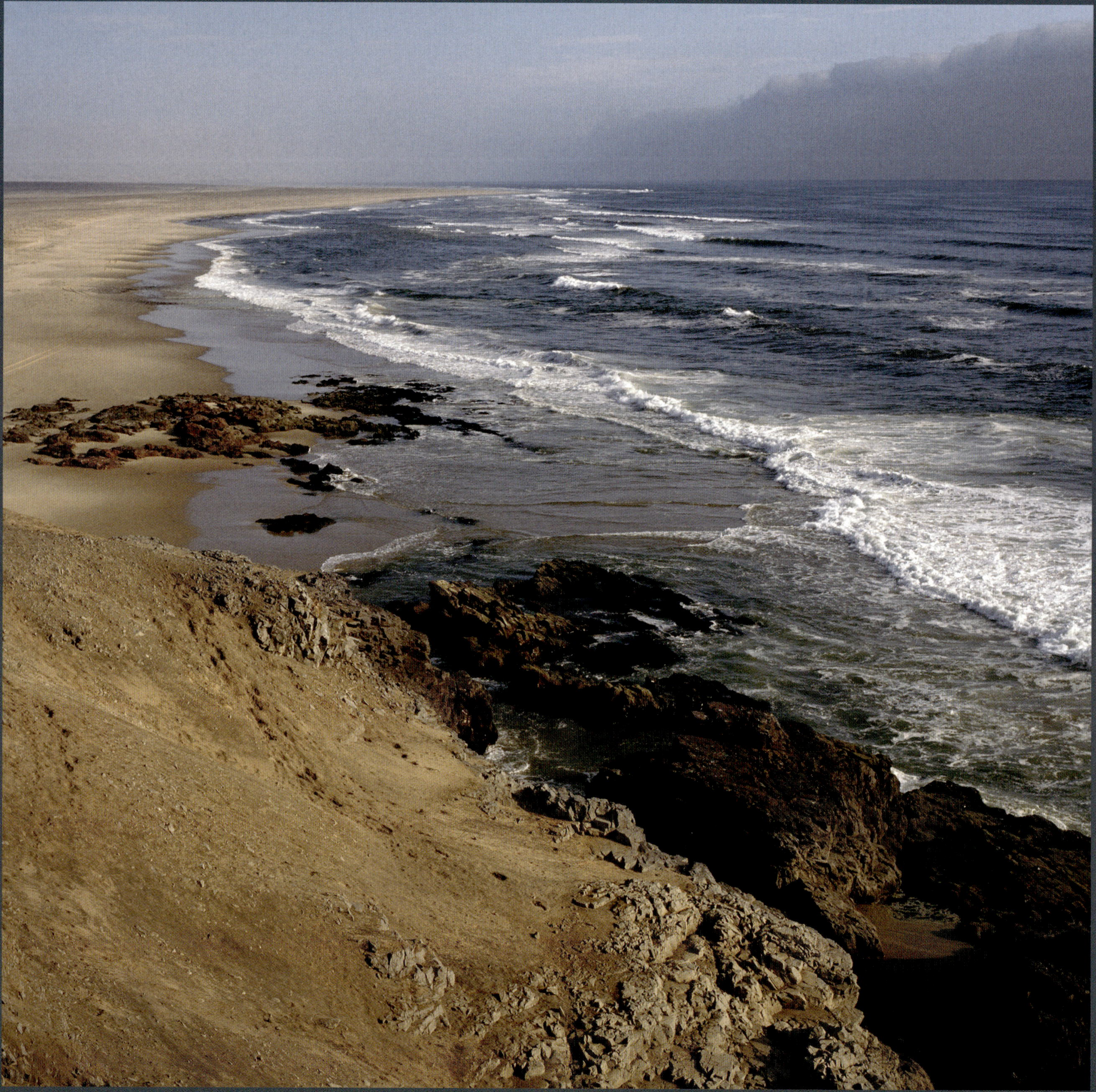

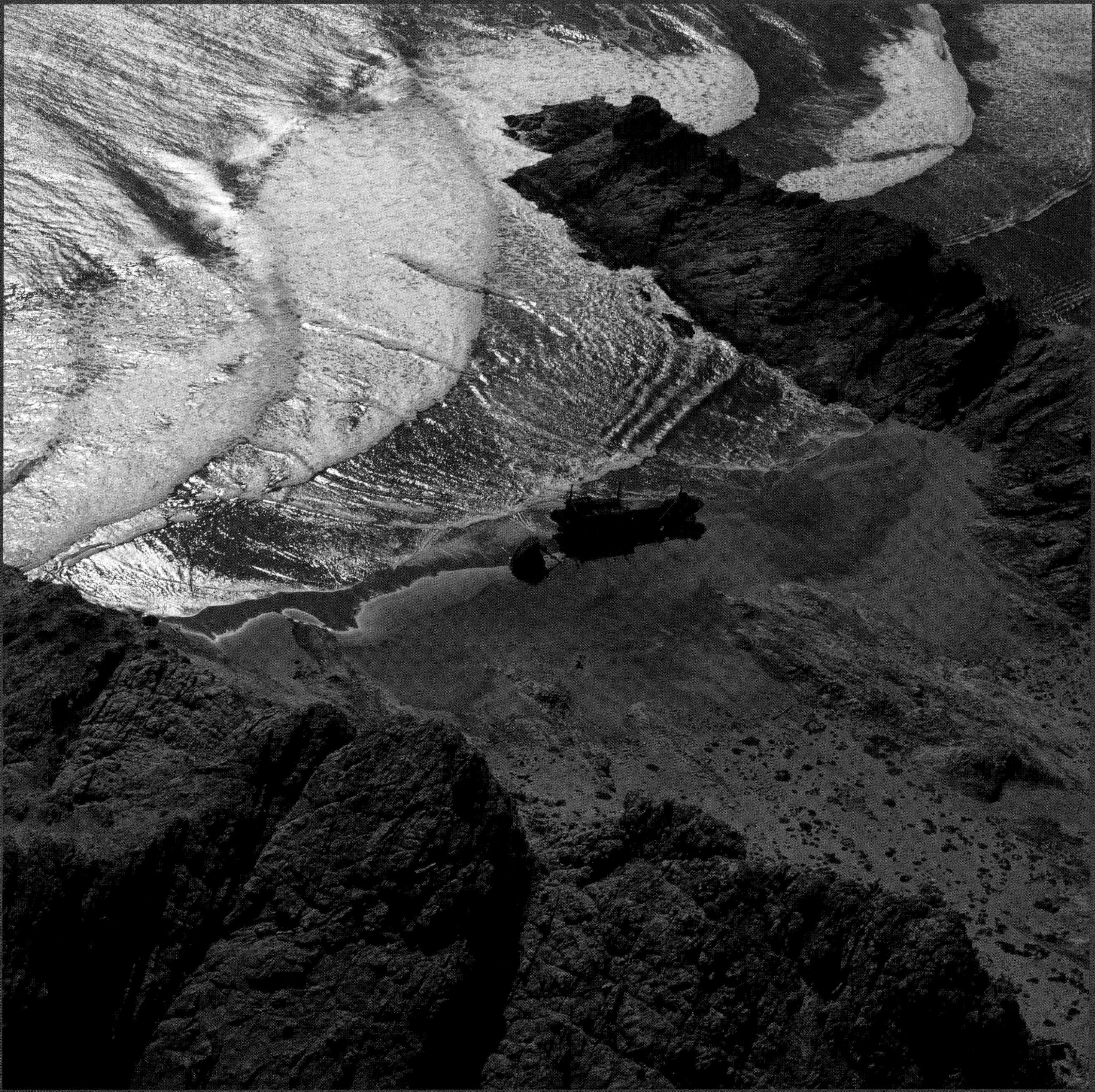

(OPPOSITE) Rocky Point (ABOVE) Wreck of the *Otavi*, Spencer Bay

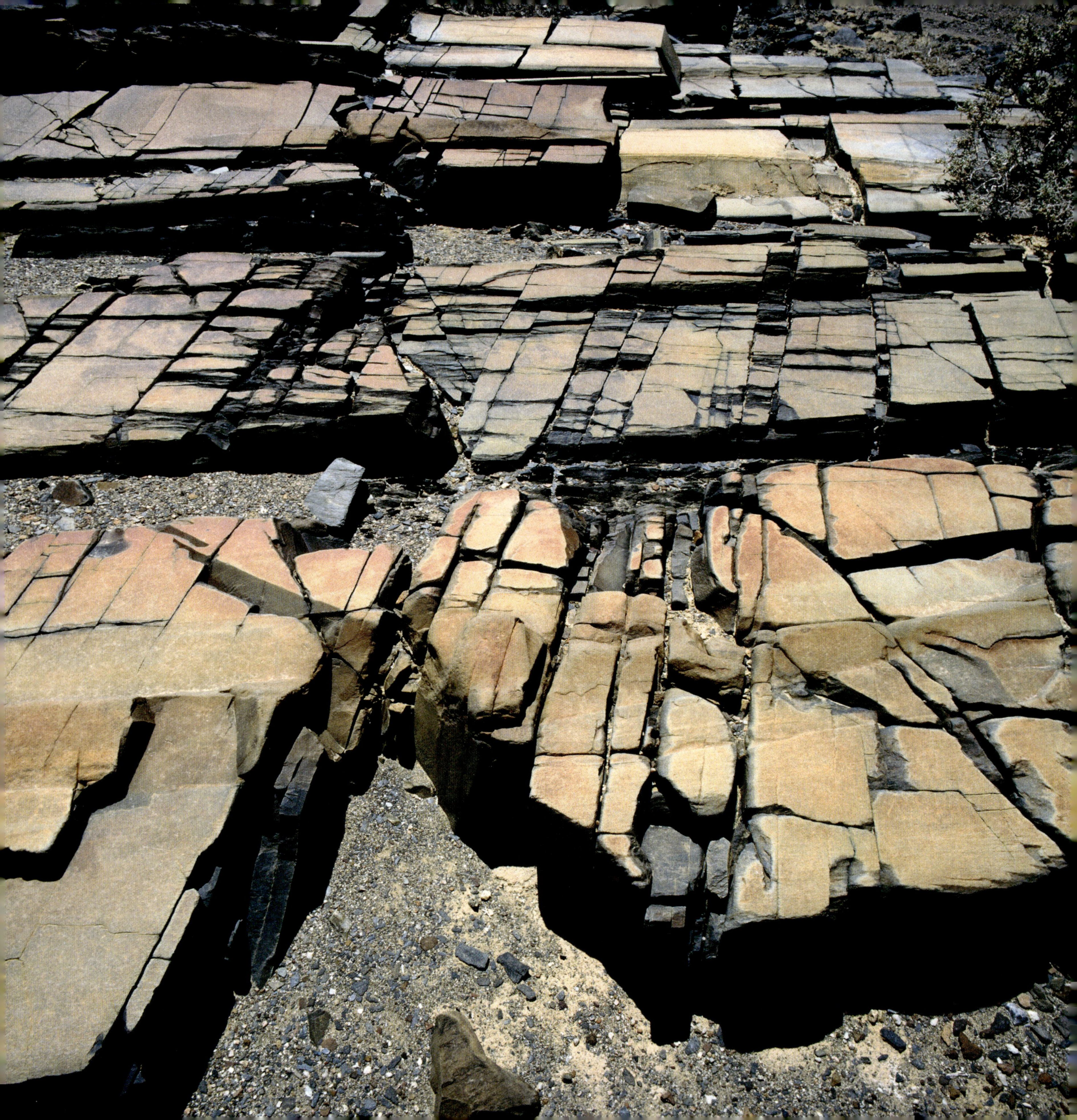

Portfolio 6

ROCK RENDEZVOUS

When photographing in Kaokoland, Damaraland and the Skeleton Coast, my themes developed from general landscape to specific themes, such as mirages, dune formations, textures, artefacts left by man in the desert, and this razzmatazz with rocks. These phases often lasted two to three years before evolving to the next theme.

My focus when photographing rocks was as much on their structure, colours and textures as on their durable, robust and solid nature. Areas to which I returned many times were the Kunene environs, the Huab, Khumib and Hoarusib riverbanks and surroundings, and the Ugab formations west of the Brandberg. Especially challenging were the rock-strewn slopes in the Brandberg West area, a daunting and forsaken landscape where Louw and I camped several nights, enabling me to photograph the rocky environs from different angles at different times of day. These rugged surroundings proved to be a veritable wonderland of ridges, rifts and ravines. The birth of *Rock Rendezvous* stems from a creative connection I had with Kurt Johannessen, the founder and for many years director of the Cancer Association of Namibia. One of his drives to raise funds for the Association was the publication of an annual calendar. The first Cancer Association calendar featuring my work was launched in 1993 for the 1994 calender year. This was the debut of the *Presence of the Past* series. The second one was for the 1999 calender year, and was the debut of the *Rock Rendezvous* series. I was inspired by both topics, and when devising titles for the images, also played around with words in an attempt to express what drew me to focus on these themes and develop them as portfolios.

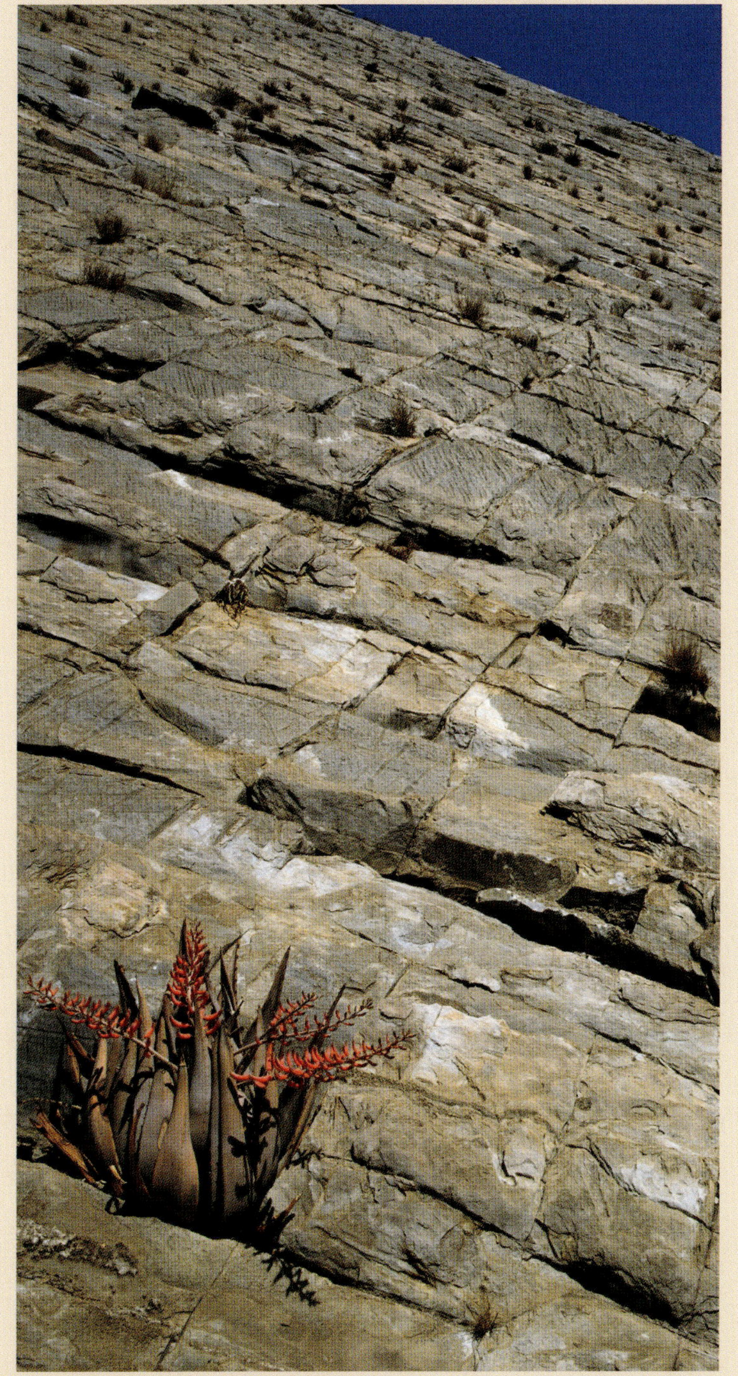

(OPPOSITE) Shimmering Schistose (ABOVE) Aloe Aerial

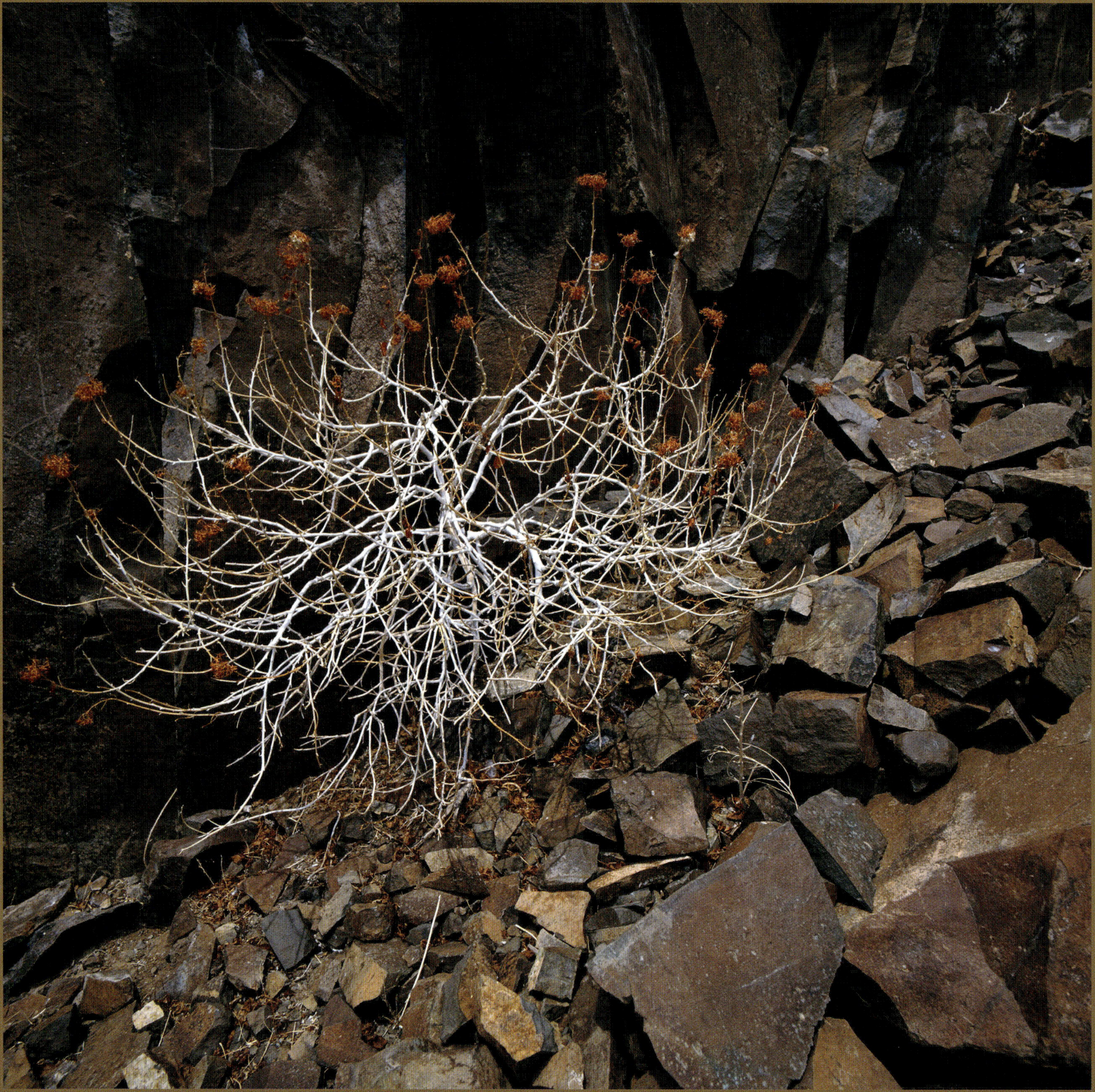

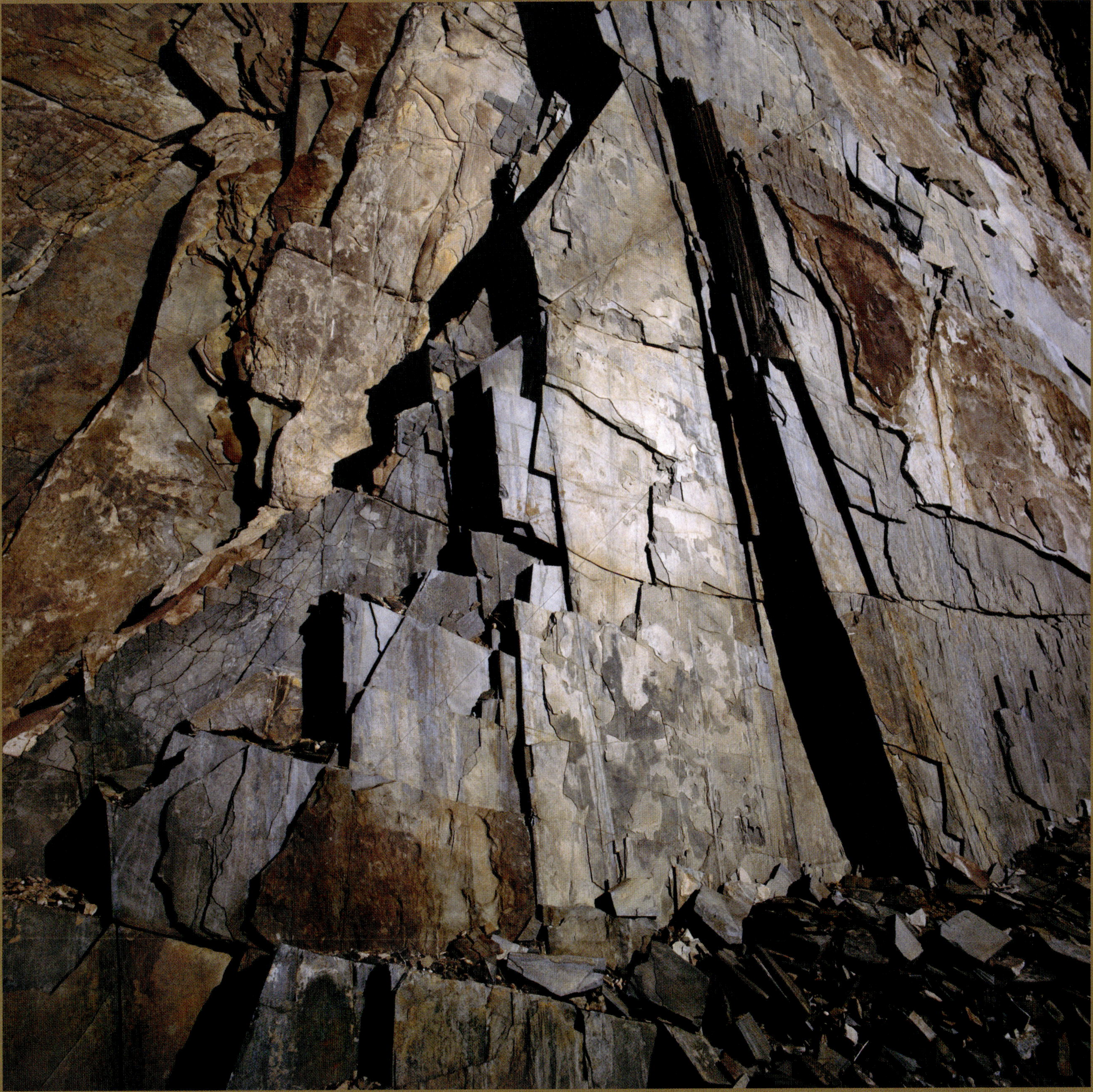

(OPPOSITE) Candelabra (ABOVE) Slanting Staircase

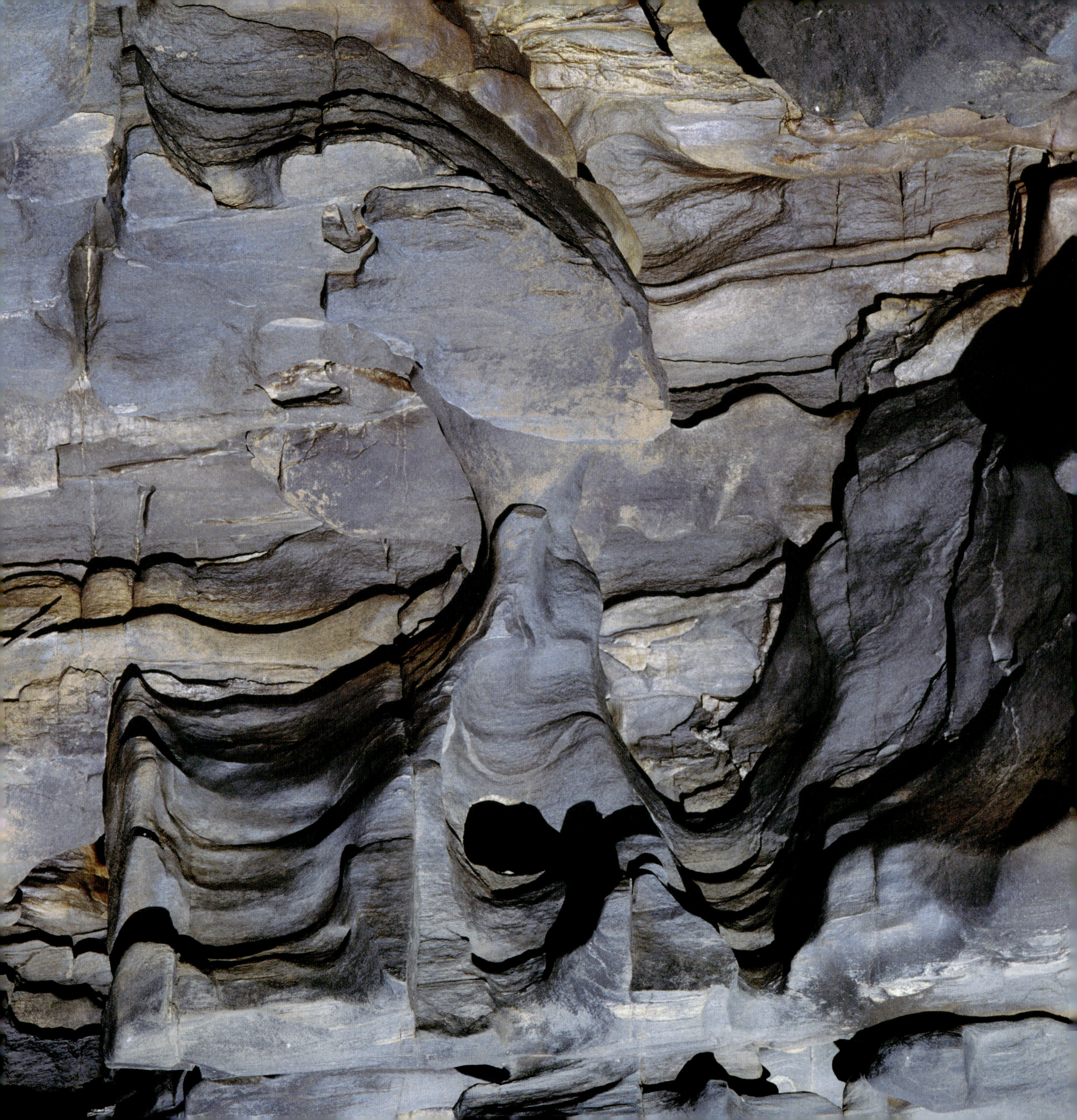

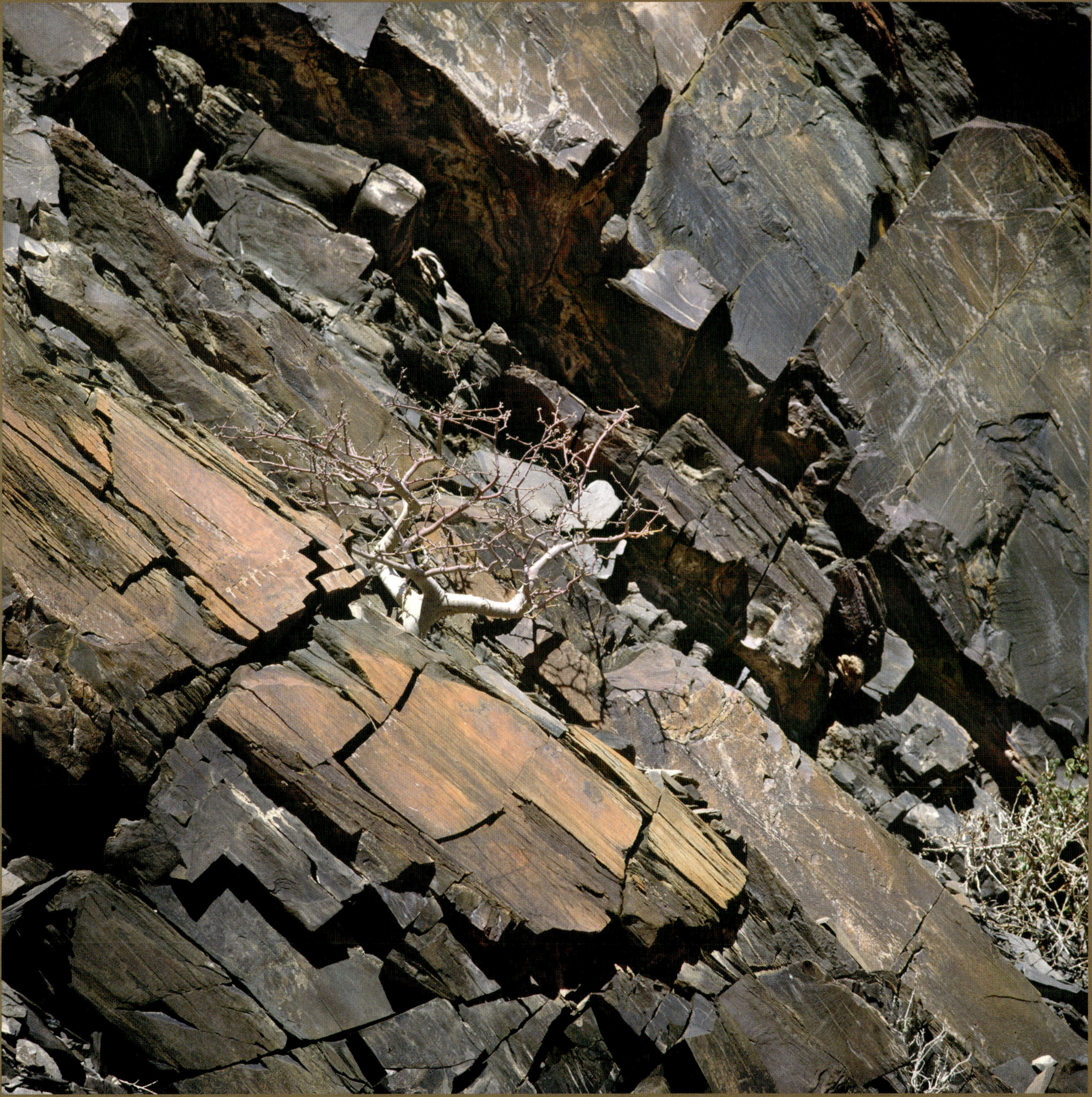

(OPPOSITE) Kunene Rocks (ABOVE) Commiphora Queen

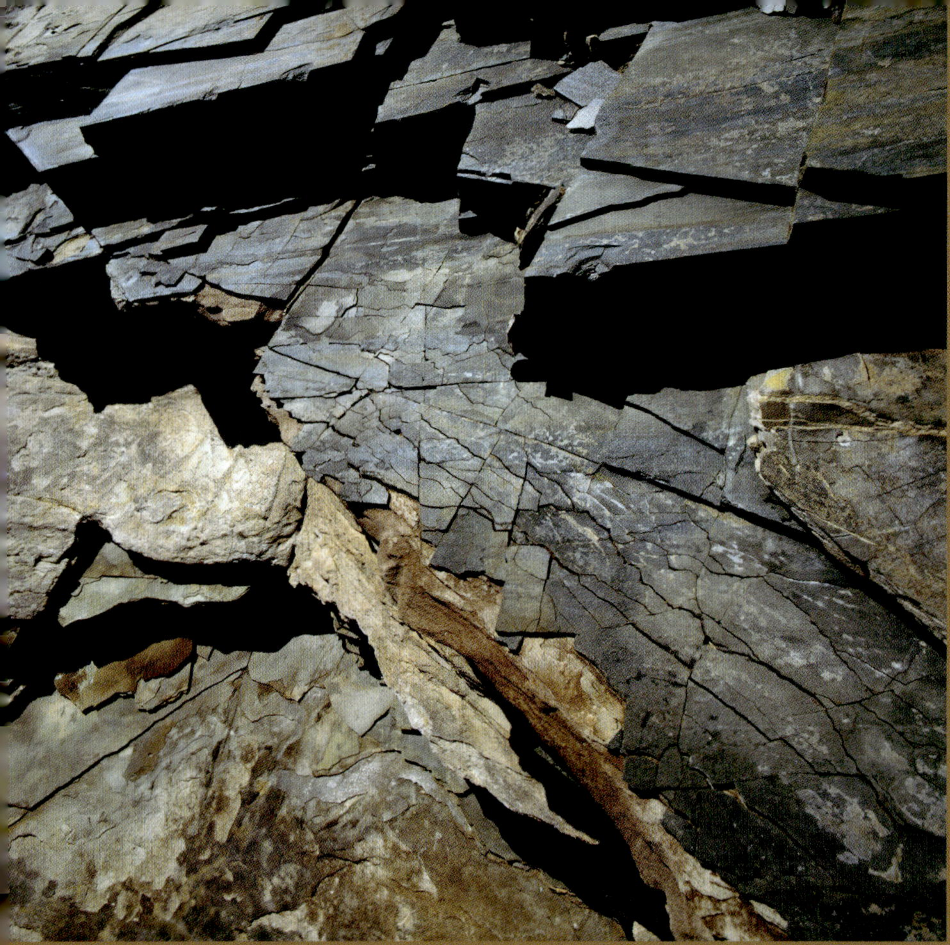
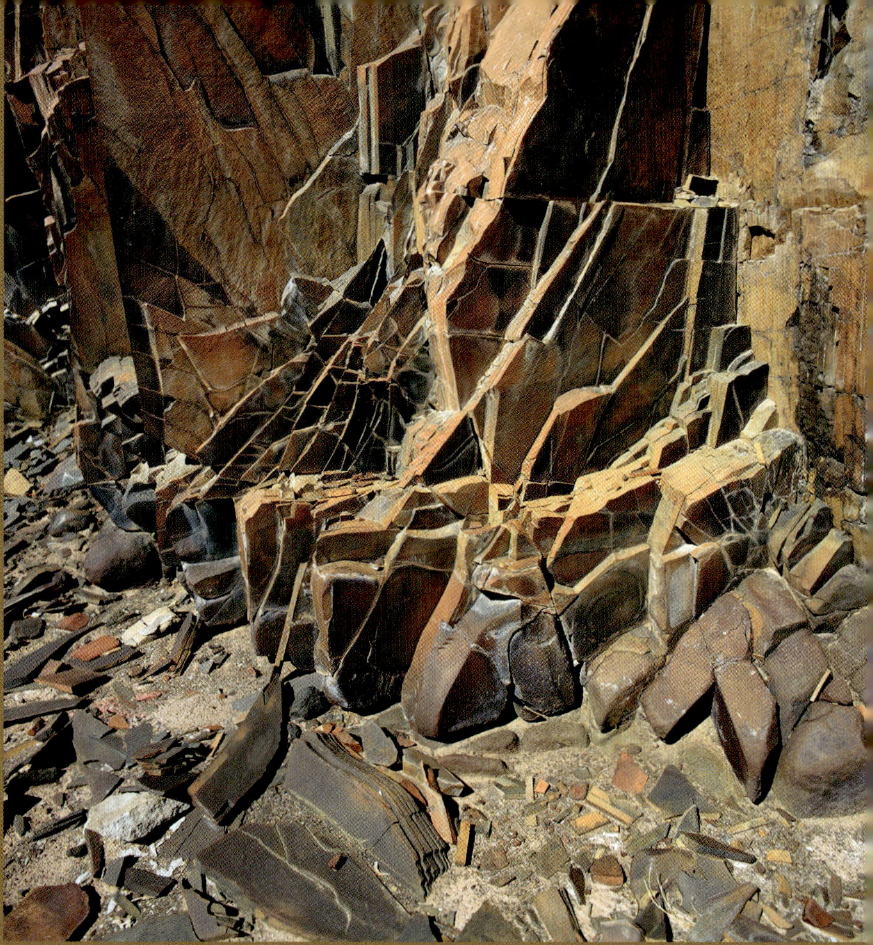
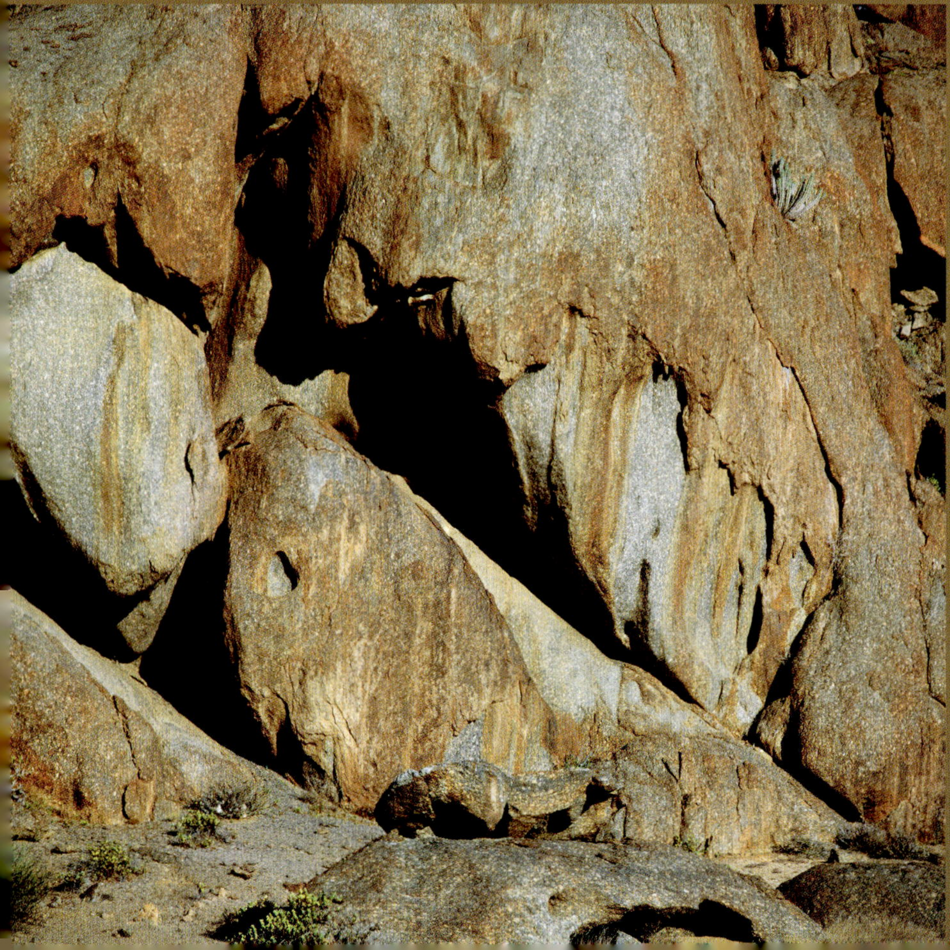
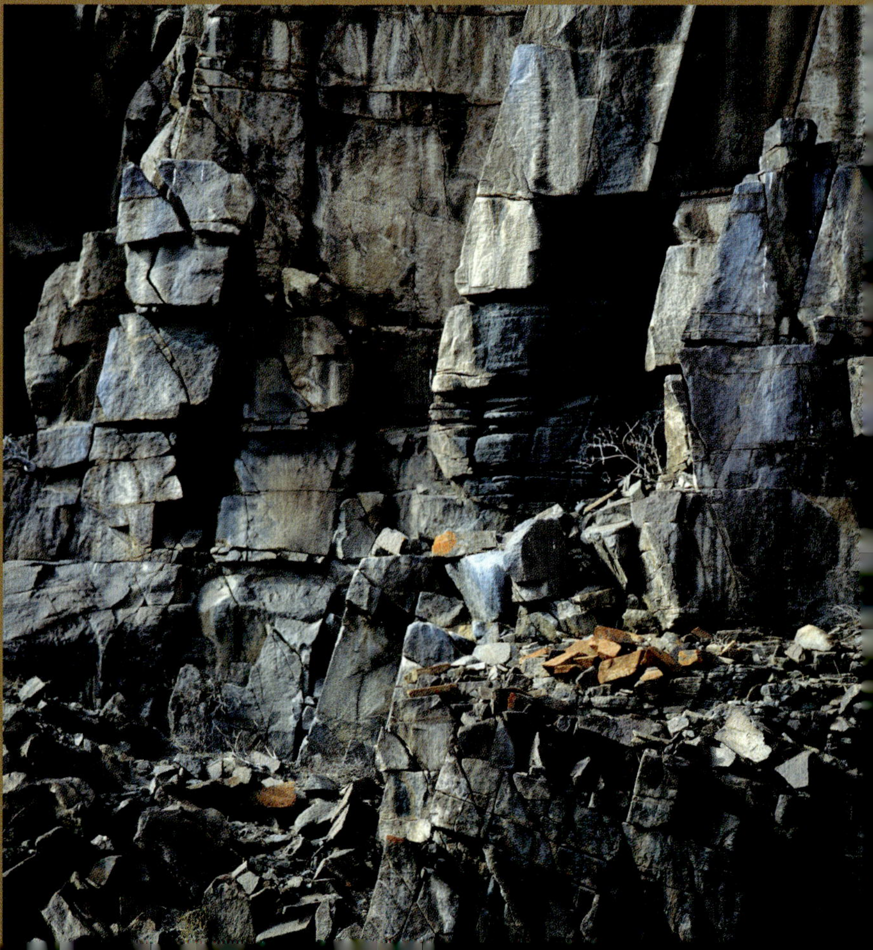

ROTSTEKENING

wat sien ons op die klipoppervlak:
'n maan wat oor 'n einder sak
'n jagter skiet 'n mannetjiesvolstruis

maar toe hy die eerste vere pluk
kom 'n warrelwind aan sy hande ruk
die wind skep 'n bloedbevlekte veer
en sit dit op 'n blink pan water neer

ons weet dis slegs die maan
en die mannetjiesvolstruis
wat kan sterf en groei
omdat hy vlam én vuuras is
as hy die vuurdans dans

so wil die tekening ons wys
dat maan, jagter en volstruis
betekenis aan die landskap gee

van wat gesien is
van wat ons nie sien nie

Piet van Rooyen, *Goedsmoeds*,
Pretoria: Protea Boekhuis, 2002: 22

(OPPOSITE TOP LEFT) Slanting Staircase (OPPOSITE TOP RIGHT) Damaraland Descent
(OPPOSITE BOTTOM LEFT) Rock Stalagtites (OPPOSITE BOTTOM RIGHT) Lichen Ledge, Huab River Wall

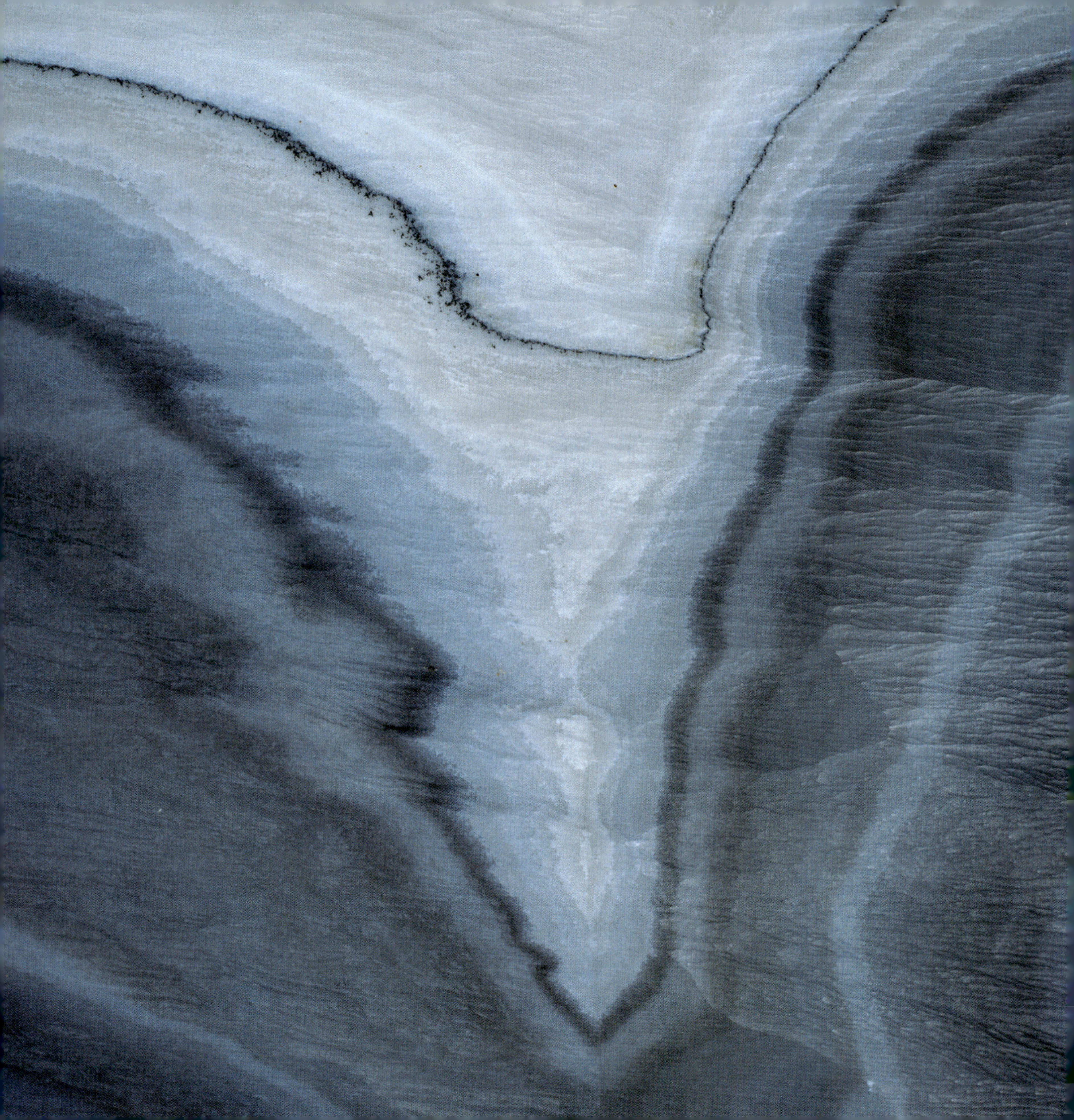

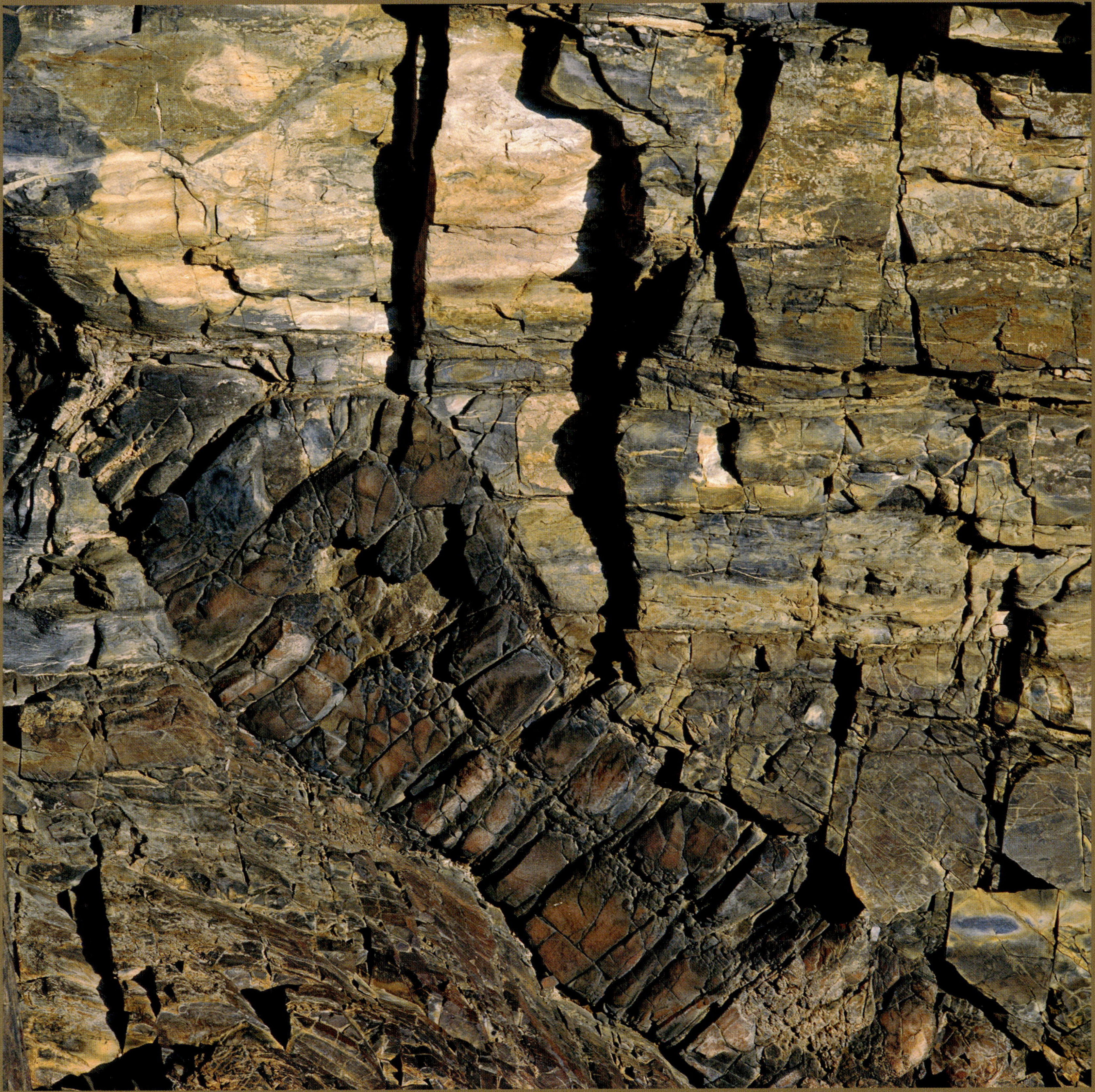

(OPPOSITE) Aragonite of Africa (ABOVE) Rocky Realm

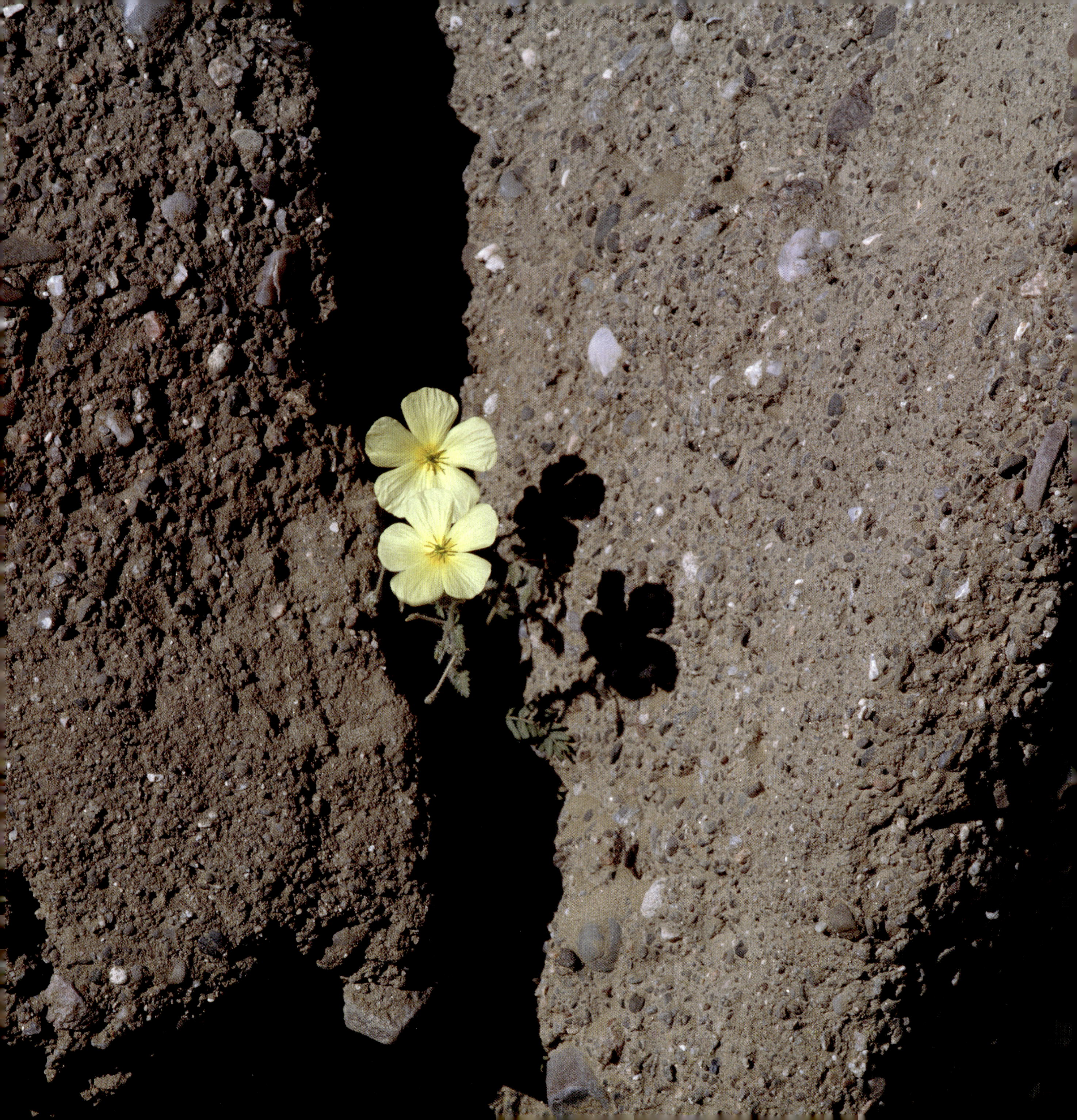

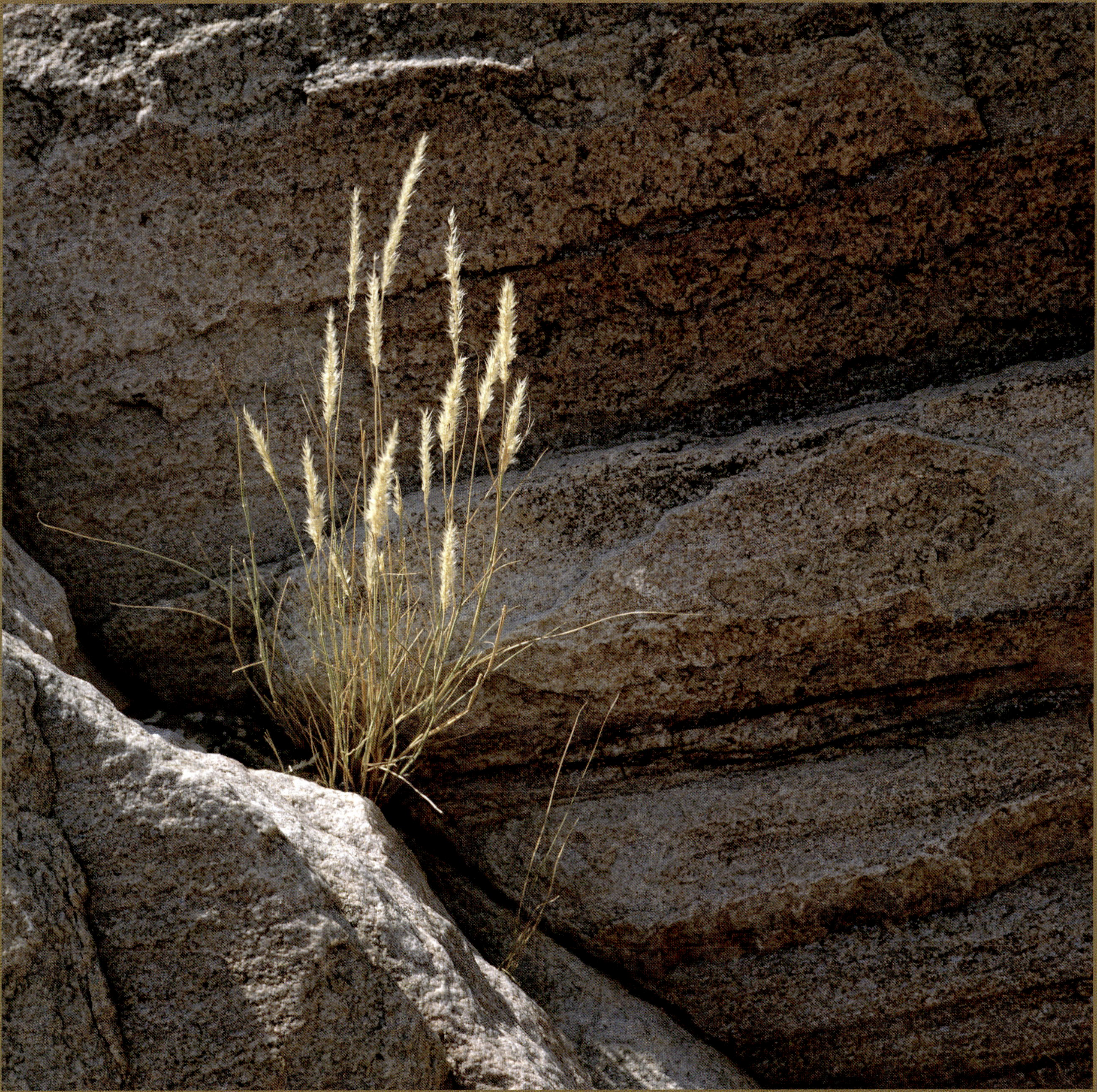

(OPPOSITE) Morgenstern (ABOVE) Sentinel Grass

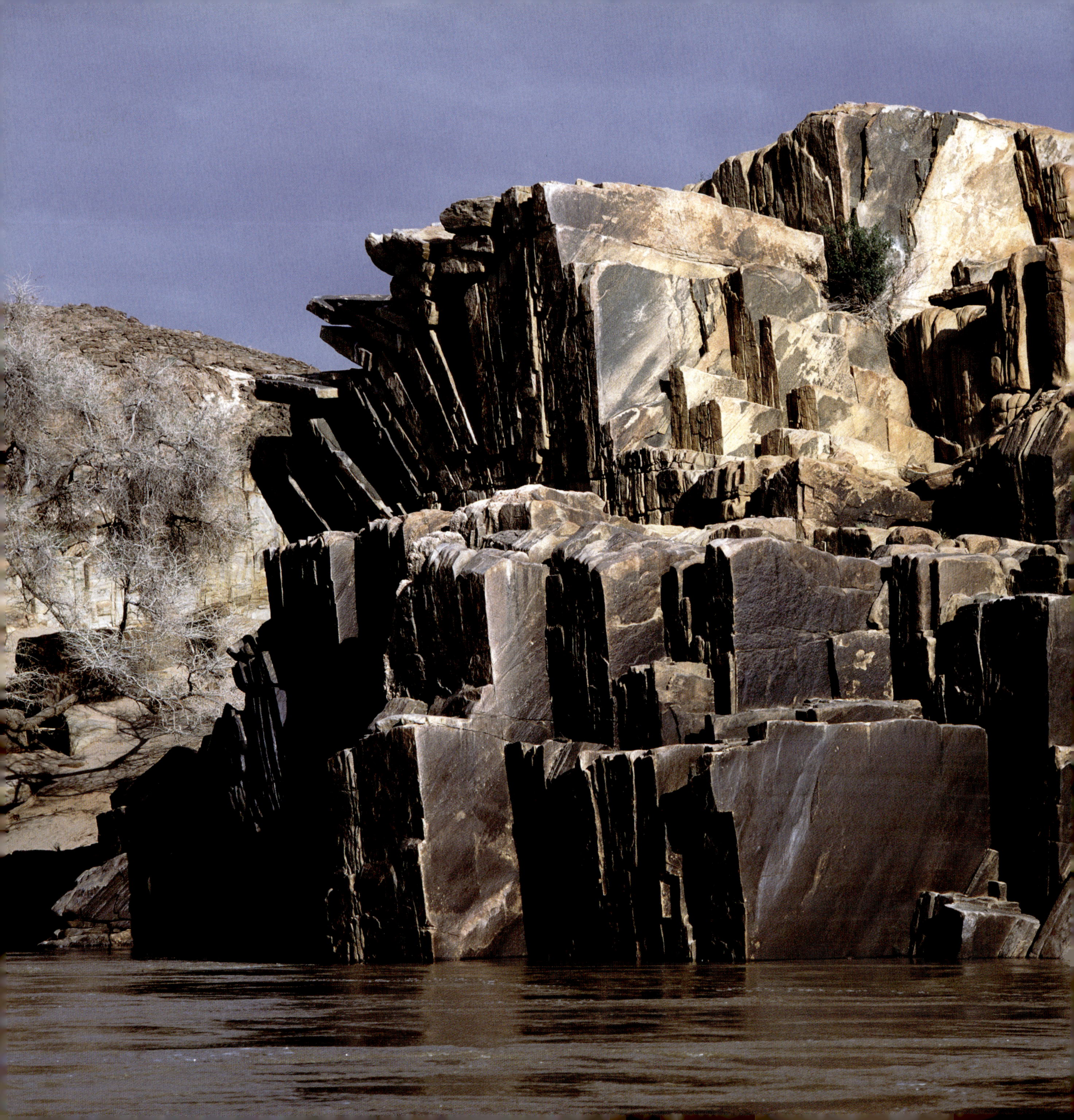

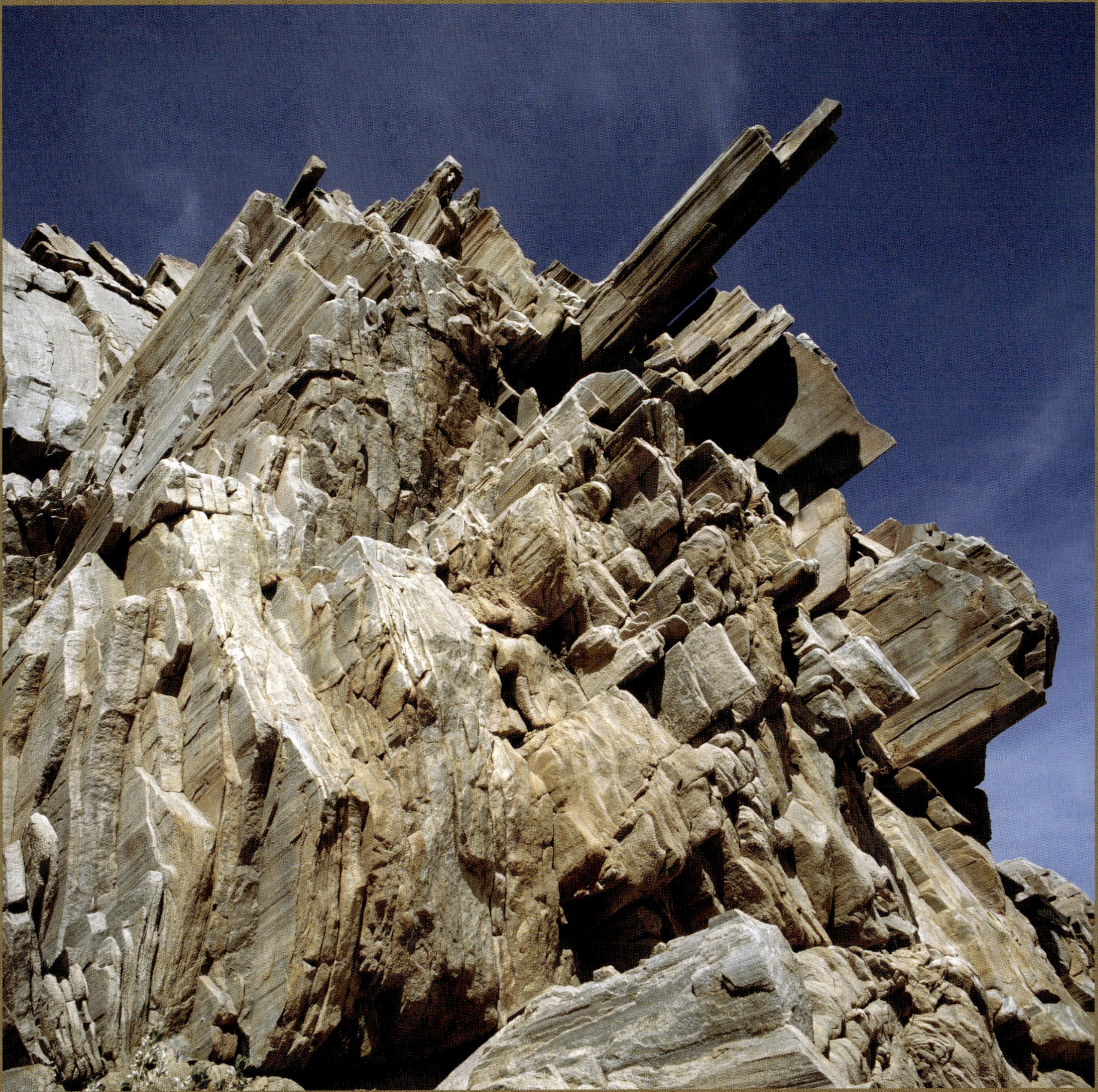

(OPPOSITE) Kunene Dominoes (ABOVE) Finger Rock

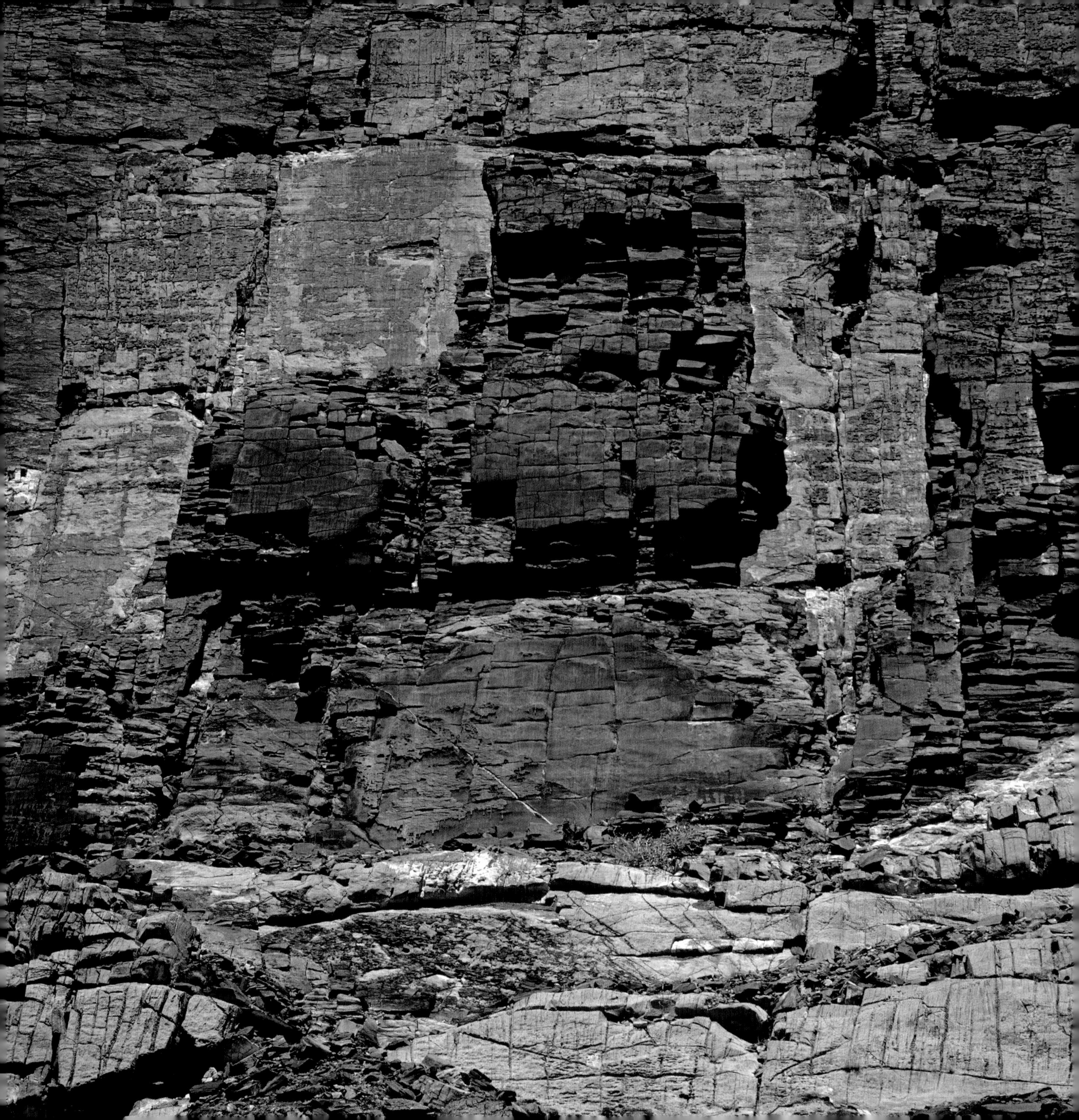

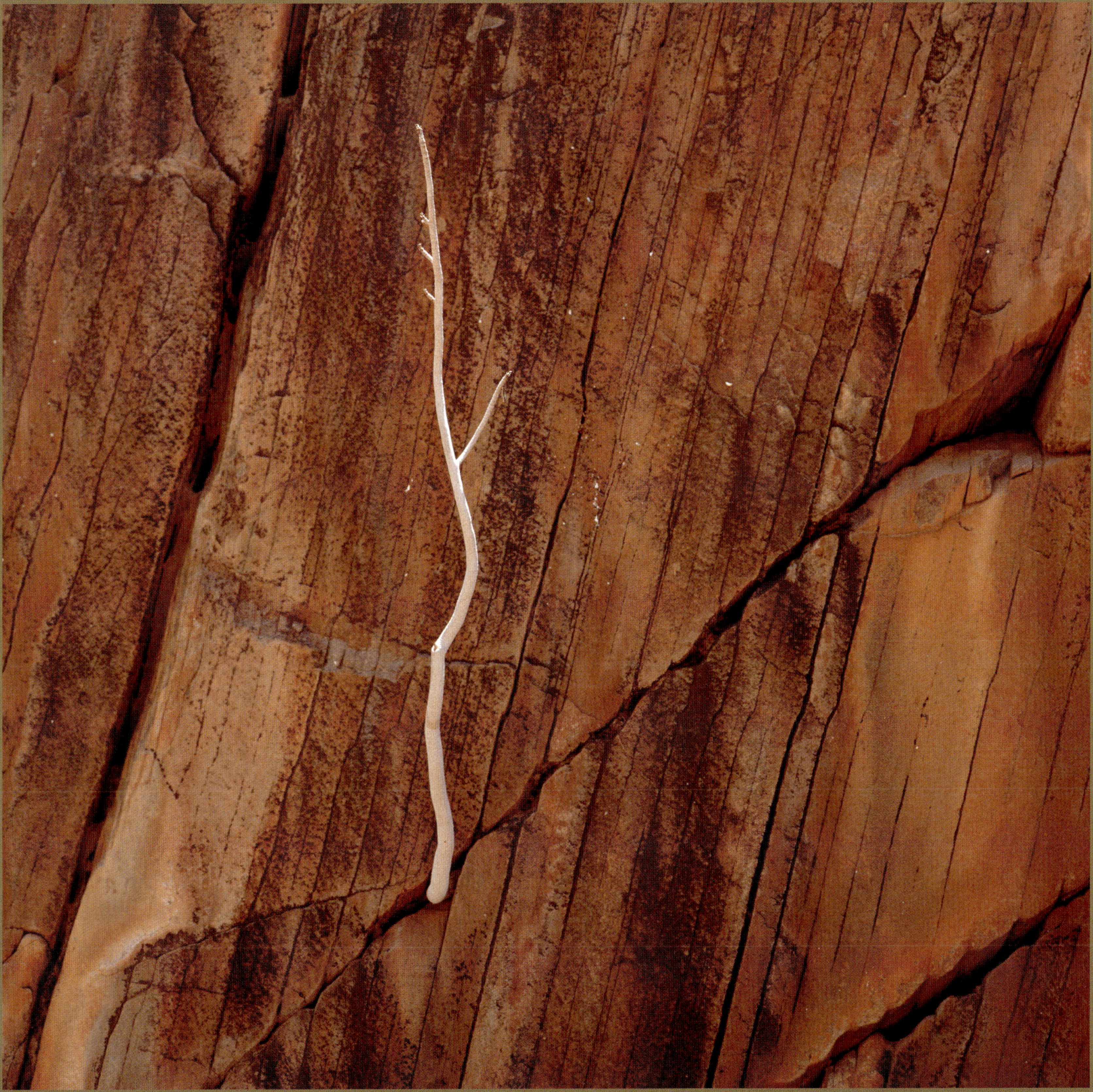

(OPPOSITE) Multiple Mosaic, Ugab River Wall (ABOVE) Kunene Commiphora

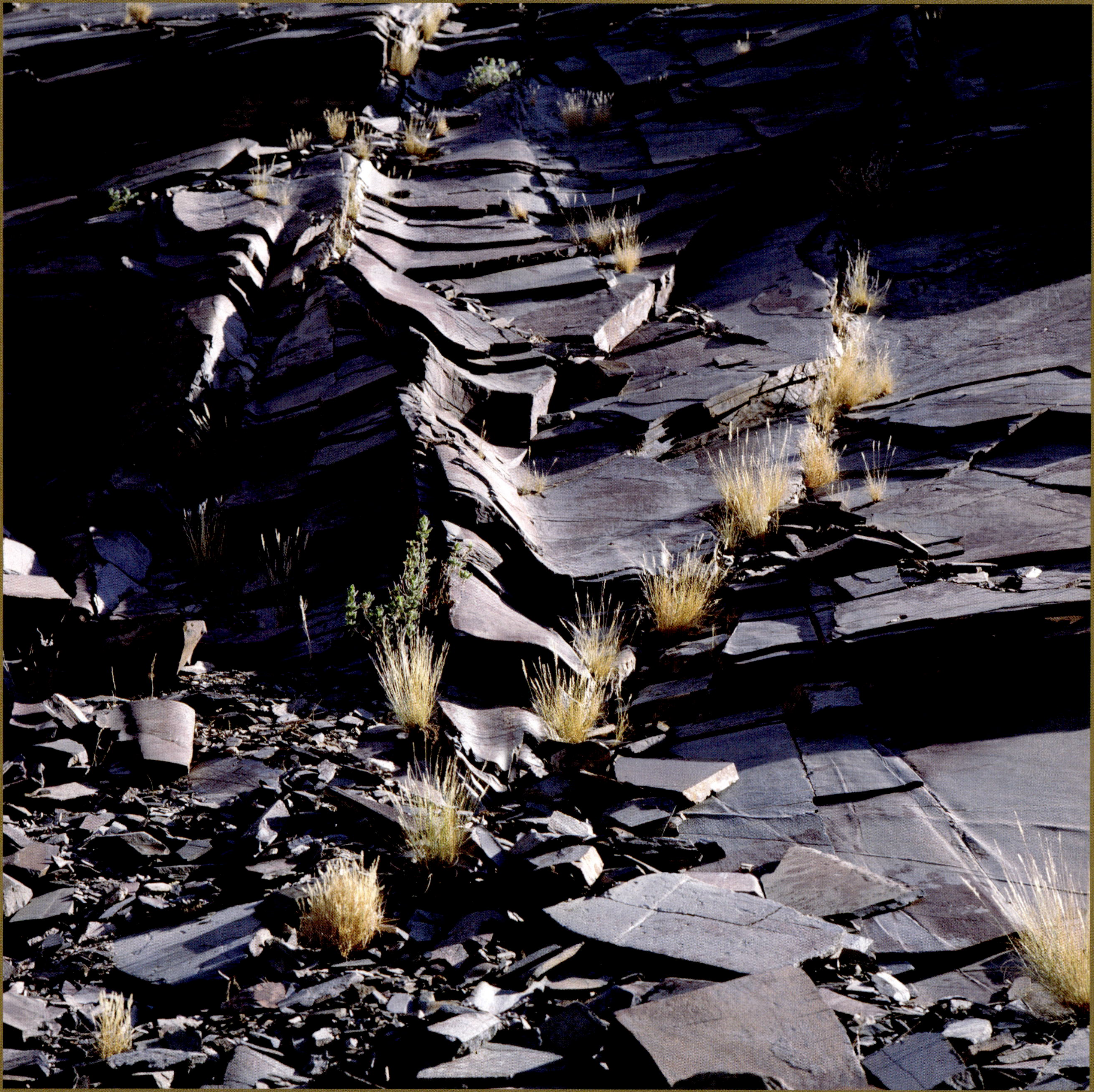

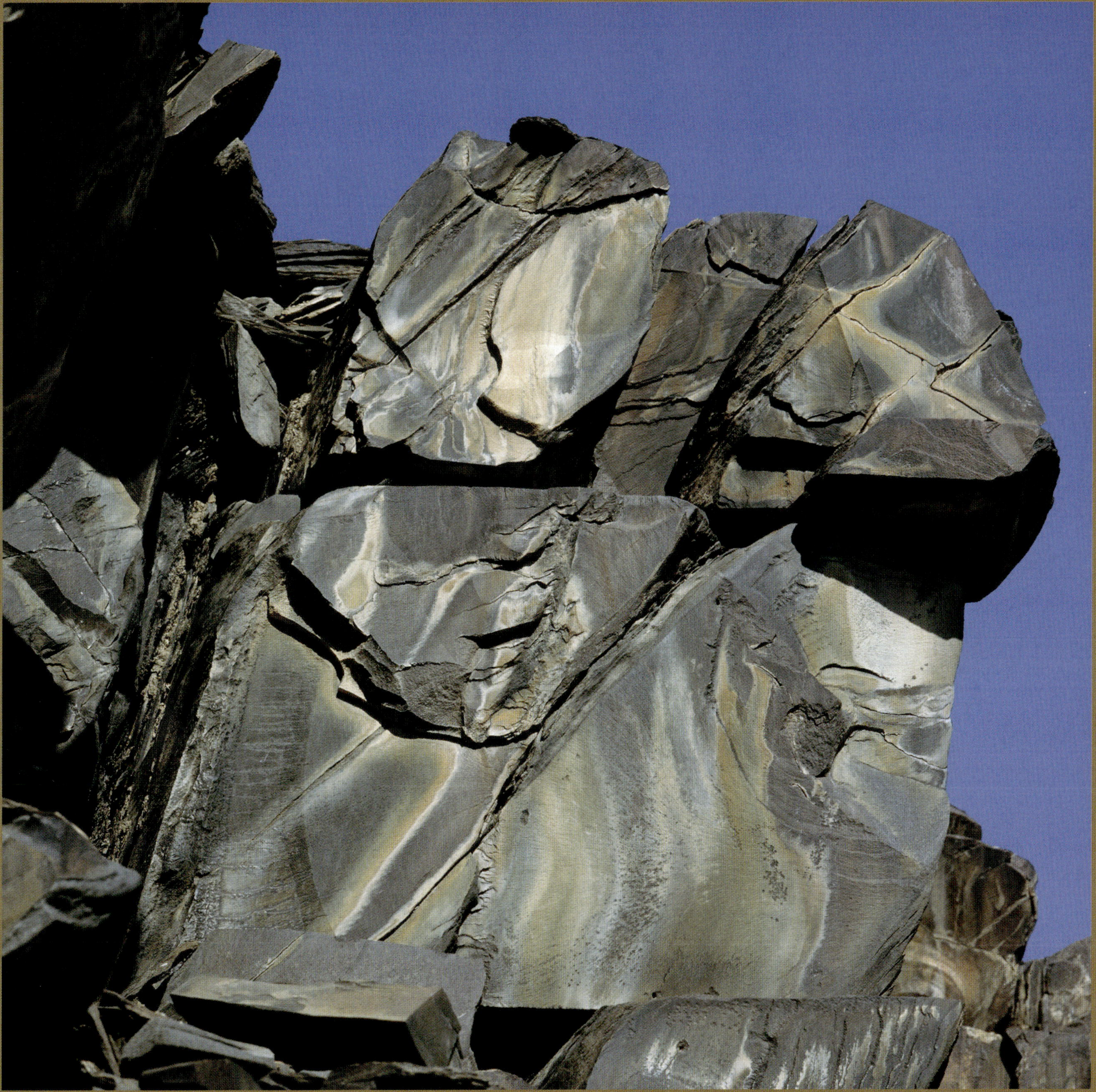

(OPPOSITE) Ugab Undulations, Brandberg West (ABOVE) Rock of Ages

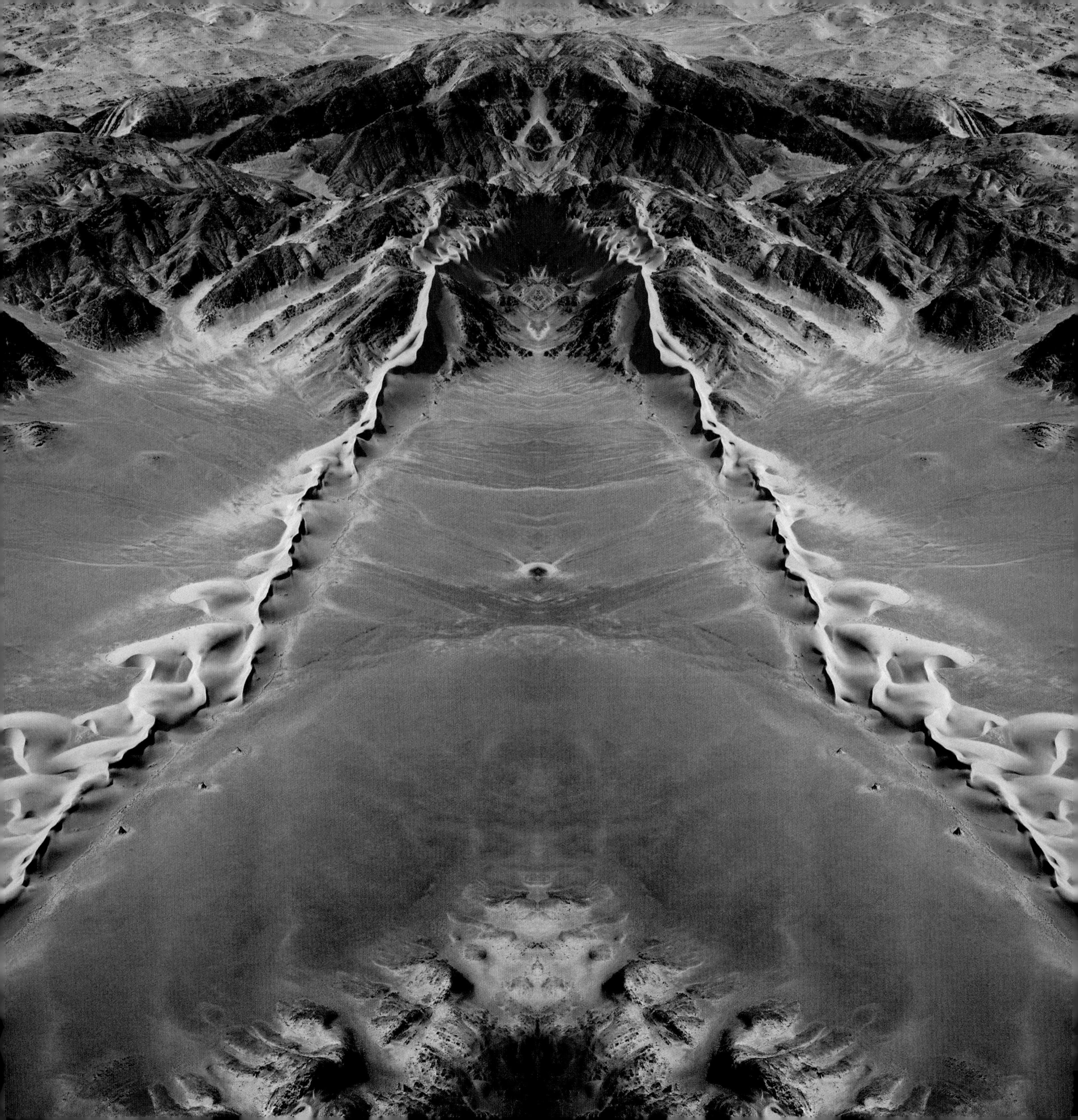

Portfolio 7

MYSTIC DESERT

The development of this portfolio was initiated by Andreas Kahlau of Silvertone International, who devised the introductory image, *The Portals of Discovery*, sparking off an exhilarating creative adventure that kept me agog for nights on end. The computer-manipulated interpretations were developed from photography I'd done in the Namib and Kalahari deserts over some 25 years, the images ranging from close-ups to aerial views and depicting primarily the abstract, graphic and textural qualities of the arid landscape. All the images in this portfolio have a desert connotation – sometimes entering into a mythical, fantasy or dream world – and a philosophical, inspirational or spiritual content that relates to my sense-impressions while spending time in the desert.

One of the key images of the series is *Isis*, the ancient Egyptian goddess who was both sister and wife of Osiris, to whom she bore Horus. Isis absorbed numerous other Egyptian divinities, especially that of the harvest goddess Ernutete (Thermutis). She was also worshipped around the Mediterranean countries as a mystical mother goddess.

The "guru" in *The Sorcerer* is don Juan Matus, a Yaqui Indian shaman from Sonora, Mexico, who is the central figure in a series of books written by anthropologist Carlos Castaneda. To achieve the status of sorcerer, Castaneda did an arduous ten-year apprenticeship with don Juan, during which he was taught to "see" rather than merely look.

The Magic Circle represents the Jungian mandala as the symbol of the central goal or self, represented by the circle, square or quaternity through symmetrical arrangements of the number four and its multiples.

In *Odyssey*, the *Eduard Bohlen* sails through the Namib Sand Sea, symbolising life's journey as a long wandering in search of self-realisation and enlightenment.

Several of the *Mystic Desert* images won recognition in the Fujifilm Photographic Awards of Southern Africa and the /Ae//Gams Arts & Cultural Festival in Namibia, in which the image *Isis* was crowned as overall winner of the Art Category in 2006, and was bought by the National Art Gallery of Namibia for its Permanent Collection.

(OPPOSITE) Dark Mountain

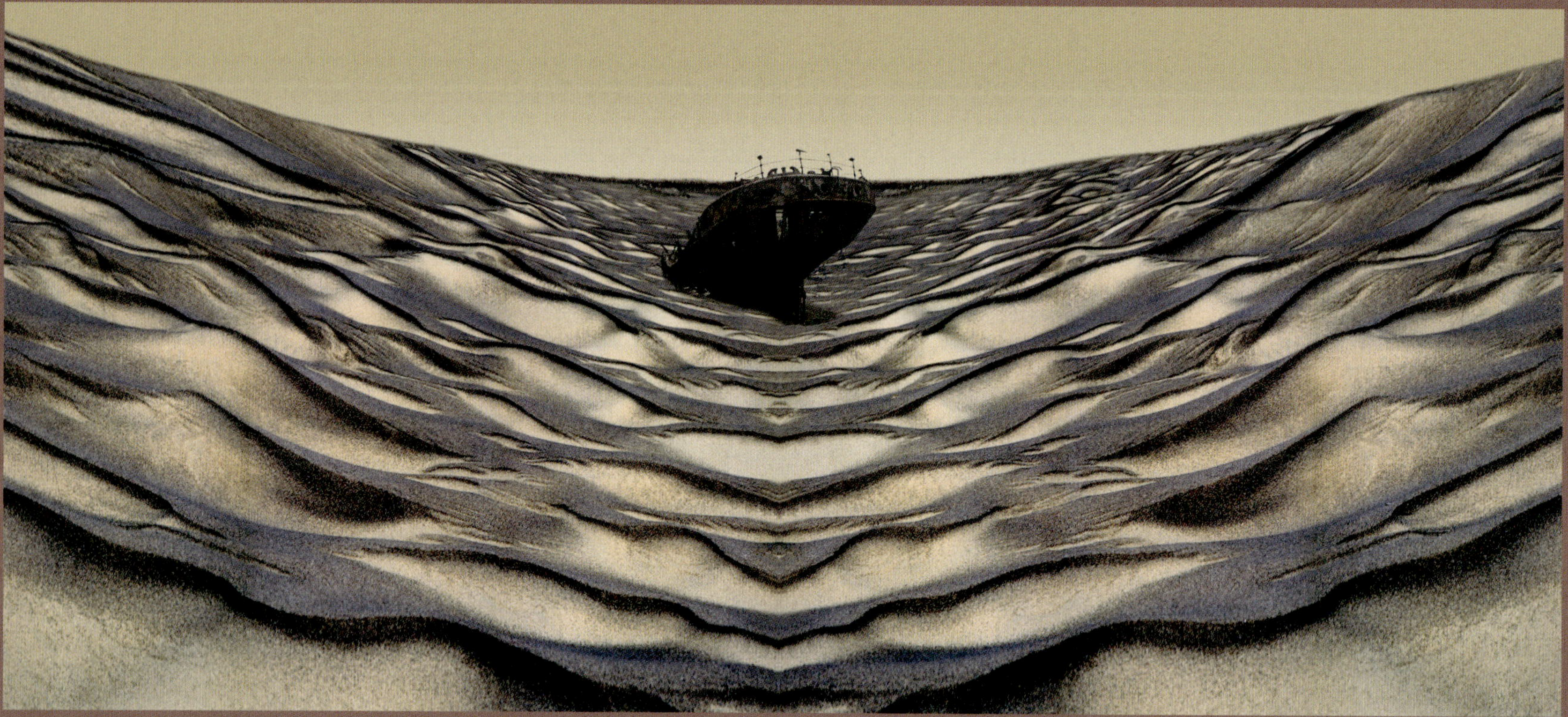

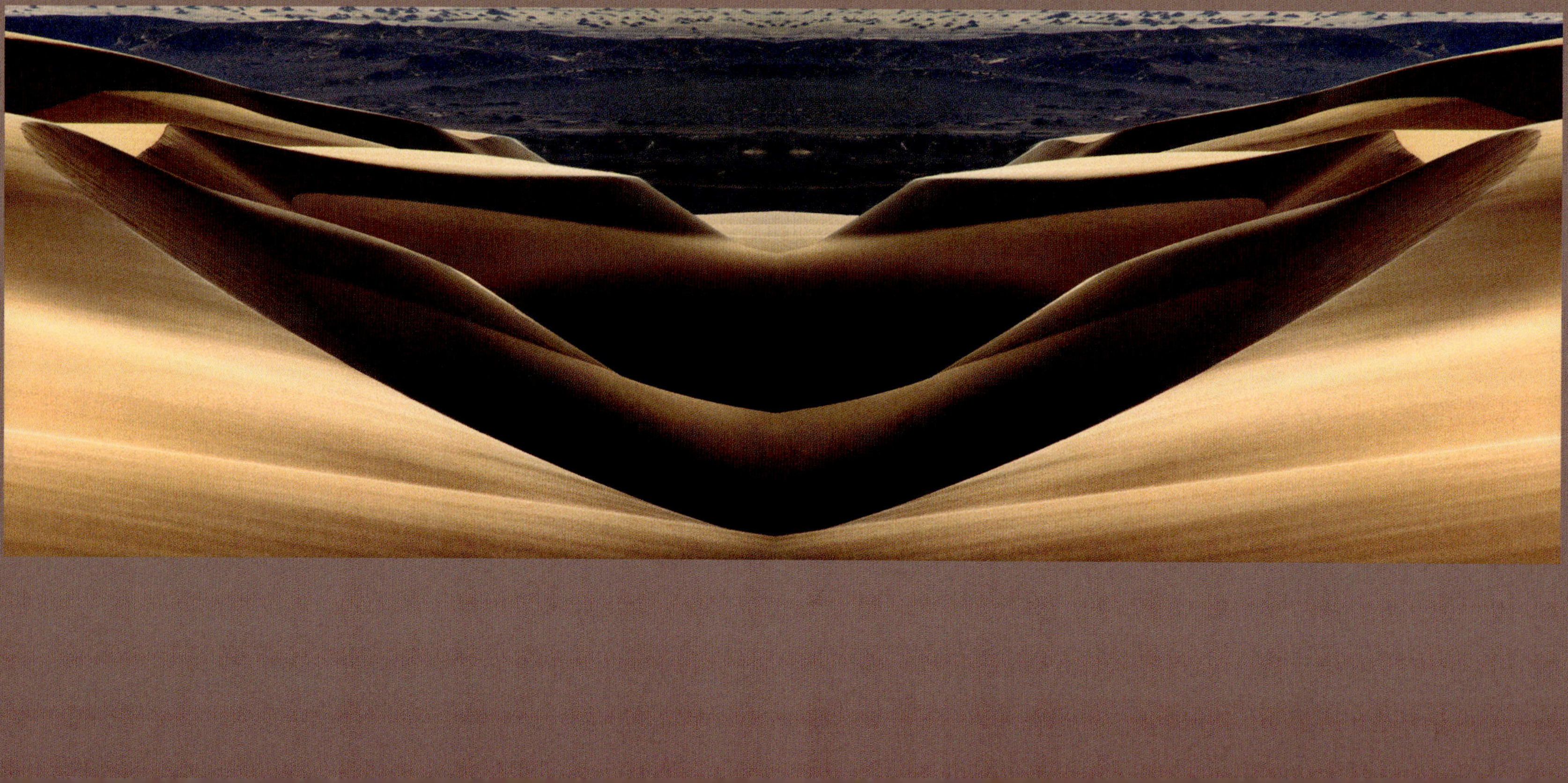

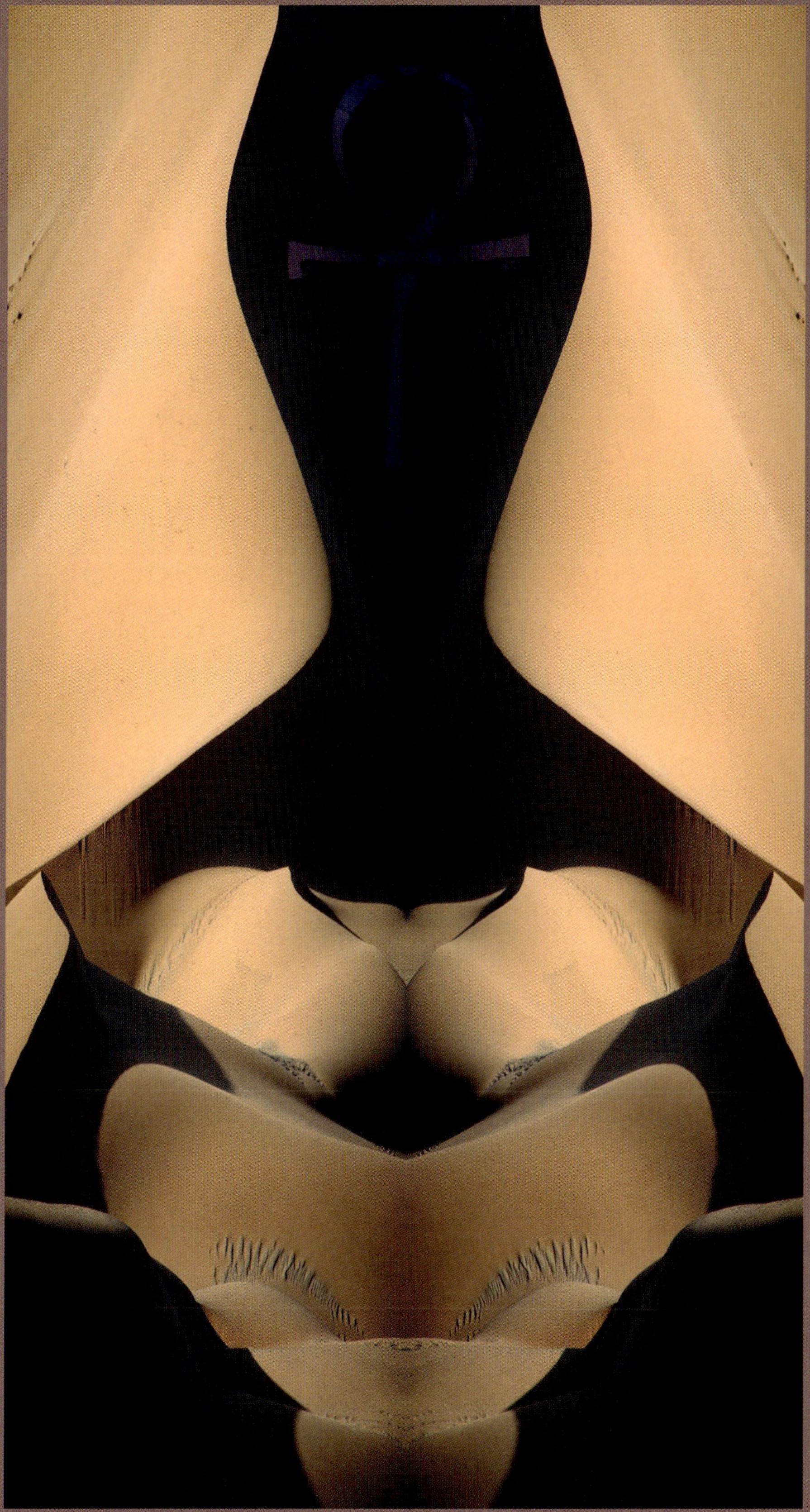

NAMIBIA

I've returned here to be in the deserts
I love to hear the sound made by sand dunes
I am one of those who perceive the rhythm
Of a landscape as recorded in many paintings
I am one of thousands who know I am finally home

Mvula Ya Nangolo, *Watering the Beloved Desert, New and Selected Poems*, Makanda, Illinois: Brown Turtle Press, 2008: 51

(OPPOSITE ABOVE) Odyssey (OPPOSITE BELOW) The Portals of Discovery (ABOVE) Isis

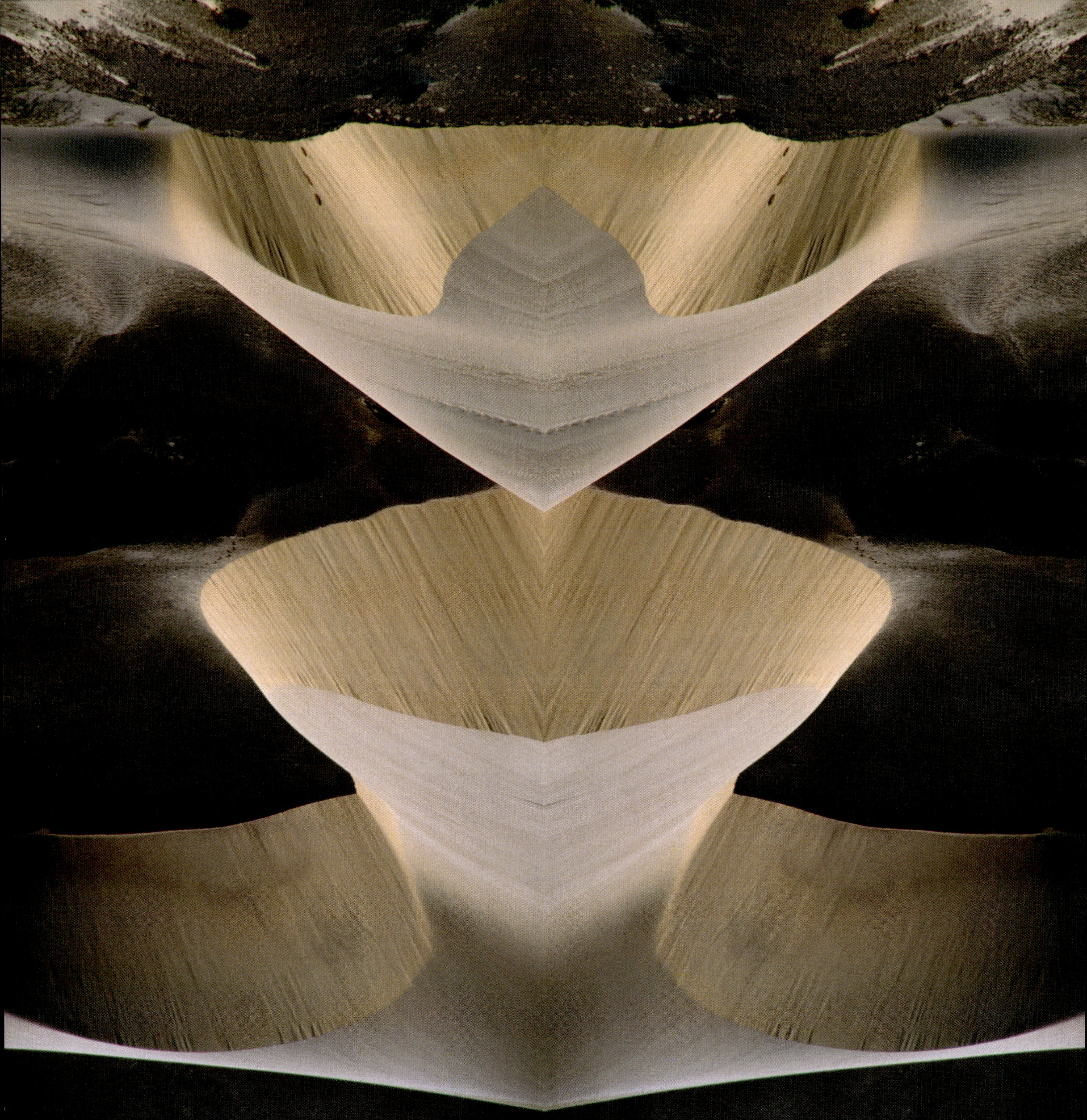

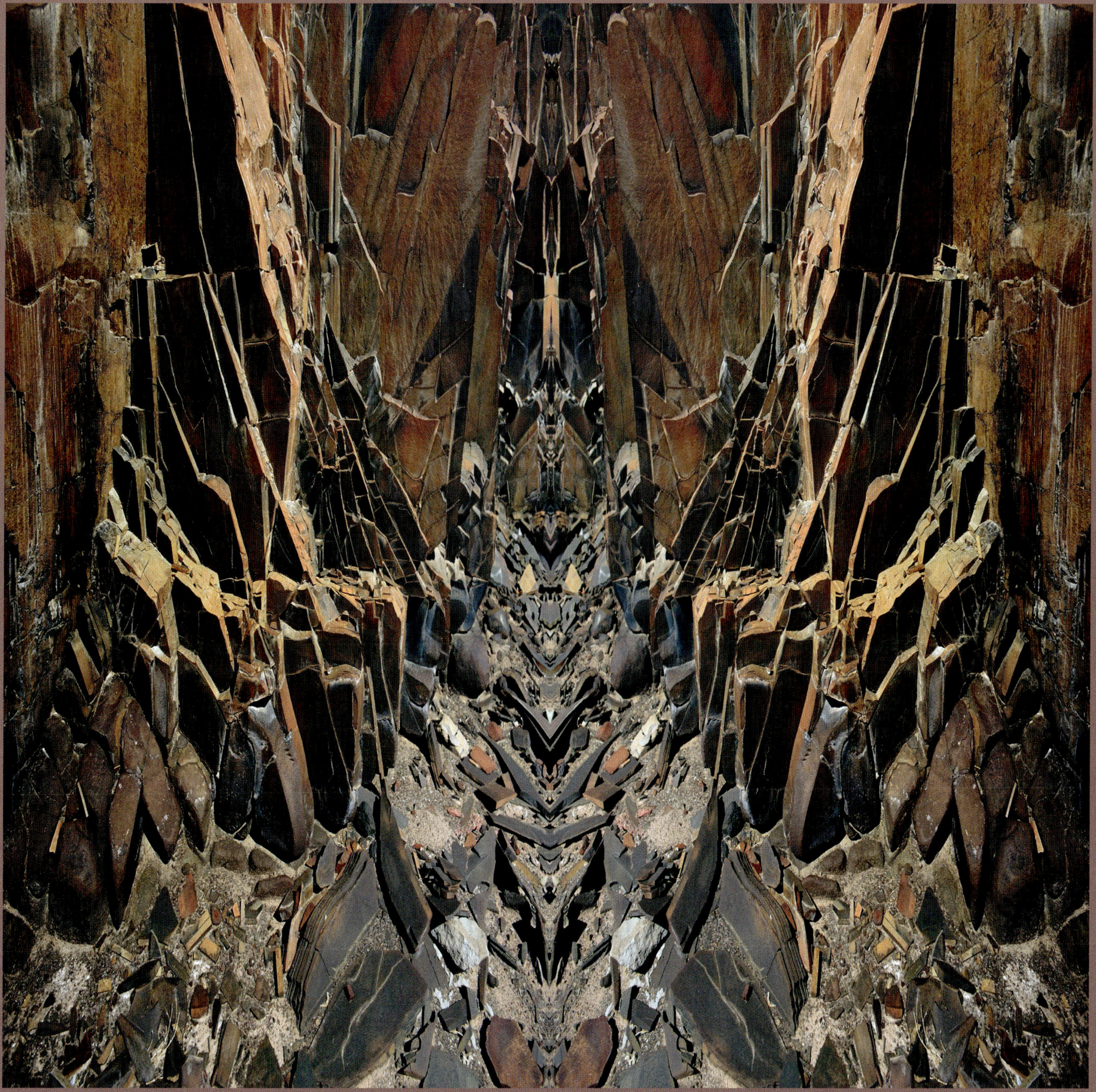

(OPPOSITE) The Holy Grail (ABOVE) The Namibian Ark

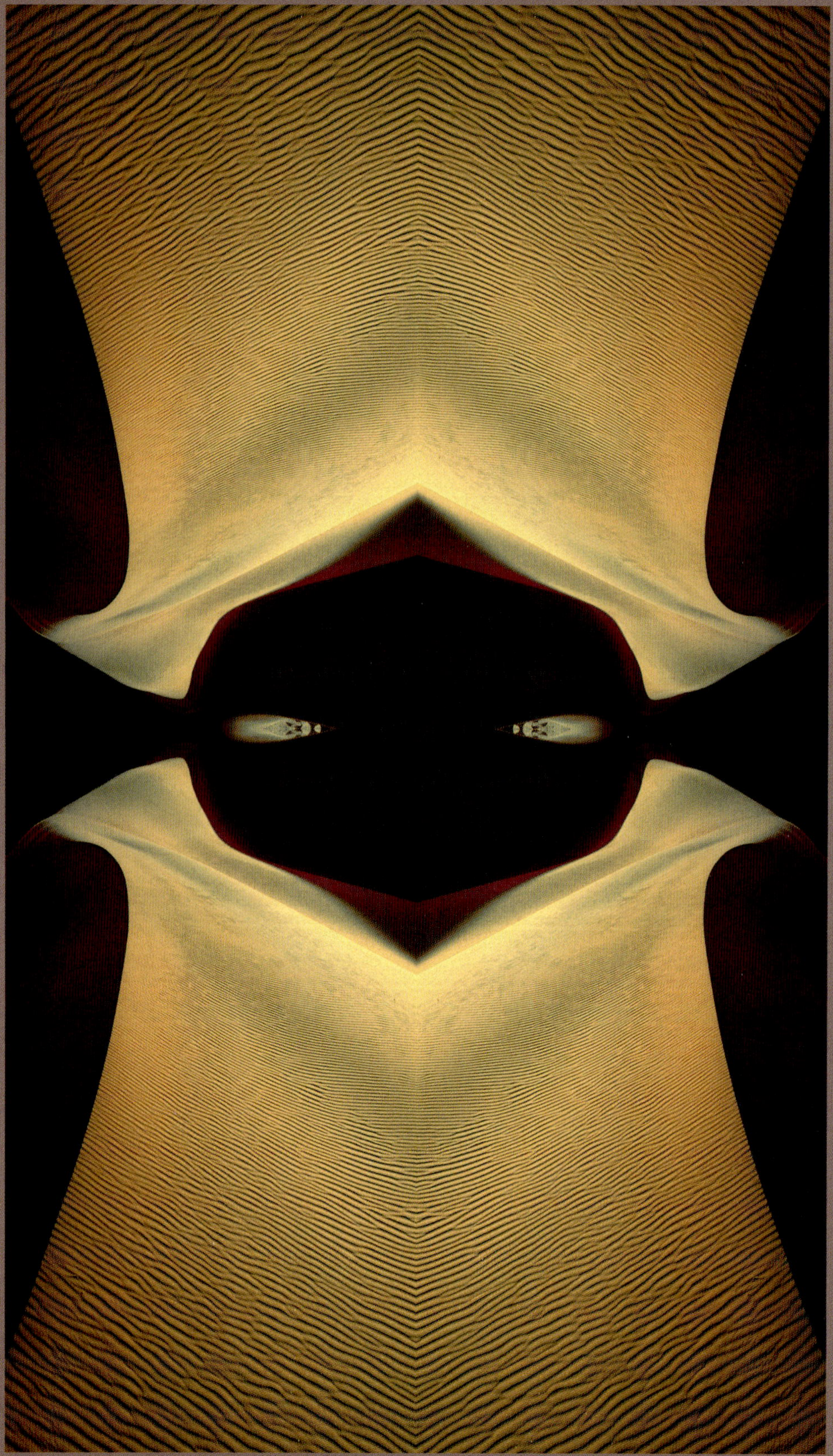

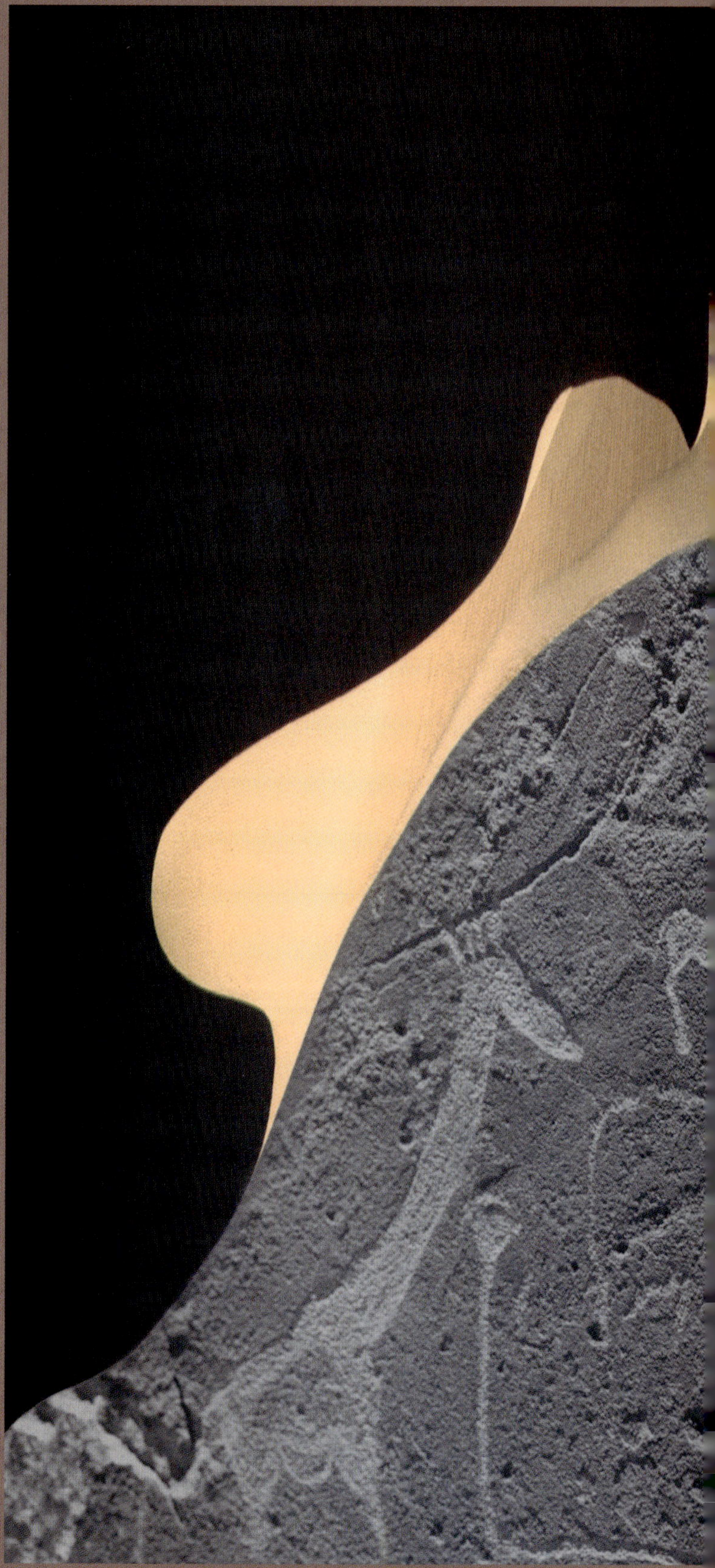

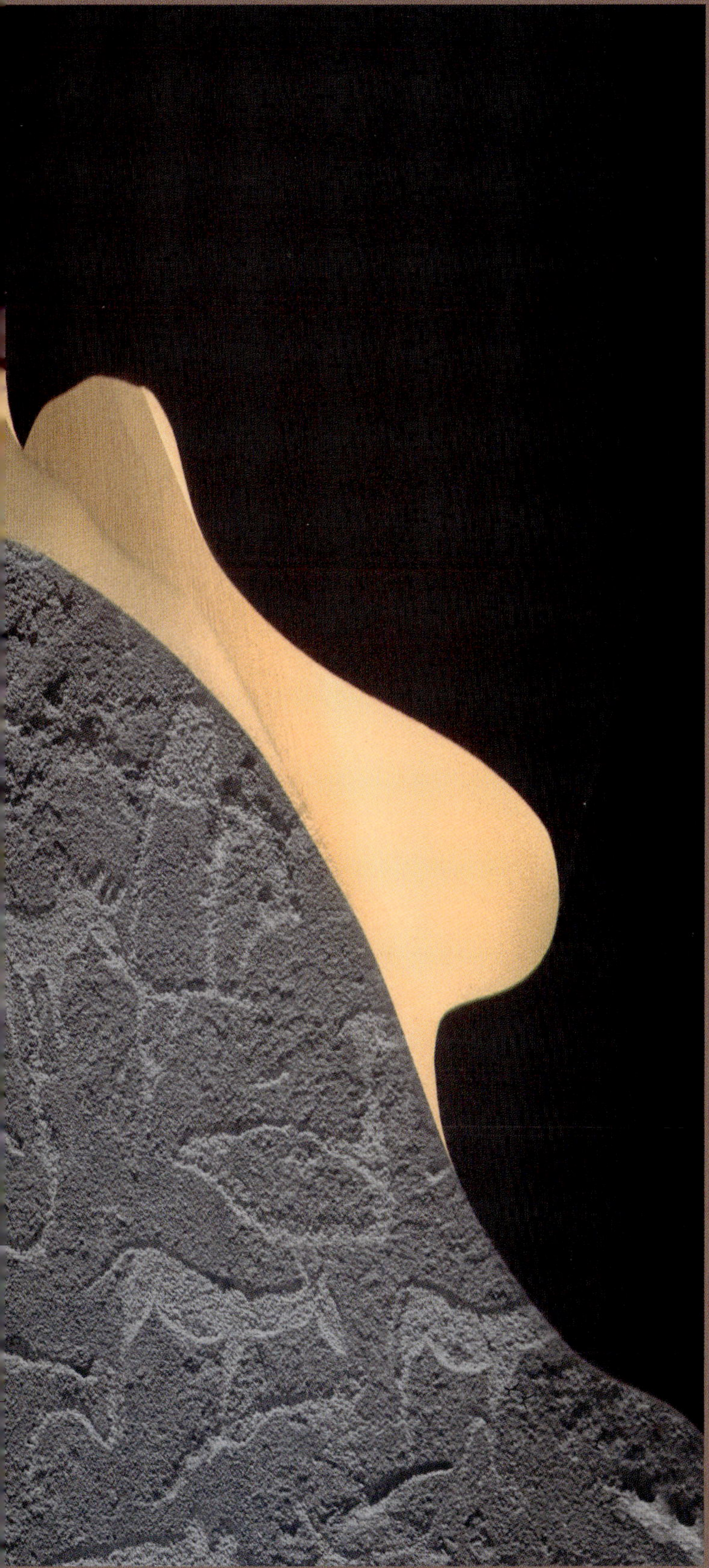

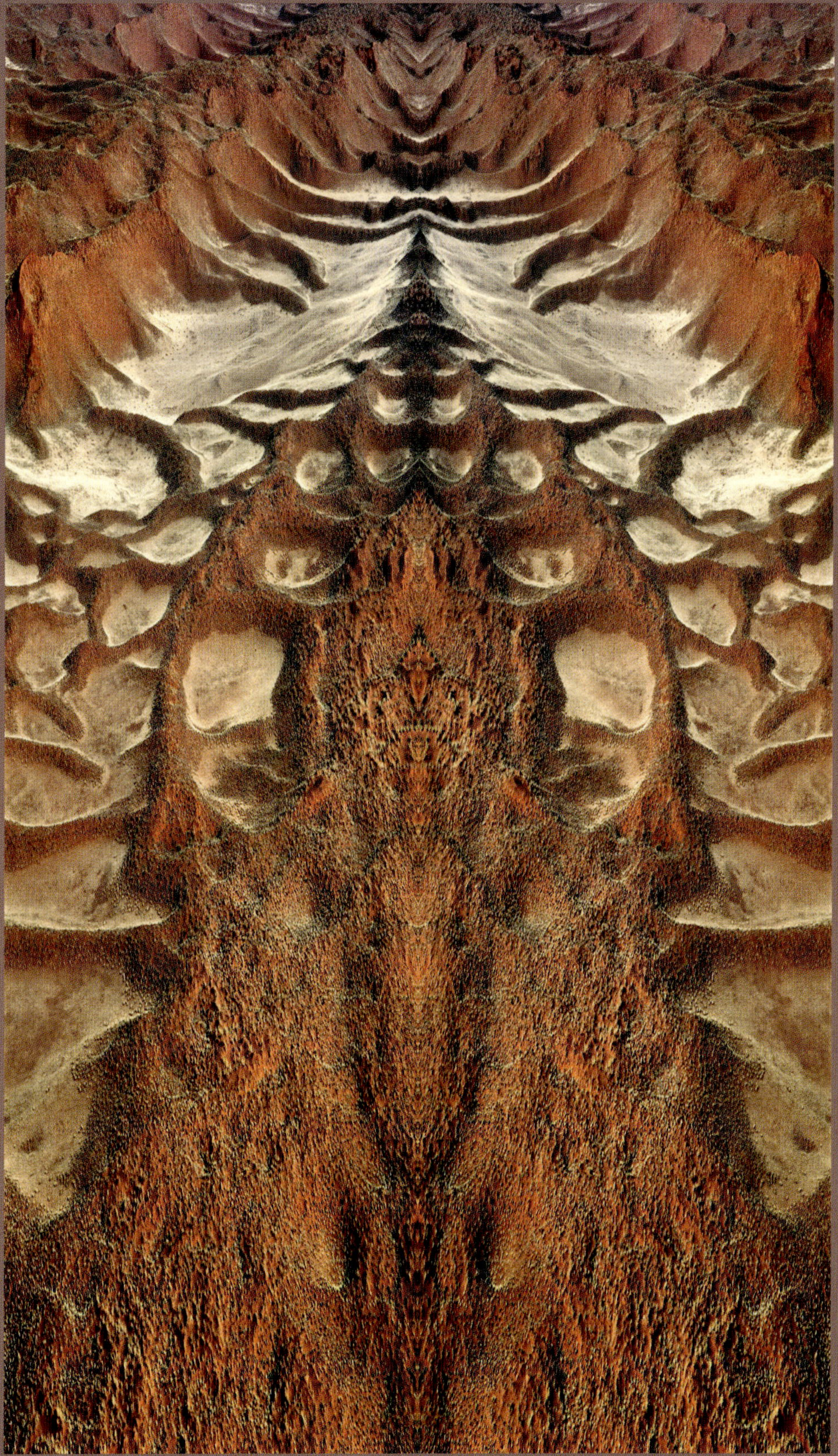

(LEFT) Messenger from Mars (MIDDLE) Trance Kalahari (RIGHT) Stopping the World

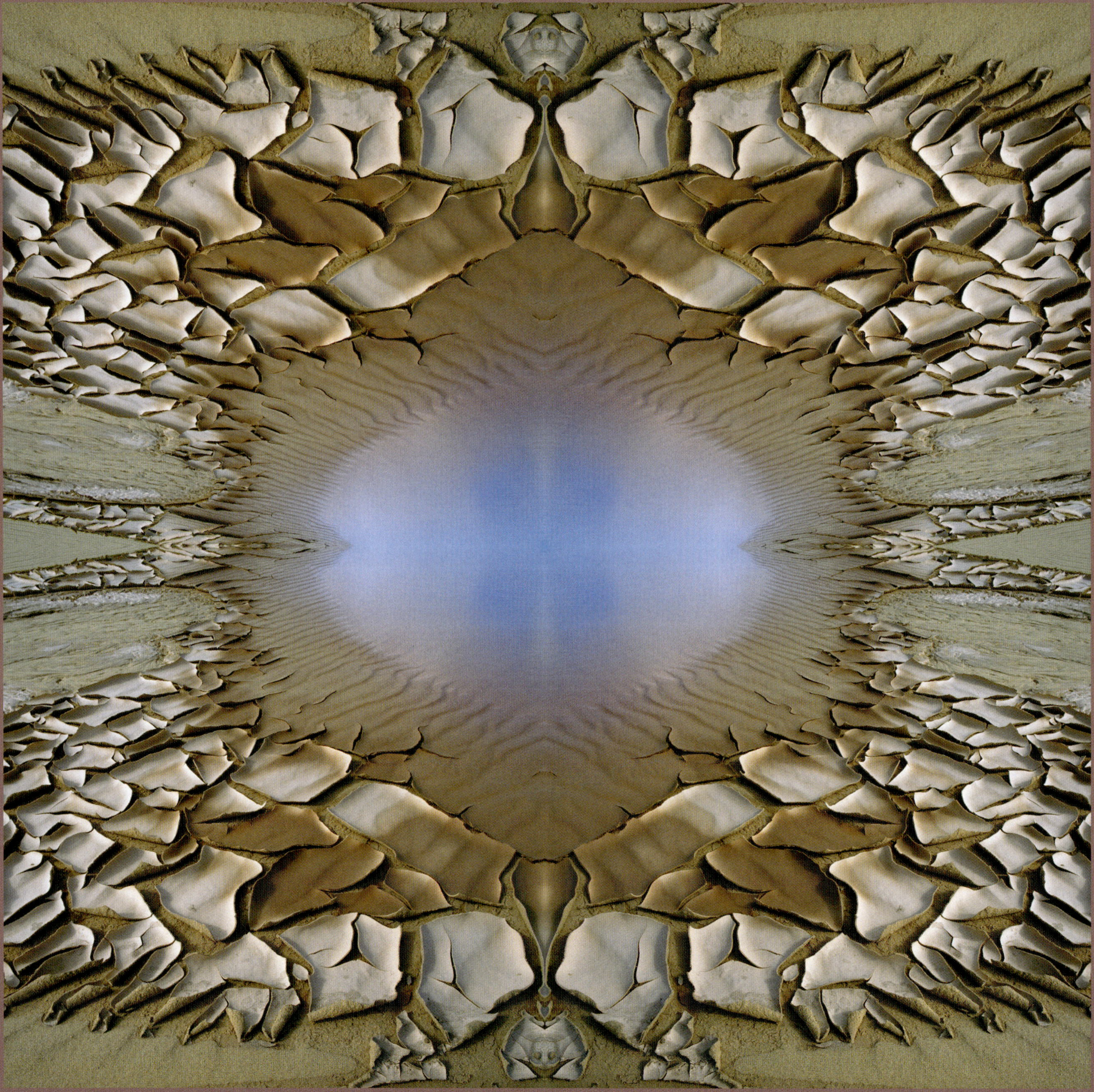

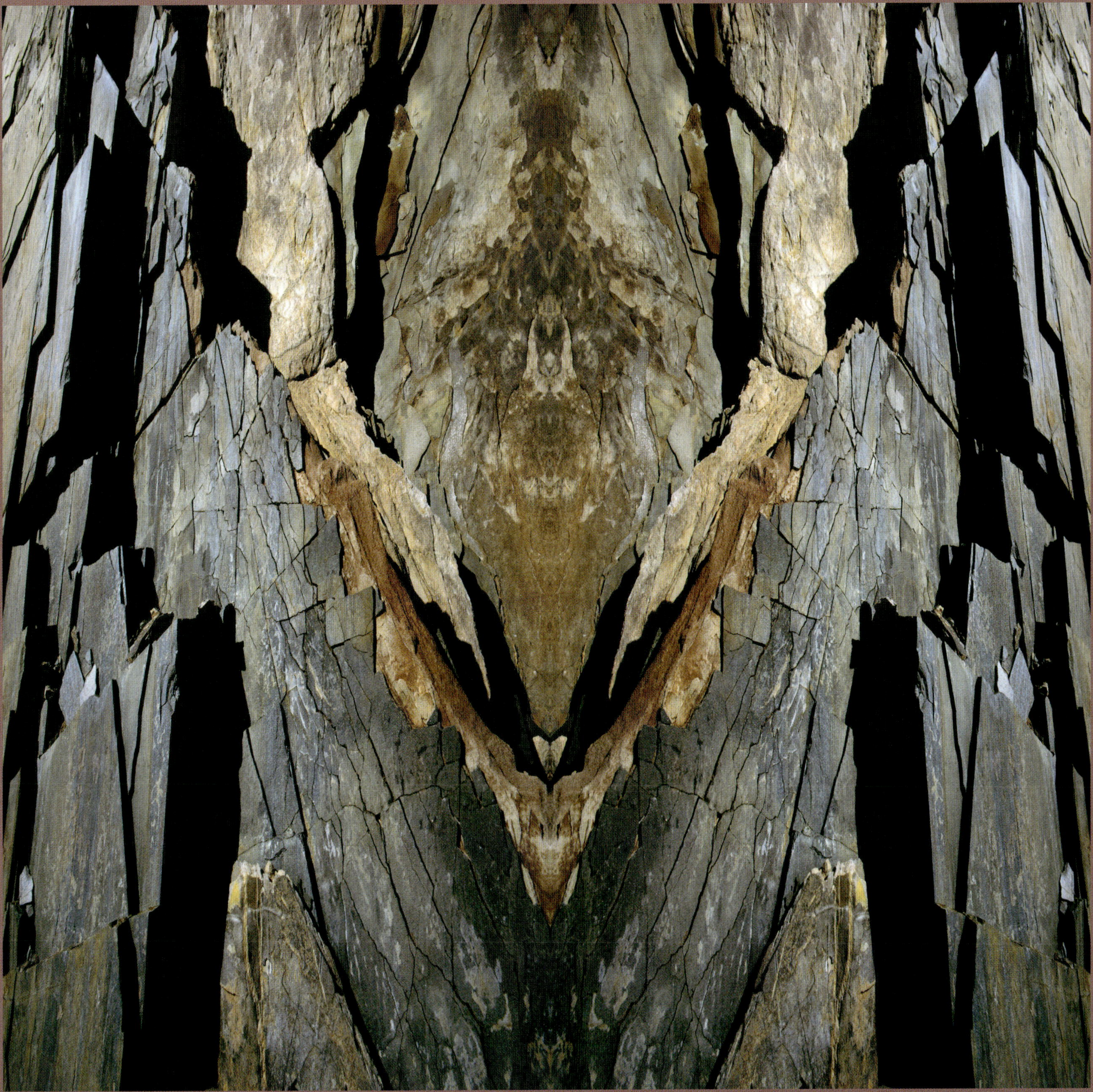

(OPPOSITE) The Magic Circle (ABOVE) Birth of the Mantis

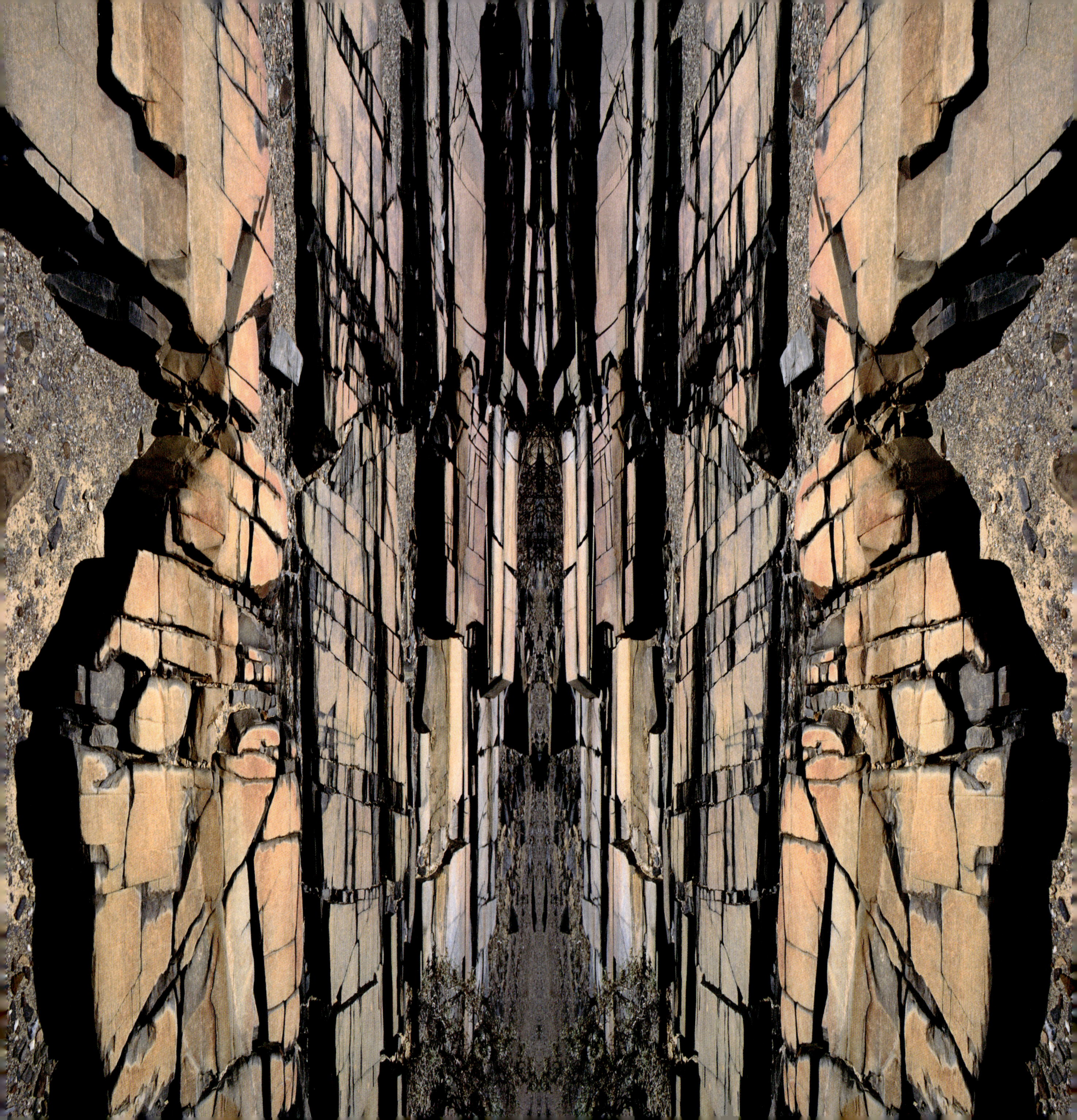

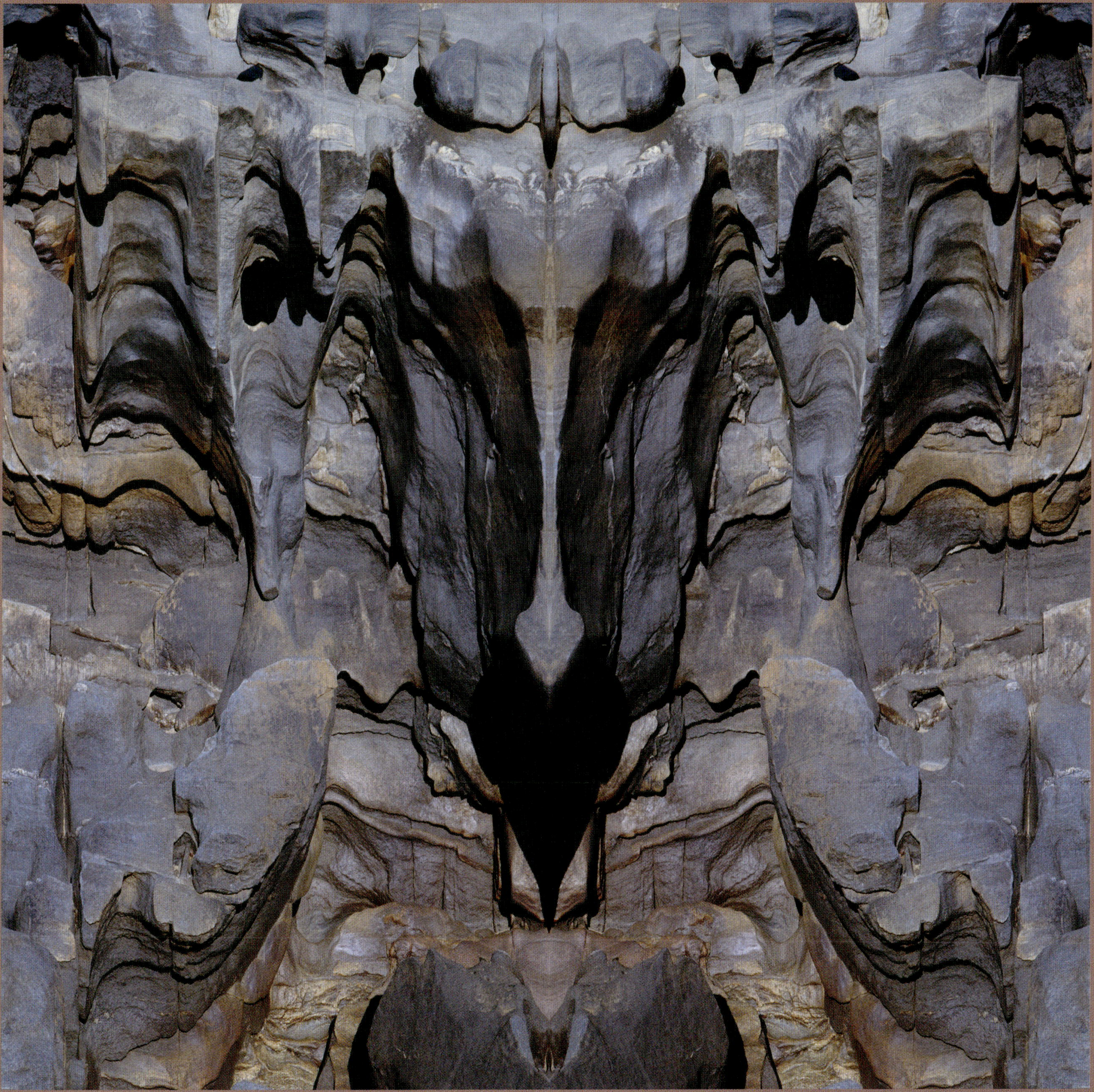

(OPPOSITE) In the Vast Cathedral of Time (ABOVE) The Darkness Within

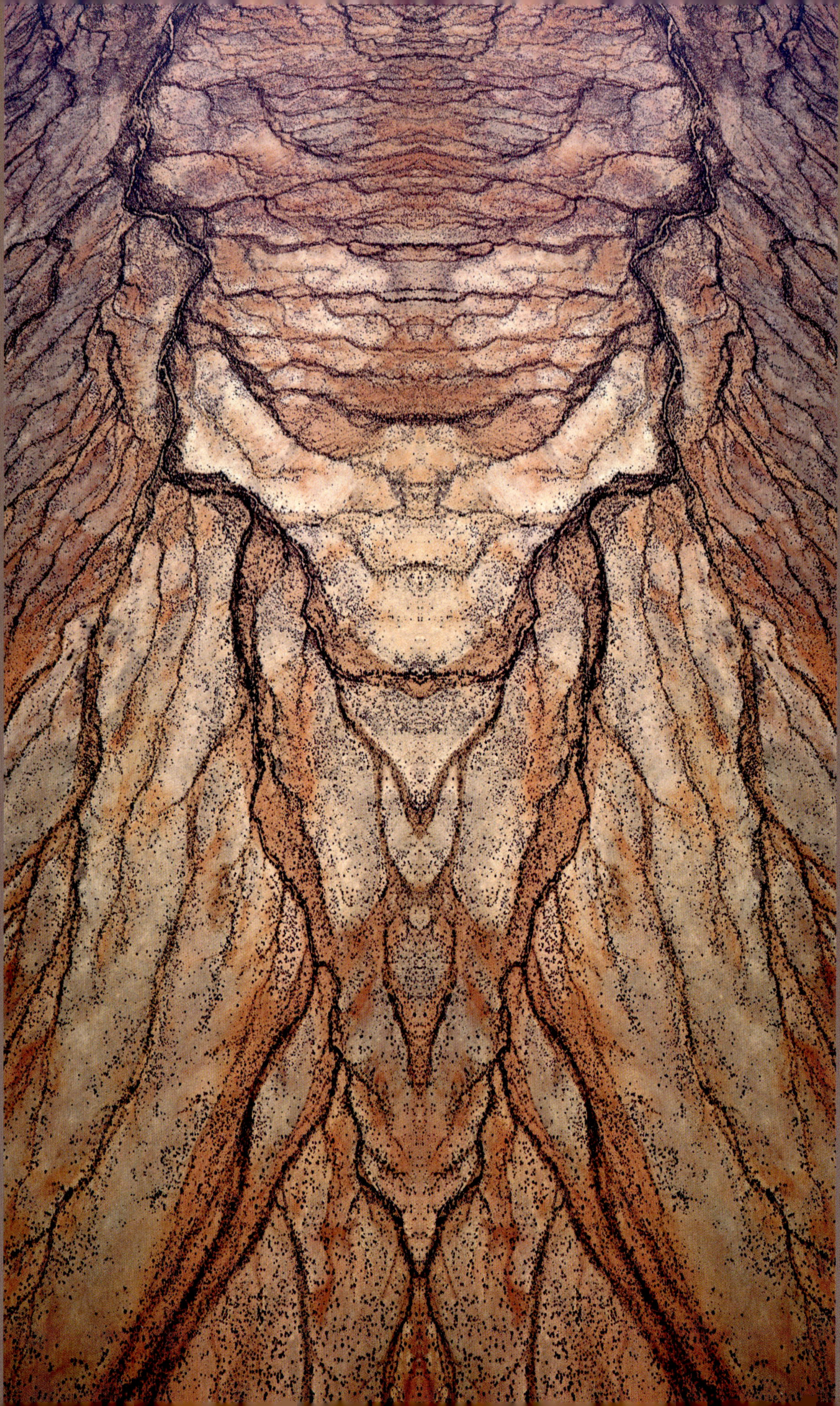

Laat toch den poort voor ons open weezen op wij zullen voorbij trekken om een aander land te zoeken. Opdat onze menschen komen ook van ver af, zulke vrede wensch ik laat ook een enkele mensch loopen en slapen waar hij wil.

Hendrik Witbooi in a letter to Captain Maharero written on 27 June 1884.
(From the diary of Hendrik Witbooi, captain of the Witbooi-Hottentotte, 1884–1905, Cape Town: Van Riebeeck Society, 1929: 10

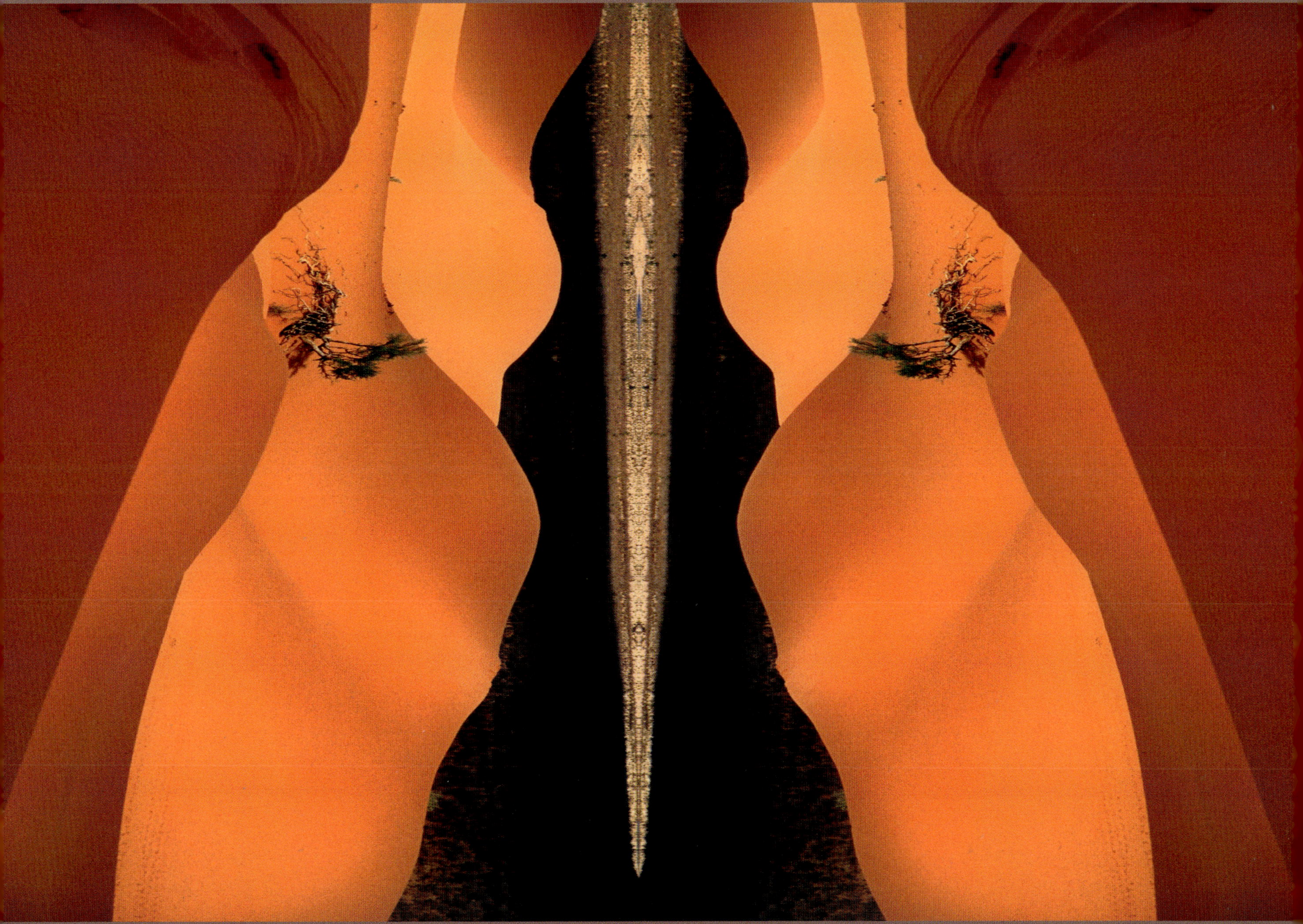

(OPPOSITE) The Sorcerer (ABOVE) Kalahari !King

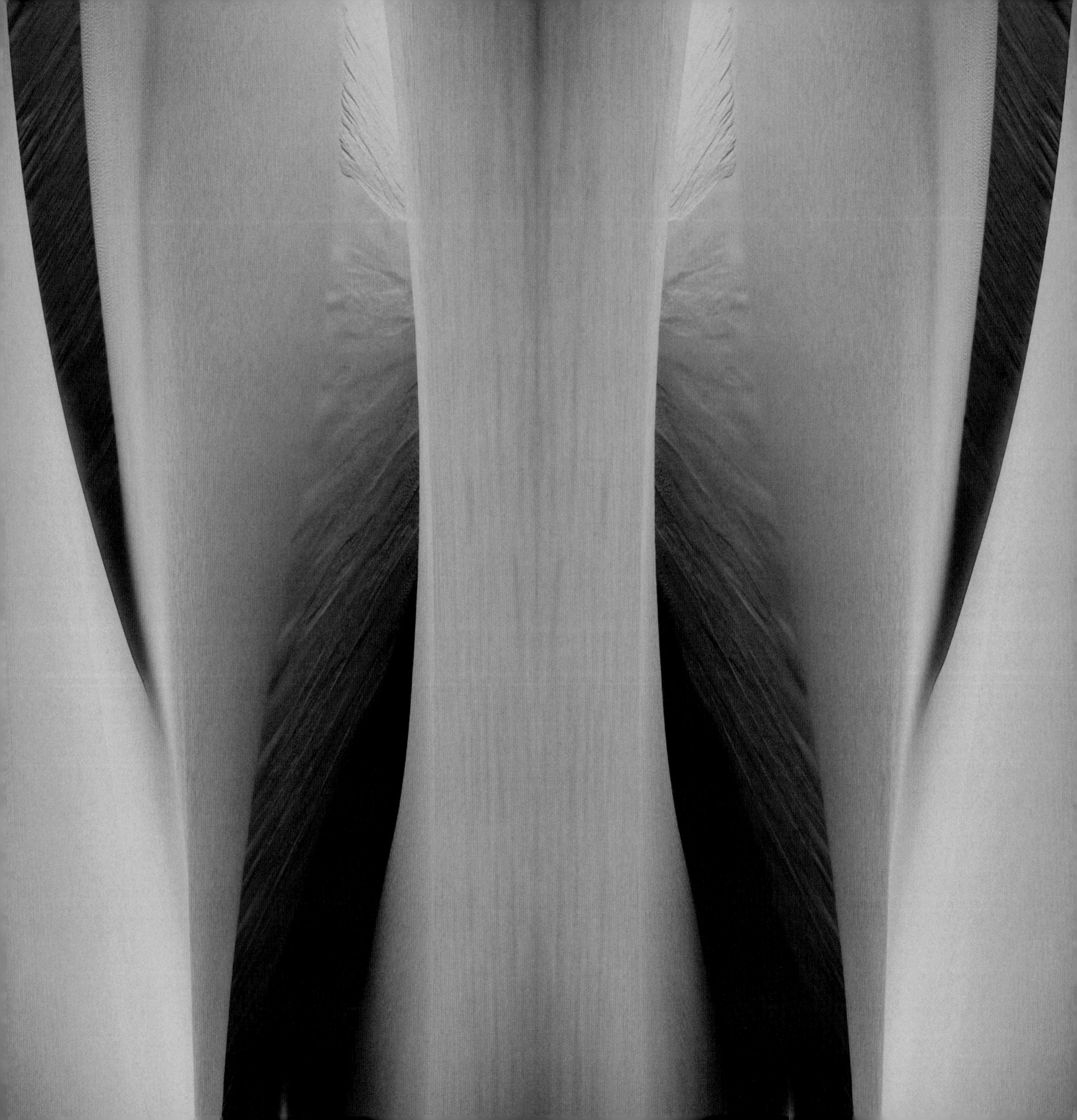

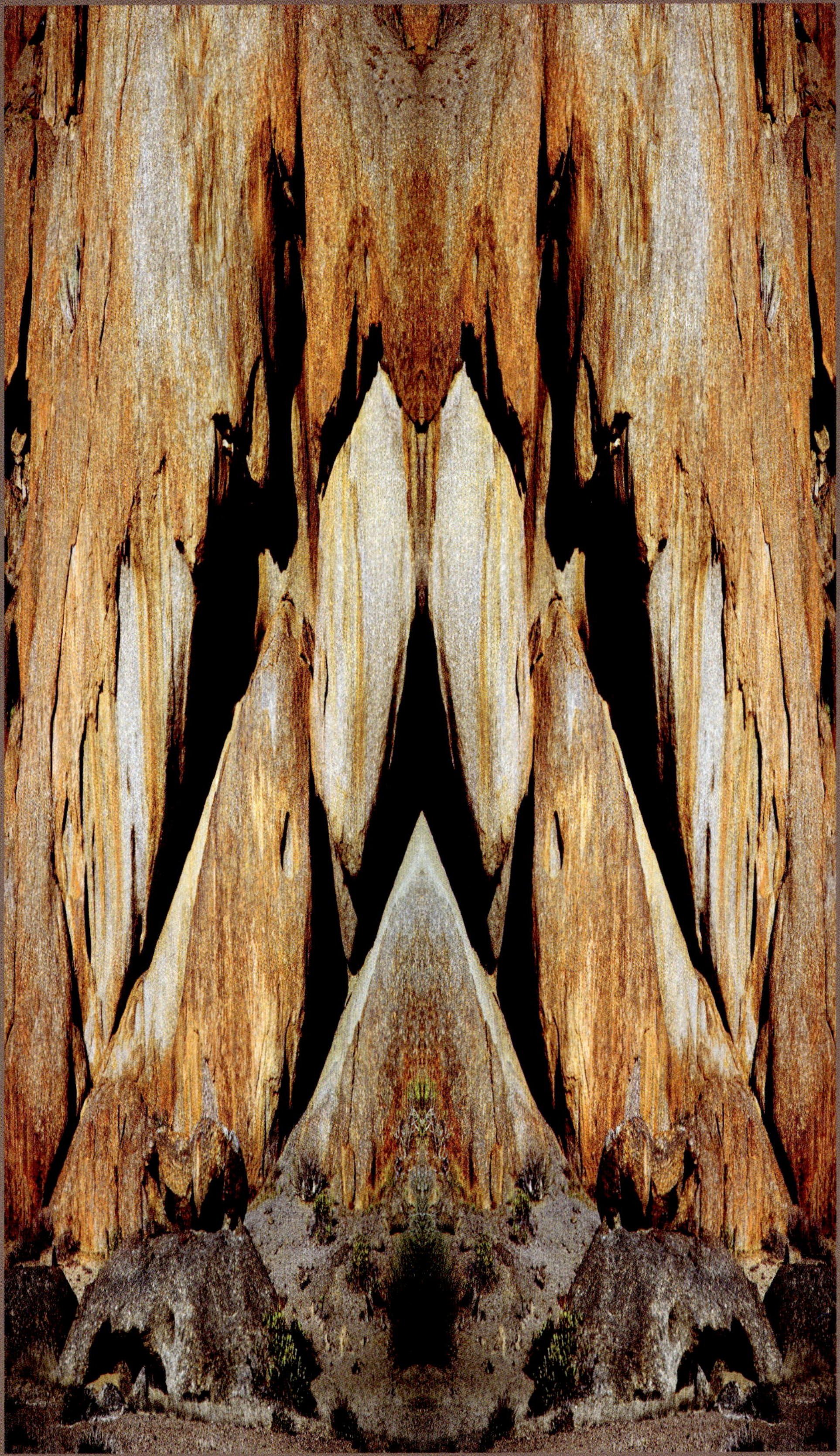

(OPPOSITE) The Manifestation of the God-Self (ABOVE) The Buddha Shrine

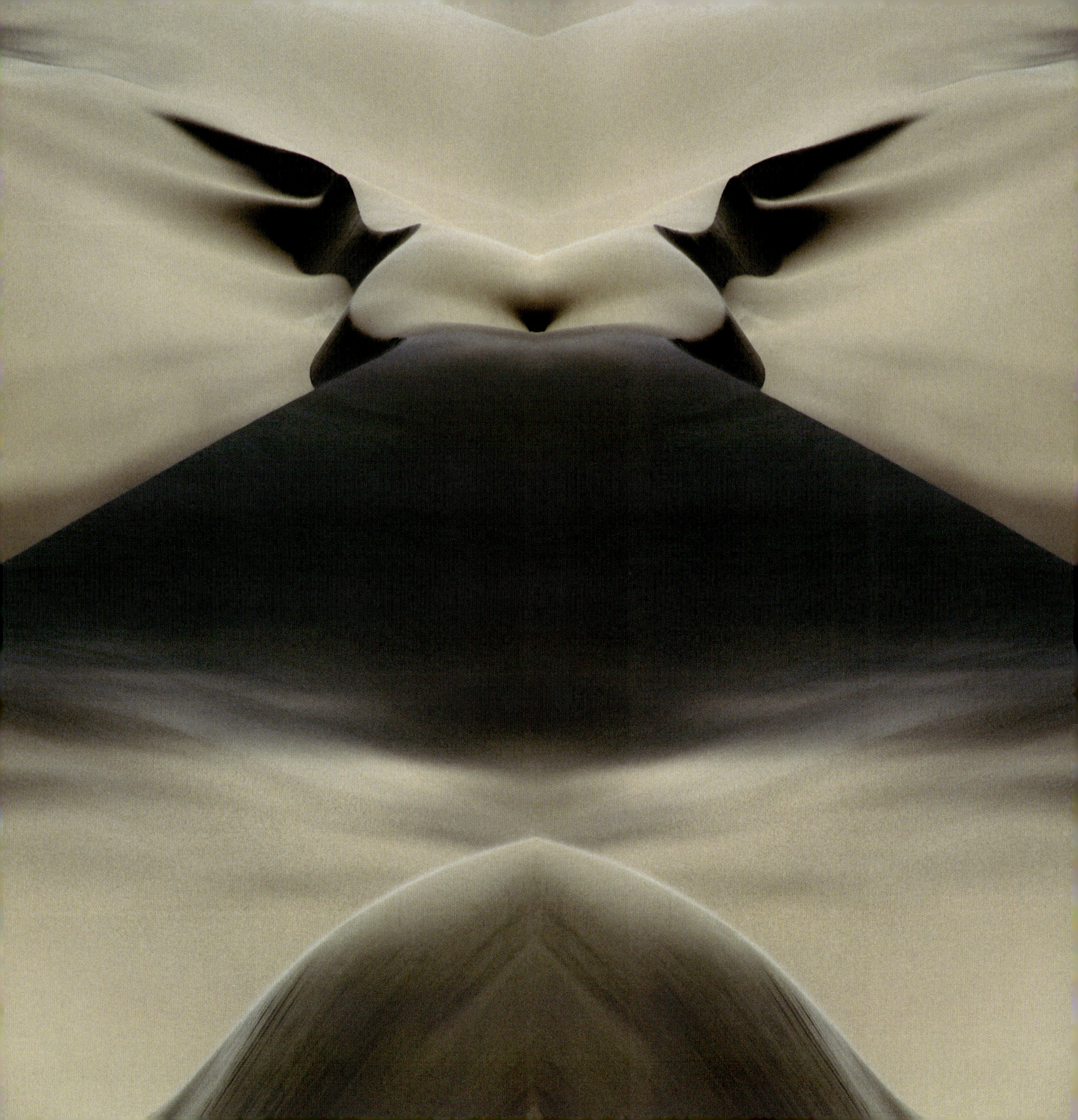

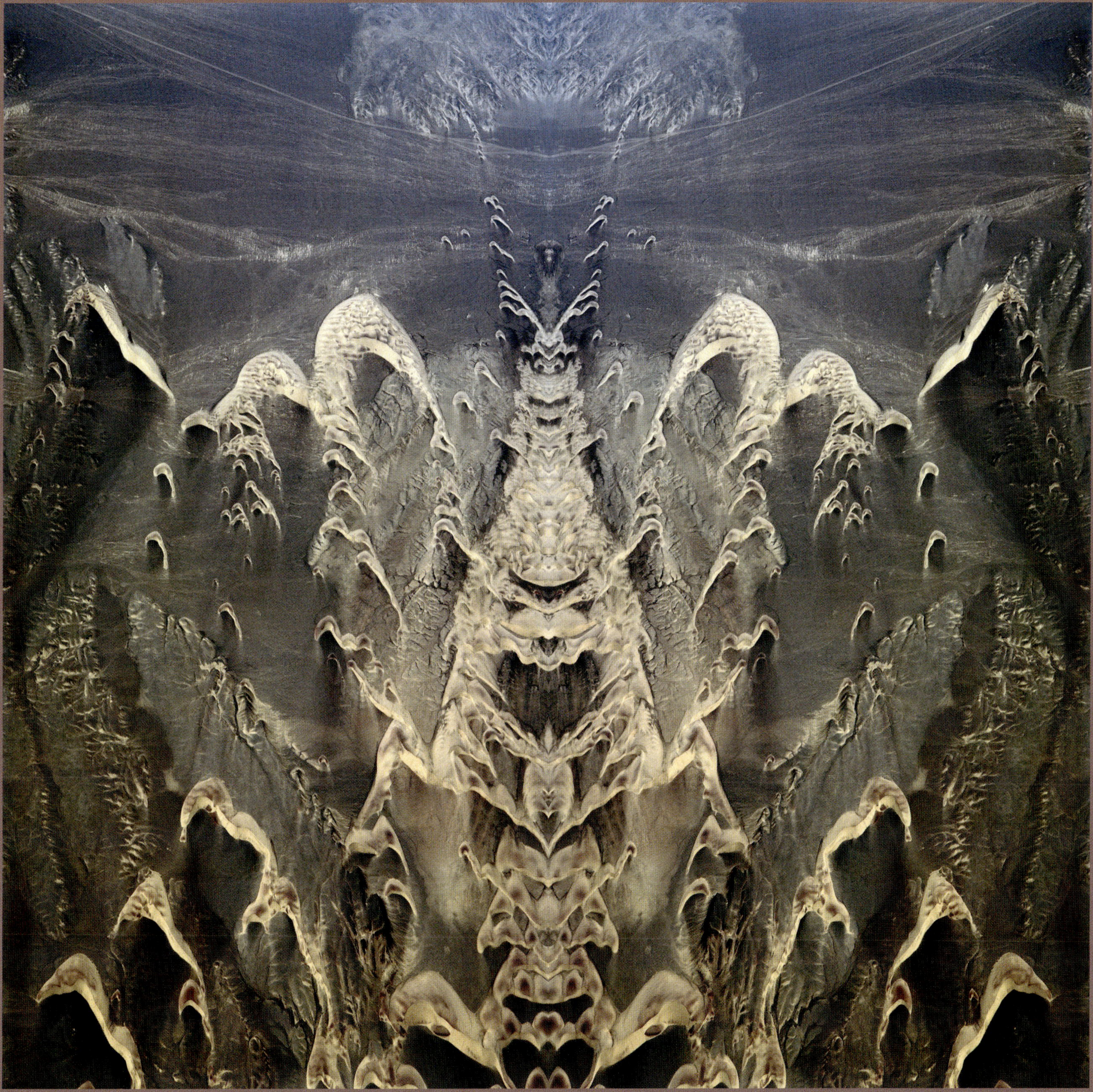

(OPPOSITE) The Beast (ABOVE) Middle Earth

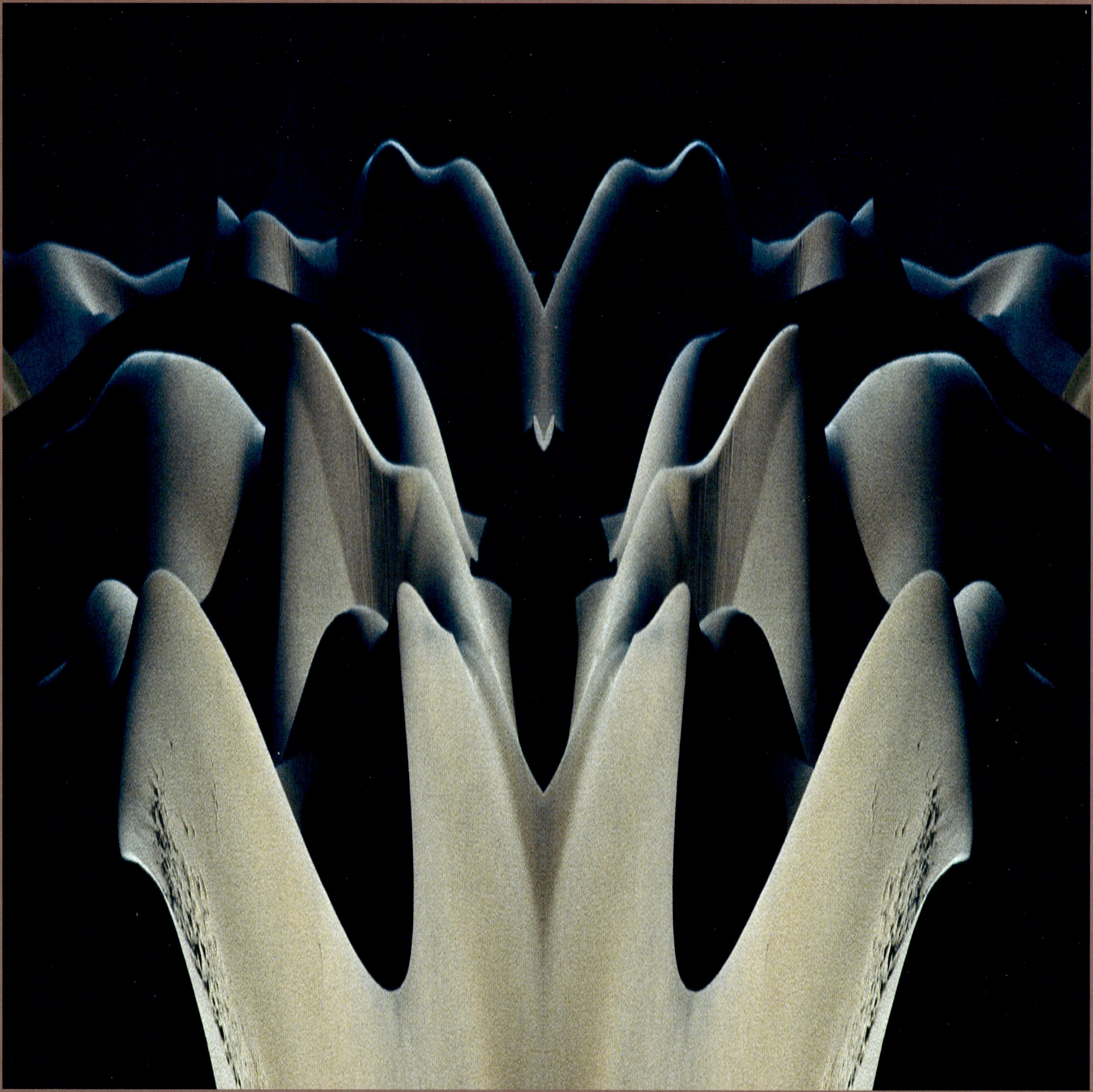

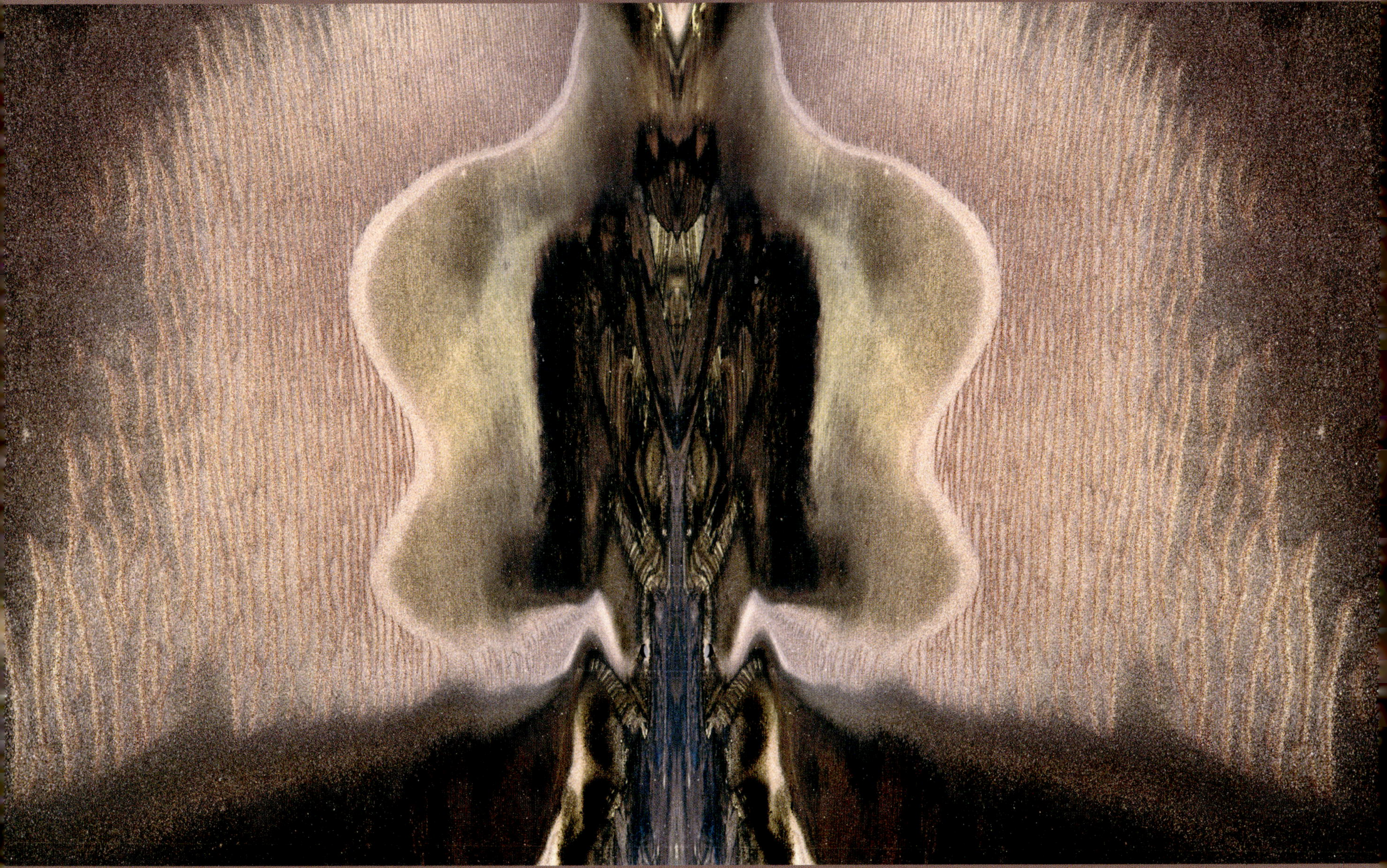

(OPPOSITE) Mountains on the Moon (ABOVE) Beyond the Big Bang

PLACE NAMES INDEX

Numbers in **bold** denote pages with photographs.